Professor Margaret Schlauch, author of *English Medieval Literature and Its Social Foundations*, received her Ph.D. degree from Columbia University in 1927 and was for many years on the staff of the English Department at New York University. Since 1951 she has been lecturing as Professor at the University of Warsaw, and was chairman of its Department of English Philology from 1953 to 1965. In 1961 she was elected corresponding member of the Polish Academy of Sciences. Her studies have dealt with comparative medieval literature, the history of the English language, and problems of poetics. Her latest volume, *Antecedents of the English Novel*, was issued jointly by Polish Scientific Publishers in Warsaw and Oxford University Press in London (first edition 1963, reprinted 1965). She is at present working on problems of English prose style in the late Middle Ages, and planning a textbook on English stylistics for foreign students of the language.

SCHLAUCH, Margaret. English medieval literature and its social foundations. Cooper Square, 1971 (orig. pub. in 1956). 366p il map 74-158962. 12.95. ISBN 0-8154-0387-0

CHOICE   DEC. '7'

Language & Literature

An acceptable work that, despite a bibliography that is dated, could serve as an introduction for undergraduates. Despite Schlauch's being at the University of Warsaw, and several times citing Engels, one is not excessively concerned about her bias. There is much on Chaucer, but more than one-half the book is concerned with the 14th and earlier centuries. An index to the footnotes triples as a bibliography and index. There is not much about "social foundations," but the standard literature is all included and some attention is paid to the historical setting.

ENGLISH
MEDIEVAL LITERATURE
AND
ITS SOCIAL FOUNDATIONS

UNREVISED REPRODUCTION

BY

MARGARET SCHLAUCH

WARSZAWA PWN • POLISH SCIENTIFIC PUBLISHERS
LONDON OXFORD UNIVERSITY PRESS

Reprinted in Poland

CONTENTS

LIST OF ILLUSTRATIONS

(Arranged in order of appearance in the book)

On p.   32.   The Expulsion of Adam and Eve from Paradise (from the Caedmonian MS., British Museum).

> Richard Wülker, *Geschichte der englischen Literatur* (Leipzig and Vienna: Bibliographisches Institut, 1900), p. 39.

Opp. p.   56.   Life of St. Guthlac. The hermit is carried through the air by demons.

> British Museum, Harley Roll. Y.6, late 12th century.
>
> O. Elfrida Saunders, *op. cit.*, vol. II, plate 60.

On. p.   78.   The Anglo-Saxon Heptarchy.

> George K. Anderson, op. cit., opp. **p. 22.**

On. p.   79.   England after the Danish Conquest.

> George K. Anderson, *op. cit.*, opp. p. 23

Opp. p.   80.   Decorated leaf of Bede's *Ecclesiastical History*. Ornamented initial B.

> British Museum, MS. Cotton Tiberius C. II., ninth century, fol. 5b.
>
> O. Elfrida Saunders, *op. cit.*, vol. I, plate 16.

Opp. p.   88.   Monstrous Creatures Described in *Wonders of the East* (from an 11th-century MS. in the British Museum).

> Wülker, *op. cit.*, p. 72.

Opp. p. 104.   Donnington Castle, Early Norman Period, Berkshire, viewing the Trent and the Soar valleys, north of Bath.

> *Antiquities of Great Britain, Illustrated in views of Monasteries, Castles and Churches now existing*, printed by James Phillips in George-Yard, Lombard Street, and published by the Proprietors T. Hearne and W. Byrne (London, 1786), plate II.

On. p. 115.   The Angevin Empire

> A.L. Morton, *A People's History of England* (London: Victor Gollancz Ltd., 1938), map opp. p. 102.

Opp. p. 128.   Malmesbury Abbey, Wiltshire.

> *Antiquities of Great Britain, op. cit.*, plate XXVIII.

Opp. p. 216. "Fro spot my spyryt þer sprang in space": The Dreamer of the *Pearl*-poem, from the Cotton MS. Nero A.x. in the British Museum.

> *Pearl*, edited by E.V. Gordon (Oxford: Clarendon Press, 1953), frontispiece.

On p. 235. Chaucer's *Parlement of Fowles*.
A woodcut by the printer Robert Pynson, Caxton's assistant.

> Edward Hodnett, *English Woodcuts* (London: Oxford University Press for the Bibliographical Society, 1935 for 1934).

Opp. p. 240. Boethius being taught by Philosophy. *The Consolation of Philosophy*.
Paul Durrieu, *op. cit.*, plate LXIX.

On p. 242. Caxton's edition of Chaucer's *Troylus and Oreseyde*.
A woodcut by Robert Pynson.

> Edward Hodnett, *op. cit.*, fig. 158, no. 1953.

Opp. p. 256 Front Page of the *Canterbury Tales* from a 15th-century MS. in the British Museum.
Wülker, *op. cit.*, plate following p. 156.

On p. 257. *Canterbury Tales*: Pilgrims at table.
Engraving of the 16th century.

> Arthur M. Hind, *Engraving in England in the Sixteenth & Seventeenth Centuries, A Descriptive Catalogue*, Part I: The Tudor Period (Cambridge: At The University Press, 1952), plate 2.

On p. 262. *Canterbury Tales*: The Yonge Squyer.
A woodcut by Pynson.

> Edward Hodnett, *op. cit.*, fig. 149, no. 1642.

On p. 263. *Canterbury Tales*: The Wife of Bath.

> Chaucer's Pilgrims, from the 1532 folio edition of Chaucer's Works, p. 98.

> From the facsimile reprint of the first complete folio ed. with introduction by W.W. Skeat (London: Oxford University Press, 1905).

On p. 268. *Canterbury Tales*: The Friar, printed by W. Caxton.
Edward Hodnett, *op. cit.*, fig. 4, no. 219.

FOREWORD

This book is intended for students and amateurs of medieval English literature wishing to obtain an initial general view of the subject. The treatment has had to be broad rather than detailed, therefore, and the bibliographical references make no pretension to exhaustiveness. At the same time an effort has been made to include such items as would enable a student to embark on the further study of any special theme for himself. To this end basic editions have been noted, and also a choice of leading articles and monographs. Emphasis has been placed on recent contributions, since these studies often include summaries of previous research, with annotations.

There was a time when the culture of the Middle Ages was ignorantly condemned as barbarous and unworthy of serious study. Later, in the period of the romantics and their successors, the foundations were laid for a more just appraisal of the great achievements realised during the millenium which followed the extinction of the Western Roman empire. In the case of some specialists the pendulum may be said to have swung too far, and a blind enthusiasm for all medieval culture has with them replaced the previous contemptuous ignorance. Occasionally the cult of medievalism has assumed a frankly political significance, as when it has been invoked to justify systems like the fascist corporate state in Italy. Less deliberately, certain individual writers, alarmed by the crises and dangers of our own times, have created for themselves an idealised concept of medieval orderliness and have turned to it as a refuge. Using the greatest masterpieces only as a foundation for their cult, they have glorified the medieval way of life as offering a plan of escape from present anxieties.

Such idealisation of medieval culture is possible only at the price of ignoring the many aspects of disorder and cruelty and ignorance which existed in the real life of the times. Of these aspects too students should be reminded, with the help of social and economic history. It is to be hoped that a middle line of interpretation has been followed in the present sketch, avoiding both the extremes of a specialist's enthusiasm and the equally unwarranted belittling by the prejudiced sceptic.

Writing in a country still handicapped by the effects of war-time destruction, the author was not able to check on the accuracy of all citations and references at first hand, nor to obtain fresh materials for the purposes of illustration. For all such inadequacies she asks pardon in advance.

MARGARET SCHLAUCH

Warsaw. 12 February 1956

PART I
OLD ENGLISH

CHAPTER I

THE PERIOD OF ORIGINS

1. THE ANGLO-SAXON CONQUEST

The first period of English culture in England begins abruptly, as is well known, with a series of attacks, invasions and forcible settlements upon the island in the fifth century. The invaders were tribesmen from the Germanic territory extending from the lower Rhine region north-eastwards along the shoreland as far as the Southern part of Jutland in Denmark. Raids had been made in the early part of this century, but the first major entry took place about A.D. 450 (the traditional date given is 449). By about 500 the Eastern sections of the country had been subdued. Later, in the sixth century, a second advance carried the invaders westward to the hilly and mountainous territory (Wales and Strathclyde) in which the original Celtic inhabitants were able to defend and maintain themselves unconquered.

The country thus overrun from the Northern European continent had been a Roman province, an integral part of the unified system of political domination which up to about A.D. 375 had embraced most of the known ancient world. Previously, Britain had been inhabited by Celtic tribes — themselves early invaders who had mixed with the prehistoric populations of the islands — organised in small political units lacking effective coordination. From the last century of the previous era onwards, the Romans had established an increasingly strong rule in England proper, but they had never conquered Ireland nor Scotland. The latter territory was barricaded from the subdued regions by a fortified wall built by the Emperor Hadrian in A.D. 120, and Ireland remained detached, though not uninfluenced, during the entire period of Roman rule.

As a Roman province, Britain had developed the type of urban life familiar in other cities of the empire. It had baths and libraries, forums, schools and theatres, and — what was very conspicuous in provincial life — its army, military roads and camps (*castra*, whence the English place-name Chester and the final element in Lan-caster). The Britons

2

were taxed by Rome, ruled by Roman generals and governors, administered in the Latin language, conscripted into the imperial army system. But in time there arose a mixed wealthy aristocracy including not merely temporary visitors from the world capital on the Tiber, but permanent residents who allied themselves with the native nobility, intermarried with them, and produced finally a Britano-Roman ruling class made up largely of Celtic elements. As in neighbouring Gaul, many of the names commemorated in historical texts and on inscriptions of the period are Celtic cognomens adorned with Latin suffixes. The mass of the army itself, in the last century of provincial life, appears to have been composed of Romanised Britons who had never seen Rome, though many of the officers and most of the generals may well have come from the capital. The language of the provincial cities was Latin, but we may assume that Celtic dialects still prevailed in the countryside and many persons living in the cities were bilingual.

The economic basis of Romanised British culture was the ancient institution of slavery. Slave labour was used on a very large scale, as elsewhere in the Roman world, to build the towns and cities, work the mines, navigate the ships, and above all to farm the land of the great wealthy estates producing the food for the ancient world. Such was the material foundation of classical culture. The Roman ruling class, together with their native allies in the provinces, had organised a vast system to exploit slave labour. Wasteful as it was, and inhumanly cruel, it still succeeded for a time in producing very imposing results. But it was subject to fatal internal contradictions which had begun to undermine the whole imperial system, social and political, even before the barbarian tribes like the Anglo-Saxons began their attacks from the outside. The *latifundia* or great estates had ruined the small farmers in Italy and were threatening to do so elsewhere, thus dislocating large numbers of the still-free population and reducing them to paupers. The cheap commodities produced by slaves and the declassed free workers (now "proletarianised," if the word may be thus loosely employed) were unable to find sufficient markets for purchase, because of the pauperisation of the masses and because of the inadequate means of transportation, which hindered a profitable exchange with and among the provinces.[1]

Underneath the show of Roman wealth and prosperity, then, provinces like Britain were subject to economic decay which affected the entire social system. There are signs that the households living in the Roman villas on the large landed estates had been undergoing crisis, and many of them were simply abandoned as unprofitable in the fourth century. The land may have been reverting to farming on a smaller scale, by more primitive methods, before the invasions. And it must be remembered that large sections of the land of Britain had remained uncultivated from prehistoric times: forests still covered much of it, and there were wastes and swamps never converted to productive use.

Nevertheless the level of provincial cultural life remained relatively high to the end, as compared with that prevailing among the little-known tribes in Northern Europe. Celtic skill in handicrafts, combined with Roman techniques, produced objects of ornament and utility of a high order: decorated domestic utensils, furniture, jewels, buildings for public and private use, as well as the military roads and installations visible to this day in England. By the end of the fourth century Britain had become Christian, and was tied to Eastern as well as Western city-centres of the new religion by fresh cultural bonds (exchange of books, teachers and priests), though these centres had not yet become strictly organised in an institution having a supreme authority in Rome. [2] It is not certain to what extent the new religion, or even the Roman governmental system in general, had affected the Celtic rural population not close to the towns. These people may well have offered passive resistance to Christianity as well as to the pagan cosmopolitan culture imported to the island from the Mediterranean area. But the towns and cities were, we may assume, quite thoroughly Christianised as well as Romanised by A.D. 400, and churches were conspicuous among the public buildings to be found in them.

Concerning the origins and background of the Germanic invaders there is considerable discussion, nor is opinion agreed as to the precise areas from which came the Angles, Saxons and Jutes. Bede's account in the *Historia Ecclesiastica Gentis Anglorum* has been found to be over-simple and out of harmony with other known facts and the evidence of archaeology. [3] Kent was settled by a group who were indeed called Jutes in the early sources, though this name early passed out of use and its origin is in doubt. They appear to have emigrated from Jutland, Denmark, late in the second century, and to have occupied a region vacated by the Saxons when the latter moved southwestwards to land in the lower Rhine area (to the Northeast of that river). The Angles, originally located in a section of Schleswig called Angel, between the Saxons and the Jutes, left their homeland en masse and moved Southwest; they had probably begun to mingle with the Saxons on the continent before the invasion. [4] In fact, it has been suggested that the first leaders, traditionally designated as Hengist and Horsa, gathered their followers from the entire stretch of the low-lying German coastland, chiefly the lower Rhine and Holland. Professor Chadwick has stated categorically that the invaders were linguistically homogeneous, and that the dialectal distinctions of Old English developed later as a result of political divisions in England, thus proving "absolutely nothing as to the presence of different nationalities among the invaders."[5] However that may be, the situation was at least a complex one. The Jutes may have settled predominantly in Kent, the Saxons in the South and Southwest, and the Angles in Anglia and northwards, but the divisions were not sharp.

Few materials are available describing the protracted invasions and conquest from the Romano-Celtic point of view, and no contemporary records have been left by the invaders themselves, since they were analphabetic. What evidence we have is partly archaeological and partly to be deduced from texts of doubtful historical value, like the tract by Gildas called *De Excidio et Conquestu Britanniae* (ca. 540) and the composite *Historia Britonum* attributed to a certain "Nennius" (materials written down about A.D. 800 and later). The sources are sufficient, however, to indicate a condition of thorough devastation: the shattering of an older culture, the flight of town dwellers to wild lands, the wreckage of entire cities, the wholesale slaughter of such families as did not escape to the fens or mountains. A recent historian has thus evoked impressions of the catastrophic change: "at Canterbury the [Jutish] king's hall and the houses of his immediate followers, standing self-consciously among the tumbled wreckage of Roman shops, tenements, and churches, bore witness at once to the new Teutonic order and to a precarious continuity with the Roman past. But beyond the limits of Kent that continuity had already all but disappeared. In the waste of broken buildings that had once been Roman London an unusually acute eye might detect a handful of squatters or refugees, men of dubious ancestry and uncertain occupation..., the walls of Verulam enclosed in all probability a city of the dead, though, on the hill-side a mile away, the half-forgotten sanctuary of St Alban may never have quite lost the service of its devotees..."[6]

In the Southwest, resistance continued. The Roman names of Aurelius Ambrosius and Arthur (the latter perhaps equivalent to the Latin name Artorius) and the possibly historical core of the legends gathered about them, indicate that organised military campaigns were conducted for a time by the native army in the Roman fashion (early sixth century), but this led to no permanent success. The task of the next age was the assimilation of the conquerors to settled life and the creation of a new culture.

That culture developed independently, having no contact with, or stimulus from, the Romanised Celts. There is no evidence, either, that the natives and provincials made any attempt to Christianise the Anglo-Saxons. The latter remained pagan, continuing to worship the Germanic gods like Woden and Thunor (corresponding to Scandinavian Odin and Thor), about whose cult little is known to us. The period of the sixth and early seventh centuries, obscure to the historian, reveals nothing of cultural contacts between the races, yet it is difficult to believe that these did not occur when villages of Anglo-Saxon peasant-farmers began to till the soil in proximity to Celts, especially where these had been least Romanised and Christianised.

2. THE SOCIAL LIFE OF ANGLO-SAXON ENGLAND

The social organisation of the Germanic settlers was, as compared to the Roman, simple and based on small political units, recalling in many ways that of the Celts whom the Romans themselves had conquered.[7] The chiefs or leaders of the expeditions had an authority which dated back to the life on the continent. They became the founders of the royal dynasties in the kingdoms (some of them impermanent) of Kent, Wessex, Surrey, Mercia, Anglia and Northumbria, and among the Hwicce (in the Western counties bordering on Wales).[8] Such chieftains assigned the land of the new country to their followers, recognising traditional ranks of nobility and also rewarding special services performed by less distinguished warriors. The group of leading nobles around the king constituted his court and acted as his advisers. Seasoned retainers were known collectively as the *duguð*, younger men as the *geoguð*, in later times. The entire group, called the *þegnas*, are sometimes referred to as the *comitatus*, a term borrowed from Tacitus. The Anglo-Saxon collective equivalent was *gesið*. In early times its members claimed equally distinguished lineage with that of the king, who was regarded as a *primus inter pares*, and was chosen by them. Hereditary succession was a matter of custom rather than legal principle among the Germanic peoples.

The oldest laws distinguish, besides the nobility later known as the earls or *eorlas*, a large group of free peasants called the *ceorlas*, another of the *lætas* (freedmen, perhaps including some surviving Celtic peasants) holding smaller pieces of land, and finally the group of slaves (*þeowas*). The laws inform us about the money value (*wergild*) of an individual's life in each group. One of the outstanding features about Anglo-Saxon society is the lack of an elaborate social hierarchy separating the *ceorlas* from the king. The peasant farmers of Kent were most fortunate of all in this respect. Their units of land (*sulungs*), which varied from about 150 to 200 acres, were larger than those in other parts of England, elsewhere called hides, and varying from 40 to 120 acres. The social value of the men of Kent was reckoned higher than that of others, as expressed in terms of *wergild*, and they were subject to no lord except the king himself.[9] The socio-economic advantages of the Kentish peasantry—which can be traced into later periods of the Middle Ages—have been thought to have their origin in the close association of the Jutes with the neighbouring Franks on the continent. And the situation among the Franks, as Engels has pointed out, was important for the development of medieval society in the West, as contrasted with the ancient Roman. [10]

Elsewhere in England the *ceorlas* were also in a rather advantageous social position, though not standing as high as the men of Kent. A group of families forming a village held their privately owned land in unenclosed adjacent strips — the "open fields," as they have been called — on which crops were rotated by individual peasants who often cultivated widely separated units. [11] In addition there was meadowland used as commons for grazing while it lay fallow, and there was usually an adjacent forest and wasteland from which families had the right to take their wood supply. [12] The peasants paid the king directly for their land holdings. The rent was delivered in kind: for instance, the owner of ten hides paid 300 loaves of bread a year, ten jars of honey, 12 *ambers* (casks) of Welsh beer and 30 of clear beer, two oxen, 10 wethers, 20 fowl, ten cheeses, an *amber* of butter, five salmon, 20 measures of fodder and 100 eels. [13] The royal tax was supplemented by others to the nearest district lord. In time the obligations to the *eorlas* increased, as these noblemen multiplied in number and assumed tighter authority over the villages. More and more the *ceorlas* were subordinated to members of the noble class, and later to church lords also — abbots and bishops — as these too were endowed with lands by the kings. [14]

The earliest political organisation of communities and counties is not known in detail. It is to be assumed that landholders in the villages held local meetings to discuss matters of immediate interest. [15] An early local unit was the "hundred," a geographical unit of varying extent, originally equivalent to the area of 100 hides approximately. These local areas eventually developed regular meetings, primarily to execute the justice of customary law. Each was presided over by the king's reeve, while the peasants carried out the justice themselves. However, there is no evidence to suggest the existence of general assemblies for shires or entire tribes, such as we find in Iceland, for instance, from the earliest times. The Anglo-Saxon kingdoms seem to have had nothing [16] to correspond to the Scandinavian *thing* or *Althing*, institutions of annual general meetings of all free farmers who enacted laws and judged cases brought to trial before an elected commission. The Anglo-Saxon political structure was centred rather on the king and his councillors, and much depended on the initiative and leadership of these men. The military organisation was a levy of free *ceorlas* into an army (called the *fyrd*) on the summons of the king, whether directly or by the nobles around him, as the case might be.

Offa, King of Angel, in a Fight

British Museum

One of the striking characteristics of the early Germanic kingdoms in England was the mutability of their fortunes. We know the history of the heptarchy in some detail only after the coming of Christianity and the art of writing. What is revealed for the seventh and eighth centuries was probably true, though on a smaller scale, in the first period as well. A struggle for advantage was conducted among the small realms, with one or another temporarily obtaining domination over one or more neighbours, and with transitory alliances formed and broken among them. Within the royal dynasties there was frequent conspiracy, violence and killing, with members of the same family readily assassinating one another to obtain a petty crown. This violence continued to mark the Anglo-Saxon royal families after Christianity had been introduced. It was characteristic of the entire period of Old English culture. Both literature and historical evidence suggest that the ties of blood relationship were no stronger than those uniting a grateful *þegn* to his royal master, if indeed they were as strong. A like situation may be found among other primitive Germanic dynasties, according to traditional accounts, despite the emphasis on ties of blood relationship calling for revenge in feuds with outsiders.

3. THE SOCIAL ROLE OF THE EARLIEST LITERATURE

The pagan invaders of England brought with them an oral literature, as we can deduce from later survivals, but concerning its precise nature we are forced to speculate. In dividing Anglo-Saxon literature into early and late pre-Christian, or non-Christian and Christian, it must be remembered that we are dealing with a body of texts, most of which have come down to us in late forms. They must have been copied and recopied over a period of time which we can estimate only indirectly, from such evidence as archaic linguistic forms, scansion, and internal references (e. g., to pagan divinities). Hence, when such literary products are here assigned to the chronological and social groups indicated, the division is made partly for convenience and partly as a result of deductive reasoning about chronology which as a matter of fact may err in its conclusions about any specific text.

We may begin with some of the most elemental forms of expression known to Germanic peoples in quite primitive times, including the ancestors of the Anglo-Saxons while they were still on the continent. First to be considered are the simple literary types associated with the experiences of the community as a whole, not restricted to a small class within it. These expressions are connected with forms of work, and with magic rituals which attempt to control nature for the use of

man, especially in connection with his labour and general welfare, his
sickness and health and the like.

From such an early stratum of popular literature, long antedating
Christianity and surviving beyond its advent, we have some curious
examples in the form of charms. We know that the Anglo-Saxons shared
the general primitive belief that the course of nature—the rainfalls and
droughts, fertility or sterility of cattle and fields—could be controlled
by mimetic acts accompanied by appropriate words in rhythmical composition. The Anglo-Saxon had their witches and spell-binders thought
by them to be especially efficacious in obtaining desired magic effects,[17]
but the ordinary peasant also used charms independently, we gather,
in the course of his work. Those which survive are scattered in various
manuscripts which of course postdate Christianity. Thirteen are in verse,
at least in part. They deal with such matters as controlling a swarm
of bees, getting rid of a wen or a sudden sharp pain in the side, curing
diseases and the effects of poisons, regaining stolen cattle, lightening
a difficult childbirth. The texts as preserved contain Christian elements,
but there are also pagan references within them which show the antiquity of the sources from which they come. The sentences are simple and
employ repetition, the units of speech are short, and the lines habitually
end-stopped. Such traits differentiate the versified charms from the style
of the courtly and religious epics known to have been composed in historical
times. A few charms contain phrases of Old Irish, somewhat distorted,
indicating some sort of contact with Celtic practitioners.[18]

The charm used to get back stolen cattle appeals for help to a certain
supernatural patron (a saint, replacing a pagan divinity?) named Gar-
mund, and concludes with a curse on the thief. It contains repeated elementary imperatives and also a simple, quite forceful curse. Noticeable
are the doubling of subjects, the loose construction of the last lines,
and other traits of untutored colloquial language:

> ȝarmund   ȝodes ðeȝn,
> find þæt feoh   and fere þæt feoh
> and hafa þæt feoh   and heald þæt feoh
> and fere ham þæt feoh.

> Garmund,   thane of God,
> find the cattle   and lead the cattle,
> and have the cattle   and hold the cattle,
> and guide the cattle home.

The curse runs as follows:

> þæt he næfre næbbe landes,   þæt he hit oðlæde,
> ne foldan,   þæt hit oðferie,
> ne husa,   þæt he hit oðhealde.
> ȝif hyt hwa ȝedo,   —ne ȝediȝe hit him næfre!

Let him never have any land,   he that may lead it away,
nor any earth,   he that may take it away,
nor houses,   he that may keep it away.
Should anyone do so,   —may it never prosper for him!

Conspicuous in the Nine Herbs Charm is a reference to Woden which evokes a bit of lost mythology concerning the god as serpent-killer:

Wyrm com snican,   toslat he man;
ða ʒenam Woden   viiii wuldortanas,
sloh ða þa næddran,   þæt heo on viiii tofleah.

A worm came creeping,   he cut at a man,
then Woden took   nine glory-rods,
then he struck the adder   so it burst into nine.

Very interesting is the charm for unfruitful land. Its formulas and instructions, as preserved in writing of a later period, are predominantly Christian, but it contains lines which appeal to a pre-Christian earth goddess of indeterminate antiquity:

Erce, Erce, Erce,   eorþan modor,
ʒeunne þe se alwalda,   ece drihten,
æcera wexendra   and wridendra,
eacniendra   and elniendra.

Erce, Erce, Erce,   mother of earth,
may the all-ruler grant thee,   eternal lord,
fields that are growing   and flourishing,
increasing   and strength-giving.

Some of the lines have the majesty of a hymn and suggest a formal religious cult:

Hal wes þu, folde,   fira modor!
Beo þu ʒrowende   on ʒodes fæþme,
fodre ʒefylled   firum to nytte.

Hale be thou, earth,   mother of men!
Be thou fruitful   in God's embrace,
filled with food   for the good of men.

There is evidence that England knew the primitive custom of proclaiming a workman's pride in his finished work by means of an inscription. On the continent, early Germanic labels in the runic alphabet (see below), written on a sword, a brooch or a drinking horn, sometimes announced the name of the craftsman who had made it. Thus the Gallehus horn of Denmark is inscribed with the eloquent words:

ek Hlewagastir Holti[n]gar   horna tawido.
I, Hlewagastir a Holting,   made this horn.[19]

No early inscriptions of precisely this sort are extant in English; but we do have an inscription on a jewel which is made to proclaim (in the first person) what king ordered it made: "Ælfred mec heht gewyrcan." However, this belongs to the period about A.D. 900, by no means primitive, when the convention by which an art object is thus made to speak was also used elaborately in formal verse.

Among the earliest forms of popular literary expression are various wise sayings and memory jingles. Primitive laws and genealogies, popular lore about the weather and peasant wisdom gathered from practical experience are often expressed in these rhythmical forms. The catalogues of names embodied in *Widsith* (see below, section 5) probably represent such primitive memory verses. A Christian form of mnemonic verse, the Menology extant in an eleventh-century manuscript, may well have had pagan precursors in the form of heroic nomenclatures. [20] It has been pointed out that the tradition of metrical composition affected the phraseology of law codes, some of which contain passages that could readily be printed as verse. [21] Rhythm must have been a distinct aid in the period when (as in Iceland also) legal prescriptions were transmitted entirely by memory.

The miscellaneous wise sayings generally called gnomes also represent an early literary type. In origin they may well be the product of versified peasant experience: a genuine village product; but their extant form shows signs of literary redaction. They comment sententiously on weather and crops, the forces of nature and the behaviour of people, and although generally banal, they at times have the touch of poetic imagination. [22] Curiously, the collections of these maxims are so arranged that the separate units very often end in the middle of a line, with the pattern of scansion left unfinished. This has suggested the possibility [23] that the concatenation of sayings resulted from a kind of game in which each speaker's contribution had to be "capped" by his neighbour. On the other hand, the rather artificial breaks in mid-line may be due to learned remodelling of primitive traditional material. [24]

```
                        Stream sceal on yðum
mencȝan mereflode.   Mæst sceal on ceole
seȝelȝyrd seomian.   Sweord sceal on bearme,
drihtlic isern.   Draca sceal on hlæwe,
frod, frætwum wlanc.   Fisc sceal on wætere
cynren cennan.   Cyninȝ sceal on healle
beaȝas dælan.
```

```
                        A stream with the sea
shall mingle its waves.   The mast on a boat
as sailyard shall stand.   A sword —lordly iron—
```

> shall be on one's bosom.   Old dragon shall live
> in a cave with its riches.   The fish in the water
> shall bring forth their kind. The king in the hall
> shall deal out treasure.

Closely akin to the gnomes are some moralising poems called *The Gifts of Men* and *The Fates of Men*.[25] The former deals with the callings of men and the occupations in which they show their gifts, and the latter tells the ways (mostly violent) by which men may die. The mood of these catalogues is sombre, and the phraseology indicates Christian origin. But the type appears to be older than Christianity. There are parallels for the Anglo-Saxon gnomes in other Germanic literature, notably a poem of the Old Icelandic *Edda* called the "Hövamál" ("Speech of the High One"), which in its substance at least appears to antedate Christianity.

Such is the extent of the verse which may by any plausible argument be attached to the social milieu of the Anglo-Saxon farming population.[26] The position of the rural poets is quite obscure. They were nameless members of the community who of course did not regard the composition of verses as a profession. Village wisdom is typically anonymous.

4. THE FORM OF THE OLDEST POETRY

Before turning to the literature of the pre-Christian upper classes, it will be well to glance at the poetic form of some of the verses that have already been quoted. It will be noticed that they do not employ rime, as do memory jingles and versified gnomes current today, like this:

> Evening red and morning grey
> Sets the traveler on his way;
> But evening grey and morning red
> Bring down showers on his head.

Instead, the sound patterns rely on repetition of the initial sounds of words (alliteration) in order to establish auditory echoes. Words beginning with the same consonants or certain groups of consonants are said to alliterate, as in such modern catch phrases as "hale and hearty," "spick and span," and many others. In addition, any vowel was able to alliterate with any other,[27] as in the phrase "eagle-eyed aviator."

The typical Anglo-Saxon line of verse was divided by a caesura into two approximately equal half lines, with two strongly stressed syllables in each. (A relatively small number of lines had six stresses, three to each half-line.) The first initial sound of the second half-line gave the alliteration for the entire line, and it was repeated in at least one other stressed syllable, as in "a gristly ghost, Grendel by name." The numbers of unstressed syllables separating stressed ones were not regularly fixed as in modern English. Since they were variable in number, the effect may appear highly irregular to a modern reader unacquainted with the principles of Old English scansion. As a matter of fact, the arrangement of stresses in the typical two-stressed hemistichs (i.e., half-lines) has been found to follow some quite clear patterns, limited in number and showing few irregularities. The variations in the number of unstressed syllables may be thought of as subject to control by variations in the tempo, as in musical delivery, where a long series of rapid notes is made to occupy the same span of time as a short series of slower ones.

It must be remembered that at first all poetry was probably intoned or chanted, and that narrative verse had some sort of musical accompaniment. Pauses were used like rests in music. The principle was quite different from that of modern verse, which is today read silently or spoken aloud with very little declamatory effect. The oral mode of transmitting Anglo-Saxon verse conditioned its literary form in the earliest times.

The subject of Old English scansion is complicated and the proper analysis of it is still a matter of discussion. [28] In his pioneer work on the general subject, Eduard Sievers [29] defined the types of syllables which were qualified to bear the four chief stresses of a normal line of verse, and the situations in which secondary stress appeared as well. Stress-bearing syllables had to occur in syntactically prominent words (e.g., nouns, pronouns, adjectives, etc., but not prepositions or conjunctions); and they had usually to be metrically long: that is, they had to contain a long vowel or diphthong, like *dūn* or *dēop*, or a short vowel or diphthong followed by two consonants, as in *deorc*. Occasionally a stress was distributed over a metrically short syllable plus a following unaccented one. These two together then bore the "resolved" stress and functioned as a single stressed syllable (for instance, the word *sele* taken as a whole). Occasionally too, by exception, a short syllable alone was found to bear the stress. Sivers distinguinshed five types of half-lines, which may be thus schematically represented if ˊ stands for a stressed long syllable, ˘ for a stressed short one, ˏ for a long with secondary stress, ˛ for a short with secondary stress, and x for one or more unstressed syllables.

A	ˊ x ˊ x	hȳran scolde
B	x ˊ x ˘	ond Halga til
C	x ˊ ˊ x	oft Scyld Scēfing
D (a)	ˊ ˊ ˏ x	fēond mancynnes
(b)	ˊ ˊ x ˏ	wēold wīdeferhð
E	ˊ ˏ x ˊ	weorðmyndum þāh

One or more unstressed syllables, constituting anacrusis, may appear
before lines requiring initial stress (types A, D, E), as unaccented notes
may precede the first bar in a musical composition. Most of the classics
of Anglo-Saxon poetry will be found to be scannable by these main
patterns, but there are exceptions even in the most conventional verse.

The Sievers method of scansion by these five main patterns, long
accepted with little dissent, has in the last few decades been critically
reexamined. The general tendency in newer interpretations has been
to stress the musical aspects of Anglo-Saxon poetry, to demand more
attention for such matters as rests and elasticity of tempo, and to get
away from the rather formalistic (visually expressed) patterns of Sievers.
Thus the importance of anacrusis and other musical effects was stressed
by Andreas Heusler, and the analogy with musical rhythm was worked
out in further detail by John C. Pope.[30]

In the earliest verse, the custom was to use end-stopped lines: that
is, the divisions between sentences and between major sentence parts
coincided with the ends of lines. Thus the individual lines were either
complete statements or complete syntactic units. The "run-on" line
was developed later in what may be called the classical period, among
courtly and learned poets. It is typical of the age of written composition.

In the period here being discussed, before the introduction of the
Latin alphabet, Germanic peoples made a limited use of a special alphabet composed of runes. These characters reveal a certain kinship with
both the Latin and the Greek alphabets, but their precise origin is a
matter of conjecture. Like the picture writing of other primitive peoples,
runic writing was looked upon as a magic art. It served not only to record
statements, but also actively (so its users thought) to produce magic
effects designed for the control of nature. Runic inscriptions on wood
or metal were supposed to evoke illness or to cure it (an incident in the
Icelandic *Saga of Egil Skallagrim's Son* exemplifies this), to help obtain
victory, to bring about good or bad luck. The very nature of the writing
was thought to have an influence upon nature comparable to that exercised
by the spoken charms. Knowledge of runes was limited, therefore, to
persons having pretentions to magic power, who obviously had an interest
in keeping that knowledge restricted and surrounded by an aura of
mystery.

Each letter in the runic alphabet stood not only for a spoken sound,
but also for a specific word (a noun) beginning with that sound. Hence
a series of runes could not only spell a single word, but also represent
a series of images. For example, þ represented the initial sound (a voiceless
dental spirant) of the word *þyncan* (*think*), and at the same time it stood
for the word *thorn* and was called by that name. The memorising of runic

characters and their meanings was aided by explantory verses which somewhat resembled an adult magician's *A B C*-book. What the earliest rune-poems were like we do not know, but we can surmise their character from a later Old English example (probably of the eighth century), and two still later Scandinavian rune poems (an Old Norse one, twelfth or thirteenth century; an Icelandic, fifteenth century).[31] A vivid example is this explanation of the letter I, the rune called after *ice*:

I (is) byþ oferceald,   ungemetum slidor,
glistnaþ glæshluttur,   gimmum gelicust,
flor forste geworuht,   fæger ansyne.

Ice is most cold,   immeasurably slippery,
it glitters glass-bright,   to gems it is likest,
a frost-wrought flower,   a right fair sight.

The full series of runes used by the Anglo-Saxons is as follows:[32]

ᚠ   ᚢ   ᚦ   ᚩ ᚱ ᚳ   ᚷ   ᚹ   ᚻ[ᚺ]   ᚾ ᛁ ᚸ
f   u   þ   o r c   �   w   h   n i j
feoh (feh) ur thorn os rad cen gyfu wen haegl nyd is ger

ᛇ[Z]   ᚼ   ᛈ   ᛉ ᛏ ᛒ ᛖ ᛗ   ᛚ   ᛝ[ᛟ] ᛟ[ᛟ]
i(h)   p   z   s t b e m   l   ng   oe
eoh peorth eolh sigel tir beac eh man lagu ing ethel

ᛞ   ᚪ   ᚫ   ᚣ   ᛡ   ᛠ ᚸ ᛏ ᛥ ᛤ ᚸ
d   a   ae   y   io   ea cw c? st g
daeg ac aesc yr iar ear   —   —   —   —

Runic Characters with Word Equivalents

This represents a larger set of characters than those used in the earliest Scandinavian texts and inscriptions. As we shall see, the runes were employed in close association with the arts of decoration. (See chapter 3, section 3, under the discussion of the Ruthwell Cross in relation to the *Dream of the Rood*.)

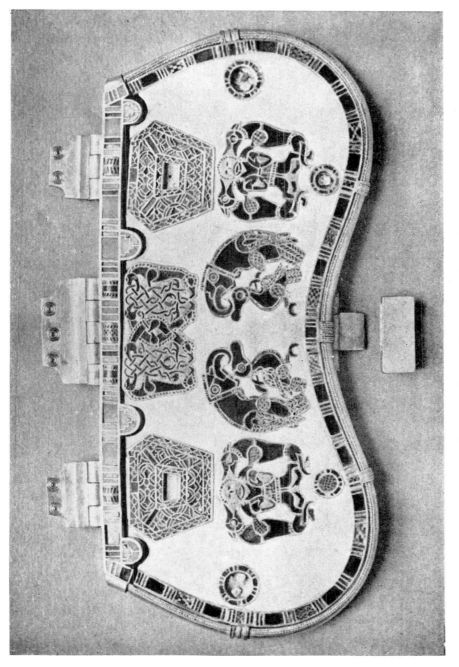

From the Buried Treasure at Sutton Hoo

A purse-lid with gold frame

5. EVIDENCE FOR COURTLY POETRY BEFORE THE AGE OF WRITING

Poetic creation was cultivated among the warriors as well as the peasants. Specially recognised and talented members of the military caste produced verses to glorify leaders, to commemorate events in tribal history, and to entertain their fellows at court. That this practice was general throughout the Germanic world we know indirectly from a number of sources. Later legends, evoking the age of migration (fourth to eighth centuries) as a period distant but unforgotten, include typical figures of warriors of high rank who produced poems urging to combat, recalling past glories, admonishing to revenge. These men recited at funerals and entertained in the royal halls after banquets. Significantly, they were not of a different, lower class, but belonged themselves to the aristocracy. They were sure of their audience, and sure of their position in society.

They received their rewards as other fighters did, in the shape of treasures or land granted by the king. Sometimes the reward was for a twofold service: both for fighting and for composing verse. The economic foundation of their status is clearly reflected in passages of several extant Anglo-Saxon poems dealing retrospectively with the heroic age. Very revealing is the lament of a poet calling himself Deor (see ch. 3, sec. 5), who has forfeited the favour of his lord and now sees a rival enjoying the "land-right" or estate he had once held.[33]

> 38   Ahte ic fela wintra   folзað tilne
> holdne hlaford,   oþ þæt Heorrenda nu
> leoðcræftig monn,   londryht зeþah
> þæt me eorla hleo   ær зesealde.
>
> I held many winters   a handsome post,
> had a kindly lord,   till Heorrenda now,
> the song-skilled man   received my land-right
> which the earls' protector   in past time gave me.

Another poet with the generic fictional name of Widsith (literally, Wide-Journey), tells about receiving a rich gold treasure from the celebrated King Ermanaric of the Goths. This treasure he gave to his own king later in gratitude for the confirmation of the right to hold land that had been his father's:[34]

> 93 Þone ic Eadзilse   on æht sealde
> minum hleodryhtne,   þa ic to ham becwom,
> leofum to leane,   þæs þe he me lond forзeaf,
> mines fæder eþel,   frea Myrзinзa.
>
> That then I gave   to Eadgils to own,
> to my lord protector,   when I had come home,

as reward to my dear one   because he endowed me with land,
—my father's estate—   that lord of the Myrgings.

Thus the social and economic ties binding early professional poets
to their patrons and associates are fairly clear. We can guess with some
likelihood of accuracy what were the materials they drew upon when
they were composing for pure entertainment — aside from occasional
pieces such as eulogies, funeral laments and battle-songs. One of the
most striking features of Germanic literary narrative in the pre-feudal
age is that it is intertribal. Events and personalities of the migration
age—the fates of Ermanaric the East Goth, Theodoric the West Goth,
Attila the Hun, the kings of sixth-century Franks and Burgundians—
were celebrated in widely sundered parts of the Germanic world, furnish-
ing materials for epic verse from Iceland to Germanised Gaul. [35] These
epic traditions are replete with deeds of violence; ruthless ambition and
the desire for revenge are among the most conspicuous motives for the
action. In this they reflect the historic actuality as portrayed by Latin
writers such as Jordanes the Goth, Gregory of Tours chronicling Frankish
history, and Paul the Deacon telling of the Lombard kings in Italy.

Out of this historical past, made fabulous by the imagination of
unknown narrators, there developed the famous legend of the fall of the
Burgundian tribe, re-named the Nibelungen in Germany (Niflungar
in Scandinavia), with its historical personages freely intermingled with
fictitious ones. The Nibelung cycle shows us Gunther and Gibich and
Giselher (historic Burgundian rulers) Attila the Hun (called Etzel in German), Hagen and Sigmund and Brynhild (attested Frankish names),
the Goths Ermanaric and Theodoric, consorting with giants and dwarves,
a dragon-killer and a bespelled warrior maiden, in a complex feud over
the ownership of a death-bringing, accursed treasure.

In Iceland, a whole series of shorter narrative poems about these
and other legendary heroes was developed and finally written down
in a collection known as the *Elder Edda*. A certain number of these lays
must have originated in Norway before the emigration to Iceland in the
ninth century; others were composed in the Icelandic colony. The poems
are stanzaic. They deal with single events in the heroes' careers: Sigurd's
fight with the dragon, his murder at the hands of his brothers-in-law;
their death at the court of King Atli (Attila), the adventures of another
hero named Helgi with a supernatural warrior-maiden, and so on. The
action is swift and it is portrayed with abrupt leaps from climax to climax. Scholars have speculated on the possibility that similar short lays,
now lost, existed in other Germanic languages—including Old Frankish
and Old English—before the age of literacy. If they did exist in prehistoric
Old English, they have disappeared, and we have little foundation for

speculation about their existence. Short passages do exist, treating of separate incidents of various heroic cycles, including that of the Nibelungen, but they are either fragments of ampler lost poems told in broad epic style, or are embedded in the long, fully developed epic of *Beowulf*, as digressions on the main theme. The technique of epic narration is quite different from that of lays, and there is no reason why we must assume that lays in the Eddic style always preceded the elaboration of longer stories into epics. As for shorter epic units, such as *Waldere* (see ch. 2, sec. 3), the evidence for them is also late. [36]

Nevertheless, it is generally conceded that the materials of the Anglo-Saxon epic, the stories about Scandinavian and other figures of the heroic age, were brought to England in the period of invasions: probably in the first part of the sixth century. We have no reason to believe that significant contacts were maintained after the end of the invasions between the Saxons of England and those of the continent in the pre-Christian age; hence the later borrowing of heroic pagan material is unlikely. Curiously, too, there were no epic legends developed about English heroes of the invasions proper—men like the shadowy Hengist and Horsa—which might have displaced the continental traditions. We can only say that these latter traditions were transplanted, but we can not say in what form. It would be unwise to hazard theories on the basis of our late and indirect evidence. [37]

Non-narrative verse no doubt existed in courtly circles also. Various social occasions would have favoured its composition, such as funerals, marriages, and feasts celebrating victories. To surmise what these poems may have been like, however, we are forced once again to examine later Old English literature on the one hand, and the analogous forms in Old Norse and Old Icelandic on the other. Here, in an essentially lyrical form, the differences between English and Scandinavian are not so great. Eulogies of kings, drinking songs, laments for fallen heroes and so on, are attested for a number of Germanic tribes, partly from the observations of classical writers and partly by the Scandinavian records. *Beowulf* describes situations in which such songs were said to be delivered. Especially impressive is the account of the hero's obsequies, during which solemn lamentations were chanted by twelve "earls" while the ashes of the hero's body, collected from the funeral pyre, were consigned to a monumental cairn.

3178   Swa beȝnornodon   ȝeata leode
       hlafordes (hry)re,   heorðȝeneatas;
       cwædon þæt he wære   wyruldcyninȝ[a]
       manna mildust   ond mon(ðw)ærust,
       leodum liðost   ond lofȝeorncst.

> Thus the Geatish folk   gave voice to their grief
> for the fall of their lord,   his followers true,
> they claimed that he was   among kings of the world
> mildest of men   and mannered the gentlest,
> to his people kindest,   most eager for praise.

Other passages tell about the lamentations spoken by a widow, a sister or a mother while standing before the hero's funeral pyre. Thus Hildeburh in the Finnsburg story mourns a son and a brother slain in her family's feud with her husband Finn (see ch. 2. sec. 4). Cremation of bodies antedated Christianity; hence the literary expressions associated with it have their roots in the prehistoric past. The scenes described in *Beowulf*, including the Finnsburg episode, recall the death of Sigurd and Brynhild's lament in the Scandinavian *Edda* and *Völsunga Saga*, also the funerals of the historical Attila and Alaric as reported in the Gothic history of Jordanes (see especially ch. 49), and more remotely the classical accounts of funerals in Homer (*Iliad*, lib. xxiii, 138 ff., xxiv, 785 ff.; *Odyssey*, xxiv, 43 ff.) and Virgil (*Aeneid*, lib. vi, 176 ff., xi, 59 ff.). The similarities are due to like social practices in various societies during the heroic age.[38]

Another type of burial for tribal leaders—inhumation of bodies on a ship, together with armour and treasures—may also have been accompanied by the recitation of poems in eulogy and lament.[39] Recent archaeological excavations at Sutton Hoo have indicated that these burials were also occasions of ceremony. The opening passage of *Beowulf* describes a not dissimilar occasion on which the body of a dead chieftain, richly apparelled, is consigned to the currents of the sea in a solitary, unguided ship.

It may be said in summary that the Anglo-Saxons quite surely brought with them from the continent a considerable body of materials which entered into the creation of later recorded literature. Among their most certain possessions were versified heathen charms and spells and memory verses perpetuating such information as tribal law and genealogies and gnomic wisdom. They also had legends of the Germanic heroic age; but whether these were told in prose or verse, in short lyrical-dramatic units or longer narrative ones, we can only guess. For concrete materials we must turn to the written texts, all of which were recorded in the period following after the advent of the Latin alphabet, in the seventh century of our era.

[1] J.N.L. Myres in Collingwood and Myres, *Roman Britain and the English Settlements* (Oxford, 2nd ed., 1937). Cf. Friedrich Engels, *The Origin of the Family* (New York, 1942), ch. 8; K. Kautsky, *Foundations of Chistianity* (New York, 1953), bk. ii: "Society in the Roman Empire".

[2] Charles Oman, *England before the Norman Conquest* (London, 1913).

[3] Myres, *op. cit.*, p. 346.

[4] H. Munro Chadwick, *The Origin of the English Nation* (Cambridge, 1924), ch. 5, p. 97.

[5] Chadwick, *op. cit.*, p. 67.

[6] Myres, *op. cit.*, p. 452.

[7] F.M. Stenton, *Anglo-Saxon England* (Oxford, 1946).

[8] See Chadwick, *op. cit.*, map accompanying ch. 1.

[9] Stenton, *op. cit.*, ch. 9.

[10] Engels, *op. cit.*, ch. 8.

[11] C.S. and C.S. Orwin, *The Open Fields* (Oxford, 1938).

[12] Oman, *op. cit.*, p. 358 f.

[13] *Ibid.*, p. 363.

[14] "The organisation of the folk reflected in the Tribal Hidage implies a state of society in which kings were seeking their rents and services directly from the holders of the ancient family lands. But from an age which was already remote in Alfred's reign, this primitive simplicity had been complicated by the creation of territorial lordships for nobles in the king's service and for churches," Stenton, *op. cit.*, p. 298. Charters for such awards by the kings appear from the seventh century onwards.

[15] Stenton, *op. cit.*, p. 295.

[16] Chadwick, *op. cit.*, pp. 144 ff.

[17] See the reference in the Penitential of Archbishop Theodore of Canterbury (A.D. 668—90): "si mulier incantationes vel divinationes fecerit....," cited by Alois Brandl, *Geschichte der altenglischen Literatur* (Strassburg, 1908), p. 15.

[18] Kemp Malone, ch. 1 in A.C. Baugh, *Literary History of England* (New York, 1948), pp. 38—42. The most recent edition is by Elliott van Kirk Dobbie, *The Anglo-Saxon Minor Poems* (New York: Columbia University Press, 1942), here used for citations. Important earlier editions are those in R.P. Wülker, *Bibliothek der angelsächsischen Poesie*, I (Hamburg, 1921) and F. Grendon, *The Anglo-Saxon Charms* (New York, 1909; reprinted 1930). Note: cited passages are taken when available from the series *Anglo-Saxon Poetic Records* (New York: Columbia University Press) edited by Krapp and Dobbie. Marks for vowel quantities, though given by some editors (for instance by Klaeber in his edition of *Beowulf*), are omitted in the quotations here given. A recent study of the whole problem is by Godfrid Storms, *Anglo-Saxon Magic* (The Hague, 1949). On Irish contacts see H. Meroney in *Speculum*, XX (1945), 172 ff. For bibliography of this and other types see Martin Lehnert, *Poetry and Prose of the Anglo-Saxons*, (Berlin, 1955).

[19] W. Krause, *Runenschriften im älteren Futhark* (Halle, 1937).

[20] Dobbie, *Anglo-Saxon Minor Poems*, pp. 49—55.

[21] Malone, *loc. cit.*, p. 35 f.

[22] Blanche C. Williams, *Gnomic Poetry in Anglo-Saxon* (New York, 1914 and 1937). Most gnomes are in the Exeter MS., but some appear elsewhere. The Maxims come from the Cotton Tiberius manuscript B.i, edited by Dobbie, *Minor Poems*, pp. 55—57.

[23] The suggestion is made by Stenton in his *Anglo-Saxon England*. Others regard the run-on lines as evidence of a late date.

[24] Andreas Heusler, *Zeitschrift des Vereins für Volkskunde*, XXVI (1916), 52.

[25] Edited by Krapp and Dobbie from the Exeter MS. in *The Exeter Book* (New York, 1936).

[26] The Riddles in Anglo-Saxon, though resembling gnomic verse in some respects, are demonstrably modeled on Latin poems. Their origin is therefore not popular.

[27] Actually, it was an initial glottal stop before each vowel which probably served as the alliterating element.

[28] For a brief account of the subject see Roman Dybowski, *Literatura i Język Średniowiecznej Anglii* (Kraków—Warszawa, 1910), pp. 79—82, or George K. Anderson, *The Literature of the Anglo-Saxons* (Princeton, 1949), pp. 51—54. Examples here given are from Fr. Klaeber, *Beowulf* (1936 ed.), p. 281.

[29] Eduard Sievers, *Altgermanische Metrik* (Halle, 1893).

[30] Andreas Heusler, *Deutsche Versgeschichte*, in Paul's *Grundriss*, VIII [1—3] (Berlin, 1925—29), especially part I, pp. 126 ff.; John C. Pope, *The Rhythm of Beowulf* (Yale University Press, 1942); J. Kuryłowicz in *Biuletyn Polskiego Towarzystwa Językoznawczego*, X (1950), pp. 25—44.

[31] Bruce Dickins, *Runic and Heroic Poems of the Old Teutonic Peoples* (Cambridge, 1915). The MS. of the Old English poem is lost, having been destroyed by a fire in the Cotton Library in 1731; George Hickes had printed it in 1705, and modern editions depend on his.

[32] Taken from Anderson, *op. cit.*, p. 181.

[33] *Deor*, edited by Kemp Malone (London, 1933); also Krapp and Dobbie, *Exeter Book*.

[34] *Widsith*, edited by Kemp Malone (London, 1936); Krapp and Dobbie, *op. cit.*

[35] The Frankish treatments, now lost, must be surmised from extant versions and from references in Gregory of Tours, *Historia Francorum* (sixth century). See Andreas Heusler, *Nibelungensage und Nibelungenlied* (Dortmund, 1921); Hermann Schneider, *Germanische Heldensage*, I (Berlin, 1928).

[36] A. Brandl, *op. cit.*, p. 12. Brandl assumes that existing verse had to be remodeled after certain linguistic changes had taken place, thus differentiating it from Old Saxon and creating a new Anglo-Saxon poetry, but this is not directly supoprted by extant evidence.

[37] Ritchie Girvan, *Beowulf and the Seventh Century* (London, 1935), ch. 2.

[38] H. Munro Chadwick, *The Heroic Age* (Cambridge, 1912).

[39] On the archaeological evidence see D. Elizabeth Martin-Clarke, *Culture in Anglo-Saxon England* (Baltimore: Johns Hopkins University Press, 1947), especially chs. 1 and 5. The artifacts of the Sutton Hoo Ship Burial are described by Bruce Mitford in an illustrated pamphlet published by the British museum (1947); see the bibliography by F. P. Magoun, Jr. in *Speculum*, XXIX (1954), 116—24. A general discussion of Anglo Saxon art and Viking art in England has been given by T.D. Kendrick in 2 vols. (London, 1949).

LATIN LITERATURE OF THE SCHOOLS AND VERNACULAR LITERATURE OF THE COURTS

1. EARLY KINGDOMS AND THE COMING OF CHRISTIANITY

During the sixth century the most important political development in England was the establishment of seven small kingdoms on the Germanic continental model, which were able to achieve a relative degree of stability. Despite much small-scale warfare, and the internal rivalries for local crowns, some of the dynasties were able to maintain themselves uninterruptedly for a century and more. By the end of the eighth century these seven were, however, in effect reduced to three: Northumbria, Mercia and West Saxony. The last of these directed the fortunes of Kent, which retained nominal independence.

Culturally, the Anglo-Saxons made their first significant contacts outside of their own sphere in the area of Northumbria. Here an early convert to Christianity, King Edwin, was overthrown (in 633) by a coalition expediently formed between the still-pagan King Penda of Mercia and a Celtic chieftain of the Western territory named Ceadwalla who was presumably a Christian; but a successor of Edwin's, King Oswald, reunited Northumbria and actively favoured missionary work in his lands by representatives of Celtic Christianity coming from Ireland. Most of the early kings of England, as later in Scandinavia, were predisposed to welcome the new religion because it helped to consolidate the small and otherwise unstable political units they ruled.

At this time Ireland was the leading centre of Celtic Christianity, and in fact one of the few areas in Western Europe where Roman literature and learning, combined with the new Christian doctrine, enjoyed peaceful cultivation during these disturbed times. After the missionary activity of St. Patrick (son of a Roman senator in Boulogne, died 493), Irish schools had been established, and the arts of writing, manuscript illumination and book-making had been zealously fostered. Irish scribes not only made decorative copies of Biblical and other religious texts in Latin; they also, in time, devoted care and energy to the recording of a wealth of heroic native legends in the prose vernacular. Thus a rich store of pre-Christian epic tales in Old Irish has been preserved to modern times — many, of course, in late and modified versions based on lost originals. The conservation of pagan literature was not felt to be inconsistent with a devotion to the new cult.

While Ireland was still keeping up close connections with neighbouring Gaul in the fifth and sixth centuries, it was affected by the strong influence exercised by Eastern Christianity upon the Romanised Celts of the mainland. Egypt, Syria and Palestine sent teachers to Marseilles and other centres of Southern Gaul. Old Roman schools of oratory were replaced by monastic establishments devoted to the study of theology according to the principles being laid down in the writings of the church Fathers in this transitional period. Here as elsewhere in the Greek and Roman world, the basic creed of the new world religion was being interwoven with the heritage of Platonism and the subtle unworldly fantasies of Neo-Platonism, so largely concerned with supra-mundane matters and so unconcerned with direct knowledge of the natural world. There was a strong tendency, sprung from the confusions of the age and reinforced by them, to take refuge in the most fruitless and abstract speculations dealing with the supernatural aspects of religion. Dionysius the so-called Areopagite, reputed to have been a missionary in Gaul, left a body of eschatological writings symptomatic of this intellectual trend. It was not shared to so great an extent, however, by writers like St. Augustine, who did not permit their Platonism to carry them so far away from the affairs of the real world about them.

The monastic institutions fostered in Southern Gaul were of a type familiar in Asia Minor and in Egypt. They were made up of hermits living in separate clustered cells, with far less emphasis on communal life than was to appear later when monasticism was organised on an international scale. These Gaulish monks studied Greek, Hebrew and Syrian texts as well as Latin ones. Manuscripts, epistles and instructions were received quite regularly from communities near Alexandria and Bethlehem; there is evidence that Syrian practices and even the Syrian language were taught at Lerins monastery in France at the time when Patrick was living there.[1] As a result, Christianised themes of Oriental thought, Oriental attitudes and Oriental motifs in art were transmitted to Ireland by way of Gaul. The effect of Coptic Christianity on early Irish sculpture, monastic architecture and manuscript decorations has been noticed by art historians.[2] A lively interest in the theme of souls facing judgment after death was common to Egypt and Ireland at this time, expressed in both countries in terms that can be proved to have been directly

borrowed from the much older pre-Christian cults of the Nile valley.[3]
As in Egypt, Irish hermits frequently retired into wild desert places,
either singly or in small groups. The very word "desert" was used to
denote a monastery, and a hymn praising the one at Bangor called it
"vinea vera/Ex Aegypte transducta". Many early Irish legends about
anchorite saints report that these solitaries made friends of wild beasts,
precisely as the Egyptian and Palestinian hermits are said to have done.

Thus varied was the cultural background of the first Christian
missionaries to reach Northern England. They were men of Ireland,
whose visits were encouraged by King Oswald of Northumbria. From
the remote monastic settlement of Hy Island (Iona) in the Hebrides
came St. Colomba, late in the sixth century. From Hy also came Aidan
in 634 (he died in 651), to whom Oswald granted the island of Lindisfarne
off the Northumbrian coast for the organisation of a monastic settlement,
Irish style. Lindisfarne served as headquarters for Aidan's roving missions.
The death of the Mercian King Penda (655) removed the ruler who had
been the most threatening foe at once of the new religion and of the
political independence of Northumbria. Under King Oswin (died 670)
the organisation of Celtic Christianity went forward peacefully in that
kingdom.

In the meantime, Christian missionaries had reached Southern
England from Rome, sent thither by Pope Gregory the Great. The first
group led by Augustine landed in Kent (597); they were immediately
successful in converting King Aethelbert (563-616). The organisation
they represented was far broader and at the same time more strictly
unified than the Celtic church. It was closely allied with the capital city
of the Western Empire, a connection which still had the value of great
historic prestige. It fostered unified methods of instruction and religious
observation (though these were not as yet accepted everywhere in the
West), and it had already worked out, in the Rule of St. Benedict, a form
of disciplined monastic life stressing communal activities and unified
procedures throughout an order which was to have important educational
significance in many countries. In these respects Roman monasticism
differed from the less formal, provincial and even individualistic institution of Irish hermit monks in their smaller groups. The Celtic and Roman
churches also differed in their methods of reckoning Easter. So far as
cultural history is concerned, the most important distinction between
the two lay in the fact that the Irish church, despite its considerable
services to learning, art and religion, had become isolated by the course
of historic events and was developing along provincial lines, whereas the
Roman church, soon to be accepted in Italy, France and the Christian
parts of Spain, Germany and Southern England, represented a carry-over

of tradition from the unified political world of the Western Mediterranean in classical antiquity.

The choice before the kinglets and chieftains of England was easily resolved. The advantages of allegiance to the more central authority of Rome were obvious, quite apart from the less ponderable claims of sentiment and cultural tradition. The issue was peaceably settled at a Synod called by King Oswin in Whitby (664), and after the triumph of the Roman party the Irish missionaries quietly withdrew. The establishment of church unity was facilitated by an agreement among the then reigning kings of Northumbria, Kent and Mercia, who recognised the value of the stability contributed by the new institution. Ecclesiastical unity was thus realised long before political unity in England.

Instruction on the Roman model was quickly begun, and it (like early Celtic learning) at first included some of the heritage of Eastern as well as Western Mediterranean culture. Roman law, which had largely aided the doctrinal and institutional unification of the Western church, both in basic concepts (sin as "transgression") and in regional organisation (bishoprics), was soon being studied in England. It was however Theodore of Tarsus, a Greek scholar originating from Asia Minor, and trained at Athens, who founded the centre of teaching at Canterbury. He was accompanied by Hadrian of Nicidia, who was born in Byzantine Africa and trained in Italy when it was still politically dependent upon Byzantium. At Malmesbury, a monastic settlement founded under Celtic auspices by the Irish Maildulf (Maildubh) was now transferred to the Roman organisation, but it still maintained some contacts with Irish scholarship.[4] In the latter seventh century there were a number of centres, apparently, where Greek and even Hebrew were taught in addition to Latin. In the North, besides the monastic foundation at Lindisfarne, there were schools at Whitby, Jarrow and Wearmouth; in the eighth century at York and Lichfield also.

There is evidence from both Latin and vernacular literature that Irish Christianity, with its strong Oriental elements, continued to influence the Anglo-Saxon church for some time after the Synod of Whitby. The Irish version of the Roman alphabet, modified by Saxon usage, appears in the earliest Latin manuscripts in the North. A copy of the Gospels made at Lindisfarne is preserved in a fine volume decorated on the outside with metal work and jewels. The text itself is written in the Hiberno-Saxon script and adorned with intricate designs in the style of Irish artists exemplified in the Book of Kells (now preserved in Trinity College, Dublin). The Lindisfarne manuscript was written about the year 720. It represents a triumph of the art of fine book-making, and is a monument to the combined talents of the Irish and English schools.[5]

2. LATIN SCHOLARS AND TEACHERS TO CA. 800

The founders of the church schools in Anglo-Saxon England considered that they had a two-fold task. The first was, obviously, to provide copies of the basic texts of the new religion: the Old and New Testaments, the expositions and liturgies, the tracts and handbooks embodying the rules of the new way of life. Next came the task of dissemination and instruction. A considerable effort was required to bring the revised values before Germanic clansmen nurtured on a tribal ideology of touchy caste honour, feuds and revenge. The ideological themes of humility and resignation and official pacifism (regardless of current practice to the contrary) had been projected out of the ancient cultures in a period of world crisis and decline of the dominant system. Among several very popular cults of Asia Minor glorifying these non-martial virtues and expressing the aspirations of various oppressed peoples, Christianity rapidly assumed leadership and eventually triumphed.[6] Its commandments were singularly out of keeping with the bloody feuds and predatory expeditions of the military aristocracies of the North, just as they had been discordant with the political realities of the ancient world; and the discrepancy between officially accepted doctrine and violent practice among the ruling dynasties was not to be resolved.

Only within the special religious groups where asceticism and community of goods were the official rule, was any serious effort made to adjust the practice with the theory of the new faith. As economic units they were at the time still negligible. The religious orders, informal as they were at the beginning, were nevertheless the sole agencies of learning and instruction, and they demanded also a certain measure of constructive physical work from their members. They attracted a number of intellectually gifted men and of women as well in the first generations of Christianity in England. From the biographies known to us, it would appear that the outstanding teachers and scholars, the abbots, abbesses, librarians, writers and so on were generally recruited from the ruling class. In more than one instance, too, the much-harassed kings of Northumbria, wearied of palace revolutions and bloodshed in the family, sought refuge in monasteries in order to escape the distasteful risks of their position.

Mastery of the art of writing on manuscripts was put into the service of native vernacular and of Latin literature almost simultaneously, but what has survived from the late seventh and early eighth centuries is chiefly Latin. Anglian texts of the period have mostly come down to us in later copies.

In the Southern part of England Aldhelm (ca. 640—709) was the first outstanding Latin writer.[7] A member of the West Saxon royal family, he studied with Maildubh the Scot (i.e., Irishman) at Malmesbury, later at Canterbury under the direction of Theodore and Hadrian. He became Abbot of Malmesbury and later Bishop of Sherborne, and he supervised the founding of additional monasteries and the building of a number of churches. He is said to have known Hebrew, Greek and Latin. According to a later authority, William of Malmesbury, who was in a position to have reliable information, Aldhelm was skilled in music, song and the composition of vernacular poetry. He is reported to have lured people to religious services by first performing for them as a minstrel out of doors. King Alfred is said to have loved the poems, now lost, which were attributed to Aldhelm. What we do have of Aldhelm is prose tracts, letters and verses in an artificial Latin at the opposite pole from an engaging popular style. His turgidly written letters are full of word-play, alliteration, Latinised Hebrew and Greek loan words, and formalistic patterns in word order;[8] his verses contain elaborate acrostics and curious out-of-the-way epithets. The style probably reflects the influence of the early teachers, Theodore and Hadrian, who appear to have had the obvious defects of their quite cosmopolitan training in the schools of the late empire. Very indirectly one can detect traces of the so-called "Asiatic" school of oratory, which had a centre in Tarsus of Asia Minor. Its artificial style had also indirectly affected the Latinity of Ireland, by way of the rhetorical tradition in Gaul.

Some aspects of Aldhelm's writing had a certain importance for vernacular literature. His ingenious riddles, imitated from those of Symphosius (late Roman empire, date unknown) were composed within the frame-work of a treatise on metrics, but the author looked upon them, it seems, as examples demonstrating the wonders of nature. The concluding riddle, No. 100, is a poem representing a speech by "Creatura" (that is, created nature) who theologically expounds her role in relation to the divine creator in terms of Christianised Platonism:

> Conditor, aeternis fulcit qui saecula columnis,
> Rector regnorum, frenans et fulmina lege,
> Pendula dum patuli vertuntur culmina caeli,
> Me varium fecit, primo dum conderet orbem.

Behind the alliterations and epithets of this passage it is perhaps possible to sense a parallel with vernacular poetry. On the other hand Aldhelm's two short tracts in praise of virginity, one in prose and one in verse, show no such connections. They are purely didactic, and are constructed largely on a series of examples illustrating the qualities being praised. Such catalogues of *exempla* became a favourite type of didactic literature in ensuing centuries.

Other Anglo-Saxon writers of Latin in the South shared a number of Aldhelm's interests and stylistic traits. Tatwine, Archbishop of Canterbury (died 734) also wrote riddles and adorned the verses with acrostics. Eusebius Abbot of Wearmouth in the North (after 716) wrote riddles modeled on Tatwine's.[9] Wynferth, otherwise known as St. Boniface, outdid Aldhelm in the intricacy of the acrostic patterns in his verses. This is the same Boniface (died 755) whose ambitious missionary activities in Germany, carried out in perilous circumstances, were widely celebrated throughout the West.

Northern Latinity in England produced a figure of far more impressive literary achievements than any of these others, in the person of the Venerable Bede (ca. 673—735). He was trained by Benedict Biscop, Abbot of Wearmouth, who had been instrumental in having the Benedictine Rule introduced to replace Celtic monastic practices.[10] Later Bede transferred to the monastery at Jarrow where he spent the rest of his life teaching and writing. He was interested in a wide variety of subjects, and his works constitute the most ambitious effort to absorb and recreate the heritage of classical and patristic learning for the use of the Anglo-Saxon schools. In performing this task of transmission, he avoided the excesses of the Neo-Platonists like Dionysius the Areopagite. He and the later Alcuin show familiarity with classical epic (Virgil, Statius, Lucan, Ovid and others), besides the works of the Latin church Fathers.[11] Of course, when they cite such authorities, we can not be sure whether they knew the entire works, or merely select passages such as were frequently current in anthologies of extracts.

It may be said that one of the themes which most conspicuously challenged the attention of Latin scholars at this period was the problem of physical creation or the beginning of things. In this sense Aldhelm's Riddle No. 100 is symptomatic. Bede, like others, turned to two sources for enlightenment: both theological (Biblical and patristic) and classical-scientific. Among the former sources, it is noteworthy that the Pentateuch, especially Genesis, engaged so much of the attention of English church writers at this time. In this respect they were continuing a preoccupation already apparent in Gaul and Spain of the fifth and sixth centuries.

Bede, following patristic models which go back to Basil of Caesarea (fourth century) wrote a *Hexameron* or discussion of the Biblical six days of creation,[12] followed by commentaries on more of Genesis and the rest of the Pentateuch, as well as the four Gospels, the Apocalypse, and other texts. Much of this exegesis follows the widespread system of allegorical interpretation promulgated by Saints Ambrose and Augustine. It subordinated historical fact to moral instruction. Bede's scientific interest, on the other hand, was reflected in books dealing with geography, the heavenly bodies, the reckoning of time, problems of climate, eclipses and seasons. [13] In addition, Bede wrote on orthography and metrics, and he composed homilies and poems in Latin. Among the latter are some which also treat of time and the seasons, and a metrical life of St. Cuthbert of Lindisfarne. In all his works, Bede's straightforward style contrasts strikingly with the tortuous Latinity affected by writers like Aldhelm.

But his greatest achievement was of course the writing of his *Ecclesiastical History of the English Nation* (*Historia Ecclesiastica Gentis Anglorum*, completed in 731). Although restricted in scope as the title indicates, the work is also of great value for our knowledge of the course of secular political history in Anglo-Saxon England. Bede was a judicious and sober historian for the most part; elements of credulous fantasy are less conspicuous in his writing than in that of most of his contemporaries. He gives a clear, animated, reliable account, and he is able, on certain occasions, to write with an unaffected eloquence imparting a truly poetic quality to his Latin prose. These qualities were, as we shall see, successfully transferred to the Anglo-Saxon version of the *Historia* which was made in the reign of King Alfred.

In the decades after Bede's death, the most distinguished Latinist was a Northumbrian compatriot of his, Alcuin or Ealhwine of York (ca. 735—804). Educated by contemporaries of Bede, librarian and director of the York school, closely associated with princes of church and state, Alcuin never himself advanced beyond the rank of deacon by ordination. His learning and prestige were so great, however, that he was invited by Charlemagne to join him in efforts to establish learning among the Frankish ruling class, particularly in the organisation of the palace school at Aachen and in the direction of monastic studies. Alcuin finally settled permanently in France in 793 as head of St. Martin's monastery, and also of houses at Troyes and Ferrères. Some of his works, being written expressly for Charlemagne, are not strictly a part of Anglo-Latin literature. Such is his *Rhetoric*, for instance, which reworks and expands classical sources like Cicero's *De Inventione*, Julius Victor's *Ars Rhetorica* and some others, recasting the whole in the form of a dialogue between scholar and emperor. Alcuin showed his independence by using Biblical situations along with others to exemplify the principles of Roman legal oratory. [14]

The scope of Alcuin's works, regardless of their place of composition, is significant of the intellectual needs and interests of his age. The concern with astronomy and the reckoning of time is again reflected in a number of letters to Charlemagne. Like Bede, Alcuin wrote also on grammar and orthography besides hagiography and technical theoological problems (e.g., the nature of the Trinity). He too composed a commentary on Genesis, using the question-and-answer form; his poems include an historical survey of the missionary teachers and bishops of York church drawn largely from Bede. Alcuin's epistles reflect wide and amicable connections among important persons of his time, and he shows the solicitude of a conscientious teacher about the welfare of his disciples.

Alcuin's later poems and letters contain frequent references to the catastrophe which overwhelmed Northern English culture with the onset of the Scandinavian raids and invasions beginning in 787. There are personal cries of distress in his epistles to friends, and a lamentation on the destruction of Lindisfarne monastery (793). Alcuin echoes here a theme already familiar in the lamentations for the fall of Rome and other continental cities before barbarian attacks of the fifth to eighth centuries. The memories of past learning and splendour are merged with images of present desolation. Unaware of the deeper historical causes for their dreadful experiences, about which very limited information was at their disposal, the poets attribute them exclusively to God's anger at moral corruption. The poems are none the less moving for that. Alcuin's elegy on Lindisfarne expresses a deep sense of public and private loss, and at the same time it gives us valuable insight into the nature of the treasures which were annihilated or carried away by the Vikings.

The period beginning about A.D. 800 marks indeed the end of the first literary age in England, especially in the far North. The turmoil and slaughter of the ensuing century was not favourable to the preservation of literature. There is evidence that its creation was not entirely terminated, either in Latin or in the vernacular, with the onset of Scandinavian raids. Mercia in particular seems to have carried forward literary production; but much was destroyed completely, much has survived only in later transcriptions, and we can not even surmise how much was prevented from coming into existence as death and destruction once more walked the land.

3. FIRST VERNACULAR CHRISTIAN POETRY

The earliest pieces of Old English verse surviving in their original form were composed in Northern England, the homeland of Bede. [15] One of them, indeed, purports to be the Death-Song of Bede himself, and is embodied in a Latin letter by Cuthbert describing Bede's last days. There is nothing about the language or other evidence to prevent our assuming that Bede actually composed the simple lines about man's need to be wise in thought as he faces the departure of his soul for judgment after death.

Another bit of poetry from about the same time, or even earlier, is a Hymn celebrating the wonders of creation, composed by a countryman of Bede's named Caedmon. All that we know about this Anglo-Saxon poet is reported in the *Historia Ecclesiastica* (bk. iv, ch. 24). According to it, Caedmon was a simple farm labourer, turned lay brother, who received the gifts of song and versification in a special vision of super-natural origin. (This is a not unusual anecdote found attached to the biographies of other early poets.) However they were inspired, Caedmon's

The Expulsion of Adam and Eve from Paradise
From the Junius MS.

gifts brought him to the attention of Abbess Hild, a scholarly lady in charge (657—80) of a dual monastery for men and women at Whitby. She wel-comed Caedmon into the community as monk and encouraged him to write more religious verses in the vernacular. According to Bede, he responded by composing poems based on—or inspired by—the first books of the Bible: the ones which, containing the narration of the world's origin and primeval history, held a particular attraction for the Anglo-Saxon imagination. He is also said to have treated themes from the New Testament, and visions of doomsday to come. The Hymn itself is pre-served in manuscripts of the later English version of Bede's history. The nine lines in the original Northern dialect are worth quoting because of their historical importance:

Decorated Leaf of the Lindisfarne Gospel

British Museum

Nu scylun herȝan   hefænricæs uard,
metudæs mæcti   end his modȝidanc,
uerc uuldurfadur   sue he uundra ȝihuæs,
eci dryctin,   or astelidæ.
He ærist scop   ælda barnum
heben til hrofe,   haleȝ scepen,
tha middanȝeard   moncynnæs uard,
eci dryctin   æfter tiadæ
firum foldu,   frea allmectiȝ.

Now shall we praise   the heaven-keeper's warden,
the might of God   and his mood-thought,
work of the glory-father   as he of all wonders,
the eternal lord   established the start.
He first created   for the children of men
heaven as a roof,   the holy creator.
Next the middle realm   did mankind's ward —
the eternal lord —   afterwards fashion
for men of the earth,   the ruler almighty.[16]

Here we have the main characteristics of epic verse clearly exemplified: the patterns of scansion, the epithets and appositions, the parallel constructions, interruptions and repetitions in the sentences. But the lines are still prevailingly end-stopped.

Nothing else of Caedmon's work remains to us, at least not in the form in which he wrote it. We do possess, however, a manuscript of later date (11th century) containing poems in the West Saxon dialect closely corresponding in subject matter with those described by Bede. This is the Junius manuscript,[17] so called from the name of the Dutch scholar who acquired it in the seventeenth century. Its contents are: *Genesis*, *Exodus* and *Daniel* (that is, poetic paraphrases of sections of those books), and a composite piece called *Christ and Satan* by modern editors.[18] No scholar now believes that these poems were all Caedmon's and it is most unlikely, even, that any of them is even a direct redaction of one of his writings. It is very likely, however, that the poems were inspired by Caedmon's example and the term Caedmonian poetry may well be applied to them. (For discussion see ch. 3, sec. 1.) It has been suggested that Caedmon's treatment of the Biblical themes was lyrical, in the style of his extant Hymn, but of this we can not be sure.

4. COURTLY EPIC: THE SHORTER PIECES

While the earliest Christian verse was being composed, some of the non-Christian epic materials were being worked up into final shape and written down for the first time. At least some of them appear to have been composed first in the Northern regions. In a letter of A.D. 797, Alcuin advises Bishop Hygbald of Lindisfarne[19] to have his monks listen to works of the church Fathers at their meals, not to the songs of pagans (*carmina gentilium*), for what, he asks, has the old Germanic hero Ingeld got to do with Christ? (*Quid Hinieldus cum Christo?*) Since Ingeld was a son-in-law of King Hrothgar in the epic poem *Beowulf*, and the subject of separate epic treatment in Scandinavia, Alcuin's hostile words testify to the existence of narratives from the borrowed Danish courtly cycle already in existence in Northumbria.[20] These are lost. But it is fortunate that in Anglo-Saxon England, as in Ireland, the hostility of men like Alcuin to secular narrative was not so great as to prevent the recording of at least some part of it in durable manuscripts. For this reason we still possess literary treasures that would otherwise have been lost.

The Northumbrian versions put down in such manuscripts at the time of Alcuin have vanished. They did not survive the ravages of the Scandinavian invaders beginning late in this century. Yet a number of the extant epic texts in the West Saxon dialect show internal evidence of having been composed originally in Anglian territory and later transcribed and modified linguistically in the South. It will be simplest to discuss all of the surviving epic materials at this point, though their chronological relations may have been more complex than the grouping indicates.

A typical theme of early Germanic poetry was the defense of a royal hall from attacking enemies. Many a tribal king thus ended his rule, falling in defensive combat while the hall burnt above him. Such a situation is central to *The Fight at Finnsburg*,[21] a fragment which recounts the sudden attack made upon the hall in which some visiting warriors are lodged, and their brave resistance to the attacker, who is their host. The motive is an ancient feud. From certain passages in *Beowulf* (see below) we learn that the attacker is King Finn of the Frisians, the defenders are a band of Danish guests under King Hnaef, whose sister Hildeburh had been married to Finn. We also learn that Hildeburh lost both brother and son in the combat. After a truce and a winter's respite, the Danes took revenge by killing Finn and carrying Hildeburh back to her people.

The separate fragment dealing with the first fight is powerful though conventional in its expression. It is analogous to descriptions of other beleaguered and bloodily contested strongholds in Germanic legend: the destruction of Hrolf Kraki recounted in the Old Icelandic saga named for him, of the Burgundian princes, Kriemhild's brothers, in the German *Nibelungenlied*, and others. Thus the Old English text, though surviving in a late form, is replete with the atmosphere of a more primitive society, and with the *mores* of the class in it that lived by an exacting code of honour and revenge.

The same spirit breathes through another fragmentary text, *Waldere*, [22] which belongs to the same cycle as the *Nibelungenlied*. Two passages of what was perhaps a rather ambitious poem (eighth century?) deal with an episode in the adventures of Walter of Aquitaine and Hildigund, both of whom had been hostages at the court of King Attila the Hun. They fled from it in secret, but on the way home were attacked by King Guthhere of the Burgundians, who coveted their treasure. Hagena, a former companion of theirs in exile, reluctantly gave support to King Guthhere in the attack. The first fragment is an inspiriting speech by Hildigund, urging Waldere to valorous exploits; the second is the end of a boastful challenge to Waldere, and the beginning of his reply. These speeches are typical of the bellicose "flyting" which enlivens combat scenes in other Germanic narratives of the same type. Significantly enough, this same legend was treated on the continent in a Latin epic of the ninth or tenth century, called *Waltharius* and doubtfully ascribed to the monk Ekkehard I of St. Gall in Switzerland. Not all monastic writers in Latin shared Alcuin's scruples about the value of Germanic legends as subjects for serious treatment. To the author of *Waltharius* we are indebted for an important text preserving Germanic lore of the heroic age in the alien garb of Virgilian hexameters. A version of the same legend was known in Poland by the 13th century. It was incorporated (perhaps from oral sources) in the *Chronicon* of Bishop Boguphal of Poznań (died 1253). [23]

A third short piece of Anglo-Saxon verse is likewise valuable for its preservation of epic allusions and topics — unelaborated, to be sure — which would otherwise be lost to us. The poem *Widsith*, as has been said (see ch. 1, sec. 5), purports to be the chronicle of a poet's (scop's) visits among the fabled princes of the epic age, together with catalogues of the names of other princes, offered without comment. Since the references extend from Egyptians and Israelites and ancient Greeks (these may well constitute, it is true, a late interpolation) to Germanic tribes and rulers of the fourth to the sixth centuries, they obviously are not founded on a literal biography. [24] Despite possible interpolations, the theme is simple. The poem may be taken as a dramatic statement by the poet of the materials he has at his disposal for epic declamation if he should be invited to entertain at a king's court. The Old Norse sagas of a later date have analogous situations of poetic repertoires thus dramatised and offered in autobiographical form, and they may be found in Celtic literature too. In Widsith's catalogue we find tantalising references to celebrated heroes such as Ermanaric of the Goths, Guthhere of the Burgundians (the German Gunther of the Nibelung story), Aelfwine of the Lombard kingdom in Italy, Offa of the continental Angles, Hrothgar and Hrothulf and Ingeld of the dynasty celebrated in *Beowulf*. The mere catalogue of names suggests how much epic tradition then known, in whatever form, is now hopelessly lost.

5. *BEOWULF*: PLOT, STRUCTURE, ART FORM

The one epic theme which has been preserved for us in full literary treatment is the celebrated narrative of *Beowulf*. Described in outline, its subject matter appears simple enough. It tells of a champion of the Geats (a tribe dwelling in Southern Sweden) who twice perfomed feats of prodigious valour to save a people oppressed by supernatural forces of destruction. In his youth he visited the royal court of the Danes, which had been devastated by the nocturnal visits of a man-eating monster named Grendel, and he slew the gristly invader in unarmed single combat. When the depredations were renewed by Grendel's gigantic mother, seeking revenge, Beowulf pursued her to her under-water lair in a haunted lake, and there killed her after long struggle, with the help of a magic sword. Later, in his old age, after ruling for fifty years as king of the Geats, he fought a second time in the role of slayer of monsters. This time he sought out a dragon which had been afflicting his people, and killed it in a remote mountain cave. He himself succumbed to the injuries received in the combat. He died and was buried under a cairn on a headland by the sea, amidst the lamentations of his devoted followers.

The text of *Beowulf*, a poem of 3182 lines in length, is the single instance of a fully developed and sustained epic narrative that has come down to us. It shows many of the literary characteristics of other epics in various languages. It is told in a broad and dignified manner. The action is not hurried; it is retarded by passages of description, by direct speeches in lofty tone (more than 1300 lines of these), by inserted minor narratives or "epic digressions." [25] Among these latter are summaries of other epic tales recounted by court singers, such as the attack on Finnsburg hall, an exploit of Sigmund the dragon-killer, a reminiscence of Beowulf's own early deeds. As befits the poetry of a courtly milieu, there is emphasis on the etiquette of social intercourse: the colloquy of the visiting Geats with the Danish coast guard, Beowulf's presentation of himself at Heorot, King Hrothgar's hall, his later report of his adventures to his uncle, King Hygelac of the Geats—all of these are handled with appropriate amplitude and formality. There is dignity and even a touch of warning against pride in Hrothgar's speech of thanks to

Beowulf, and the Danish Queen Wealhtheow contrives to express a tactful appeal for future aid and friendship in the gracious language of seasoned diplomacy.

The style of the poem elsewhere bears out the impression of epic formality. It is typical of an art consciously cultivated and adapted to its purpose. To a certain extent the art appears in all of Anglo-Saxon narrative, both Christian and pagan. But nowhere is it marked by more careful elaboration than in *Beowulf*. Though the material of the story may well have been transplanted to England in a simple form, the extant poem is anything but primitive.

In matters of detail, the effect of formality is borne out by the use of compound nouns and phrases, called "kennings," which designate by indirect means rather than by immediate designation, as is more usual in prose. Examples are: "heath-stepper" (*hæðstapa*) applied to a stag; "wave-traverser" (*yðlida*) applied to a ship, "distributor of treasure" (*synces brytta*) for a prince, and so on. [26] Some of these appear frequently as stereotypes. The single words entering into the composition of such kennings are usually quite simple and familiar in prose, but the nominal compounding itself is a trait of the poetic style. There are verbal stereotypes too. Especially noticeable are the repeated expressions which announce a speech: "Then spoke X, the son of Y" (e.g., *Beowulf maþelode, bearn Ecgþeowes*). Repetition or echoing of phrases is employed for a specific rhetorical effect, it has been pointed out, namely to mark off the beginning and end of a subdivision — a speech, a description, a section corresponding to a paragraph in prose. There is also a fine sense of appropriateness in handling antitheses and parallels of phraseology, direct and indirect discourse. [27]

Beowulf contains some memorable descriptions, usually interwoven with the action in such a way that they accompany it and elucidate it without arresting it. The poet sketches rapidly yet vividly the voyage of Beowulf from Geatland to Denmark and then homewards again; he paints a picture and at the same time evokes an atmosphere and forwards the action when he delineates Grendel's mist-covered and spooky advance upon Heorot, or the vigil of Beowulf's companions at the lakeside while he fights in the watery depths, or the approach of Beowulf to the dragon's cave. At times the descriptions are so heightened as to give a bravura effect. Justly famous is the shivery account of Grendel's stealthy invasion of the silent hall where the Geats lie waiting for him: [28]

710   Ða com of more   under misthleoþum
    Ʒrendel ʒonʒan,   ʒodes yrre bær;
    mynte se manscaða   manna cynnes
    sumne besyrwan   in sele þam hean.

Wod under wolcnum   to þæs þe he winreced,
ʒoldsele ʒumena   ʒearwost wisse
fættum fahne...

720   Com þa to recede   rinc siðian
dreamum bedæled.   Duru sona onarn
fyrbendum fæst,   syððan he hire folmum æthran,
onbræd þa bealohydiʒ,   ða he abolʒen wæs,
recedes muþan.   Raþe æfter þon
on faʒne flor   feond treddode,
eode yrremod;   him of eaʒum stod
liʒʒe ʒelicost   leoht unfæʒer.

     Then from the moorland   from misty cliffs
Grendel came gliding;   God's wrath he bore.
The monster was minded   from among those men
One to entrap   within the high hall.
He moved under clouds   till he saw most clear
the wine-hall of warriors   with gold adorned
plated and gleaming...
So came to the building   the creature advancing
bereft of all joy.   The door sprang asunder
though fastened by fetters   when his fist had grasped it,
and purposing evil   —for in passion he raged—
he tore wide the entrance.   Thereafter he trod
on the gleaming floor,   that fiendly foe;
he entered in anger   and from his eyes there flared
a hideous light   most like unto flame.

Another celebrated passage of description, almost indeed a purple
patch on the epic, is Hrothgar's word-painting of the haunted lake, surrounded by crags, mountain torrents and frost-bitten groves, where Grendel's
dam lurks in her underwater cave. Fire has been seen flickering over
its surface; no one knows how deep it is; the terror associated with it
is so great that a wild hart pursued by hounds will rather suffer death
on its shores than spring into that water to save itself. Here the deliberate romanticising of nature is so marked and so untypical that some
non-Germanic influence on the style has been suspected.[29] No immediate model has been discovered, however, though Virgilian echoes have
been detected by some from the *Aeneid* (lib. iv).

Besides speeches and descriptions, there are passages of distinctly
lyrical quality which further help to diversify the narrative and at the
same time to make more stately its deliberate tempo. The lyrical mood
is chiefly elegiac. Among the themes treated are Hrothgar's grief for
his fallen thanes, regret for past youth and past glories, the nostalgia
of a single surviving clansman for the brave company that once surrounded him. Beowulf's reminiscent review of his life before the final combat
is also melancholy in tone. All of these passages intensify the rather somber

mood prevailing in the poem. Even when the feasting and light and good company of the mead-hall are portrayed, we are never long permitted to forget that "Baleful death hath sent away before us many races of men!"

Concerning the plot of *Beowulf* as a whole it may be said that the first part—the action in Denmark—is unified and is well constructed; though there are two different climaxes represented by the fights with the two monsters, there is no slackening of interest. The second fight has so many new elements, and is so effectively heightened by its strange surroundings, that its course is followed with increasing attention on the part of the listener. The latter part of the poem, with its action in Geatland, is also well constructed. The fight with the dragon is carefully prepared, its significance is underscored by Beowulf's faithful companion Wiglaf, and (as befits an epic) the concluding action after it—embracing the speech of the dying hero, his obsequies, and the lament for him—is recounted in some detail. The weakness in the plot is the tenuous connection between the first and second parts. We have not only to transfer our attention from Denmark to Sweden, but from the youth to the old age of the hero, when the very people surrounding him are different. The only tie with past action is the generic similarity of the struggle: the same hero versus another supernatural adversary.

Aside from a natural lapse of interest during the transition from part one to part two, the composition as a whole commands respect. It progresses, it represents an organic whole, and it amalgamates minor themes and plots into a unified major one. The subordinate themes accentuate rather than disturb the total unified effect.

6. *BEOWULF*: MATERIALS OF THE STORY

A single reading of *Beowulf* is enough to reveal that two types of material have entered into the making of it. On the one hand, we find in it the characters of Scandinavian and other chieftains who have an air of historical reality about them, and are in fact real people attested by reliable external evidence. On the other hand, we have the unclear horrific shapes of trolls and water-monsters and fire-spewing dragons, who obviously belong in the supernatural realm of fairy tales (*märchen*). In analysing the components of the finished epic it is desirable to treat these two main divisions separately.

Among the historical personages, the one most readily identified is Hygelac, Beowulf's uncle and king. He is the same as the Chochilaicus of whom Gregory of Tours (died 594) relates that he perished some time about A.D. 520 during a raid in Western Frisia while Theuderic was king of the Franks. [30] The event is referred to in *Beowulf* with concrete details, geographical and other. It is told by anticipation, as a future calamity of the Geats, while Beowulf is still in Denmark (1202 ff.); and it is twice recalled through reminiscence when Beowulf is an old man (2354 ff., 2910 ff.). The Old Norse *Ynglinga Saga* tells us more about Hygelac under the name of Hugleikr. The Latin *Gesta Danorum* of Saxo Grammaticus (ca. 1200) adds to our information about the Danish royal house: Hrothgar, his sons, and his nephew Hrothulf; and this can be supplemented by the Icelandic saga about Hrothulf, which calls him Hrolf Kraki (*Hrolfs Saga Kraka,* surviving in a redaction of the fourteenth century).

It is true that Saxo's history and the sagas, being later authorities, are less reliable than the early Frankish historians. Still, the names are recognisable as the same ones, and many relationships among their bearers are consistently preserved. The feuds and violence and family betrayals of Germanic chiefs living about A.D. 500, their ferocity tempered by qualities of endurance and loyalty and generous behaviour towards persons within their own social group, are not unfaithfully mirrored in the English epic composed some centuries later, long after emigration had occurred from the scene of the action. Other historical personages mentioned or briefly treated are Emanaric of the East Goths (fourth century), Offa of the continental Angles (fifth century), the Merovingian dynasty in the person of an eponymous king, and the Swedish King Onela, whose death occurred ca. 535.

Turning from the historical to the fictional elements, we find ourselves at once in the enchanted world of international myth and folklore. For the beneficent Geatish dragon-killer, the slayer of water monsters, suggests innumerable analogous champions in the legends of many peoples. All of them are heroes larger than life, approaching the stature of demigods or gods. A Beowulf, a Sigurd (Siegfried) or a Perseus battling with a gigantic serpent recalls the god Apollo in combat with the Python, St. George victorious over a dragon, and even the Archangel Michael engaged in cosmic struggle with evil in the guise of a serpent. [31] Indeed there is a suggestion of universal forces in the exploits of even the purely human heroes of minor legends, and their role as rescuers liberating a whole people from terror suggests the welcome intervention by supernatural powers friendly to man. Although nothing is said in the poem to indicate that Beowulf himself is a god, his very function is in a sense godlike, according to the primitive imagination. It is no wonder that nineteenth century criticism often sought mythological explanations for the type of plot in which he appeared. [32] The favourite interpretation was that all such dragon-killers were reflexes of sun-gods, engaged in eternal warfare against the powers of darkness, freeing men from its terrors.

Such an interpretation is no longer followed. Instead, the plot of *Beowulf* has more recently been investigated in extensive comparison with the innumerable folktales of the world which contain similar situations.[33] An elaborate study has demonstrated, for instance, that many *märchen* of the type known as "The Bear's Son" contain the adventures of a hero supernaturally born, slow in maturing (as Beowulf is said to have been, ll. 2183 ff.[34]), powerful beyond ordinary men, who distinguishes himself later by pursuing and slaying a monster residing in a lower subterranean world to which it has abducted a princess. Some faithless companions abandon him at the entrance to that other world and steal the princess from him—temporarily. (Thus the Danes, though not the Geats, went away and left Beowulf in the under-water cave when they thought he had died there.) Or the hero is sometimes the younger of two brothers who succeeds in rescuing a princess when his senior had failed, and he too may be temporarily robbed of his reward by a treacherous attendant. The endlessly varied analogues to be found in folklore serve to evoke for readers today the general world of popular fantasy out of which the plot of *Beowulf* took shape. There is an entire group of Irish *märchen* standing closer to *Beowulf* than others in certain respects; hence some have looked to Ireland rather than Scandinavia for the ultimate origin of the basic plot.[35] But the similarity in all such cases is at best generic. The nameless heroes of fairy tales who kill monsters and win princesses can help only in a very general way towards the understanding of *Beowulf's* remoter origins in folklore. They do not live in the milieu of courtly etiquette and epic conventions; they are not associated with historical personalities, as are the characters in the Old English epic.

In the neighbouring Germanic literature of Iceland there are two stories of monster-killings in historical settings which furnish much closer analogues to *Beowulf* than does any recorded *märchen*. One of these is the exploit of Böðvar Bjarki, a hero at the court of the Danish king Hrolf Kraki (the Hroðulf of *Beowulf*). It is recounted in both the prose Icelandic *Hrolfs Saga Kraka*, mentioned above, and likewise in the *Gesta Danorum* of Saxo Grammaticus (bk. ii. Bjarki, the youngest of three sons whose father was transformed into a bear, began his life as a coward and was later transformed into a brave champion.[36] So far, he resembles a hero of *märchen* rather than one of an epic founded on history. But like Beowulf he comes from Geatland, he serves Hrolf at the very scene of Beowulf's exploits in Denmark, and he delivers king and court from the ravages of a terrible monster, thus winning friendship and praise. These parallels have led some to identify Beowulf with Bjarki. Though the similarities are too general to permit of conclusive identification, the *Hrolfs Saga* shows kinship with both the magic world of fairy tales on the one hand and that of heroic tradition on the other, just as *Beowulf* does. Springing from the same type of background, it aids in the understanding of the poem.

Another prose Icelandic tale, the *Grettis Saga Ásmundarsonar* (written ca. 1300 about persons living in the late tenth century), throws considerable light by analogy on the hero's struggle with Grendel's dam. The Icelandic hero Grettir was a great wrestler, and according to tradition a great victor over monsters. At a certain farm-house he once fought all night long a female troll who had been accustomed to carry off one of the workers on the place every Christmas eve; having hewed off the arm of the giantess (as Beowulf twisted off Grendel's), he succeeded in casting her over the steep edge of a neighbouring river, close to a waterfall. Later he descended to this torrent with the aid of a rope, swam up under the waterfall, climbed into a cave behind it, and there killed another giant in a combat much resembling Beowulf's with Grendel's mother under the lake. The companion supposed to wait for Grettir and draw him up by the rope was discouraged at the sight of quantities of blood and guts being washed downstream from under the waterfall. Convinced that Grettir must have been killed, he—like the Danes in Beowulf—abandoned his post. Grettir mounted the rope unaided. After that the district was free of troll-visitors.

In several still later and more fantastic Icelandic tales such as the *Saga of Samson the Fair*,[37] there are other heroes who fight combats with trolls living behind waterfalls. Their caves too are reached by a combination of swimming and climbing. Thus the episode may be said to have had a certain vogue, at least in one part of Scandinavia. It is valuable for an understanding of the second troll-fight in *Beowulf*. There the scene of action had been hard to visualise, we observed: the hero is shown as diving into a lake, swimming far down—and then in the lower depths suddenly finding himself within a dry cave where a fire burns brightly. The change is inexplicable. On the other hand, the Scandinavian scenes are sharply clear and realistically accurate.

It seems plausible that since Scandinavian landscape as described in the sagas offers a more coherent, credible setting for this important event, a continental origin may be assumed for the entire account of the double combat, first in the hall and then under water.[38] The social setting is of course different in the two literatures. The Icelandic, on the one hand, has adapted the episode to the customs and realistic outlook of independent farmers who themselves tilled the soil and acknowledged no king above them; the Old English, on the other, to the formal etiquette and lofty style of small royal courts concerned rather with warfare than the processes of agricultural production. Nevertheless the sequence of events is quite clearly similar. The blurred effect of the landscape in *Beowulf* may well be due to composition of the poem in a country lacking waterfalls like the Norwegian and Icelandic, though the plot originally required such a setting to be completely clear.

7. *BEOWULF*: LITERARY MODELS AND IDEOLOGY; DATE

The fundamental plot of *Beowulf*, no matter what its specific origin, suggests as we have seen a struggle of vaster implications than a mere wrestling match, even one with a supernaturally strong adversary. Critics may disagree as to the extent and significance of the symbolic element,[39] but most of them admit its presence. The impression is heightened by the interweaving of short passages and references revealing Christian faith on the part of the narrator.

At an earlier period in *Beowulf* criticism, it was frequently argued that the poem, originating as a collection of separate parts by different authors, had finally been further diversified by the deliberate interpolations of a late Christian redactor.[40] The insertions made by this "monkish writer", as he was called, were regarded as disharmonious patches on an otherwise consistently pagan epic.

Negative evidence, however, speaks strongly against this theory. There is no linguistic or metrical evidence marking off the Christian passages and references from the remainder of the text. Moreover, it has been noted more than once that the main story (if not the digressions) is pervasively imbued with Christian attitudes; they do not appear merely in patches.[41] The sum total of their effect is to suggest subtle parallels between the folklore elements and theological concepts, to temper the fierce attitudes of the original plot with admonitions, warnings against pride and vainglory, vengefulness and pagan concepts of fatalism, idolatry, and so on: to affirm in general a faith in the Christian God and the victorious justice of his rule.[42] It may well be that the folklore theme was chosen by the poet because it avoided the vengeful situations so typical of Germanic tribal struggles portrayed in other epics.

On the other hand, it has been noticed that the Christianity of the poem is rather vague and undogmatic. Though Grendel is provided with a Biblical ancestor, Cain (a detail to be found in Old Irish legends also), and the age-long warfare of God and Satan is also alluded to in this connection, nothing is said about Christ or the cross, angels, saints, relics, or specific details of dogma. One can, it is true, detect a general consonance with the work of St. Augustine, particularly *The City of God* with its argued rejection of pagan cults, and there is a certain similarity to the ideas contained in Bede's *Commentary on Genesis*, where the quarrel between Cain and Abel is likened to the struggle of evil versus good. But the resemblance to such patristic thought is likewise vague and—once again—it is focussed upon the underlying idea of a dualistic struggle, so expressed that it can be interpreted in terms of non-Christian ideas also. The permeation of pagan heroic material by the new ideology was apparently the work of a thoughtful poet educated in the new doctrine, but he has left little trace of his attitude on definite theological problems. Fortunately for our knowlegde of heroic legend, he has been content to transmute rather than to change markedly or to distort the old plot of Germanic history and folklore.

There is another strong cultural influence which has possibly helped to shape the structure of *Beowulf* as a completed epic. This is the tradition of Latin epic narrative, with its well-defined structure and conventions of language. The tradition is preeminently represented in the *Aeneid* of Virgil. There are various parallels to be found in the structure of the Old English poem. There is a likeness between the narrative of Aeneas to Dido and the long report of his deeds by Beowulf to Hygelac upon his return home to Geatland. This is the more likely to be an imitation by the Anglo-Saxon poet because a narrative is not needed at this point. Beowulf is repeating what the reader already knows, whereas Aeneas is describing the fall of Troy for the first time. The descent into the haunted lake is to a certain extent reminiscent of Aeneas's descent into Hades. The felicitous rule of Beowulf over the Geats recalls the rule of Aeneas over the kingdom he founded in Italy. Above all, the missions of the two epic heroes are comparable. Virgil, writing in the heyday of the Roman empire, was using epic narrative modelled after Homer's *Iliad* and *Odyssey*, in order to glorify the Emperor Augustus, and with him the dominating political role of Italy in the ancient world. To do so he borrowed the machinery of the pre-imperial tribal epic in which individual heroes are closely identified with the welfare of small tribal units. The *Beowulf* poet, himself living in such a tribal society, could easily have drawn upon the pseudo-tribal poem of the ancient Roman. Beowulf is a hero devoted to the welfare of his people, according to the theory if not the practice of the ruling-class tribal code, just as Aeneas pretends to be such a simple unselfish hero while revealing the historical traits of the world-ruling Augustus.

The likelihood that the *Beowulf*-poet knew and used Virgil is reinforced by details in style and language, especially such linguistic details in the Old English as may possibly be explained as Latinisms in translation.[43] A certain number of these can indeed be found, though their number has been exaggerated by some critics. The funeral of Beowulf has been compared with that of Hercules.[44] Such comparisons are of course often misleading: the similarities may be due rather to like social backgrounds than to direct literary influences. But the likelihood of some classical influence in England is heightened in view of the Latin books studied there, among the clergy at least, rather soon after the introduction of Christianity.[45] In this respect England had unusually abundant materials for the grafting of Latin literary forms and conventions upon the heritage of Germanic tradition. The combination of the two types of heritage goes far to explain why England alone, in so early a period, produced an epic narrative of such length and dignity, such sustained power and significance, as *Beowulf*.[46] The very adaptation of the Germanic alliterative line, its recasting from the end-stopped closed unit to the run-on variety, is thought to be due to classical influence.[47]

Most opinion is agreed, then, that *Beowulf* is a unified poem with aesthetic qualities of a high order, composed more or less as we have it today.[48] A single author shaped its materials (of whatever kind, however obtained) according to his ideology, and that ideology was the product of tribal history modified through recent conversion to Christianity.[49] His aesthetic values are generally thought to have been affected by classical models, though scholars differ as to the extent of the influence. The "national spirit" in *Beowulf* has been stressed by a number of critics, from Taine onwards,[50] but not always with sufficient awareness of the changed significance of the word "national" as applied to various periods of English history.

In one important respect a parallel may be drawn between the social context of *Beowulf* and that of classical epic. In both instances, poets were retelling stories widely known and presumably already familiar to their audiences. Therefore, the aesthetic pleasure gained from listening sprang, not from suspense as to the general outcome of the action, but from interest in the *manner* in which known action was made to lead to known outcome.[51] Hence a doubled obligation was laid upon the poet to re-shape the plot effectively. The *Beowulf*-poet is successful in meeting this challenge. His speeches and descriptions help. So does his emphasis upon the suspense of the actors within the story. These could not be sure of the outcome as they listened to the eerie wrestling of Beowulf with Grendel in darkened Heorot, or waited for a sign of his return to the surface of the haunted lake, or clustered fearful at the base of the dragon's mountain. In such scenes the poet uses powerful factors of collective emotion to reawaken memory of suspense in his listeners, despite their probable familiarity with the ancient tale.

The problems of origin, of ideology and literary indebtedness have a bearing on the problem of date. If we accept the fact that the composer of *Beowulf* as a single unified poem was himself a Christian, with at least general knowledge of the new religion and of classical epic, then the date of composition must be placed some time after about A.D. 600, probably allowing a number of generations for the establishment of schools and the teaching of Latin. At the other extreme of time we have the date of the extant manuscript of the poem (Cotton Vitellius A. 15 in the British Museum), which was transcribed in the West Saxon dialect about A.D. 1000. The language of our unique copy, however, shows archaisms and dialect forms which point to an original composition some centuries earlier in a more northerly region. The consensus of opinion favours a date shortly before or shortly after 700, the place being Northumbria (or perhaps Mercia), since literary culture was then at its height in these regions. If Northumbria was the homeland of *Beowulf*, as of other early writings, then it is unlikely that it was composed after the Scandinavian raids, beginning in 787, had wrecked the material foundation of a cultural life. On the other hand, the social situation in the Northern provinces was auspicious for the cultivation of heroic epic and for its preservation in writing before the coming of the Vikings.[52]

Notes to Chapter II

[1] George T. Stokes, *Ireland and the Celtic Church* (London, 1899), pp. 166—88.

[2] Arthur Kingsley Porter, *The Crosses and Culture of Ireland* (Yale University Press, 1931), pp. 18 ff.

[3] See M. Schlauch in *Journal of Celtic Studies*, I (1950), 152—66, for a summary of evidence collected by specialists.

[4] Cf. Aldhelm's letter to an Irish scholar named Eahfrid ex Hibernia, Migne, *Patrologia Latina*, LXXXIX, Epistola 3.

[5] Stenton, *op. cit.*, pp. 181—91.

[6] Franz Cumont, *Les Religions orientales dans le paganisme romain*, 4th ed. (Paris, 1929); Edward Carpenter, *Pagan and Christian Creeds* (London, 1920); miscellaneous information in Sir James Frazer, *The Golden Bough* (London, 1911—26); also K. Kautsky, *Foundations of Christianity*, as cited ch. 1, n.1; also Archibald Robertson, *The Origins of Christianity* (New York, 1954).

[7] For a sketch of Aldhelm see Eleanor S. Duckett, *Anglo-Saxon Saints and Scholars* (New York, 1948). His works are edited by R. Ewald, *Monumenta Germaniae Historica*, Auct. Antiq., XV (Berlin, 1919), with introduction. For the Latin poetry and poetics of Aldhelm, Bede and Alcuin, see F.J.E. Raby, *A History of Christian Latin Poetry* (Oxford, 1927), and his *History of Secular Latin Poetry*, I (Oxford, 1934); J.W.H. Atkins, *English Literary Criticism: The Medieval Phase* (Cambridge, 1943), pp. 36—58.

[8] Cf. the first sentence of a letter addressed to Eahfrid after his return to Ireland: "Primitus (pantorum procerum praetorumque pio potissimum, paternoque praesertim privilegio) panegyricum poemataque passim prosatori sub polo promulgantes, stridula vocum symphonia, ac melodiae cantilenaeque carmina modulaturi, hymnizemus," Epistola 3. Such strained decoration by alliteration is derived from late classical models, with exaggeration, rather than from Germanic. Aldhelm's effort may have been a humorous attempt to impress an Irish colleague whose own style had been affected by the same models.

[9] Ed. E. Dümmler, *Poetae Latini Aevi Caroli*, I, in *Monumenta Germaniae Historica*, *Poetae Latini Medii Aevi* I (Berlin, 1881). See E. Winkelmann, *Geschichte der Angel-sachsen* (Berlin, 1883), p. 75 f.

[10] Cf. Eleanor Duckett, *op. cit.*

[11] J.D. A. Ogilvy, *Books Known to Anglo-Latin Writers from Aldhelm to Alcuin* (Cambridge: Medieval Academy of America, 1936).

[12] Raby, *Latin Secular Poetry*, I, p. 68 f.

[13] For Bede's *Commentaries*, see Migne, *Patrologia Latina*, XCI; his complete works are in XC—XCV.

[14] The most recent biographical study is by E.S. Duckett, *Alcuin, Friend of Charlemagne* (New York, 1951); it gives full bibliographical references. Wilbur Samuel Howell, *The Rhetoric of Alcuin and Charlemagne* (Princeton University Press, 1941) gives discussion, text and translation. Alcuin's *Rhetoric* is edited with others

of the same type by C. Halm, *Rhetores Latini Minores* (Leipzig, 1863). For Alcuin's interest in astronomy and related subject see Migne, *Pat. Lat.*, C, Epistolae 80—86.

[15] Ed. A.H. Smith, *Three Northumbrian Poems* (London, 1933).

[16] The text is that of Smith's edition, with slight changes in punctuation. On the tale of Caedmon's supernatural inspiration, see G. Shepherd in *Review of English Studies*, N.S. (=New Series), V (1954), 113—22.

[17] Ed. George Philip Krapp (New York: Columbia University Press, 1931); first edition by Francis Junius, who attributed the poems to Caedmon (Amsterdam, 1655).

[18] The first editor to do so was Chr. W.M. Grein in his *Bibliothek der angelsächsischen Poesie*, 1 st ed., I (Göttingen, 1857).

[19] Ed. E. Dümmler, *Epistolae* IV (Berlin, 1895), p. 183; discussion by Brandl, *op. cit.*, p. 40.

[20] Late Icelandic sagas and the *Gesta Danorum* of Saxo Grammaticus (ca. 1200) give us most of our information about Ingeld.

[21] The MS. is now lost. The text was printed by George Hickes from a leaf in Lambeth Palace Library (1705). It is edited by Elliott van Kirk Dobbie in *Anglo-Saxon Minor Poems* (New York, 1942) and in Klaeber's edition of *Beowulf* (see note 28).

[22] *Waldere* is preserved on two leaves of a MS. in the Royal Library, Copenhagen. Text edited by Dobbie, *Minor Poems*, and by F. Norman (London, 1934). For discussion see H. Schneider, *Germanische Heldensage*, I (Berlin, 1928), pp. 331—44; M.D. Learned, *PMLA*, VII (1892), 1—208.

[23] F.P. Magoun and H. Smyser, *Walter of Aquitaine: Materials for the Study of his Legend* (New London: Connecticut College, 1950). The Polish version by Boguphal, and others derived from it, are edited by M.D. Learned, *op. cit.*

[24] *Widsith*, ed. by R.W. Chambers (Cambridge, 1912) and Kemp Malone (London, 1936). On the literary type, see M. Schlauch in *PMLA*, XLVI (1931), 969—87 and W.H. French, *ibid.*, LX (1945), 623—30.

[25] Adrien Bonjour, *The Digressions in Beowulf* (Oxford, 1950).

[26] Caroline Brady, "The Synonyms for 'Sea' in *Beowulf*," *Studies* in Honor of Albert Morey Sturtevant (University of Kansas Press, 1952), pp. 22—46, has recently argued that many of these terms are to be taken in a literal sense rather than metaphorically. See also her article "The Old English Nominal Compounds in -*RAD*," *PMLA*, LVII (1952), 538—71. Their literal sense does not prevent their stereotyped use from being an epic mannerism.

[27] Adeline E. Bartlett, *The Larger Rhetorical Patterns in Beowulf* (Columbia University Press, 1935); see also G.J. Engelhardt in *PMLA*, LXX (1955), 825-52

[28] Citation from the third edition by Fr. Klaeber (Boston, 1950), but without diacritical marks. Elliot Van Kirk Dobbie has done an edition in *The Anglo Saxon Poetic Records* (New York, 1951); also C.L. Wrenn (London, 1953).

[29] The Icelandic sagas, for instance, do not contain set nature descriptions. Surroundings (landscape, seascape, weather, etc.) are indirectly portrayed.

[30] *Historia Francorum*, lib. iii, cap. 3, ed. W. Arndt in *Mon. Germ. Hist.*, Scriptores Merov., I, p. 110 f. The eighth-century *Liber Historiae Francorum*, cap. 19, based on Gregory, more accurately spells it Chochilaicus. See K. Malone, "Hygelac," *English Studies*, XXI (1939), 108—19; also F.P. Magoun, "Beowulf and King Hygelac," *English Studies*, XXXV (1954), 1—12.

[31] Edwin Sidney Hartland, *The Legend of Perseus*, 3 vols. (London, 1894); also Hans Honti, *Volksmärchen und Heldensage*, FFC (Folklore Fellows Communications) No. 95 (Helsinki, 1931), pp. 33 ff.: "Die Beowulfsage."

[32] Karl Müllenhof, "Der Mythus von Beowulf," *Zeitschrift für deutsches Althertum*, VII (1870), 419—41.

[33] Friedrich Panzer, *Beowulf* (Munich, 1912).

[34] But K. Malone thinks not. See *Anglia*, LXIX (1950), 295—300.

[35] E.g., H. Dehmer in *Primitives Erzählungsgut in den Islendinga Sögur* (Leipzig, 1927).

[36] On the relation of this to *märchen* see J.R. Caldwell, "The Origin of the Story of Böðvar-Bjarki," *Arkiv för Nordisk Filologi*, LV (1940), 223—75. For general discussion of origins and analogues see R.W. Chambers, *Beowulf: An Introduction* (Cambridge, 1932) and W.W. Lawrence, *Beowulf and Epic Tradition* (Harvard University Press, 1930). On the specific relations between *Beowulf* and the saga, see Axel Olrik, *Heroic Legends of Denmark* (New York, 1919), especially pp. 245 ff.; Oscar Ludwig Olson, *The Relation of the Hrolfs Saga Kraka and the Bjarkarimur to Beowulf* (University of Chicago Press, 1916); C.W. von Sydow, *Beowulf och Bjarke* (Helsingfors, 1923).

[37] Described by W.W. Lawrence, *op. cit.*, and M. Schlauch, *Romance in Iceland* (New York and London, 1933).

[38] There has been disagreement on this. See W.S. Mackie in *Journal of English and Germanic Philology*, XXXVII (1938), 455—61 and the reply by W.W Lawrence, *ibid.*, XXXVIII (1939), 477—80.

[39] J.R. Tolkien argued in "Beowulf: The Monsters and the Critics," *Proceedings of the British Academy*, XXII (1936), 245 ff., that all three combats of Beowulf against supernatural creatures suggest the struggle with evil. T.M. Gang has objected that while the first two may be so regarded, the fight with the dragon is a comparatively matter-of-fact affair. See his "Approaches to *Beowulf*," *Review of English Studies*, III, N.S. No. 9 (1952), 1—12. Replying in *PMLA*, LXVIII (1952), 304—12, Adrien Bonjour reverts to a position similar to Tolkien's. Both recent critics cite Dorothy Whitelock's *The Audience of Beowulf* (Oxford, 1951), which by historical criticism helps us to see these monsters as did the poet and his contemporaries.

[40] E.g., Bernhard ten Brink, *Altenglische Literatur* (Strassburg, 1893).

[41] Klaeber edition, introduction, p. 1.

[42] Fr. Klaeber, "Die christlichen Elemente im Beowulf," *Anglia*, XXXV (1911), three articles, and XXXVI (1912), conclusion; also O.F. Emerson, "Legends of Cain," *PMLA*, XIV (1906), pp. 909 ff; Marie Padgett Hamilton, "The Religious Principle in *Beowulf*," *ibid.*, LXI (1946), 309—30.

[43] Tom Burns Haber, *A Comparative Study of the Beowulf and the Aeneid* (Princeton University Press, 1931); Alois Brandl, "Beowulf-Epos und Aeneis in systematischer Vergleichung," *Archiv*, CLXXI (1937), 161—73.

[44] By A.S. Cook in *Philological Quarterly*, V (1926), 226—34.

[45] See Ogilvy as cited in note 11 above. It must be remembered, however, that Latin writers referred to in Anglo-Latin texts were often known by fragments only, as preserved in anthologies.

[46] James R. Hulbert, "*Beowulf* and the Classical Epic," *Modern Philology*, XLIV (1946—47), 65—75. On the ideology of the poem and its dual heritage see

Bertha L. Phillpotts in *Essays and Studies* of the English Association, XIII (1928), 7—27.

[47] A. Heusler, "Heliand, Liedstil und Epenstil," *Zeitschr. f. deut. Alt.*, LVII (1920), pp. 5 ff., discusses the debt to classical run-on lines. See also John C. Pope as cited in ch. 1, n. 30; also Paull F. Baum, "The Meter of *Beowulf*," *Modern Philology*, XLVI (1948—49), 73—91.

[48] E.g., by H.M. Chadwick, *The Heroic Age* (Cambridge, 1912) and *The Growth of Literature* (Cambridge, 1932). Cf. J.R. Hulbert, "The Genesis of *Beowulf*: A Caveat," *PMLA*, LXVI (1951), 1168—76. Hulbert returns to a modified form of the theory of lays as a source in "Surmises concerning the *Beowulf*-Poet's Source," *Journal of English and Germanic Philology*, L (1951), 11—18. The oral narrative character of *Beowulf* (and other poems) has been stressed by Magoun in *Speculum*, XXVIII (1953), 446—67. For a convenient review of recent studies see J.C. van Meurs, "*Beowulf* and Literary Criticism," *Neophilologus*, XXXIX (1955), 114—30.

[49] Arthur E. Du Bois, "The Unity of *Beowulf*," *PMLA*, XLIX (1934), pp. 374 ff.; J.L.N. O'Loughlin, "*Beowulf*—Its Unity and Purpose," *Medium Aevum*, XXI (1952), 1—14; on special artistic effects see A.G. Brodeur, "Design for Terror in the Purging of Heorot", *PMLA*, LIII (1954) 503—13.

[50] E. Wadstein, "The Beowulf Poem as an English National Epos," *Acta Philologica Scandinavica*, VIII (1933), 273—91.

[51] This point is well made by M. Lumiansky, "The Dramatic Audience in *Beowulf*," *Journal of English and Germanic Philology*, LI (1952), 545—50.

[52] L. Schücking, "Wann entstand der Beowulf?" *Paul and Braune's Beiträge*, XLII (1917), 347—410, has suggested composition in the midst of Scandinavian settlements in England (late ninth century). The proposal of so late a date has not been generally accepted.

RELIGIOUS POETRY: EPIC, DIDACTIC, VISIONARY

1. THE CAEDMONIAN SCHOOL

While the nameless poets of the royal courts were shaping heroic narratives for the delight of noble audiences, a new kind of vernacular poetry was being produced in connection with the monastic schools. About the authors we know little or nothing. About their training we can only guess, on the basis of internal evidence, but it would appear that they were acquainted not only with Biblical texts, but also with some of the extensive Latin commentaries upon them written by churchmen of the fifth to the eighth century. It was through the commentaries chiefly that the poets were subjected to that strong influence of Christianised Neo-Platonism, which was to direct general European thought away from investigation of the natural world and towards inner speculation for centuries to come. The social forms emerging from economic foundations in the Middle Ages confirmed this tendency.

The early Christian poetry of England makes its appearance quite suddenly somewhere about A.D. 700. Considering how little time had elapsed since the conversion of the island, the authors appear to have mastered a remarkable amount of knowledge and instruction in the new ideology within a short period. Anglo-Saxon Christian narrative, viewed from one point of view, is a literary innovation, for it presents new, imported materials and expresses values and beliefs but recently acquired in the authors' homeland. On the other hand, it is in many ways conservative, since it continues to use what were probably the well-established techniques of Germanic pagan narrative. Sometimes, it is true, the influence of Latin models and Latin rhetorical and poetic doctrine can be detected through the Old English verses, but the general effect is, so far as style is concerned, largely that of undistorted native writing. There is some modification in technique—for instance the increased tendency, already mentioned, to use run-on-lines—which probably results from the custom of reading texts aloud rather than reciting them[1]—but this constitutes no striking departure from the older usage. Certainly it does not appear conspicuous in such texts as have come down to us in writing. Neither is the new device of rime conspicuous, though there are scattered examples of lines and half-lines employing it, in imitation of a practice already widely prevalent in the composition of Latin hymns.

The materials worked upon by Anglo-Saxon religious poets were borrowed from the Bible and Apocrypha, from hagiography and homilies and didactic expositions of various kinds, sometimes expressed in the form of visionary experiences. Though the sources were varied, however, the subjects chosen were not widely diversified. A few major themes emerge which suggest the predominant trend of intellectual interests at the time. One very striking theme now treated with epic breadth and dignity is the creation of the universe as briefly described in Genesis. Preoccupation with this subject was already foreshadowed in poems like Aldhelm's *De Creatura*, Caedmon's Hymn, and the poem chanted by the scop in *Beowulf* (11. 90—98). Anglo-Saxon poets quickly absorbed, it seems, the limited scientific heritage handed down by Roman writers from the Greeks; in their own age little new was added.

Another topic of absorbing interest is the conflict between good and evil as presented in vivid pictorial contrasts, in action of intense struggle. The literary treatments reveal a sharply dichotomised universe, a dual world of conflicting absolutes. The concept was of course implicit in the earliest Christian texts (the Gospels), but was heightened, as has previously been noted, by further Oriental influences—chiefly Zoroastrian—which affected Asia Minor and Europe during the early centuries of Christianity. Such influences are traceable even in the late cults of Germanic paganism, in myths like the Scandinavian ones about struggles among the gods and the fall of Valhalla. Here as in the tale of the angels' fall, the enemy is a rebel against the group, one who becomes a lordless man (Old English *hlafordleas*) through his own act.[2] Thus the dualistic concept may have affected Anglo-Saxon Christianity indirectly, in the form of a pagan survival embodying old social attitudes. Whatever its origin and mode of transmission, the myth of a negative cosmic force appears in such favoured plots and situations as: the revolt of the angels (several times treated), Satan's struggles to regain power by tempting Christ and struggling against God at doomsday; the efforts of sundry devils to weaken the strength of saints facing martyrdom. These last are but modifications of the larger theme, translated into terms of human frailty and human steadfastness.

There is, finally, a predilection for the theme of military combat drawn from Biblical and hagiographical sources but elaborated in terms of contemporary Germanic warfare. The Vulgate offered situations in plenty for such descriptions. Old English poetry made use of them in terms already familiar to poets and audiences, thus reflecting inherited tastes, perhaps as a concession (conscious or unconscious) to popular demand. For it is likely, in view of the stories about deliberate competition between ecclesiastical and lay poets, that Christian narratives may have been recited as part of a propaganda campaign directed to wider audiences than those within monastery walls.

The earliest Christian poetic narratives are very free adaptations of parts of the books of Genesis, Exodus and Daniel. They are those texts of the Junius manuscript which were formerly (see ch. 2, sec. 2) attributed to Caedmon but are now thought to represent the work of his followers.[3] The language is West Saxon of a later period, but early Anglian forms embedded in it suggest original composition in Northern England about A.D. 700. The themes obviously coincide with Caedmon's interests as reported by Bede.

Genesis is not only a poem of considerable literary merit, but its contents reveal significant debts of Anglo-Saxon culture to foreign sources. In the first place, the story does not begin (as in the Bible) with the creation of earth and man, but with the war in heaven and Satan's fall, that primary and most impressive instance of the strife which was thought to divide the universe into two opposing principles. The account is simple and stark. Then comes the creation of earth, described in words recalling Caedmon's Hymn:

112
   Her ærest ʒesceop ece drihten
  helm eallwihta, heofon and eorðan,
  rodor arærde, and þis rume land
  ʒestaþelode stranʒum mihtum,
  frea ælmihtiʒ.

   Here first there created the king eternal
  the helm of all creatures, heaven and earth,
  set aloft the skies, and this spacious land
  firmly founded with mighty force,
  the lord all-mighty.

With line 235 of *Genesis* there is a break in the continuity of the text. We find ourselves in the midst of God's instructions to Adam and Eve: "...enjoy all else, but avoid this tree alone..." The ensuing section, through line 851 (called *Genesis B*) has been proved to be an Anglo-Saxon adaptation of an Old Saxon poem, not an original composition.[4] The date of the original text from which the English poet borrowed is the early ninth century; hence the adaptation must be still later. It must post-date the composition of *Genesis A*, within which it is found. The action covered in the insertion is that of Milton's *Paradise Lost*: the fall of Satan (here repeated at greater length than in *Genesis A*), his journey to earth and the Garden of Eden, the temptation and fall of Eve, followed by that of Adam. *Genesis A* then picks up the story with the expulsion from Eden, and continues the Biblical account of early mankind down to the story of Abraham and Isaac.

In treating the majestic theme of Satan's fall, *Genesis B* reaches great heights of imaginative power. There are echoes in it of the rebellious type of Germanic underling who has defied his overlord and hates his successor in that lord's favour: "I can be God as well as He" (1. 283), and "For me it is the greatest of griefs that Adam—who was wrought of the earth—shall hold my mighty throne" (11. 364—66), and "Then God's foe, equipped in his trappings, began to gird himself forth; he had a faithless heart" (1. 442 f.). But the issues are vaster. The Saxon poet and his Anglo-Saxon adapter do not let us forget that the forces here pitted against each other embrace more than a tribal society. It is the universe of moral values, which (since the days of the Roman empire) were being thought of in terms of all mankind. The type of imagination at work in *Genesis B*, though separated from his by many centuries, irresistibly suggests that of John Milton, and it is not impossible that the poet of the Puritan Commonwealth may have had an opportunity to study the Junius manuscript, whose owner he could have known personally.[5] The speeches of the main characters—Satan, Eve, Adam—are constructed in a style appropriate to epics, and they are marked with many vivid descriptive touches.

There is in fact much in *Genesis B* to remind us that with the advent of Christianity, Old English poetry was subjected to new literary influences. Among them were the Latin epic conventions and Latin rhetorical doctrines.[6] Ecclesiastical schooling was shaping the poets towards a new way of approaching experience and transforming experience into an art. They began to adopt a point of view which was to dominate European art until the sixteenth century, and which we may justifiably call the characteristic medieval attitude in matters aesthetic. The single word which most aptly designates it is the attitude of *symbolism*. According to this approach, all of manifest nature is regarded—not primarily as an environment to be grasped by scientific processes and mastered socially for the use of man—but primarily as a huge panorama presenting opportunities for moral instruction. In all of the arts, the symbolic method looks beneath physical facts to general meanings of an abstract nature. The physical make-up and physical charm of an individual lily, for instance—its shape and scent and tactile smoothness—are of small consequence beside its ability to suggest abstract ideas and issues, including moral and

theological ones such as innocence, temptation, fall, redemption, and
so on. The origins of this attitude to nature and history are to be traced
in Latin Christian writers like St. Ambrose, Prudentius, Boethius and
others. (See ch. 6 on the rise of allegory.)

In the coming centuries the symbolic treatment of nature became
highly elaborate and all but universal in medieval art. Its aesthetic
consequences for good and ill must be deferred for later discussion. For
the moment, what is of interest here is that in vernacular English, as
early as the eighth century, approximately, we already find signs of this
new attitude in the poetry of *Genesis B*. Speaking of Adam's yielding
to Eve's persuasion, the poet says:

717
>   He æt þam wife onfenȝ
> helle and hinnsið,   þeah hit nære haten swa,
> ac hit ofetes noman   aȝan sceolde;
> hit wæs þeah deaðes swefn   and deofles ȝespon,
> hell and hinnsið   and hæleða forlor
> menniscra morð,   þæt hie to mete dædon,
> ofet unfæle.

>   From the woman he took
> hell and perdition,   though not so hight,
> but by name of a fruit   it was to be called;
> it was sleep of death   and spell of the devil,
> hell and perdition   and downfall of men,
> mankind's murder   that they took for meat,
> the unholy fruit.

This is an exposition of symbolic meanings that were clustered about
an external object of the tale, one that "bore the name of a fruit."
Henceforth the apple was to be a symbolic means of suggesting the
whole complex of theological ideas gathered about the story of man's
fall through disobedience.

The rest of *Genesis*, the latter part of the A-text, is less elaborate
than the interpolation, but it too has overtones of symbolic meaning.
The story of creation and early history, for instance, is indebted to the
patristic commentaries known as *Hexamera* (from the Six Days of creation),
a type of symbolic exposition of Genesis which originated with Basil
of Caesarea (bishop 370—79 A.D.) and was imitated by other church
Fathers, including Bede.[7] Throughout, there is a constant interweaving
of materials and styles in the poem: the echoes of Germanic tradition
persist, most clearly apparent in the scenes of struggle; there is a tendency
to develop speeches with an oratorical fulness, and to insert nature
descriptions which heighten both the pictorial effect and the moral
significance. For instance, the dark waters of Noah's flood and the dark
flames of the fire consuming Sodom and Gomorrah—"sweartan lige,"

(1. 2507) —suggest the nature of the evil being punished rather than the physical aspect of the elements.

The same combination of qualities is to be found in *Exodus*.[8] The story of the departure of the Hebrews from Egypt and their passage through the Red Sea has been interpreted symbolically, in the manner of the commentaries, as signifying preparation for and experience of baptism.[9] If such is the hidden meaning, little of it appears on the surface. Rather, there are vivid descriptions with symbolic overtones, as when the brilliant sunrise pours light over the Children of Israel in the desert, or when the walls of the Red Sea divide to "hold them in safety in its firm embraces." At the same time, nothing could be more faithful to pagan Germanic tradition, both Anglo-Saxon and Scandinavian, than the stereotyped account of the "birds of prey, greedy for battle, dewy-feathered, dark lovers of carrion, [which] screamed in wheeling flight," waiting for the expected slaughter of the Hebrews by the Egyptians.

Somewhat less striking is the paraphrase of Daniel, which follows its source fairly closely, down to the feast of Belshazzar. The high point is the account of the three Hebrew lads protected by an angel in the fiery furnace to which they have been condemned. The passage is made lyrical by means of a prayer spoken by Azarias,[10] and a song chanted by all three victims. The lyrical interlude, though effective in itself, delays the action at a moment of great suspense. Some have suspected it of being an interpolation by a later writer. The prayer is independently treated elsewhere (see below, sec. 4).

The last item in the Junius colection is a poem comprising three parts not closely connected. The subjects are: (1) the fall of Satan and the rebellious angels (once more), (2) the triumph of Christ over the powers of hell, (3) the temptation of Christ by Satan. Modern editors appropriately call this group *Christ and Satan*, for a kind of unity does result from the delineation of Satan in all three as God's adversary. In the first section we again hear Satan lamenting his present condition and Dantesque surroundings, again in terms of a Germanic declassed warrior in a state of exile because of treason. The second subject is rather hastily treated in three episodes: the harrowing of Hell, the resurrection and ascension, and the last judgment. The third subject, which remains a fragment, is developed chiefly by dialogue. This imparts liveliness to what is basically a conflict lacking suspense, for the conclusion is of course foreseen throughout.

Though *Christ and Satan* does not possess the unity and sustained power of the other Caedmonian texts, it shares their gift for vivid portrayal, for the construction of impressive speeches, and for a technique of sentence structure revealing planned mastery of the linguistic medium.

Life of St. Guthlac

British Museum

A detailed analysis of the syntactic and structural traits revealed throughout the Junius manuscript would probably bring to light many signs of rhetorical training on the part of the author or authors. The compositions are not, as critics have sometimes patronisingly remarked, simple products of untutored imagination such as one finds among "children and savage peoples."[11] Even this earliest creation of Christianised Old English verse can not be understood without grasping the dual inheritance already being firmly welded in the Northumbrian and Mercian monasteries: native poetics united with patristic theology and Roman rhetoric.

2. THE WORK OF CYNEWULF

One other writer of the Northern school of Christian poetry, besides Caedmon, is known to us by name. The signature of someone named Cynewulf appears towards the end of four religious narrative poems. The name is written in runic characters standing, in the sentences where they are used, for the objects which their names designate. The passages in question express moral reflections of a commonplace nature, giving no key to the writer's personality, nor (as was formerly thought) to his biography.[12] On linguistic evidence—the preservation of the unstressed medial vowel of his name in the form of -e- —the poems are generally assigned to the late eighth or early ninth century. In the past he has been identified tentatively with the Bishop of Lindisfarne of the same name (died ca. 780), or with a certain Cynewulf priest of Dunwich, otherwise obscure (ca. 800).[13] More recently, however, it has been suggested that he was a Mercian writer of the ninth century. Despite the severity of Viking raids after 800 (see ch. 4), some monastic schools in England continued to train scholars and produce materials for instruction in the two Latin traditions, classical and Christian.

Cynewulf shows by his work that he was rather deeply saturated in these two traditions, especially the latter.[14] His four subjects are definitely ecclesiastical, but like the writers of the Caedmonian school, Cynewulf is also indebted to the tradition of secular heroic epics. The signed poems are: *The Fates of the Apostles*, briefly recording the ends of the lives of the twelve disciples or "athelings"; a poem on the Ascension, otherwise called *Christ B* (the second of three possibly connected poems on Christ's role and mission); *Juliana* and *Elene*, both hagiographical narratives. The latter of them deals with the finding of the cross by Helena, mother of the Emperor Constantine.[15] *The Fates* and *Elene* are found in the Vercelli Book, an Old English manuscript of verse and prose texts preserved in the chapter library of Vercelli Cathedral in Northern Italy.[16]

The *Christ*-poem and *Juliana* are contained in the Exeter Book, a poetic miscellany belonging to the chapter library of Exeter Cathedral in England.

The Fates of the Apostles is the simplest and shortest of the four signed poems. It is relatively bare of descriptive embellishment, and may be compared with catalogues designed to help memory, like the Menology already discussed. The purpose of such works is chiefly practical, and the artistic element is not conspicuous.

Christ B narrates the Ascension, including the speech of Christ in farewell to the twelve disciples, the joyous salutation by angels in heaven, their address to the disciples explaining the event, and some remarks by the poet of a general and not very unified character, commenting on the importance of the event. The poems preceding and following, *Christ A* and *Christ C* (see below, sec. 3), are separated in the manuscript by conventional marks elsewhere used by the scribe to show divisions between poems; hence there is reason to suppose that all three sections are independent, and that Cynewulf wrote only part *B*.[17] On the other hand, the style does not show any obvious change. Moreover, the themes treated here in sequence—Nativity, Ascension, Last Judgment—were often combined in the sculptures and relief carvings of early Christian iconography.[18] The association of the main ideas may have led to simultaneous composition, or at least to the combination of the three texts in the one manuscript, whether or not Cynewulf was the sole author. It should be added that the signed poem is the shortest, the least unified, and perhaps the least interesting of the three. Its comments on the meaning of the Ascension are derived from a homily by St. Gregory, and from a Latin hymn on the Ascension, attributed to Bede. There is a not clearly relevant section (11. 664—82) resembling the gnomic verses on the *Gifts of Men* (also contained in the Exeter Book; see ch. 1., sec. 3, note 25). Here Cynewulf's borrowings, though effective in detail, do not appear to be well assimilated. He adapts some phraseology of the tribal Germanic epic when he speaks of Christ as a "giver of treasure" (*brega mæra*) and the disciples as a band of thanes (*þegna gedryht*, 1. 456 f.).

Juliana is more unified.[19] It offers a rather conventional piece of hagiography treated in epic style. Like other early saints' lives originally told in Latin, it concerns a beautiful and steadfast maiden who was denounced as a Christian by kinsfolk and betrothed, condemned to prison and torture by the state authorities, vainly tempted by the devil, miraculously protected from death during various attemps to execute her, and finally (when she is quite ready) crowned with a martyr's death. (Just why she was not done to death on the first attempt of the hard-working executioner is not made clear. She was supposed to die at his hands in any event.) The colloquy of Juliana with the devil creates an opportunity for the poet to embroider upon the favourite theme of absolute evil in conflict with good. The devil's speech avowing his destructive role (11. 352—417) has a certain dramatic intensity, but in general the poem does not show any great literary independence in the treatment of a familiar type of plot.

Elene, on the other hand, is a rather varied and colourful treatment of St. Helena's legendary voyage to Jerusalem and the efforts made by her, finally crowned with success, to discover the buried cross. Here too Cynewulf was faithful to his source, a version of the Latin *Vita Sancti Quiriaci* (*Life of St. Cyriac*) probably composed in Ireland from a Greek original;[20] but he elaborated it and heightened its effectiveness by descriptions and dialogues in the epic style. The opening account of the Emperor Constantine's victorious battle presents him as a powerful Germanic chieftain. Helena journeys over the seas like a pagan Valkyrie, a true "battle queen." Her arguments with the Jewish spokesman Judas show, however, the effects of training in Roman rhetoric. When the devil appears to dissuade Judas from cooperation with her, their interchange suggests the type of *disputatio* that was to be popular in vernacular literature from the thirteenth century to the end of the Middle Ages. These lively elements, both old and new, impart a certain vigour unknown to the conventional narrative of wonder-working relics upon which Cynewulf drew. Normally this literary type did not inspire very independent treatment in the vernacular. The interest in legends of the cross was conspicuous in ecclesiastical circles during this age, for Pope Sergius I had instituted the feast of the Elevation of the Cross in 701. The cult was reflected in liturgy and iconography as well as vernacular poetry.[21] (See discussion of the *Dream of the Rood*, sec. 3 below.) Thus it is possible that Cynewulf composed his poem in connection with some specific event such as the consecration of a church or the reception of a relic, much as Alcuin composed Latin *carmina* for the dedication of altars and tombs.

3. CYNEWULFIAN POEMS

Closely associated with the signed poems of Cynewulf are a number of others which have been tentatively assigned to him, either because they occur closely connected with his in the manuscripts, or because they show similarity of style and themes, or both. It may be that some of them were actually written by him.

Christ A and *C*, preceding and following the unquestioned authentic poem by Cynewulf, in the Exeter Manuscript, are two obvious instances. These deal with the Nativity and the Last Judgment respectively. In fact, there is a certain continuity in words and ideas covering the end of *Christ A* and the beginning of *B*. The Nativity poem is more lyrical than the other two. It is based upon church antiphons of the season of Advent, and the very structure of the verse passages shows their liturgical inspiration. There is a short passage of direct dialogue between Mary and Joseph, embedded in the lyrical sequence. It anticipates the earliest mediaeval church drama by many centuries, but there is nothing to indicate that it was to be performed or even read aloud by impersonators of the two characters.

Christ C is the most effective of the three, with its abrupt introduction of the Day of Judgment—"suddenly at midnight it will fall"—, its vivid depiction of the world's destruction, its stern account of mankind's division into the saved and the damned. The panorama of events is partly inspired by Latin writers like St. Augustine, St. Gregory and Bede, and at the same time it is creatively handled. The reproaches addressed to sinners [22] at the final reckoning include a few lines recalling with some eloquence the historical origins of Christianity among the lowest ranks of the oppressed in the Roman empire:

1499   "Bibead ic eow þæt ʒe broþor mine
  in woruldrice wel aretten
  of þam æhtum þe ic eow on eorðan ʒeaf,
  earmra hulpen. Earʒe ʒe þæt læstun,
  þearfum forwyrndon þæt hi under eowrum þæce mosten
  in ʒebuʒan, ond him æʒhwæs oftuʒon,
  þurh heardne hyʒe, hræʒles nacedum,
  moses meteleasum...

1512   Eall ʒe þæt me dydan,
  to hynþum heofoncyninʒe. Pæs ʒe sceolon hearde adreoʒan
  wite to widan ealdre, wræc mid deoflum ʒeþolian."

   "My bidding to you was that ye my brothers
  in this world's kingdom well should comfort
  with the earthly goods I gave you to use, —
  ye should help the needy. In niggardly wise
  ye denied the destitute a dwelling place
  under your roof, and ruthless refused them
  clothing when naked and food when starving.
        ...To me ye have done this,
  scorning heaven's king. Ye must hard requite it
  in age-long anguish, suffer exile with devils."

Like an early Dante, the poet is moved by a lively sense of justice and demands punishment in the terms of his experience and instruction. He strives to delineate the fate of the damned in vigorous language of horror and despair, and to contrast this picture with a final glimpse of supreme joy in heaven.

Andreas is another poem often assigned to Cynewulf, though without any certain evidence. In the Vercelli Book it precedes the signed *Fates of the Apostles*, and the latter has been regarded by some (not very convincingly) as a kind of appendix to the longer poem. Andreas is St. Andrew, who is supposed (according to the apocryphal and sensation-crammed *Acts of St. Andrew* in Greek) to have had some extraordinary adventures in rescuing St. Matthew from imprisonment and threatened death among a tribe of loathsome cannibals called the Mermidons. The elements of exaggerated fantasy and crude supernaturalism rob the tale of human appeal. The Mermidons are sub-human, the saints are superhuman: there is no common ground between them. The best part of the tale is the description of Andrew's sea voyage from Achaia to Mermidonia. Here the Anglo-Saxon fondness for seascapes receives ample expression. The account is much more elaborate than the comparable passages in *Beowulf* (the voyages to and from Denmark), and much longer. The likenesses are less probably due to borrowing than to a common epic tradition of extraordinary vitality.[23] The leaping fish, the wheeling gulls, the winds and tempest, form a background as arresting for a saint's voyage as for a hero's. But miracles and apparitions are here added in rather bewildering profusion. The sea journey of Andrew is so greatly expanded that one almost forgets the purpose of the interlude, which is to carry the hero to the scene of the rescue he is to perform. Such elaboration for its own sake, or for the sake of didactic instruction, never occurred in *Beowulf*.

Guðlac is also a piece of hagiography in verse, this time dealing with an English saint of Mercia who died in 714. The original composition of the poetic treatment may be assigned to Mercia. The text appears as a single unit in the Exeter Book, but is obviously a composite of two poems, for a fresh start is made with 1. 819. The two versions, called *A* and *B* respectively, both tell how Guðlac went out into the wilderness of Croyland in Lincolnshire, to live there as a hermit; how he wrestled with demons who taunted and tempted him, as was to be expected in these circumstances, and how he was rewarded for his steadfastness by eternal bliss after death. The *A*-version in its original form appears to have been written soon after Guðlac's demise; the *B*-version is later, being based on a Latin *vita* by Felix of Croyland, and could not have been written by Cynewulf.

What is interesting in both accounts is the evidence that solitary anchorites existed in England in the eighth century, modeled on the early Irish hermits who in turn imitated those of Egypt and Asia Minor. The sociology of English religious experience is still faithful in this period to that of its foreign predecessors. A number of details confirm the relationship. The friendship of birds and beasts for the demon-haunted solitary is a trait frequently encountered in Irish hagiography, as it is in *Guðlac*. The idyllic description of blossoming mead and cuckoos singing in the early year (A 722—59) contains details strongly reminiscent of early Irish nature poetry, and testifies once more to the direct cultural contacts existing between England and Ireland in the first period of Old English literature. [24]

The Dream of the Rood, in the Vercelli Book, is an outstanding achievement of Old English poetry, superior to any of the four signed works of Cynewulf, and yet sometimes attributed to him because of a generic similarity of style. [25] But where the authentic works and the others of the same school thus far discussed are faulty in structure, being in parts discursive, exaggerated or repetitious, the *Dream* is simple, intense, unified and highly imaginative. The poet relates a vision in which he beheld the cross, bright with gold and jewels but stained with blood, and heard it speak to him with a human voice. It retold to him the events of the crucifixion from its own point of view, like a sentient creature, using the first person singular. The action is symbolically rather than literally described; Christ is said to have behaved like a young hero voluntarily stripping himself for action and mounting the cross like a steed. The suffering too is shared by the inanimate wood.

Such attribution of feelings and speech to an inanimate object goes back, of course, to very primitive ideas about animism throughout all forms of nature, non-living as well as living. As a sophisticated literary device it is exemplified on a less exalted level in some of the Latin riddles which served as models for the Old English. In the *Dream*, however, the power of expression is far greater [26]. Deep feeling underlies this poem, whereas other examples of prosopopoeia are merely ingenious. The theme is obviously related to that of *Elene*.

The Dream of the Rood is directly connected with the history of sculpture in Anglo-Saxon England. A cross erected at Ruthwell in Dumfriesshire, Scotland, probably early in the eighth century, is decorated on one face by an inscription in runic characters which are close to about ten lines of the poem (between ll. 44 and 64), [27] and there is an inscription of two lines reminiscent of the poem's wording (ll. 44 and 48) on a later Anglo-Saxon cruciform reliquary now preserved in the church of St. Gudule, Brussels. The dialect of the Ruthwell runic inscription is Northern, of the middle eighth century approximately, thus providing strong evidence that the poem also originated in the North, likewise at an early date. The figures sculptured in relief upon the cross show, once more, a debt to Celtic and Oriental motives, including solitary saints and friendly animals.

The Phoenix represents another instance of the close contact between Anglo-Saxon and Latin culture. It is a descriptive-symbolic poem freely adapting one in Latin on the same subject which has been attributed to Lactantius (died ca. 340).[28] The legend tells of the self-destroying, self-regenerating bird in a remote blessed grove, whose remains were worshipped in Heliopolis, City of the Sun, in ancient Egypt. The bird is obviously a symbol for the sun itself, being daily consumed in its own flames and daily reborn. In view of Christian indebtedness to such ancient cults of nature's resurrections, there was no difficulty in adapting the symbolism of the phoenix to Christ's resurrection. The Latin author himself makes no such overt connection. The Anglo-Saxon poet not only expands and embroiders the description of fabulous natural beauty in the earthly paradise where the phoenix dwells; he adds a long interpretation applying the general ideas to the fall of man and the resurrection of humanity at the final judgment. Thus the purely decorative myth, as treated by Lactantius, is transformed into an admonitory discourse on several of the rather somber themes which dominated Anglo-Saxon religious thought.

The author of *Phoenix* shows his knowledge of the Bible by paraphrasing and expanding (11. 552—69) some verses from the Book of Job (29: 18 and 19: 25—26). He concludes the poem with a group of eleven macaronic lines in which each second hemistich is in Latin, but alliterates with the preceding Anglo-Saxon hemistich. The tendency to use run-on lines, to begin sentences in mid-line, to build parallels of sentence structure, all mark the writer who has studied poetic art in the schools. Parallelism of the sentence parts is sometimes reinforced by the use of identical inflectional suffixes at the ends of the like units, thus producing unaccented rimes. Aside from these echoes of sound, there are also occasional inner rimes and near-rimes between hemistiches, as in this group of lines:

14
                        ne mæȝ þer ren ne snaw,
ne forstes fnæst   ne fyres blæst.
ne hæȝles hryre,   ne hrimes dryre,
ne sunnan hætu,   ne sincaldu,
ne wearm weder,   ne winterscur
wihte ȝewyrdan,   ac se wonȝ seomað
eadiȝ ond onsund.

                    There may no rain nor snow
nor frosty bite   nor fiery blight
nor chilling flail   of frost or hail
nor sun's heat blasting   nor dire cold lasting
nor summer weather   nor shower of winter
cause aught of harm,—   but meadows ever
lie happy and wholesome...

The poet was obviously a well-read man, an experimenter interested in his craft, a lover of sound and colour. Somewhat self-consciously, he was trying to enrich still further the dual heritage of Anglo-Saxon poetry. He made use of many devices alien to the signed Cynewulf poems. Hence, although some critics have claimed *Phoenix* for Cynewulf, it was most probably composed by another. [29] In general, the group of poems just surveyed, variously and loosely connected with the name of Cynewulf, have a certain kinship. In their style, point of view and subject matter, they show varied aspects of one and the same literary effort in which Cynewulf shared: the struggle to adapt native poetics to foreign themes brought to England by several channels.

4. MISCELLANEOUS RELIGIOUS-DIDACTIC POEMS

Other religious poems on various themes have come down to us in the extant manuscripts. Some may have been composed in the time of Cynewulf, others later: it is difficult to assign them to specific periods because of the form in which they have been preserved. These are shorter texts, often rather lyrical than narrative in form and inspiration.

Doomsday, a poem contained in a manuscript of Corpus Christi College (Cambridge) is a meditation on the subject of final judgment. [30] That theme was, as we have seen, treated on a large scale more than once in Old English. Here the elements of dramatic action and vivid portrayal are subordinated to the melancholy reflections on the subject which occur to the poet in a quiet murmuring forest. The peaceful setting contrasts sharply with the dreadful theme. The point of view is introspective, and the general effect, though stirring, is less so than in *Christ C*. The source is Bede's poem called *De Die Judicii*, but the vernacular poet has treated the material with some independence, and has expanded it. [31]

There is a shorter and less distinguished poem on the same subject in the Exeter Book, which may be called *Judgment Day* to distinguish it from the longer one. Here too the imagined end, the consumption of the world in flames, is invoked to underscore admonitory reflections. Studies of the vocabulary and linguistic forms of these two poems indicate that the shorter one, *Judgment Day*, was probably an Anglian composition originally, and therefore may well belong to the period of Cynewulf. *Doomsday*, on the other hand, was probably composed in Southwest Saxon to begin with and probably belongs to a considerably later period. [32]

A Soul's Address to its Body is another theme twice treated in Old English poetry, one version being preserved in the Exeter and one in the Vercelli Book. Again, the cultural background is of considerable interest. In this case, it is indeed more interesting than the poems themselves, which are relatively undistinguished. The subject is a speech of reproach delivered by the soul of a dead man after his death, just before its departure to face judgment. The Russian scholar F.D. Batiushkov has shown that this literary type of discourse originated among the Greek Fathers of the Eastern church, particularly in Egypt, a country which for centuries previously had been preoccupied with thoughts of death and the soul's preparation for judgment in an another world.[33] The soul's discourse can be traced back from the writings of Coptic Christians to the pre-Christian *Book of the Dead*. The path of transmission is not difficult to surmise, in view of the contacts of Celtic Christianity with the East by way of Gaul. Treatment of the same theme in Old Irish texts—though these are of doubtful date—suggests that here again Old English religious literature was indebted to Hiberno-Oriental tradition. Later in the Middle Ages, as we shall see, the soul's address to the body was elaborated into a full dialogue.

The Descent into Hell (Exeter Book) describes briefly the visit of the two Marys to Christ's sepulchre and the resurrection, and then goes back to tell about the saviour's reception in Hell by the patriarchs and prophets awaiting deliverance. It stops short before their departure for Paradise (the "harrowing" proper). The ultimate source is the Greek apocryphal Gospel of Nicodemus. Irish influence has been suggested here too,[34] but it is not clearly demonstrable. The theme was popular in homilies and was reflected in later mediaeval art.

Moral pieces of a general character include short poems on such subjects as vainglory, the order of the world, the seasons of fasting, alms-giving and resignation, most of them contained in the Exeter Book. There are also homiletic fragments in verse. Gnomic verses on moral subjects may also be mentioned here, though proverbs as a type belong to an older literary stratum (see ch. 1, sec. 3).

Azarias has been mentioned previously in relation to the Caedmonian *Daniel* (above, sec. 1). The Prayer and the Song of the youths in the fiery furnace may have belonged to a more extensive treatment of the story, but they are complete as they stand, and there is no reason to assume the existence of a second poetic version of *Daniel* in Old English.

5. LYRICAL POEMS AND RIDDLES

Among the poems referring to early Germanic pagan traditions there was one, we have seen, which was expressed in lyrical form. That was *Deor*, the lament of a scop supplanted in his lord's favour and deprived of the land which he had formerly held. The personal tone produces a lyrical effect, heightened by the technical device of a refrain identically repeated at the end of stanzaic units of varying length. Moreover, the elements of story-telling are very much subordinated to the delineation of a mood. *Deor* is preserved in the Exeter Book, and with it appears a group of poems sharing its lyrical tone although they lack refrain. Several of these compositions are monologues portraying both a subjective mood and an objective human situation involving other persons. All of them are pervaded by an elegiac atmosphere. In this respect they are closely akin to certain elegiac passages in *Beowulf*, where lyrical expression has a dramatic function within the epic setting, being inspired by themes like the loss of a chieftain or the solitude of one who has outlived his fellows in warfare.

The independent lyrics echo the same moods. They are also pervaded with a sympathetic feeling for nature in certain aspects which favour serious meditation, as in the *Doomsday* poem already cited. In this respect they show that curious and felicitous combination of seemingly contradictory traits which is characteristic of Old English poetry: epic sternness, sensitivity to natural environment, and a tendency to melancholy reflectiveness. The presence of very similar themes in Celtic nature poetry, notably Welsh, suggests that the Anglo-Saxon lyric was probably influenced by contact with the older culture of Britain. The coincidences of detail can hardly be accidental.[35] And the moralising strain, though no doubt present from the beginning (as the Scandinavian parallels indicate), must have been fortified by Latin poetry known to have been studied in England at the time.

The Wife's Lament and *The Husband's Message* are titles given by modern editors to two moving yet baffling lyrical pieces, one in the form of a dramatic monologue, the other, of prosopopoeia. In the first, a wife laments her condition of exile in the absence of her husband. She has been the victim of intrigue conducted by her husband's enemies; she now dwells alone in a cave regretting the past and cursing her foes. In the second poem, a piece of engraved wood speaks in the first person, telling how it came to be used as a letter, and what message it bore to the receiver. It conveys an invitation from a loving husband to his wife bidding her journey overseas in the spring and join him when the cuckoo sings. Here the tone is relatively cheerful. It has been thought that the two poems may refer to the same situation, the same husband and wife.

The Wanderer and *The Seafarer* are elegiac speeches by solitary men who describe the rigours of their lives. The former expresses the profound sense of isolation of one who has lost native land, kinsmen and "gold-friend" (that is, chief) and has been forced to travel over the icy seas in wintry sorrow, seeking for a new lord to protect him. At times he dreams that he still lives in the safe and radiant past, happily dependent upon some local patron, but he awakens to the harsh reality of black waves, sea-birds crying, "frost and snow falling mingled with hail." *The Seafarer* too portrays the rigours of life at sea in the winter, as seen through the eyes of a homesick exile. With all its deprivation, however, such a life calls to those who are by temperament wanderers. All things pass; their transitoriness evokes moral and religious reflections on the part of the poet.

Both these poems combine two themes similarly: depiction of the fate of an exile in Germanic tribal society, and a homelitic conclusion vaguely Christian in character on the instability of worldly happiness. Some critics have thought that such a combination points to dual authorship in both cases,[36] but the present tendency is to avoid catagorical statements on the matter. Another problem in connection with *The Seafarer* is the question whether one person is speaking in two moods, or two different persons—perhaps an old, hardened, disillusioned sailor and an eager youth who finds the hard life romantically attractive.[37] The issue is not very important so far as one's appreciation of the poem is concerned. Classical parallels have been suggested, as is natural, for the situation and theme are richly exemplified in ancient Latin literature. The use of monologue by an exile is to be found, for instance, in Virgil, and also in Ovid's *Tristia*.[38] The pairing off and constrasting of present misery in our transitory lives with a vision of more permanent felicity to be hoped for later may be due to the influence of Boethius.[39] Certainly there was possibility of more than one influence operating upon an English poet of the eighth or ninth century, granted the conditions under which he worked; and in view of the dual heritage of all such writers, the ambivalent attitudes of these lyrics could as well be expressed by individual speakers in monologue, as by two in dialogues.[40]

More unified in tone and very typical of its period is *The Ruin*, a lamentation for the past splendours and present desolation of a city now lying destroyed. Real experience and literary precedent alike offered inspiration for such composition. Here and there in England the imposing monuments of Roman culture were still visible in a state of decay which invited an Anglo-Saxon poet to meditate on the civilisation which had been overthrown by his ancestors' conquest of the island. By A.D. 800 there were newer-ruins to be seen in the North which were due to the raids of Scandinavian Vikings on the coast settlements. The literature of the late Roman empire, known to scholarly circles, was replete with lamentations for the fall of ancient cities, especially Rome, which lay in partial desolation after the long-continued inroads by barbarians akin to the Anglo-

Saxons themselves. The sermons of Gregory the Great were full of such lamentations for the fate of Rome and all Italy; minor Latin poets like Paulinus of Nola and Venantius Fortunatus had given voice to similar elegies in verse. Alcuin did the same for Lindisfarne when he received news of its destruction at the hands of the Vikings in 793. Like a plangent leit-motif of the times we read the words of the Old English poem:

3 Hrofas sind ȝehrorene, hreorȝe torras,
   hrunȝeat berofen, hrim on lime,
   scearde scurbeorȝe scorene, ȝedrorene,
   ældo undereotone.

   Fallen the roofs and prostrate the towers,
   despoiled the mansions and riven the mortar,
   in shards the shelter shattered and levelled,
   consumed with age.

We do not know the precise location of the ruined town which is here delineated. The references to bath houses and hot springs make likely the identification with the Roman city of Bath, but the Wall of Hadrian in the North has also been suggested. If the former identification is accepted, it poses the question: were not many of these shorter anonymous poems composed in Southern England in the first place, instead of being translated into West Saxon from the Northumbrian dialect, as has generally been believed?[41] The wintry seascapes of *The Wanderer* and *Seafarer* had formerly been thought to suggest Northumbria, but this need not be so necessarily. Winter at sea can be cold off the Southern coast too. Perhaps too much emphasis has been placed in the past upon sporadic linguistic forms appearing in texts like the shorter poems of the Exeter Book, which have been thought to indicate a "lost original in the Northumbrian dialect." Recent studies of dialect geography, showing the nuances occurring within one and the same linguistic area, as well as the diffusion of traits in an irregular manner, make us doubtful about the older tendency to lay down strict categorical divisions within a language unless evidence is full and unequivocal. It may be that most of the poems here being described, if not all, were first composed in the West Saxon dialect and only slightly modified when transcribed into the Exeter Book which now preserves them.

The most baffling and perhaps the most powerful of the group is an untitled poem called *Wulf and Eadwacer*. It precedes the Riddles (see below) and was at one time thought to be a riddle itself. Instead, it appears to be a dramatic monologue spoken by a woman who is somehow allied to Eadwacer, a man she hates—her husband?—while she passionately yearns for the exiled Wulf who once embraced her, giving her joy and sorrow, and leaving her with sick memories. The situation is obscure. Ingenious surmises have linked it with the story of Sigmund (also an exile, like Wulf), the father of Sigurd Dragon-killer in the Icelandic *Völsunga Saga*. In that case the speaker would be Signy, Sigmund's sister, who was married to the hateful Siggeir. Whatever the background, the lyric is conceived with amazing intensity. Its oblique portrayal is heightened by the occasional use of the hemistich refrain "Ungelic is us" ("Our fates are unlike"). Here and in *Deor* we have precursors of the typical stanzaic form of lyrics.

Exile and hatred, separation and the woes of men and women; the need to maintain stoic integrity in time of stress and to esteem lightly the pleasures of this world—these are the themes of the Old English lyrics. In them the melancholy of a warrior caste glorifying grim endurance is enhanced by the mood of abnegation inculcated by Christianity. The individual who speaks is doubly alone: on the one hand he is cut off from society by being declassed, by surviving the deaths of his fellows, by incurring the hostility of a husband or husband's family; and on the other he is alone because (like the poet of *Doomsday*) he is wrapped up in meditations about destinies lying beyond this life. Thus exile is the theme of all of the poems, whether in the literal or the metaphorical sense. Nature descriptions at times offer a lightening contrast, at times intensify the gloom. The agreement in mood and point of view gives an impression that more than an individual poet is speaking in each case. The voice we hear is that of a whole community expressing its uncertainties in uncertain times.

The *Riddles* in Old English verse are closely related to those written in Latin by Aldhelm, Tatwine and Eusebius; some are in fact modeled directly on these learned forerunners. Most of them appear in the Exeter Book, a few being scattered elsewhere. One is preserved in the Northumbrian dialect.[42] Some riddles give indirect and slightly humorous descriptions of familiar objects to be identified. Such are the ones with answers like Weathercock, Key, Bookworm or A One-Eyed Seller of Garlic. A considerable number are cast in the form of prosopopoeia and expressed with rather lofty poetic imagery, as when the Sun proclaims its functions in the universe, the Swan depicts its own feathered flight and sad cry, the Shield, Horn, Sword and Anchor announce their uses in veiled language. Several give expression to the preeminence of the human spirit over lower ranks of creation, as in Soul and Body and the speech of the Reed. The latter marvels how "a man's mind, united with a blade," can convert a dumb stalk into a musical instrument. The hierarchic beauty of the world of nature is consciously hailed in a group of riddles dealing with natural phenomena such as storms, sun, moon, and icebergs.

The cosmology revealed in these allusive lyrical descriptions has been proved to have strong Platonic and Neo-Platonic affinities.[43] It is fitting, therefore, that a paraphrase of Aldhelm's *De Creatura* should appear among them, although it makes no pretense of being a riddle. Again the role of created nature is portrayed as subordinate to the creator's will; the contradictions and harmonies in its vast range are made vivid: foul and innocent, old yet ever new, harsh yet soft, ever changing, it reveals an inner consonance throughout all its constrasting manifestations.

The Riddles are no mere playful exercise for intellectual clerics. They show once again how deeply the writers were preoccupied with the wonders of creation, how eager to learn what the past had to tell about them. Here Anglo-Saxon England fell heir to a conception of nature transmitted from Athens to Alexandria, thence by way of Rome and Gaul to England: a nature poetically envisaged in hierarchical ranks of being, orderly and obedient beneath surface conflicts, a nature regarded as handmaiden to theology and as yet but slightly esteemed as a subject of independent study. The Old English poems stress the poetic view and leave the theology unobtrusive, but at the same time they indirectly reveal an entire philosophy of nature, one which was to remain typical in the Middle Ages. The same attitude to nature was reflected in poems about animals, derived from the Latin moralising collection known as *Physiologus* (see ch. 4, sec. 4), perhaps contemporary with these. Together with the lyrics and the shorter poetical pieces such poems are indicative of the diversified culture prevailing among the educated groups, both secular and ecclesiastical, in English society of the eighth and ninth centuries.

[1] The suggestion is made by K. Malone in Baugh's *Literary History*, p. 63.

[2] Cf. R.E. Woolf, "The Devil in Old English Poetry," *Review of English Studies*, IV, N.S., No. 13 (1953), 1—12.

[3] For the Junius MS. see the Krapp edition (New York, 1931); also I. Gollancz, *The Cædmon Manuscript* (Oxford, 1927). Opinions differ as to whether the Biblical paraphrases in it preceded or followed *Beowulf*. *Exodus* l. 58 is identical with *Beowulf* l. 1410: "enge anpaðas, uncuð gelad," but the borrowing could have occurred in either direction. Arguments for the priority of *Beowulf* appear somewhat the more convincing.

[4] Internal evidence—differences in meter, style and vocabulary—convinced E. Sievers in 1875 that this section must be a translation from Old Saxon. Later, in 1894, his surmise was confirmed when a fragment of the original was discovered in the Vatican Library, with lines corresponding to ll. 791—817 of the Old English text. A few hemistiches will show the closeness of the wording:

Old Saxon	Old English
"Uuela that thu, Eua, habas," quað Aðam,	"Hwæt, þu Eue, hæfst
"ubilo ʒimarakot unkaro selbaro sið.	yfele ʒemearcod uncer sylfra sið.
Nu maht thu sean thia suarton hell	ʒesyhst þu nu þa sweartan helle
ʒinon gradaʒa..."	ʒrædiʒe and ʒifre..."

Modern English

"Alas, O Eve, thou hast (quoth Adam) with evil marked out
Our journey together. Swart hell thou mayest see
Greedy and grasping..."

[5] For bibliography of the discussion, see G. Anderson, *op. cit.*, p. 146 f. A recent argument in favour of Milton's indebtedness is given by J.W. Lever, "Paradise Lost and the Anglo-Saxon Tradition," *Review of English Studies*, XXIII (1947), 97—106. Junius was in England in 1651 when he received the MS. from Bishop Ussher.

[6] Notice, for example, the artful use of aposiopesis in *Genesis* l. 370, and the eight-line periodic sentence with a series of parallel dependent clauses, ll. 523—31. Cf. also the emphatic repetition in ll. 718 and 720, cited in the text.

[7] Bede, *Hexameron*, in Migne, *Patrologia Latina*, XCI (= *Bedae Opera*, II). In the seventh century Eugene of Toledo had written a poem on creation called *Heptameron de Primordio Mundi*, and had revised a commentary on the same theme,

Dracontii Hexaemeron... emendatum, Pat. Lat., LXXXVII. It is noteworthy that Bede's commentary ends at approximately the same point (ch. 21) as the Caedmonian *Genesis* (ch. 22).

[8] On internal evidence of grammar and metre, see Brandl, who dates this before *Genesis, op. cit.,* p. 87. *Exodus* has recently been edited by E.B. Irving, Jr. (Yale University Press, 1953).

[9] C.W. Kennedy, *The Earliest English Poetry* (Oxford University Press, 1943), p. 177.

[10] A variant form of the prayer, called *Azarias,* exists in the Exeter MS. Its presence in *Daniel* may be due to interpolation. See Krapp ed. of the Exeter Book, p. xxxiii f. Malone dates the *Azarias* section (*Daniel B*) later than the rest, partly on the evidence of differing use of the run-on lines. He suggests that the author of *Daniel B* may have been a Northumbrian writing about 875.

[11] E. Legouis and L. Cazamian, *A History of English Literature* (New York, 1935), p. 38 f. The authors speak of the "childish realism" of *Exodus,* but do not mention the signs of symbolism in the handling of themes.

[12] Carleton Brown, "The Autobiographical Element in the Cynewulfian Rune Passages," *Englische Studien,* XXXVIII (1909), 196—233. But cf. K. Sisam, *Studies,* ch. 1. as cited in the following note.

[13] See Carleton Brown, *loc. cit.* and in *PMLA,* XVIII (1903), 308—34; A.S. Cook, ed. of *Christ* (Boston, 1900), introd.; Kenneth Sisam, "Cynewulf and His Poetry", *Proceedings* of the British Academy, XVIII (1932), reprinted in his *Studies in the History of Old English Literature* (Oxford, 1953).

[14] Marguerite-Marie Dubois, *Les Éléments latins dans la poésie de Cynewulf* (Paris, 1943). The author gives numerous parallels in phraseology between Cynewulf's verses and the Biblical-patristic writings. Not all instances are convincing, but the evidence is none the less impressive. Many of the echoes of the Vulgate pointed out by her are to be found in the Psalms.

[15] Brandl attempts to establish a chronological order: *Christ, Elene, Juliana, Fates,* on the basis of vague personal remarks in the signature passages. Kennedy and Anderson follow the order *Juliana, Elene, Christ, Fates,* since the more recent form of the name Cynwulf (without medial -*e*-) appears in the signatures of the latter two. For recent discussion of the runic signatures, see R.W.V. Elliott in *English Studies,* XXXIV (1953), 193—204 and Tamotsu Matsunami in *Anglica* (Hiroshima, 1954), 3—15. But both forms existed about 800. The order here followed, which is that of Malone, is convenient because it groups the poems by literary types.

[16] Ed. by G. P. Krapp (New York, 1932). The poem probably reached Vercelli by way of the pilgrimage route, much frequented by English visitors to Rome in the Middle Ages. See Krapp's edition of *Andreas and the Fates of the Apostles* (Boston, 1906), introduction.

[17] Augustine Philip, "The Exeter Scribe and the Unity of the *Crist,*" *PMLA,* LV (1940), 903—09.

[18] K. Mildenberger, "The Unity of Cynewulf's *Christ* in the Light of Iconography," *Speculum,* XXIII (1948), 426—32.

[19] The source is to be found in the *Acta Sanctorum* ed. by the Bollandist Society, *sub die* Feb. 16: "Acta Auctore anonymo ex xi veteribus MSS.," Feb., II, 875—79.

[20] Krapp, *Vercelli Book,* introduction, p. xli. The legend is given in a form close to Cynewulf's source in *Acta Sanctorum,* May, I, 445—48.

[21] William O. Stevens, *The Cross in the Life and Literature of the Anglo-Saxons,* Yale Studies in English, XXIII (1904).

[22] The address of Christ to ungrateful humanity may be based on Sermon 249 by Caesarius of Arles; see M.M. Dubois, *op. cit.,* p. 120, citing A.S. Cook.

[23] Leonard J. Peters, "The Relationship of the Old English *Andreas* to *Beowulf,*" *PMLA,* LXVI (1951), 844—63.

[24] Cf. Kenneth Jackson, *Early Celtic Nature Poetry* (Harvard University Press, 1935).

[25] Albert S. Cook, *The Dream of the Rood* (Oxford, 1905), argued for Cynewulf's authorship. But Krapp was doubtful. In their edition of the poem (London, 1934), Bruce Dickins and A.S.C. Ross see no evidence in favour of Cynewulf. S.K. Das, *Cynewulf and the Cynewulf Canon* (Calcutta, 1942), denies his authorship.

[23] M. Schlauch, "The Dream of the Rood as Prosopopoeia," *Essays and Studies in Honor of Carleton Brown* (New York, 1940), pp. 23—34.

[27] G. Baldwin Brown, *The Arts in Early England,* V (London, 1921); F. Saxl, *The Ruthwell Cross* (London, 1943); Meyer Shapiro in *Art Bulletin,* XXVI (New York, 1944), 232—45.

[28] Text of the Latin *Phoenix* in Migne, *Pat. Lat.,* II, 277. For the literary theme of the earthly paradise, both pagan and Christian, see Howard R. Patch, *The Other World* (Harvard University Press, 1950).

[29] In his *Critical Studies in the Cynewulf Group* (Lund, 1949), Claes Schaar concludes on the basis of studies in sentence structure that *Phoenix, Christ C, Guðlac A* and *Andreas* are not by Cynewulf; *Dream of the Rood, Christ A* and *Guðlac B* are closer to his style but may well be by other poets also.

[30] Edited by Dobbie in *Anglo-Saxon Minor Poems* (New York, 1942).

[31] Though sometimes claimed for Alcuin, it is now accepted as Bede's. See L. Whitbread, "A Study of Bede's Versus de Die Judicii," *Philological Quarterly,* XXIII (1944), 193—221.

[32] R.J. Menner, "The Vocabulary of the Old English Poems on Judgment Day," *PMLA,* LXII (1947), 583—97.

[33] *Zhurnal Ministerstva Prosveshchenia (Журнал Министерства Просвещения),* (1890, Parts 1—2 and 1891, Parts 3—8); also *Romania,* XX (1891), 1—55 and 513—78; Louise Dudley, *The Egyptian Elements of the Legend of the Body and Soul* (Baltimore, 1911). For the Anglo-Irish connections see M. Schlauch as cited in ch. 2, n. 3.

[34] Genevieve Crotty, "The Exeter Harrowing of Hell," *PMLA,* LIV (1939), 349 ff.

[35] Émile Pons, *Le Thème et le sentiment de la nature dans la poésie anglo-saxonne* (Strasbourg, 1925); also Emil Seiper, *Die altenglische Elegie* (Strassburg, 1915); Kenneth Jackson, *Early Celtic Nature Poetry,* already cited.

[36] R. Imelmann, *Forschungen zur altenglischen Poesie* (Berlin, 1920), argued that a redactor added homiletic elements in both. G.K. Anderson agrees that the moralising conclusion is "intrusive," at least in the case of *The Wanderer,* and nothing more than "a sop to Christianity from the hands of some pious scribe," *op. cit.,* p. 159. But B. Huppé argues for unity in *Journal of English and Germanic Philology,* XLII (1943), 516—38.

[37] Huppé thinks, *loc. cit.,* that two persons are involved. Stanley B. Greenfield, *ibid.,* L (1951), 451—65 and *Studies in Philology,* LI (1954), 15—20, maintains that there is only one. See also Dorothy Whitelock, "An Interpretation of 'The Seafarer'"

in the volume: *Early Cultures of North East Europe*, ed. Cyril Fox and Bruce Dickins (Cambridge, 1953), pp. 261—72. I.L. Gordon dissents from these authors' stress on Christian moral interpretation, *Review of English Studies*, N.S., V (1954), 1—13.

[38] Imelmann, *op. cit.*, pointed out that Aeneas's long discourse to Dido is a speech by an exile recounting past glories and lamenting fallen comrades; he also suggests a parallel between Dido and the Banished Wife. Helga Reuschel, "Ovid und die ags. Elegien," *Beiträge zur Geschichte der deutschen Sprache und Literatur*, LXII (1938), 132—42, drew attention to the similarities with Ovid's work. In neither case is borrowing conclusively established.

[39] R.M. Lumiansky, "The Old English Wanderer," *Neophilologus*, XXXIV (1950), 104—12.

[40] Cf. Bertha Phillpotts, "Wyrd and Providence in Anglo-Saxon Thought," *Essays and Studies* of the English association, XIII (Oxford, 1928); J. Rosteutscher, "Germanischer Schicksalsglaube und Angelsächsische Elegiendichtung," *Englische Studien*, LXXIII (1938), 1—31.

[41] Older scholars like Leo and Earle had surmised that *The Ruin* refers to the city of Bath. S.J. Herben, *Modern Language Notes*, LIV (1939), 37—39 and LIX (1944), 72—74, has argued that it refers to Hadrian's Wall. Cecilia Hotchner, *Wessex and Old English Poetry* (New York, 1939), has reinforced the arguments in favour of Bath, and raised the question of original composition in West Saxon. K. Sisam, *Studies*, ch. 8, warns against over-confident assignment of poems to specific dialect areas.

[42] A Northumbrian version of Exeter Riddle No. 35 is published by A. H. Smith, *Three Northumbrian Poems* (London, 1933), p. 36 f.; Dobbie, *Minor Poems*, p. 109.

[43] See Erika von Erhardt-Siebold, "English Storm Riddles," *PMLA*, LXIX (1949), 884—89; also her discussion of Riddle 39, *ibid.*, LXI (1946), 910—15.

LATE OLD ENGLISH LITERATURE

1. THE AGES OF SCANDINAVIAN INVASIONS

From about 800 to 1066, the history of England is very much over-shadowed by that of Scandinavia. Again and again the Anglo-Saxon kingdoms were subjected to violent attacks by ship-borne invaders known as Vikings, who during this period harried and terrorised much of Europe, both East and West. Their raids and settlements included such far-flung territories as Greenland, Iceland, Ireland, Normandy, Sicily, Byzantium and the shores of the main Russian rivers. In England it was chiefly Danes who appeared first as raiders and later in great masses as permanent settlers. They were often joined however by Norwegians and Icelanders, either directly or from the colonies in Ireland and the Hebrides and Shetland Islands.

The invaders spoke varieties of North Germanic not very different from one another. Their speech was thus akin to Old English, and indeed was not difficult for natives to learn. But the linguistic kinship was less noticeable than were the social and cultural differences.

Whereas the Anglo-Saxons had long since become settled and relatively peaceful, at least in comparison with their initially destructive ancestors, the Vikings of the ninth century represented tribal warfare for expansion at its most ruthless. They were still isolated from the European trend to Christianity, and in fact the conversion of Scandinavia was not seriously undertaken much before 1000. Their social life and forms of land ownership were based on tribal organisation, with strong emphasis still placed upon the family as a collective unit responsible in matters of inheritance, marriage, and duties of revenge. Politically the Scandinavian peoples enjoyed a considerable measure of what may be called small-scale tribal democracy. Especially in a newly settled country like Iceland, law-making and communal decisions were carried out by general assemblies of all free farmers of a district. In the homelands, royal power limited the authority of the assemblies (called Things), but the kings themselves were restricted by the rival claims of powerful nobles (the jarls), who resisted efforts to unify the countries under single rulers.

The sudden outburst of piratical raids on a world-wide scale was due to several causes. Certain technological improvements in farming had reached the North before the ninth century: the use of an improved plow, the crank, the shoeing of horses (all unknown on the estates of the Roman empire). These, together with the three-field system of cultivating the soil, made for greater productivity in crops and in animal husbandry. As a result, the standard of living rose and population increased. Under the prevailing system of land ownership, many younger sons were left without land. They were driven to seek riches and permanent property abroad. Some departed also to evade the demands of kings for political subordination. Finally and most decisively, their trade expanded and their warlike expeditions were made possible by marked advances in the craft of ship-building. By the year 800 their workers had learned to use wood and iron ore to construct vessels capable of sailing far outside the traditional coast routes of the late Roman empire. They navigated with sails, also using power from crews of rowers quite commonly numbering up to 200 men, sometimes even 300. Warships were long and slender and built for speed, with iron rams on prow and stern for attacking enemy ships in naval battles. Trading vessels were broader, flatter and slower.

The first raids on England were aimed at booty, not settlement.[1] They remained infrequent until the 830's, and it was not intil 850 that they began to occur on a large scale. During this time the Mercian kingdom had reached and passed its zenith of power; by the latter ninth century Wessex had risen to the leading position and the Mercian kings were in effect subordinate to the West Saxon. The ensuing raids, carried out on a much larger scale than previously, were directed more to the South than the North of England. In the 860's a new wave of attacks began on a mass scale, this time aimed at the taking of land for permanent settlement. York was captured in 867. Thereafter East Anglia and much of Eastern Mercia were subdued by 870, leaving only Western and Southern Mercia, under hesitant rulers, to cooperate with Wessex in the now general task of resistance.

The reign of King Alfred the West Saxon (871—99)[2] was marked by ambitious operations on the part of the invaders, both North and South. The old province of Bernicia, extending up to Scotland in the East, was now conquered, and the foundations were laid for a large and relatively stable Danish colony embracing the whole Eastern territory down to the Thames, including parts of the Midlands. The conquered Mercian area was put under the control of five jarls with headquarters at the five fortified towns of Lincoln, Stamford, Nottingham, Derby and Leicester. Throughout this entire section of England, from North to South, Danish laws and customs prevailed, and therefore it was called the area of Danelaw. The settlers began to cultivate the soil and to lose their interest in piracy, but the rulers often remained belligerent and continued to draw new fighting forces from the homeland and Danish Ireland. The colonists were pagans, and remained so for some time.

Southern England, East and West, was almost overwhelmed in the latter ninth century. The Mercian Danes under King Guthrum defeated King Alfred disastrously (878), but he withdrew to the Somerset marshes, organised resistance and guerrilla campaigns, and eventually expelled the invaders after defeating and converting their king. A Christian bishop was reestablished in York. Alfred maintained his kingdom despite violations of treaties and renewed attacks from the Danes.

Alfred's successors—Edward (died 925) and Athelstan (died 939)—not only consolidated his gains but extended them, pushing the Danes backward from West Mercia and winning homage from some of the Scandinavian rulers of Anglia. Though most Danish settlers had by this time become ready for peaceful absorption, they could still be aroused to warfare upon certain occasions. Resistance to West Saxon expansions gave them such a cause. In 933 Athelstan was opposed by an alliance of Olaf Cuaran (a Viking ruler from Dublin who had claimed Yorkshire but had been expelled) and the revolted kings of Scotland and the Strathclyde Welsh. Their campaign culminated in the battle of Brunanburh (probably Birrenswark, South of Solway Firth, Scotland), a brilliant victory for Wessex, and the subject of a celebrated poem (see below, sec. 4). Athelstan became one of the most distinguished rulers of Western Europe, allied by marriage with the successors of Charlemagne.

Fortunes varied on both sides until the middle of the 10th century. In 955, the year of the death of King Eadred, the West Saxons held York and the Danes had temporarily ceased to resist them. The Danelaw, though still maintaining separate customs and organisation, became a peaceful province. The rest of England, though lacking the economic basis for genuine national unification, came closer to it in this century, under West Saxon leadership, than at any other time before the Norman conquest. Athelstan called himself "rex totius Britanniae." For about 25 years conditions favoured clerical education also, and revived Christian teaching made progress in Danelaw. St. Dunstan reorganised and reformed the church, and monasteries multiplied and extended their power and their land holdings.

THE HEPTARCHY

------ Frontier of Anglo-Saxon Occupation ------

Political Boundaries ca. 700 A.D.

ENGLAND AFTER THE
DANISH CONQUEST

Political Boundaries ca. 1030 A.D.

In 980, however, there began a decade of small violent raids from Danish Ireland and Scandinavia, and the year 991 inaugurated a fresh age of national catastrophe. In that year a fleet of 93 ships gathered from Norway, Sweden and Russia and attacked Essex by way of the Panta River and inflicted a severe defeat upon the Saxon defenders at Maldon. (For the poem on this subject, see sec. 5.) From this time on the enemy arrived in larger numbers than ever before. The continental Danes in particular had developed professional armies and navies of a type hitherto unknown: for instance, the Jomsborg Vikings had massive headquarters on the fortified harbour of today's Odraport in Poland. The Saxon armies were far less disciplined and experienced. The political organisation had deteriorated. As the attacks again took the form of mass invasions, the English King Aethelred repeatedly tried to buy off the enemy. Vast ransoms were paid to Svein of Denmark, who nevertheless continued his conquests, not even sparing Danelaw territory. By the time of his death in 1014, King Svein was acknowledged ruler of England. He was succeeded by his son Cnut (or Knut) who first subdued the country once more and was then "elected" king by the Anglo-Saxon lords. Feeling secure at last, he dismissed his Danish army and turned to peace-time activities for a period of two decades, to 1035. The Danish rule ended, however, with his son Hardaknut (died 1042).

Edward the Confessor, last but one of the Anglo-Saxon kings, was the son of King Aethelred and of Emma of Normandy, a duchy settled by Vikings in the 10th century. Upon Edward's death the *witan* or royal councillors chose his brother-in-law Harold Goodwin's son to succeed. But the illegitimate son of the Norman Duke Robert, William, used the dynastic connection through Emma in order to claim the English crown. On this pretext he launched a large-scale invasion at a moment when Harold was occupied in repelling Norse invaders in Yorkshire. At Hastings he defeated and killed Harold (1066), obtained formal election to the kingship from the *witan*, and thus attached England to the duchy of Normandy.

2. SOCIAL AND CULTURAL CHANGES, 850—1050

We have fragmentary knowledge of the transformations affecting English social life over the two centuries and more of Scandinavian raids and settlements. During much of the period, conditions were unfavourable to writing, and literacy in England declined sharply between 800 and the reign of King Alfred, then again after about 990. Even the clergy were often ignorant of reading and writing, whether in Latin or the vernacular. There were, however, some intervals of relative quiet during

Decorated leaf Bede's *Ecclesiastical History*

British Museum

which constructive social forces had a chance to reassemble themselves. Certain Midland libraries such as those at Malmesbury, Worcester and Peterborough were able to survive and transmit valuable manuscript materials for the use of chroniclers in the early 12th century. Even the North and East enjoyed some periods of reconstruction after intervals of sensational destruction, in spite of the influx and domination of pagan foreigners by no means interested in the preservation of the native literature. The churches in the Danish provinces such as York and Durham were at times able to establish pacific relations with the non-Christian rulers. And the Danish population itself was gradually transformed as it became attached to the English soil.

As invaders, the Danes had first established themselves in fortified centres, each commanded by a jarl, and they extended their rule and settlements over the surrounding territory by means of the many immigrants who later arrived with their families. Five such centres were the fortified cities mentioned above. Land was distributed to warriors under the jarls, and the recipients became free peasants called sokemen, holding their own property independently.[3] They maintained their independence until 1066 and after, never becoming serfs although they paid rent to their lords and had to attend their courts. When England was more or less unified under the later Anglo-Saxon and Danish kings, the sokemen paid taxes directly into the royal treasury, not indirectly through their lords. In the early Middle Ages (12th and 13th centuries), freemen with Danish names are still found carrying on their business and disposing of their property by themselves, without recourse to any lord.

The districts within Danelaw had a certain measure of local self-government, each with an assembly which probably corresponded to the Things in the Scandinavian homeland. At such gatherings, quarrels were settled, bargains, marriages and divorces were arranged, penalties were imposed for violations of the law. Twelve "lawmen" declared judgments and interpreted traditional customs which were the foundation of legal procedure. In the 10th century, as the Wessex kings regained sway over Danelaw territory, this special system of juridical meetings was left intact.

Concerning such assemblies in Iceland we have a rich body of information embodied in the long, very lively prose sagas about leading families of settlers and their descendants (10th to 13th centuries). The Things not only served the purposes of government and justice on a level of tribal democracy for free landowners; they were also important as a focus of social life and a stimulus to literature. The events of local feuds, items of family gossip, reports of Viking adventures abroad and tales of the supernatural were here repeated and eventually elaborated into prose narratives which were brilliant in their characterisations, their life-like dialogue and dramatic power. It was the social institution of the Thing which to a great extent explains the creation and preservation of these early monuments of realistic literary art.

Raw materials for dramatic narrative were no doubt in evidence at the corresponding assemblies in the Danelaw of England. Whether such events received fictional elaboration, either here or under like conditions in English-speaking territories, we can only guess. It has been argued that prose sagas like the Icelandic were cultivated in England,[4] either by independent development or in part by imitation. The evidence is indirect, however. Certain dramatic passages in the Anglo-Saxon Chronicle (see below, sec. 3), and in the Latin histories of the 12th and 13th centuries, show a debt to popular narrative about real poeple—often in verse, but perhaps also in prose. That the Danes and the English were drawing close is proved by the language, for a very large number of Scandinavian loan words were taken into Old English at this period, and shared in the later sound changes of the native vocabulary.

One theme which had produced much dramatic conflict in earlier life and literature was disappearing from the social consciousness of Danes and English alike during the 10th and 11th centuries. This was the conflict of family against family over questions of property rights, privileges and honour, to the accompaniment of private killings, revenges and occasional payments of wergild. In the type of Germanic societies convulsed by these struggles, the kindred was a decisive factor in a property-owner's life: he could win and survive only if he could muster relatives in large numbers to take responsibility for his deeds and to support his cause by action. But in the late Old English period the family shrank in relative importance, while society came to embrace larger and larger administrative groups under a consolidating single monarchy.

As early as King Alfred's reign, the military reorganisation was centralised and made more permanent. This was done by concentrating the responsibility: the noblemen closest to the king, together with his *ealdormen* or district representatives, received the task of direct mobilisation as professional army officers.[5] They carried out the mustering of forces through the local gentry or *thegns*. The peasant-farmers now entered service not as unclassified warriors but as followers of a specific lord. The tie with an overlord was strengthened; the immediate family and village ties were somewhat weakened.

The laws too registered the widened community control of a man's life, at the expense of the obligations of kinship. Under King Edmund (died 946) the statutes attempted to suppress blood-feuds by restricting acts of private revenge and exempting the slayer's kin from responsibility. In this way the very foundations and motives were being removed from the old heroic tales of bloodshed and revenge.

All of these shifts were conditioned upon economic changes producing broader social strata. The lords in political control of the villages were beginning even now to encroach, and permit wealthier land-holders beneath them to encroach, upon property rights formerly held in common, such as wasteland used for pasturage, meadowland, and so on.[6] The system of agriculture, requiring that strips of land rotate between productive use and lying fallow, was difficult for those holding small shares. The crushing burden of taxation laid on the Anglo-Saxons for Danegeld payments, the fortunes of war, the new forms of military service, the frequent crises in agriculture, all tended to ruin and eliminate the small holders and to aggrandise the wealth of the larger ones and of the lords. The Anglo-Saxon class known as *ceorls* declined in number during the period before 1066, having failed to remain solvent under adverse conditions.

Need, social compulsion, and finally the law required declassed men to seek protection from a lord and to serve him. Those still holding land, the wealthier peasants called *geneatas*, paid for protection in greater rents and services. A growing number of upper-class fighters entered the king's service directly, became members of his household, acted as his representatives, and often received tracts of land from him in reward. Peasants on such land worked to maintain him and his household, either directly on his estate (the *demesne*) or indirectly by contributing from the produce of their own small holdings. By the 11th century, South England was divided into larger economic units called manors,[7] which were worked by men bound to the estates. From them sprang the class of medieval serfs.

The foundations of feudalism were thus already laid in the years before the Norman conquest. The tribal period was a matter of the past; the ideals and emotional attachments it had fostered were rapidly becoming archaic, thought they persisted in literature longer than in life.

The church as a land-owning institution consolidated its claims for service and rent like any secular landlord of the time. As an educational institution, it improved and lapsed several times during the age of foreign invasion. The zeal of Alfred produced some temporary results which could scarcely have affected very wide circles, in view of the unsettled conditions. In the latter ninth century a Danish Archbishop of Canterbury named Oda (942—58) tried to bring some order into the disreputable confusion prevailing among the clergy. He had been educated in the reformed Benedictine Abbey of Fleury in France, a centre from which the Cluniac movement affected the English church through several of its leaders. Dunstan, the reformer and organiser who succeeded him at Canterbury (961—88), worked in the same tradition. He also strengthened the economic position of the church by encouraging endowments from secular lords having interests closely allied with it. In the same period, the Benedictine reform was carried out in Southern monasteries like Abingdon and Winchester, under the direction of Bishop Aethelwold. It was Aethelwold who made a translation of the Benedictine Rule into Old English. At Winchester Aelfric (see sec. 6) received the education which was to prepare him for his later activity in raising the standard of ecclesiastical learning in England.

3. LITERATURE UNDER KING ALFRED

The reign of Alfred is as notable in the realm of letters as of politics and military strategy. One of the traits distinguishing this monarch as a pioneer in statecraft was his recognition of the role of vernacular literature and learning in the construction of a unified state. He consistently stressed the importance of having a national language at a time when the sense of nationhood was still in its infancy.[8] His own translations and those he commissioned or inspired made him an innovator in the art of writing literary English prose.

Hitherto prose writings were—if we may judge from the few survivals—rather halting and artless. They included literal interlinear translations of the Psalter and Gospels (in several dialects), early laws which were later incorporated into Alfred's code, early annals which were used in the great Chronicle carried forward under his direction.

Two of the first projects undertaken by Alfred were from the works of Pope Gregory the Great.[9] The King encouraged Waerferth the Mercian Bishop of Worcester to translate the *Dialogues*, to which he provided a preface; and he himself, with the help of four professional scholars, did the *Pastoral Care*. The former is a book of relatively narrow appeal. It recounts pious tales of diabolic temptations, miracles and visions conceived in (to us) rather childish terms. The choice may have been the Bishop's, made with the tastes of cloistered readers in mind; it is to be regretted that he did not choose rather a selection of Gregory's sermons, which contain fine instances of impassioned oratory on matters of more general interest.[10] According to Bishop Asser, the biographer of Alfred, this translation was done before 884, in the time of very severe affliction for the people.

The other Gregorian text, the *Pastoral Care* (*Cura Pastoralis*),[11] being designed to instruct secular clergy in performing their duties, has a more practical and lasting interest. Alfred's preface on the state of learning in England gives not only a revealing picture of the situation, but also a deep insight into the King's understanding and solicitude. Having indicated the distressing extent of illiteracy during England's troubled times, he goes on to state his desire

that *all the freeborn youth* of England who have sufficient means to devote themselves thereto, be set to learning so long as they are not strong enough for any other occupation, until such time as they can well read English writing. Let those be taught Latin whom it is proposed to educate further, and promote to higher office.

If this aim could have been realised, it would have meant extension of reading and writing the vernacular to the children of all well-to-do *ceorlas* among the non-noble as well as the noble land-owners: a very considerable achievement in literacy for those times.

Alfred's interest in the history of his people is evidenced in the stimulus he apparently gave to the recording of it in systematic fashion. From annals already existing and known Latin sources, a compiler put together (about 891) an account of previous English history from the age of Julius Caesar. Outstanding events falling in Alfred's reign were told with breadth and detail. This original version of the so-called Anglo-Saxon Chronicle was sent to a number of centres of learning and there carried forward as official supplements were circulated for addition to it. Local materials were also used. The oldest surviving version, closest to Alfred's original project, is the Parker manuscript (thus named because it was once in the possession of Archbishop Parker; now at Corpus Christi College, Cambridge). The six other manuscripts[12] run close to it in their first parts, and then begin to diverge, though still showing indebtedness to similar sources. The one kept up longest was that at Peterborough (MS. Laud 636), which ends *sub anno* 1154. It is valuable linguistically as well as historically, for its later entries show directly the transition of the language into Middle English.

The longer entries made during Alfred's reign must have been inspired by him. They portray battles and campaigns against the Vikings in a style admirable for rapid, accurate reportage. The movements of the invaders and the strategy for the defenders are outlined against an essential background of terrain and weather. The tone is impersonal. All the more effective are the occasional short expressions of feeling, as the statement recorded *sub anno* 886 (Parker Chronicle): "The army [of invaders] had not, thanks to God, quite utterly destroyed the English people." Alfred's claim to kingship on a national scale is embodied in the comment made *sub anno* 900 in the same text: "He was king over all the English people save that part of them that was under the rule of the Danes."

In order to transmit a recognised legal system to future generations, Alfred likewise supervised the putting together of earlier law codes inherited from his predecessors. He supplemented these by Biblical commandments and by additions of his own. The texts reflect archaic stylistic usages already mentioned—alliteration, word-pairing, gnomic phraseology—which go back to the age before writing.[13] The fines and other penalties provide insight into the structure of society, revealing what violations of social behaviour were regarded as most serious and to whom the wrong-doers were responsible, according to the legal code then adopted.

Having ensured the recording of law and current history, Alfred turned to the task of more general enlightenment concerning past ages. Bede's *Ecclesiastical History* was at hand to give detailed information on the early church and early kingdoms in England. This text was made available in an adapted Old English form, partly condensed and changed, partly literally translated. The parts closest to the original are at times coloured by Latin idiom, but the best passages—for instance, the description of Caedmon's poetic inspiration and his pious end—are done with unspoiled vigour in the native style.[14]

Anglo-Saxon students also needed to be informed about their place in the panorama of world history, as seen by men of learning in the ninth century. At that time, knowledge of the older Mediterranean civilisations was not obtained directly from the eminent historians of Greece and Rome, such as Thucydides, Livy and Tacitus, but indirectly from compendia and outlines only ultimately indebted to their works. A widely known outline of the latter sort was the propaganda history of Orosius, a disciple of St. Augustine, written in the fifth century. Its purpose was to prove that Christianity was not to blame (as unconverted contemporaries were then arguing) for disasters which were overwhelming the ancient world at the time; that, on the contrary, earlier history was replete with even more sensational examples of violence than those accompanying the Germanic invasions. The aim may have been to give hope and consolation, but the pictures unrolled by Orosius were gloomy in the extreme. Even the memories of Danish violence might be expected to pale before such a chronicle. His *History against the Pagans* was popular, however, precisely because it was both compendious and didactic in tone. The Alfredian version,[15] in which the King took a special interest, is freely handled, with changes both large and small. The interpolations are especially interesting. The geographical section, for instance, being deficient in information about the Germanic world, was supplemented by reports made directly to Alfred by two voyagers, one of whom had sailed eastwards in the Baltic Sea and the other northwards along the coast of Norway to the White Sea. The former of these, named Wulfstan, had given the King a factual description of the coast from Schleswig and Pomerania (Pomorze) to the Gulf of Danzig (Gdańsk) and also an account of the tribal customs of the Esthonians dwelling still farther to the East. That first-hand account interpolated in Orosious' history is one of our first written sources dealing with the area of present-day Poland and its neighbours. [16]

Two works of a theological and philosophical nature round out the list of Alfred's translations. One of them is a composite work derived from St. Augustine's *Soliloquies*, supplemented by his *De Videndo Deo*. [17] It is extant in a late manuscript only (12th century), but is generally accepted as the king's work. It uses dialogue to expound difficult topics of dogma such as the nature of God and the soul. The interpolations include concrete metaphors such as Alfred delighted in. On the first page he compares a translator-educator to a good builder who uses tools and fetches the best wood from a forest to build city walls and houses, so that men may live there "merrily and quietly, both winter and summer, in such manner as I have not done." If not from Alfred's own hand, the work is surely done in his spirit.

The philosophical work by Boethius, *The Consolation of Philosophy*, was one which attracted medieval writers for several reasons. Its human appeal was strong, for it dealt with a man wrongfully accused of disloyalty to the king he served, stripped of wealth and friends, and left to meditate in prison upon the fundamental questions of justice in human affairs. Such had been the actual fate of Boethius, formerly an aristocratic Roman consul attached to the court of Theodoric the Great in Italy, later executed by him (524). Boethius was a Christian, we are now quite certain, [18] but he was also a trained philosopher in the Platonic tradition and he chose to debate the problems troubling him, in the form of a dialogue with Lady Philosophy, without appeal to dogma. The God whom he invokes, an otherwise unidentified power of supreme good, could have been accepted by many of the pagan philosophers who had long since rejected polytheism for some type of monotheism.

Boethius discusses, then, the causes of misfortune, the nature of chance, and men's need of an inner strength to face the hazards of an uncertain life. He tries to reconcile the sufferings of good people with an idea of divine justice, and to retain freewill for men while giving omnipotence to God. The solutions offered, especially of the latter problem, are rather unsatisfactory, but the reflections themselves are carried out in a mood of lofty yet sensitive stoicism which speaks across the divisions of time and circumstance separating Boethius from Alfred and his later admirers, down to our own day.

At points of especially intense feeling and imagination, Boethius had inserted lyrical passages, called *metra*. One version of Alfred's translation[19] renders these in prose, another in alliterative verse. The poetic versions are apparently based on the ones in prose. It is quite likely that Alfred did both (see below, sec. 4). He may have had learned assistance in the entire project, for the translation shows some use of commentaries on Boethius. Typical of Alfred's independence, however, are the numerous contractions, expansions, and inserted explanations. He never forgets the readers for whom the translation is intended. He is at pains to add brief explanations for classical names and allusions, and he at times substitutes an equivalent from Germanic mythology (for instance, Weland for Vulcan). As the literary work of one who had himself seen many changes of fortune and shared intimately in the sufferings and reverses of his countrymen, *The Consolation of Philosophy* served as a fitting crown to all of Alfred's writings. The traits of courage, human dignity and reflectiveness were common to both Latin author and Anglo-Saxon translator.

4. THE LATER RELIGIOUS POETRY

Poetry of the standard Anglo-Saxon type continued to be composed during the period of King Alfred and afterwards. In fact, the traditional forms make extremely difficult the task of assigning dates of composition to various texts, the more so since old and recent are alike preserved in late copies, affected by late changes in the language. It is possible, for instance, that *Genesis B*, already discussed, should be placed in the period here being considered.

· The fragment of a Biblical epic named *Judith*[20] is full of the old heroic spirit, but shows internal evidence of late composition (mid-ninth to mid-10th century). The author inclines strongly to the use of run-on lines and expanded ones,[21] and to long periodic sentences. The action includes the slaying of Holofernes and Judith's urging of the Hebrews to an attack upon the Assyrians. It is told with much verve and skill. Both subject matter and style may well reflect the militant spirit of the resistance to Viking invaders.

There are several metrical paraphrases of Biblical Psalms, the largest group being contained in a Paris manuscript of the early 11th century, but the translation was done about the same time as the *Judith*.[22] The verse is irregular, and contains far less alliteration than was characteristic in the typical Old English epics. The variations from standard practice may be marks of the later age, or they may be due to the influence of Biblical prose upon the translator or group of translators.

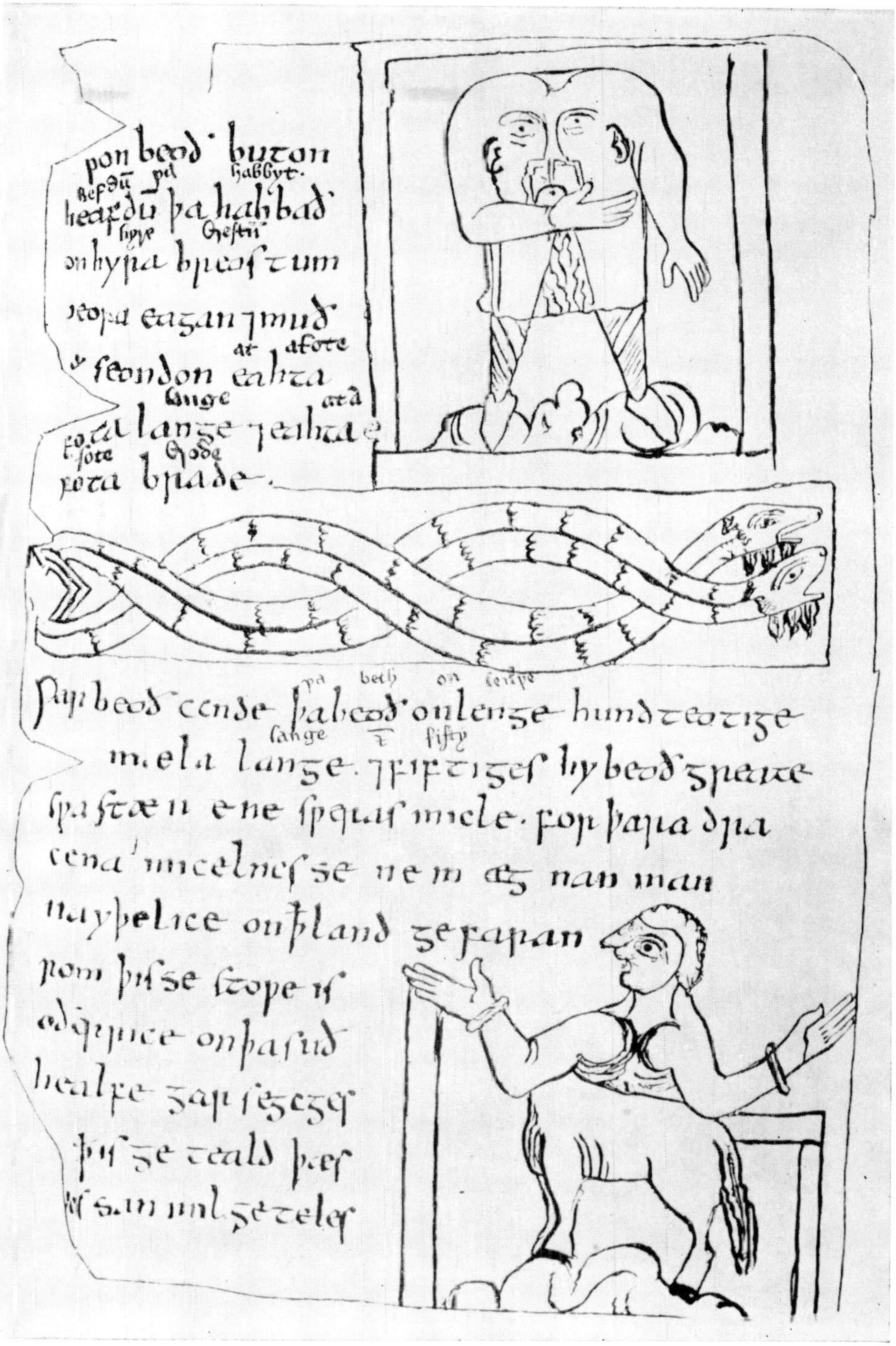

Monstrous Creatures Described in *Wonders of the East*

British Museum

in the Exeter Book, are inspired by an edifying Latin collection called *Physiologus* transmitted to Western Europe from a lost Greek original. The fantastic anecdotes were presumably put together in Alexandria, some time in the second century A.D. They betray Neo-Platonic and Oriental influences as well as Christian, but their abstruse meanings did not prevent wide popularity and general circulation in the West.

Finally, there are three separate treatments of another Oriental theme which likewise found popularity in both Western and Eastern Europe, particularly in the folklore of Slavic countries. It represents the Biblical, or rather the Talmudic King Solomon engaged in disputation with a representative of pagan wisdom—a demonic character called by names like Kitrovas, Ashmodai or Markolis—and winning a victory over him. In two Anglo-Saxon poems and a prose version, Solomon has been Christianised and his opponent is re-named Saturn. [25] Again, the chief interest of the texts is their revelation of the varied materials contributing to Old English didactic literature. The Latin original may have come to England from Ireland.

5. SECULAR VERSE AND PROSE

Worldly literature of the final Old English period also reveals a con- tinuing receptivity to foreign, even exotic, influences. For instance, two prose texts often assigned to the 11th century (though they may well be earlier) brought to Anglo-Saxon readers sections of the popular fictitious cycle of adventures dealing with Alexander the Great, originally composed in Greek. In the *Letter to Aristotle*, translated from a Latin version, Alexander tells his former tutor about his campaigns in India and the vast treasures and remarkable flora and fauna he saw there. A similar text, *Wonders of the East*, gives further reports of the same kind in the third person. [26] Still another prose text, *Apollonius of Tyre*, is a typical example of late Greek romance: a tale of improbable adven- tures, of families and pairs of lovers being separated by calamities such as shipwreck, kidnapping and selling into slavery, but reunited at the end by a series of happy accidents. This tale found its way into late Old English prose from a popular Latin version also based on a lost Greek original. As a work of art the plot has little value. It is told however with a certain simple charm in Old English, and has some interest for us because the same romance, with most of its absurdities preserved, was later adapted for the Elizabethan play *Pericles Prince of Tyre*, on which Shakespeare collaborated. The translation may have been undertaken as a school exercise, but it also offered some colourful entertainment for those who cared to read it.

A short fragment of belated Old English verse, a eulogy of the city of Durham, is interesting chiefly because it represents an exercise in the precepts of Roman rhetoric.[27] Every phrase of the poem is a stereotype illustrating what Greek and Roman text-books had prescribed as fitting ingredients for an *encomium urbis*. The synthetic result, redolent of the class room, was actually composed in the early Middle English period (soon after 1100). Both language and contents, which are typical Old English, indicate the conservatism of vernacular composition in monasteries for some time after 1066.

The later poems of the Anglo-Saxon Chronicle and a separate piece on the battle of Maldon testify on the other hand to the vitality of native warlike themes. Certain events such as battles against invaders, coronations and the deaths of kings moved the annalists to insert compositions about them in the traditional court style. The poetic techniques of the 10th and 11th century show a certain freedom as compared with earlier practice, for instance in a wider use of the less emphatic grammatical forms in the alliterative scheme. More interesting still, there are even attempts to compose in the border territory between verse and rhythmical prose. In the latter cases, the rhythms are so strong that modern editors have been in doubt as to the form in which they should print the passages concerned, whether as prose or verse.

Most famous of the Chronicle poems is the celebration of the victory of King Athelstan over the hostile alliance which fought him at Brunanburh in 933.[28] The exultant spirit runs high and the lines breathe of glory to be won in battle. In contrast, the poem on the death of Edward the Confessor (1065) stresses piety and the gentler virtues. The elegy on King Edgar's death (975) is expressed partly in Christian terms, but some of its formulas of conventional praise seem to echo the half-forgotten tribal period, before writing, when lamentations for lost chiefs were already a well established type of oral literary expression.

The Battle of Maldon, a separate longer poem of which 325 lines are extant, describes in vivid detail the heroic resistance and death of Byrhtnoth of Essex and his followers when the coast was attacked by Vikings in 991.[29] Whereas *Brunanburh* tells of a battle as reported from afar, *Maldon* could easily be the account of an eye-witness, so circumstantial is it. Courage in defence of homeland has rarely found better expression than in the words of the old fighter, Byrhtnoth's *geneat*, after their leader has fallen and most of their companions lie dead:

312   Hiӡe sceal þe heardra,   heorte þe cenre,
        mod sceal þe mare,   þe ure mæӡen lytlað.
        Her lið ure ealdor   eall forheawen,
        ӡod on ӡreote...

317 Ic eom frod feores;   fram ic ne wille,
     ac ic me be healfe   minum hlaforde,
     be swa leofan men,   licȝan þence.

Mind must be harder,   and heart the keener,
our mood be the more   as our might grows less.
Here slashed with wounds   our leader lies,
good man on the ground...
I am old in years,   nor longer would live,
but here at the side   of him, my lord,
that man so dear   it's my wish to lie.

The strong personal sentiments are still those of immediate tribal loyal-
ties, but the defensive struggle everywhere being fought against invasion
was already contributing to a sense of unity which, after long centuries
of feudalism yet to come, was to be completely realised only in early
modern times.

6. RELIGIOUS PROSE

Despite the unsettled times, some significant work was done in the
late 10th and the early 11th century in the field of ecclesiastical vernacular
prose. The main types cultivated were sermons, saints' lives and Biblical
translations.

Sermons are a literary genre of especial interest. They often reflect
contemporary *mores*, the general problems of the day, as well as church
practices and doctrines. The collection known as the Blickling homilies[30]
and various others scattered elsewhere (latter 10th century) treat with
especial vigour the apocalyptic themes concordant with the times: the
end of the world (which some preachers foresaw for the year 1000), the
harrowing of hell, the last judgment. This same vigour pervades also
the more polished work of two homilists whose names are known to us:
Aelfric and Bishop Wulfstan.

Aelfric (died ca. 1020),[31] who was trained at Winchester and later
made Abbot of Eynsham, wrote several cycles of homilies for use on
various occasions. In those entitled *Catholic Homilies* he translated and
adapted chiefly from Gregory the Great, Augustine and Bede. He applied
much skill to the task, taking pains to simplify, explain and adapt the
exposition to his audience. A long cycle dealing mostly with saints' lives,[32]
intended for delivery on the appropriate feast days, is written in a highly
rhythmical form of prose which is at times very close to, if not identical
with, scannable verse. It is English, not Latin, in its inspiration. Many
of the *vitae* concern anchorite saints of the Eastern deserts, in Egypt
and Palestine. These legends were available to Aelfric in a collection
called *Vitae Patrum*, put into Latin from various Greek originals. The

settings and attitudes of Eastern hagiography must have seemed strange to the Anglo-Saxon audiences. Throughout, Aelfric tried conscientiously to fit his alien materials to them, and to evoke the conditions of the Eastern Roman Empire (so far as he could) in terms his listeners would understand. For instance, he says himself that he avoided speaking of the system of dual emperors, since it might confuse his hearers, "as our own nation is subject to *one* king and is accustomed to speak of one king, and not of two."

The same talent for pedagogical exposition and cautious adaptation appears in other writings. Aelfric, like others of his time,[33] worked upon a Biblical translation, choosing the Heptateuch or first seven books of the Old Testament to put into idiomatic English, with judicious omissions. In his preface he revealed that he was alarmed lest uninstructed persons, reading about the doings of polygamous Hebrew patriarchs, should consider them worthy of uncritical imitation in every detail. Aelfric also translated and adapted Priscian's Latin grammar into English, and he added a graceful dialogue in Latin, later put into English, to provide exercises in Latin conversation. This Colloquy represents the young students questioning workers at the monastery, perhaps lay brothers, on their occupations of hunting, fishing, farming, and the like. Tone and subject-matter are unusually simple and close to the activities of every day life.

Wulfstan (died 1023), a contemporary and friend of Aelfric, held higher posts in the church. He was in turn Bishop of London, of Worcester and of York, and he also played a part in state affairs. Among the homilies ascribed to him,[34] the most famous and most eloquent is an address to the people of England on the evils and calamities of his times. Wulfstan of course regarded these quite simply as punishments for moral transgressions. His attitude is exactly that of Gildas who had castigated the Romanised Celts at the time of the Anglo-Saxon invasions 500 years earlier. But Wulfstan's intense feeling and his mastery of oratorical style raise his "Sermon to the English" above the more conventional ones of the time warning about an imminent end of the world.[35] It is also exceptional in the sympathy shown for common people and their woes. Many persons, he says, are reduced to poverty and humiliated:

and poor men are sorely tricked and cruelly betrayed, and [though] convicted of no crime are sold into the power of strangers far from this earth [of theirs], and for a trifling theft [by their parents], children still in the cradle are by harsh law enslaved far and wide throughout this folk; and freemen's rights are taken away and thralldom is tightened and alms-right is curtailed, and—what is quickest to tell—the law of God is hated and scorned.

In a sweeping summary Wulfstan catalogues the woes visited upon his contemporaries:

There has been devastation and hunger, burning and bloodshed in every district often and often; we have been damaged by stealing and killing, plague and pestilence, murrain and sickness, malice and craft, and very sorely by plunder of robbers; and much we have been oppressed by severe taxes [for Danegeld]; and very often stormy seasons have caused our crops to fail; for on this earth, as clearly is seen, many wrongs have prevailed for many years, and everywhere truth among men is unstable.

Something of the moralist's exaggeration appears in this, to be sure. There were intervals of relative peace in the last century or so of Anglo-Saxon England, as during the reign of King Cnut. For some generations at a time, certain centres of learning and of peaceful activity were spared, and constructive work was quietly carried forward. But for many people in those last decades, the reality of daily life must have been all too close to the dark picture painted by the eloquent bishop.

[1] See T.D. Kendrick, *A History of the Vikings* (London, 1930), ch. 8; Mary W. Williams, *Social Scandinavia in the Viking Age* (New York, 1920); Charles Haskins, *The Normans in History* (Boston, 1913).

[2] Charles Plummer, *The Life and Times of Alfred the Great* (Oxford, 1902). See also the works of Winkelmann, Oman and Stenton, already cited.

[3] G.O. Sayles, *The Medieval Foundations of England* (London, 1948), pp. 131 — 51.

[4] C.E. Wright, *The Cultivation of Saga in Anglo-Saxon England* (London, 1939). A list of possible subjects is given, pp. 72 — 77.

[5] Winkelmann, ch. 11; Sayles, pp. 97 ff.

[6] P. Vinogradoff, *The Growth of the Manor* (London, 1905), p. 176 f. "Stinting" of the common land occurred by "asserting' an individual's right to claim it for private use. The lords could approve such reclamation if enough land still remained for the villagers. See Sayles, pp. 122 — 30; Stenton, pp. 463 ff.

[7] The terms manor and demesne were not used, however, until later.

[8] М.П. Алексеев,, *История Английской Литературы* (Moscow, 1943),pp. 43 ff.

[9] *Dialogues*, ed. H. Hecht in Grein and Wülcker, *Bibliothek der angel-sächsischen Prosa*, V (Hamburg, 1905).

[10] The sermons were among those used by the homilists of the 10th and 11th centuries such as Aelfric.

[11] Ed. Henry Sweet, EETS, OS, Nos. 45 and 50 (1871 — 72). On the circumstances of the translation and dissemination of Alfred's version see Sisam, *Studies*, ch. 9.

[12] *The Parker Chronicle* (832 — 900), ed. A.H. Smith (London, 1935). See also Charles Plummer, *Two of the Saxon Chronicles Parallel* (London, 1892). For a synoptic view of six MSS., see Benjamin Thorpe's edition in the Rolls Series (London, 1861).

[13] M.H. Turk, *The Legal Code of Alfred the Great* (Halle, 1893); F. Liebrecht, *Die Gesetze der Angelsachsen* (Halle, 1903). On the problem of archaic style and oral tradition, see Dorothy Bethurum, "Stylistic Features of Old English Laws," *Modern Language Review*, XXVII (1932), 263 — 79.

[14] Ed. by Thomas Miller, EETS, OS, Nos. 95 — 96 (1890), giving evidence that the translation was the product of an unknown Mercian scholar, later revised. J.J. Campbell, "The Old English Bede," *Modern Language Notes*, LXVII (1952), 381 — 87, also concludes that more than one person worked upon this translation.

[15] Ed. Henry Sweet, EETS, OS, No. 79 (1883). See Simeon Potter, "Commentary on King Alfred's Orosius," *Anglia*, LXXXI (1953), 385 — 437 (omitting the geographical introduction).

[16] See R. Ekblom in *Studia Neophilologica*, XII (1940), 177—90 and XIV (1942), 115—44; see besides A.S.C. Ross, *The Terfinnas and Beormas of Ohtere* (Leeds, 1940).

[17] Ed. H.L. Hargrove, Yale Studies in English, VIII (New Haven, 1902).

[18] The Christian theological tracts assigned to Boethius by tradition are accepted as genuine by E.K. Rand in his edition of the *Consolatio* for the Loeb Classical Library. See also Rand's *Founders of the Middle Ages* (Harvard University Press, 1928).

[19] Alfred's translation is edited by M. Science, EETS, OS, No. 170 (1928).

[20] Ed. B.J. Timmer (London, 1952).

[21] But Timmer has pointed out, *Neophilologus*, XXXV (1951), 226—30, that the tendency to use expanded lines does not alone mean a late date. There are many such lines in the much earlier *Dream of the Rood*.

[22] G.P. Krapp, *The Paris Psalter and the Meters of Boethius* (New York, 1932), p. xvii.

[23] See the Exeter Book as edited by Krapp and Dobbie; also Dobbie, *The Anglo-Saxon Minor Poems* (New York, 1942).

[24] Ed. A. Schröder, *Anglia*, V (1882), 289 f.

[25] Robert J. Menner, *The Poetical Dialogues of Solomon and Saturn* (New York, 1941); also in Dobbie, *Minor Poems*.

[26] Stanley Rypins, *Three Old English Prose Texts*, EETS, OS, No. 161 (1924). The Alexander texts, according to Sisam, may be Mercian of the tenth century; see his *Studies*, ch. 4.

[23] See M. Schlauch, "An Old English *Encomium Urbis*," *Journal of English and Germanic Philology*, XL (1941), 14—28.

[28] The text of *Brunanburh* is to be found in Dobbie's *Minor Poems*, besides the editions of the Chronicle by Plummer and Thorpe cited in note 12.

[29] Ed. Dobbie, *Minor Poems*; also E.V. Gordon (London, 1937). The scene and course of the battle have been reconstructed in detail by S.D. Laborde, *Bryhtnoth and Maldon* (London, 1936).

[35] Ed. Richard Morris, EETS, OS, Nos. 58, 63, 73 (1874—80).

[31] See Marguerite-Marie Dubois, *Aelfric* (Paris, 1943).

[32] *Lives of the Saints*, ed. W.W. Skeat, EETS, OS, Nos. 76, 82, 94 and 114 (1881—1900). On the form see Dorothy Bethurum in *Studies in Philology*, XXIX (1932), 515—33. The source is the *Liber Vitas Patrum* (sic) discussed by Constance L. Rosenthal, *The Vitae Patrum in Old and Middle English Literature* (Philadelphia, 1936).

[33] Grein and Wülcker, *Bibliothek der angelsächsischen Prosa*, I (1872), 22 ff. See J. Raith, "Aelfric's Share in the Old English Pentateuch," *Review of English Studies*, III, New Series No. 12 (1952), 305—13. There is also a translation of the Gospels, edited J.W. Bright in four volumes (1904—06).

[34] Ed. A.S. Napier (Berlin, 1883). For recent discussion see Karl Jost, *Wulfstanstudien* (Bern, 1952).

[35] Ed. Dorothy Whitelock (London, 1939).

PART II
EARLY MIDDLE ENGLISH

EARLY FEUDALISM. THE EARLIEST SHORT TEXTS IN MIDDLE ENGLISH

1. THE ESTABLISHMENT OF FEUDALISM

When William of Normandy was crowned King of England on Christmas Day, 1066, a very great change was formally recognised in the country's social and political structure. The effects were immediately felt in the upper ranks of the ruling class, more gradually in the lower ones, and with a considerably reduced impact among the agricultural workers.

Politically, the change meant a paradoxical situation. A large geographical unit separated from the continent, which in the face of invasions had been forming itself out of loose tribal federation towards a relatively unified state organisation, now became attached, in a political sense, to a much smaller unit in France, the duchy of Normandy. The son and grandson of William continued to spend part of their time in France, and to think, speak and act as Norman dukes besides functioning as kings of England. Yet they were indebted to England for their vastly augmented importance, both economic and political, in the setting of feudal Europe. They recognised this fact in the primary attention given by them to English affairs.

Socially, England now adopted a thoroughly feudal system of class relationships. The change had been heralded by native tendencies in the previous 150 years, as we have seen, but it was now rapidly completed and made systematic. When the Conqueror divided the English lands among his followers, he created a new aristocracy bound very closely to him, and he was in a position to define clearly and imperatively the bonds of obligation attaching them to him. Their duties as English barons and lords under the king could be more definite than those they had owed as knights under the duke. At home the situation had been complicated by conflicting traditions and local customs. In England it was a new situation, following a military victory in a foreign land.

From the beginning, then, the Norman dynasty was in a strong position in relation to the social ranks just beneath it. The system of land ownership now assumed that all free subjects of the king, rich or poor, had to hold their land in tenure from somebody, except for a small group without any land at all: the declassed country workers and the vagabonds.[1] Peasants without title to land were absorbed into the ranks of unfree workers (serfs and villeins), including those farming land from which they could not depart, and owing to the landlords both products and labour in repayment for the privilege. Landowners might have direct tenure from higher lords in the shires, but all of them, small and large, held either directly or indirectly from the king. In case of internal conflict, the king's claim was supposed to be paramount. Church ownership of land was also integrated into the general feudal structure.

The correlation of land ownership with military service to the king was drawn closer.[2] From the beginning, the rulers of England struggled to realise unity of a practical nature under the king's supreme military command. They were often thwarted, as the wars against and among the powerful barons testified, but they endeavoured to establish the principle that private warfare was an offence against the king, and they enforced it with greater success than did the contemporary rulers in France. At the same time, the technique of warfare now transplanted to England was based on the more extensive use of cavalry instead of foot soldiers. The heavily armoured knight became the conspicuous figure of the armies, both in life and in literature; the old Anglo-Saxon *fyrd*, in which even the horsemen had dismounted before fighting, quickly disappeared from memory.

The transfer and tightening of relations in ownership bore hard on the Anglo-Saxon *thegns* and wealthier farmers, who had to a great extent disappeared by 1100. In the county of Cambridge, for instance, about 700 out of an original 900 prosperous farmers (sokemen) had sunk into serfdom by the early 12th century.[3] While some of the Anglo-Saxon and Scandinavian landed gentry were able to attach themselves to the new dynasty, most of the nobility was now Norman.

The European feudal aristocracy gratified its endless hunger for more land with an unscrupulous disregard for traditional boundaries both linguistic and geographical. It was a restless social element even farther removed from the incipient sense of a national entity than the class they displaced in England. When their fiefs in France or England appeared insufficient to them, these noblemen were quite willing to leave their possessions in the homeland in order to carve out new properties for themselves in North Africa, Sicily or Palestine. There is abundant reflection of their adventurous excursions (prettified into romance) in their literature of entertainment. The roving type of landlord, absent on Crusades or expeditions of less disguised robbery, was an unreal figure for the peasants working for him on his home estate and dealing with his bailiff as representative. On the other hand, many of the Norman aristocrats settled in England permanently, and in time developed close ties with the native population. They were soon absorbed into the pattern of local society.

The changes were least sharply felt in the lowest ranks of society. Under the shifts of power and the tightening of obligations to landlords, rural community life still went on with many of its old ways undisturbed. True it is that the transformation already taking place before 1066 was accelerated by the establishment of Norman feudal lords in fortified castles throughout the land. As a result, both categories of workers, villeins and serfs, were legally unfree. They were at the disposal of a specific lord within a specific boundary. They were not free to leave the lord's domain (though he could, according to law, shift them from one part of it to another); they had to pay taxes to him in connection with daughters' marriages and other private matters; they had to yield part of their time (two or three days a week) to work on the lord's estate, or deliver part of the products of their own land to him as rent, or both. But villeins, though thus subject to overlords, and restricted in their acts and movements, were free men in relation to one another, and also in their dealings with the law.[4] Serfs enjoyed less freedom both socially and legally, but both groups had the advantage of a kind of "possessorship" of the land, albeit restricted within the feudal system. Their social position had deteriorated, but not to the level of chattel slavery as known in the ancient world. And tradition and customs were strong factors preventing a complete deterioration.

Payment of labour was a very obvious form of exploitation. Here, as Marx has pointed out,[5] the rent and the surplus value appropriated by the landlord are identical; no one can fail to see the relationship. Rent paid in agricultural products is almost as obvious a form of exploitation. But unfree medieval labourers, as Marx has also pointed out, still owned the actual tools of production used by them, their plows and plough teams, spinning-wheels and churns. They were even able to accumulate some products for themselves. The relations of ownership left some margin for individual initiative, and the foundations were present for a later change in economic status. In preserving and even widening the advantages of their position, the villeins and serfs were helped by the very inconsistencies in usage in various parts of England, and by the force of custom which was recognised as fundamental in medieval law.[6]

As time passed, the unfree workers augmented their advantages by their vigorous social struggles to regain both civil freedom and freedom of movement. The slogans of the 14th century show that English peasants stubbornly adhered to the memory of their status in pre-Norman times, for one of their demands at that time was the restoration—not a first granting—of a written charter of their liberties which they believed had originally been stolen from them. Resistance accelerated and became revolutionary as villeins, serfs, poor peasants and landless workers began to find allies in the urban traders, craftsmen and apprentices who had grievances of their own against the system of feudal restrictions. The movement became vocal after 1300, but its origins go back to a time over a century earlier.

2. CONTRADICTIONS WITHIN FEUDAL SOCIETY AND ITS CULTURE

Obviously the social system of feudalism in England contained many inner contradictions which from the start made it unstable. These contradictions were more or less directly expressed in its culture, including literature.

The fundamental and ultimately decisive one was the conflict of interests between the producers and exploiters; between the vast army of those who worked upon the land or the goods yielded by the land, and those who appropriated a considerable portion of the results for their own use, without themselves contributing to the economic good and welfare of society. The class struggle which was the fundamental motive force of history in the Middle Ages was reported almost exclusively from the point of view of the exploiters. In the 14th century, however, when the great uprising of 1381 shook feudal society to its foundations, even the hostile sources make clear how deep was the cleavage and how strongly burned the fires of resistance in the lower orders beneath the silence and apparent conformity of centuries.

Within the ruling class, a very glaring conflict occurred between the kings and the groups of powerful barons, owners of huge tracts of land enabling them at times to challenge directly the power of their rulers. While the kings' interests caused them to strive for unification of authority, the barons resisted this, and tried to maintain maximum autonomy for their separate territories. The conflict of interests led to repeated revolts of the barons in the 11th to the 13th centuries, and again in later periods. Some kings like Henry II avoided major revolts, but they became violent whenever royal power seemed to be on the decline as a result of mismanagement or external reverses. Internal warfare was an all too familiar feature of medieval life.

Outside of England such conflicts were mirrored in literature produced for the magnates opposed to the kings. In France, similar struggles produced a whole body of feudal epics expressing violent partisanship for the barons and deriding the claims of the kings as supreme overlord. Such poems as *Raimond de Montauban, Maugis d'Aigremont, Ogier le Danois* and *Girard de Vienne* portray baronial warfare against the king — that is, against the legendary Charlemagne or one of his successors — with great hostility to the latter. Others, like the famous *Chanson de Roland*, favour monarchy and show the king in an auspicious light. England produced no such partisan literature from the barons' party, but some of the French epics were later translated or adapted for English readers. The best surviving manuscript of the original *Chanson de Roland* was in fact copied in England (early 12th century) and is preserved at Oxford.

Another struggle for power developed between the two institutions of monarchy and church. Ruling circles in Europe were convulsed by conflicts between empire and papacy, occurring especially between the 12th and 14th centuries, with both sides claiming supreme power to regulate the secular affairs of mankind. Dante's interest in that struggle is well known: his support of empire against papacy in matters of government colours the entire ideology of the *Divine Comedy* and was argued on theoretical grounds in his Latin prose works. Here again, English literature shows less concern with the issue. A struggle did break out between church and state over questions of jurisdiction, especially the issue of investiture (i.e., which authority should "invest" bishops with their offices). It flared up between William II and Anselm of Canterbury; it continued under Henry I, and it reached a dramatic climax in the quarrel between Henry II and Thomas à Becket (ca. 1165 — 70). Such controversies were duly reflected in the literature of learning. Most of the polemic writing connected with them was done, however, in Latin. Fortunately for English society, the struggle was kept within a restricted area, removed from the civil warfare which was afflicting the populations of Italy and Germany over the same issue. When satire was written against the church as an institution in the earlier Middle Ages, whether in Latin, French or English, it usually dealt with more general problems than the limitation of its powers of appointments and judicial administration.

A more deep-going contradiction developed within the economic sphere as trade began to expand, both nationally and internationally, and the cities increased in size and prosperity. The small, very nearly self-sufficient units like the manors, which in many cases themselves produced what was consumed upon them, began to be supplemented more and more by market towns where produce was exchanged. [7] Feudal relations did not preclude the production of surplus wares for sale by villeins on a small scale, as well as by overlords on a larger one. [8] Where political conditions became settled, the roads and transportation were improved, the cities extended their activities in trade and handicraft production. The increasing shipping trade in the Mediterranean area stimulated commerce in the Northwest of Europe also. The Crusades were closely connected with these developments, both as result and cause. The consequences for economic history are well known. The wider became the orbit of trade, the more archaic became legal and customary restrictions on people's undertakings and movements, due originally to the shrunken economic units of the early Middle Ages, when production and military security were only possible within small territories.

To a certain extent, agricultural enterprises clung to the old restrictions, which included many local fees and tolls of a protective character, while the urban world of shippings and trade and shop production tended to work against them. As the guilds expanded, one group representing special interests in production might often be found in conflict with another, thus adding to the turbulence of city life.

The growth of cities and the quickening pulse of trade had a direct influence on literature. Merchants, sailors, returned Crusaders, journeymen, peddlars at fairs, were in a position to disseminate stories heard in distant places, as well as information and misinformation about the great world lying beyond manor and village. European fiction from the 12th century onwards shows a vast increase in plots and materials directly traceable to the Eastern world of Byzantium, Asia Minor and even the Far East. While each country and each feudal community adapted and changed these materials to suit itself, the reservoir upon which they drew to obtain them was greatly augmented. Transmission from sources close at hand—for instance, the Celtic territories in England and France—was also facilitated.

Nor was the transmission limited to tradesmen, returned soldiers and professional story-tellers. Members of the clergy in monastic orders were transferred from one house to another, and were sent abroad to study and to teach. Pilgrims helped to carry both fiction and fact from one place to another. Exotic, often quite frivolous tales from the East and from Orientalised parts of Spain begin to appear in learned writings from the 12th century onwards, paralleling their appearance in the field of secular entertainment. For instance, a collection of short stories both amusing and instructive which was made by a converted Spanish Jew Petrus

Donnington Castle. Early Norman Period

Alphonsus (ca. 1100), the *Disciplina Clericalis*, was widely circulated in Latin and received French translation in England towards the end of the 12th century. Soon after 1100 a clerical traveller of more serious bent, Adelard or Athelard of Bath, went abroad to study in France, Spain, North Africa and Sicily. (See ch. 6, sec. 2.) He was a herald of the Graeco-Arabic influence which was to have widespread effects upon university circles a century later.

The transformations caused by expanding trade and city life affected England very generally. On the borders of the English-speaking territory within the island there was one further conflict which had importance for literature. It arose from the existence of two unabsorbed nationalities, the Welsh and the Scotch, which long and obstinately resisted union with the Anglo-Norman state. These groups, still organised as tribes under chiefs or local kings, were distinguished by languages of the Celtic family and by customs and traditions differing from the English. A third extensive Celtic territory, Ireland, was further marked off by its geographical separation as an island. Beginning in the 12th century, the English kings waged repeated wars attempting to integrate all these areas into their feudal state, but they met with fierce and stubborn resistance. The struggle was reflected in the native literatures and in English also, from the opposite point of view. In the later Middle Ages English was used, however, by Scottish defenders of the Lowlands. Though the people there had acquired English speech, they were attached by political and social history to the Highlanders who were struggling for independence.

These struggles of nationalities continued throughout the Middle Ages and beyond. The one in Ireland lasted, indeed, to our own times, and echoes of the Scottish struggle are still heard in the realms of politics and literary art.

3. THE LANGUAGE SITUATION AFTER 1066 AND THE CONTINUITY OF ENGLISH WRITING

After the Norman Conquest, of course, the alien French language was brought into use in the royal court and the circles immediately surrounding it. French-speaking feudal lords, with their closest followers, became the leading figures in the shires, and many clerics educated in Normandy were appointed to high posts in the English church.

All of this meant a considerable change, certainly, within the restricted spheres concerned, but until recently its importance has been rather exaggerated. The linguistic rapprochement occurred quickly in those broad circles of society where communication was imperative.

The vast majority of the people went on speaking English, and English alone, as did the clergy. Yet there is no evidence that hostility and mutual unintelligibility long separated the French settlers from the English among the lower orders.

In the law courts as in the church the native language continued to be used, supplemented for some time by Latin only, not yet by French. Later when Norman French made inroads on the legal profession, but not until about 200 years after the Conquest, it was as the result of a second, more limited period of French influence in the government under Henry III (1216—72) and his successors.[9] French was not established for court pleading until the reign of Edward I (1272—1307). The Norman overlords and their representatives who first settled throughout the countryside quickly learned English for dealings with their dependents; interpreters were necessary, we may assume, only for the first few years. The Norman aristocracy apparently did keep up French speech in their halls, for domestic use and entertainment, but the language was quickly lost in the towns, even in those which received a considerable number of foreign settlers.

The royal court, it is true, continued to use French as did the aristocracy closest to it. But bilingualism (or rather, trilingualism, if Latin is included) appeared early and soon became the rule. The longer persistence in the use of French at the English court, moreover, was not exclusively due to the impetus of the Conquest. The fashion was reinforced and prolonged because of the general vogue for French language and literature and customs throughout all of the ruling classes of Western Europe, from Norway to Italy. The extent of that vogue will be found measured in the overwhelming fashion for courtly romances (see ch. 7, sec. 3). Although considerable Anglo-Norman literature was produced in England, its circulation was limited.[10] The language was, as has been not long ago emphasised, limited rather within the narrow circle of the upper English aristocracy, while English was and remained the people's language.[11] Even the members of the aristocracy found it necessary by the 13th century to foster and preserve the use of French—that is, the Anglo-Norman dialect—in their families by means of special instruction.[12] And English itself had a noticeable influence on the French transplanted to Britain, affecting pronunciation, inflections and syntactic constructions.[13]

In view of the actual situation, then, it is not surprising that cultured English continued to be written in the literary dialect of Wessex for some time after 1066. We have already noted that several texts extant in the pre-Conquest language, such as *The Grave* and the *Eulogy of Durham*, were actually composed in the 11th century. A number of undoubted pre-Conquest texts exist in copies made in the 11th and 12th centuries. All this shows that a rigid separation of Middle from Old English literature is not easy, not even when a drastic political event like the Conquest divides the two periods.

4. NATIVE TRADITION IN EARLY HISTORY AND HAGIOGRAPHY

The most striking testimonial to the continuity of English writing is of course the post-Conquest section of the Anglo-Saxon Chronicle, as carried forward to 1154 at Peterborough. After that monastery was burned in 1116, the text was copied from a lost original resembling the versions at Worcester, Winchester and Abingdon.[14] One compiler continued this to 1131, and a second covered the years 1132—54. The latter showed great awareness of the sufferings of ordinary people in the dreary dynastic warfare being waged between two descendants of the Conqueror, Stephen and Mathilda. They were the daughter and the nephew of Henry I respectively, the former supported by the church party and the latter by the feudal, in their dispute over royal succession between 1135 and 1154. Perhaps this chronicler sprang from the ordinary people himself; certainly his sympathies for them break through in unconscious eloquence when he depicts the harsh reality of feudalism, made worse in time of internal strife:

A.D. 1137   Hi swencten swyðe þe wrecce men of þe land mid castelweorces. Pa þe castles waren maked, þa fylden hi mid deovles and yvele men. Pa namen hi þa men þe hi wenden ðat ani ʒod hefden, bathe be nihtes and be dæies, carlmen and wimmen, and diden heom in prisun after ʒold and sylver, and pined heom untellendlice pininʒ. For ne wæron nævre nan martyrs swa pined alse hi wæron; me henʒed up bi the fet and smoked heom mid ful smoke; me henʒed bi the þumbes other bi the hefed, and henʒen bryniʒes on her fet; me dide cnotted strenʒes abuton here hæved and wrythen to ðat it ʒæde to þe hærnes... Pa þe wrecce men ne hadden nan more to ʒyven, þa ræveden hi and brendon alle the tunes ðat, wel þu myhtes faren all a dæis fare, sculdest thu nevre finden man in tune sittende ne land tiled. Pa was corn dære and flesc and cæse and butere, for nan ne was o þe land. Wrecce men sturven of hunger... Wes nævere ʒæt mare wreccehed on land, ne nævre hethen men werse ne diden þan hi diden...

Translation: They drove hard the wretched men of the country with the building of castles. When the castles were built, they filled them with devils and evil men. Then they seized all the folk whom they supposed to have any goods, both by night and day, men and women, and thrust them into prison for gold and silver, and tortured them with tortures which can not be told. For never were martyrs so tortured as they: they were hanged up by the feet and smoked with foul smoke;

they were hanged by the thumbs or by the head, and coats of mail were hung on their feet; knotted strings were tied about their heads and twisted so hard that they went in to the brain... When the wretched people had no more to give, they robbed and burned all the villages so that you could travel for a whole day's journey and never find a village with any inhabitant in it, nor any land tilled. Poor people died of hunger... Never before was there such misery in the country, nor did the heathen ever act worse than they did...

In the Western part of what had been the old kingdom of Mercia, writing of the pre-Conquest type was carried on for purposes of preaching and instruction. All of the work of this general school may in a sense be called homiletic, but in some texts, such as the saints' lives to be used by preachers, the narrative element predominates, while in others dealing with more abstract matters, the emphasis is rather on exposition. It will be convenient, therefore, to separate the hagiography from the tracts because of some differences in the literary forms, although instruction is of course the underlying purpose of both.

Among the lost texts known to have existed at Worcester about 1100 A.D. was a biography of its early Bishop Wulfstan (died 1095; not to be confused with Wulfstan of York discussed in ch. 4).[15] This was done in English by a monk at the monastery named Coleman. A surviving Latin translation indicates that Wulfstan made an unusual contribution to the maintenance of the Old English literary tradition in the West. It is a pity that we do not have vernacular biography describing his career. The earliest surviving English text of the type is a 12th century account of St. Chad, a missionary to the Mercians in the seventh century. Based on Bede's narrative, it chiefly emphasises the miracles connected with the saint's activities, and has linguistic rather than literary interest for us.[16]

A group of three saint's lives—the legends of Katherine, Juliana and Margaret, composed early in the 13th century—command special attention for several reasons.[17] Here the style of narrative and also the subject matter show strikingly the continuity of early Middle English with Anglo-Saxon literature. The treatment does not recall Cynewulf's epic elaboration in his *Juliana*, but rather the hagiography of Aelfric composed in shorter units for use in sermons (see ch. 4, sec. 5). The form is certainly close to Aelfric's rhythmical alliterative prose. In fact, the patterns of ornament and of sound are so conspicuous that (again as in the case of Aelfric) editors have been undecided how the texts should be printed, whether as irregular verse lines or, as recent critics are inclined to think, as continuous prose.

So far as content is concerned, the author or authors had the same difficulties which confronted Aelfric in trying to adapt the alien and fantastic materials to native listeners or readers. Saints' lives of this type were perforce naive in style and content because of their origin among relatively unlettered people then being persecuted by the massive state apparatus of the Roman empire. The three virgin martyrs, as one critic has remarked, "address their persecutors in studiously offensive language and seem intent on securing the crown of martyrdom at whatever cost of courtesy of good manners."[18] With all their naive absurdity, however, some of the scenes are treated with a lively sense of actuality unknown to the Latin originals. The merits, such as they are, belong to the native tradition of homiletics out of which these writings blossomed.[19] The type of legendary *vita* was popular and remained so for centuries. In later times it was again cultivated in the form of larger collections, of the kind Aelfric himself had undertaken before the Conquest.

5. NATIVE TRADITION IN SHORT TRACTS

Besides saints' lives, other themes were treated in the style made classical by the West Saxon models of the Old English period. There are, for instance, various collections of homilies in the Southern dialects, both East and West, which show direct indebtedness to Anglo-Saxon models.[20] They are rather simple and straightforward, lacking both the elaborate symbolic interpretations and the elements of pure entertainment which were to become conspicuous in later sermons, after the art of popular appeal had been consciously studied by preachers.

Some poetic fragments on the old dualistic theme of body and soul have been preserved in the Worcester Cathedral Library. The style is strongly reminiscent of Old English verse. These fragments and a 12th century homily on the same subject show the continued appeal of a theme already treated several times before,[21] and destined to be treated again at some length in the 13th century.

Two short tracts may be mentioned at this point as precursors of the abundant didactic materials which were to appear in the 13th and 14th centuries. They are *Hali Meidenhad* (*Holy Virginity*) and *Sawles Warde* (*Guardian of the Soul*), both written, like the saints' lives of the Katherine group, in rhythmical alliterative prose of the Southwest (early 13th century). However, in these texts the rhythms are less insistent and the alliteration less consistently used. The former text,[22] which recounts with gloomy frankness the pains and disabilities awaiting medieval women in the married state, was a kind of propaganda tract supporting the new movement towards the foundation of regular monastic orders for women. Though addressed primarily to women with a presumed calling for the religious life and discipline, it has a more general interest because it reveals how the unfavourable conditions of medieval life tended to preserve and to fortify the asceticism originally transplanted from Eastern Christendom in a much earlier epoch. Before the composition of the Middle English text, Ailred of Rievaulx or Riedval in Yorkshire (died 1166) had written on the subject of monastic life for women. [23] The theme received ample informal treatment in the long Middle English text *Ancren Riwle* (see ch. 8, sec. 3).

Sawles Warde [24] is a homiletic tract of the same literary school as *Hali Meidenhad*. It deals with the human soul and its need for protection from the assaults of the evil foe who is active in the world outside. The underlying concept is an expanded metaphor. Man's inner self is represented as a house ruled by the soul having knowledge of what is good (Wit), and supported by the cardinal virtues, but allied to a fractious helpmeet named Will (the faculty of choice, including the choice of evil). For every virtue resident within, a corresponding vice lays siege without, under the direction of the Fiend. Fear, the messenger of Death, brings a warning to Prudence to strengthen the defenses. He has seen Hell and describes it vividly. The virtues assure Wit of their support and a messenger from Heaven brings a comforting account of the bliss awaiting there. Wit confirms his rule over his house, the better to resist assaults from the external enemy.

The source of this rather unusual bit of allegory is a chapter in the Latin treatise by Hugo of St. Victor called *De Anima*. [25] In parts the English follows the original fairly closely, but some of the speeches and descriptions are independently treated with extraordinarily effective diction. Outstanding is the description of Hell. Here the language clearly betrays its descent from Old English rhythmical prose:

Helle is wid wið ute met, ant deop wið ute ʒrunde, ful of brune uneuenlich, for ne mei nan eorðlich fur euenin þer towart; ful of stench unþolelich, for ne mahte in eorðe na cwic þing hit þolien; ful of sorhe untalelich, for ne mei na muð for wrecchedom ne for wa reckenin hit ne tellen. Se þiche is þrinne þe þeosternesse þat me hire mei ʒrapin, for þat fur ne ʒeueð na liht ah blent ham þe ehnen þe þar beoð wið a smorðrinde smoke smeche forcuðest, and tah i þat ilke swarte þeosternesse swarte þinʒes ha iseoð as deoflen þat ham meallið ant derueð aa, ant dreccheð wið alle cunnes pinen.

Hell is wide beyond measure and deep without bottom, full of fire not to be described, for no earthly fire may be compared to it; full of unbearable stench, for no living thing on earth could endure it; full of unspeakable sorrow, for no mouth can, for wretchedness nor for woe, reckon it or tell it. So thick is the darkness within it that a man can grasp it, for the fire gives no light, but blinds the eyes of those that are

there with a smothering smoke, a most baleful reek; and none the less
in that swarthy darkness black things they do see in the guise of devils
who grind them and destroy them forever, and torture them with all
kinds of pain.

It is not merely the eloquence and technical skill of *Sawles Warde*
which make it exceptionally significant in the group of shorter early
Middle English texts. Still more important is the fact that the metaphor
expressing the fundamental idea is so expanded as to produce a miniature
allegory. Wit and Will, Prudence and the other virtues and the messengers
addressing them are pale abstractions, to be sure, but they move and
speak and are given some of the traits of human beings in a story. They
are presented in a situation familiar to all who saw or participated in
medieval warfare (which meant, we may be sure, almost everybody).
This manner of conveying philosophical ideas and other kinds of doctrine
by a seeming tale was destined to have a tremendous development in the
ensuing centuries. The long allegories of the 13th to the 15th centuries,
the morality plays of the 15th and the 16th, certain aspects of Elizabethan
drama, Spenser's *Faery Queen* in the 16th century and Bunyan's writings in the 17th, are all part of that development. Medieval allegory
as a literary device is closely allied to the philosophical views and the
didactic methods of Christianised Platonism and later scholasticism. It
is also allied with much of the theory basic to medieval plastic arts in
their non-realistic aspects of symbolism.

More will be said about these problems in the coming chapters.
What is important to notice here is that *Sawles Warde* not only shows
a clear indebtedness to the literary techniques of expression cultivated
in Anglo-Saxon England, as has already been pointed out by more than
one critic; it is also prophetic of new forms and styles typical of the
more advanced Middle Ages. Its allegory is based on an image—that
of the besieged castle—which was adopted by many other writers, both
for instruction and entertainment.[26] More than most other writings of
this group, it looks forward as well as backward. This fact has not been
sufficiently emphasised by those who have remarked on the vividness
of its imagery and its fidelity to Old English style and vocabulary. In
this sense it is outstanding among the early short texts of the West Midlands
and the South which testify at this time to the continuity of English
prose.[27]

Longer English texts composed about this period, just before and
after 1200, belong more definitely in style, scope and subject matter
to the literary age to come, when vernacular literature was used more
and more in systematic attempts at lay education. These more ambitious
efforts will be discussed later (ch. 8).[28]

NOTES TO CHAPTER V

[1] Charles Petit-Dutaillis, *The Feudal Monarchy in France and England* (London, 1936), p. 67. The author inaccurately calls declassed agricultural workers the "proletariat."

[2] F. M. Stenton, *The First Century of English Feudalism* (Oxford, 1932).

[3] E. Lipson, *The Economic History of England*, I (The Middle Ages) (London, 10th ed., 1949), p. 24.

[4] For a legalistic account of this class of workers, see Paul Vinogradoff, *Villeinage in England* (Oxford, 1892).

[5] *Capital*, III, ed. by Friedrich Engels (Chicago, 1909), Part vi, ch. 47.

[6] On this subject see B. Porszniew in *Zeszyty Historyczne Nowych Dróg* (1951), No. 3, pp. 38—56; translated from *Izvestiia* Akademii Nauk SSSR, Ser. Ist. i Fil., VI (1949), No 6.

[7] The manor system was never of course completely prevalent or thoroughly organised in England. Social forms differed in various parts of the country; many towns and villages remained independent. See Sayles, *Foundations*, p. 244.

[8] Lipson, *op. cit.*, p. 87.

[9] G. E. Woodbine, "The Language of English Law," *Speculum*, XVIII (1943), 395—436.

[10] R. M. Wilson, *Early Middle English Literature* (London, 2nd ed., 1951), ch. 1.

[11] Cf. Woodbine as in n. 9 above.

[12] Cf. Walter de Bibbesworth's *Traité sur la langue française* (Paris, 1929), written to this end for use by the daughter of an English baron.

[13] The account given by A.C. Baugh, *Literary History of England* (New York, 1948), pp. 109 ff., tends to exaggerate the separateness of the French, as do many previous textbooks. Wilson's manual (see above, note 10) gives a sounder view of the situation. See also P.V.D. Shelly, *English and French in England* (Philadelphia, 1921).

[14] John Edwin Wells, *A Manual of the Writings in Middle English* (New Haven, 1916), p. 190. This important work will hereafter be cited as Wells, *Manual*.

[15] See Wilson, *op. cit.*, p. 113, and the same author's *Lost Literature of Medieval England* (New York, 1952).

[16] Ed. A.S. Napier in *Anglia*, X (1887), 131 ff.

[17] *St. Katherine*, ed. E. Einenkel, EETS, OS, No. 80 (1884); *St. Margaret*, ed. F.M. Mack, *ibid.*, No. 193 (1934); *St. Juliana*, ed. S.T.R.O. d'Ardenne (Liége, 1936).

[18] Wilson, *Early Middle English Literature*, p. 118.

[19] Dorothy Bethurum, "The Connection of the *Katherine* Group with Old English Prose," *Journal of English and Germanic Philology*, XXXIV (1935), 553 ff.

[20] Kentish and Southeast Midland collections in MS. Cotton Vespasian A. xxii and Trinity College (Cambridge) MS. B 14; Lambeth Homilies copied ca. 1180, ed. R. Morris, *Old English Homilies*, EETS, OS, Nos. 29 and 34 (1867—68).

[21] Eleanor K. Heningham, "Old English Precursors of the Worcester Fragments," *PMLA*, LV (1940), 291 ff.

[22] *Hali Meidenhad*, ed. F.J. Furnivall, EETS, OS, No. 18 (1866; re-ed. 1922); also by A.F. Colborn (Copenhagen, 1940).

[23] *Pat. Lat.*, XXXII, col. 1451 ff.

[24] Ed. (with important introduction) R.M. Wilson (Leeds, 1938). The citation is from this edition, with modified punctuation.

[25] *Opera*, III, in *Pat. Lat.*, No. 177; lib. iv, cap. 13.

[26] Roberta Cornelius, *The Figurative Castle* (Bryn Mawr, Penna., 1930).

[27] R.W. Chambers, *On the Continuity of English Prose* (London, 1932).

[28] There are other short pieces of this period, edited by R. Morris, *Old English Homilies and Homiletic Pieces*, EETS, OS, Nos. 29 and 34 (1867—68).

CHAPTER VI

EARLY ANGLO-LATIN LITERATURE:
THE ANGEVIN PERIOD

1. THE POLITICAL FRAMEWORK OF CULTURE IN THE 12TH AND EARLY 13TH CENTURIES

The governmental system growing out of feudal relations in production and land ownership was capable of a certain degree of expansion
and consolidation. At the same time, its inner weaknesses and contradictions
were constantly destroying its own political structures soon after they
were erected. Nowhere is this more clearly to be seen than in the history
of the miniature empire insecurely put together by Henry II (1154—89)
through inheritance, alliances and a series of marriages. Its territorial
extent made it seem impressive at the time, but it was an inorganic
agglomeration which was torn during his lifetime and fell apart upon
his death. Beneath the shifting political surface, however, there were
deeper forces at work which more lastingly affected social life and
produced conditions auspicious for a marked upsurge of cultural activity.

The constantly increasing prosperity of the town centres of trade
was the chief factor in bringing about the transformation. It stimulated
a colourful if not always peaceful community life and made possible an
accumulation of wealth unknown in the previous centuries. The isolated
and all but self-contained manors and the small castles of lesser feudal
lords throughout the countryside yielded precedence to the fortified towns,
in which churches and palaces of more imposing splendour now began
to be constructed. In return for financial support, feudal kings and magnates often granted special liberties and exemptions to the towns. Within
certain limits, security increased along with the advances in trade and
the organisation of production. Public buildings of various kinds could
now abandon the style of the tenebrous, thick-walled fortress and permit
the values of space and light to be realised in higher vaults and arches,
more generous window-space, bright colours in glass, painted decorations
and tapestries. The age of Gothic architecture was being prepared at
a time when rapid cultural advances were being made in other arts as well.

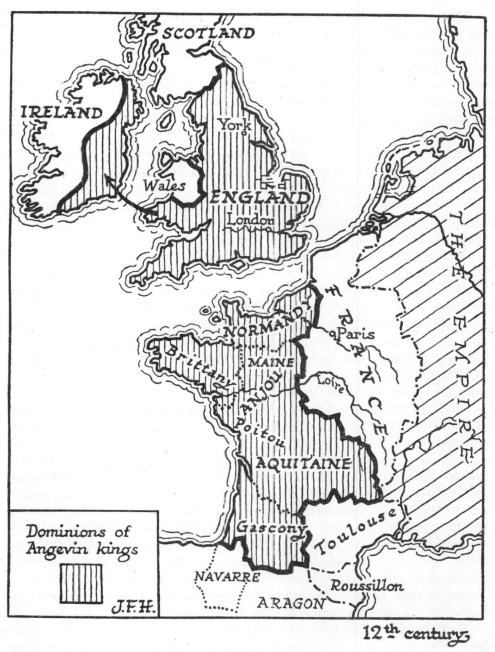

SCOTLAND

IRELAND

York

Wales

ENGLAND

London

NORMANDY

Brittany

MAINE

ANJOU

Poitou

AQUITAINE

Gascony

NAVARRE

ARAGON

FRANCE

Paris

Loire

THE EMPIRE

Toulouse

Roussillon

Dominions of
Angevin kings

J.F.H.

12th century

The Angevin Empire ca. 1175 A.D.

The advance in literary activity was noteworthy under Henry II and his successors. The royal family had in fact a direct relationship with writers and scholars, whom they attached to themselves directly as protégés by means of rewards in church and state. Their encouragement and the generally improved conditions at first augmented the writing done in Latin and French; more slowly but more essentially, that in English.

King Henry himself[1] was the son of the French Count Geoffrey of Anjou (who also held Maine and Touraine) and of Queen Mathilda, through whom he inherited the realm of England. Later he was also enfeoffed with Britanny. Through his marriage with Eleanor of Aquitaine (herself previously married to Louis VII of France, later divorced), he obtained lordship over Poitou, Aquitaine and Gascony. He thus controlled a wide and continuous block of French territory extending from Flanders on the North to the Spanish border on the South, and including the entire Western coast of France. He was therefore far more powerful than King Louis, his wife's ex-husband, to whom he technically owed feudal homage for most of the French holdings. In addition, he established at least a temporary foothold (at great cost of treasure and life) in parts of Ireland and Wales. His daughters married into the leading dynasties of Europe: Mathilda was wedded to the ruler of Saxony, Princess Eleanor to Alfonso VIII of Castile, and Joanna to the Norman King of Sicily (who also held Southern Italy).

But this loose concatenation of territories and alliances corresponded to no real unity of social and cultural interests. Its instability was sharply reflected in the bitter quarrels and warfare which repeatedly broke out among the members of the royal family. The two princes Henry and Richard the Lion-Hearted were implacable foes. Young Henry intrigued against his father, and Richard and Geoffrey conducted open war against him in the French territories, being aided and urged on by their mother Eleanor, the independent heiress of Aquitaine, by that time in close political alliance with her former husband against her present one. The family feuds of the Angevins (i.e., people of Anjou) were not an isolated phenomenon. They were connected with the struggles of independent barons against royal power on a European scale. Although Henry was victorious he paid the price of sons disaffected or dead as traitors, and a wife imprisoned for eight years for fomenting rebellion. No ties of marriage or kinship, no fear of excommunication for broken oaths, was enough to restrain the bloody greed for power through land ownership which was the actuating motive in these very typical struggles.

The leading Angevins—Henry himself and his Queen Eleanor, their sons King Richard (1189—99) and King John (1199—1216)—are important personalities not merely because they were turbulent individuals. The age produced many of these in all ranks of the nobility, whose bickerings remained however of no moment for history. The strivings and conflicts of the Angevins, however, threw into relief the entire social system of the time. More than that, history placed them in the centre of issues and events having unusual consequences for literary culture in England. The circumstances being propitious, and the situation being matured, the Angevins were able to add some impetus to certain developments already implicit in the cultural history of Europe as a whole.

Queen Eleanor, for instance, while still the young consort of King Louis of France, had accompanied him on a Crusade (ending in most horrible bloodshed, as it happens) which took her to Asia Minor by way of Byzantium. [2] She was apparently greatly impressed by the superior manners and culture, the wealth and comfort of the Greek capital. It has been surmised that her active propagation of chivalrous *mores* in France and England sprang from a desire to elevate uncouth Western manners to the standards of Eastern European courtesy and public decorum. The desire may well have been fortified by early experiences in Aquitaine and Poitou, where influences from the more refined Arabic civilisation of Spain were widely felt. (See ch. 7, sec. 2.) The wasteful and inhumanly cruel expedition of King Richard during the Third Crusade was itself but another sympton of those currents, running far deeper than warfare, which were bringing Eastern influences to Western Europe in this age by means of trade and competition for trade.

The dispute between King Henry and Thomas à Becket, Archbishop of Canterbury, threw into most dramatic relief the struggle then widely prevalent throughout Western Europe over the limits of church power in relation to .the state. Under Henry, the chief question at issue was the relation of secular courts, based on customary rights in English law, to those of the church, based on canon law. The King tried to obtain primacy for the former in the Constitutions of Clarendon (drafted 1164, revised 1166), which Becket at first recognised and later denounced. The conclusion of the quarrel was, as is well known, the murder of the Archbishop on the altar steps of the cathedral, by agents of the King's party whom Henry himself later disavowed. The event was dramatic. It received full treatment in the literature of the time, and has been frequently treated since then. It caused a revulsion in sentiment against the King and his efforts to win supreme power for the state within the judicial system of the country.

Nevertheless, the King's efforts accorded with the growing trend towards state supremacy in English institutions. In his role as ruler of England, Henry had dedicated much of his amazing activity to the improvement of administration in various branches of government — law, taxation, finance, and military service — and he himself studied these problems carefully. He attained successes that would have been impossible a century earlier. In realising them he drew about himself some outstanding men of learning. Thomas à Becket had been only one of them. Another was the legal authority Glanville, author of a pioneer work in jurisprudence, the *Tractatus de Legibus Angliae* (*Treatise on the Laws of England*), and still another was Richard son of Nigel, his treasurer, author of a pioneer work on state finance called *Dialogus de Scaccario* (*Dialogue on the Exchequer*). There was besides a whole galaxy of historians, poets, satirists, geographers, writers of compendia and commentaries, who (as we shall see) were indebted to his patronage.[3] Moreover, Queen Eleanor directly encouraged a considerable amount of writing in French, such as romanticised histories and chronicles in verse. In the latter 12th century the court of the Angevins was outstanding in Europe with respect to its prosperity, its cultural activity and its far-flung connections with other courts.

2. IDEOLOGICAL ASPECTS OF EARLY LATIN LITERATURE IN ENGLAND

Internal trade, maritime commerce, the Crusades, the consequent international journeyings of students, and similar factors were producing a new fluidity in cultural relations by the middle of the 12th century. Typical of the new restlessness was the carrer of Adelard (Aethelard) of Bath, already mentioned, who studied in Spain, North Africa, Greece and Sicily, and brought home precious gleanings of Graeco-Arabic learning. He put the elements of Euclid's geometry into Latin, wrote on topics of science and pseudo-science, and composed a dialogue *De Eodem et Diverso* (*Concerning Identity and Difference*) on the relation of the individual to the species in the light of then-known science and philosophy. Adelard was a forerunner of the philosophical allegorists who flourished towards the end of the 12th century.

At the same time certain developments occurred in intellectual life generally which were extremely important for later literature. They were related to the transformations in the practical world, and though themselves largely theoretical, they in turn affected the course taken by practical techniques and applied science.

Philosophical thought from the time of Boethius into the earlier Middle Ages had been extremely close to theology, in fact hardly separable from it, and, as we have remarked, the entire current had been overwhelmingly Platonist and Neo-Platonist. Writers like Augustine saw all creation as a hierarchy of orders of being. The lowest in rank, they thought, are the separate concrete objects with which we deal in our everyday life: individual examples of various classes of stones, plants, tools, animals and people. Somewhat higher are the species of these objects (for instance, roses, plows, domestic cats); higher still the classes, then the types and categories, and so on, until we arrive at abstract concepts such as Plants-in-General, Tools-in-General, Man. These concepts or "universals" were thought of as existing somewhere as "real" entities in an idealist universe. The ideas in the abstract, such as the essence of "flower-ness" contained in the concept of all flowers, was supposed to have existed before any flower was created on earth. The "idea" of the flower-in-general was thought to be nobler than any material flower on earth. Similarly, there were supposed to be ranks of abstract qualities, among which unity could be proved superior to duality, harmony to discord, and—more obviously to ordinary folk—love to hatred, gene- rosity to avarice, and so on. By ascending through these ranks of being and abstraction, the Platonists arrived at the concept of an absolute and unchanging being, transcending all relations yet including within itself the supreme synthesis of "the good, the true and the beautiful." This absolute being was thought to precede matter and to be separable from it. This, roughly speaking, was the form taken by idealism in ancient times. Obviously, its whole approach can be seen to be inimical to the development of experimental science.

The early Christian theologians had little difficulty in identifying this abstract and static ideal of perfection, this unchanging, undialectical being, with their God; they also used Platonic theory and methods to prove that God, identified with the Logos of the New Testament (John 1: 1) must be a trinity rather than a unity.[4] They concentrated attention on universal concepts and what they called the essence (*essentia*) of each particular individual—the man-ness of a man, the cat-ness of a cat—rather than on the individual itself. Neo-Platonic writings translated by John Scotus Eriugena in the time of Charlemagne had contributed to the elaboration of this hierarchic philosophy. Out of speculations on the relation of individuals to universal concepts developed the controversy (12th century and after) between realists, who affirmed the "real" existence of the universal ideas, and the nominalists, who considered the univer- sality to be implicit in the name (*nomen*).

As medieval society developed its social structure of hierarchies in church and state, theological speculation reflected them in its theories of the universe. The similarity between hierarchic society and hierarchic philosophy was striking throughout the Middle Ages. Of course the ideology had its roots in past authors and their works, but never before had the Platonic levels of being found such detailed and subtle exposition as precisely in this historical period when the reality of social experience evoked and sanctioned it. The view of nature was also in harmony with the rest. Repeatedly the medieval poets and philosophers express the thought that nature as a whole is *orderly*, with the members of the mineral, vegetable and lower animal kingdoms obediently functioning within the spheres assigned to them. They existed and functioned within *fixed* categories. Man alone rebels: because of original sin, he was told, and by means of his faculty of free choice. But man's supreme duty is to conform: not to try to leave the social rank into which he happens to be born, but to stay within it and cultivate the virtues of conformity fitted to the social level (*status* or estate) thus assigned to him. Obviously, this doctrine was a fine-spun justification for the *status quo*. It left no place for any revolutionary uprisings by the exploited orders of society against their exploiters.

The theory of literature[5] evolved by the theological philosophers was that it might help indirectly to reflect absolute truth to the human intellect, but at best it was only an imitation of an imitation of that truth. The reader of literature must search out the real and abiding truths more or less concealed behind the surface of the story or situation. A pagan poet like Virgil or even Ovid, if properly interpreted, could offer fragments of universal truth (Platonically conceived), whether or not he intended to do so. His heroes and heroines, their adventures and loves, could be regarded as symbols of ultimate "realities" as just defined, and of moral precepts. Thus the amours of nymphs and pagan gods could pass muster as symbols of didactic import (the soul's quest for perfection, and so on). As for the Bible itself, it more than any other book could be searched for hidden truths and inner concordances, since its presumed divine origin would be expected to charge it with an exceptional richness of meaning. The elliptic style of the Bible, its use of comparisons and parables, invited such interpretation. In this way, any event recorded in the Old Testament could be expected to have numerous symbolic meanings. Four meanings in particular, defined by St. Augustine in his *De Doctrina Christiana*, were sought for and commented upon in the Middle Ages. An event in the Old Testament could have:

(1) a literal meaning (*sensus literalis*) insofar as it was assumed to have occurred in historical reality (e.g., Jonah being swallowed by a whale as a matter of actual fact);

(2) an allegorical meaning, showing that the original event anticipated one to occur later in the New Testament (e.g., Jonah's rescue after lurking in the whale's belly anticipates the Resurrection on Easter morning);

(3) a tropological meaning, exemplifying moral precept (e.g., Jonah's hesitations and later actions exemplify the conflict of doubt and faith);

(4) an anagogical meaning, pointing to the future life (e.g., Jonah's rescue pre-figures the fate of good men at the final resurrection when time and the world are expected to end).

Not only literature, but the sculpture on the cathedrals, the figures in the stained-glass windows, the early paintings and manuscript decorations, are often conceived and executed in the spirit of these correlations.[6] If a medieval religious artist treats of a major theme like the Crucifixion or Resurection, he often surrounds it with scenes from the Old Testament which have a certain similarity to it and furnish a kind of symbolic commentary upon it. In learned literature the correlation was actually made by means of commentaries on the Scriptures, comprising a bulky part of the ecclesiastical output between Bede and the scholastics.

It is quite apparent that such a system as this Christianised Platonism, with its admiration for the generic-abstract and its low estimate of the particular, did not encourage realism (in the modern sense) as a method of expression in art. Nevertheless, realistic portrayal did find a place—a place of growing importance—in medieval art as the centuries passed. Detailed, realistic portrayal appeared in sculpture, painting and literature, primarily as a method of exemplifying abstract principles directly or by contrast. A denunciation of gluttony or greed, for instance, might well include a vivid description of an individual drunkard or miser and his actions, although presented in subordination to the general concept of a vice. Besides, grotesque figures and scenes of distorted realism were sometimes introduced in order to throw into relief and heighten the effect of more abstract portrayal, by way of contrast. They were, however, subordinate in their function. Whatever the original purpose, these elements of realistic commentary in all the medieval arts convey valuable pictures of contemporary life. They often tell us far more about conditions and emotions than the most ambitious of the abstract interpretations on literary and Biblical texts. Yet the latter reveal much too about the prevailing attitudes and values.

For us who live in the world revealed by modern science, the system of medieval Platonism is curious and strange. Its refined speculations about fixed and absolute ranks of being are far removed from our direct experience of today's natural sciences, in which the types and genera are found not to be fixed, but capable of dialectic transformations. Nevertheless, to understand the standards and postulates of medieval writing, we have to keep clearly before us its inherent ideology, and to remember at the same time how that ideology itself sprang from the social-economic foundations of living. There was little basic change in the methods and interests of speculative thought until transformations in the mode of production created conditions for the development of experimental methods in investigation.

The preference for abstractions as higher orders than concrete items of experience had one result of enormous consequence in literature. It led to the great vogue of allegory in the modern sense of the word: that is, narrative in which the actors are or somehow represent ideas and qualities rather than real people. The first noteworthy poem of this type was written in late classical times, by one who almost lived long enough to see the sacking of Rome by the Goths (A.D. 410). It was the *Psychomachia* (*Battle in the Soul*) by Prudentius, a Christian Latin poet. He portrays the chief virtues as vigilant Amazons doing combat with the corresponding vices: Chastity against Lechery, Patience against Anger, Charity against Avarice. [7] When the virtues have won final victory, they build an allegorical temple for the purified soul, in which Wisdom is enthroned as ruler. It was to this literary tradition that *Sawles Warde* belonged, with its sustained metaphor of the soul inhabiting a fortress under attack. (See ch. 5, sec. 5.) From the 13th century onwards that same tradition was to have a vast literary efflorescence.

3. ANGLO-LATIN SCHOLARS OF THE 12TH CENTURY

Latin ecclesiastical writers in England contributed to the refinement of the philosophy just outlined, after conditions became settled there. The Italian-born Lanfranc had been active in creating centres of learning at Le Bec and Caen in Normandy before the Conquest in 1066; later, as Archbishop of Canterbury, he carried out William's program of unifying and feudalising the church. Though his activity was largely administrational, he continued to be interested in developing monastic education, and he helped to create conditions favourable to it.

A countryman of Lanfranc's, St. Anselm (1033—1109), had studied under him in Normandy and became his successor at the see of Canterbury. He continued the work of stricter organisation of the church, at the same time pressing its claims for independence of feudal overlordship. Representing the papal position as against the royal, he engaged in a conflict with William Rufus which anticipated the famous struggle between Henry II and Thomas à Becket a century later. As a thinker, Anselm undertook to demonstrate how far the methods of classical argument — the "dialectic" technique of Plato's dialogues — could be used to prove the tenets of theology.

In his most original works Anselm employs the doctrine of absolute ideas in order to prove his arguments without appeal to Biblical authority. *De Veritate (Concerning Truth)*,[8] for instance, is a dialogue between Anselm and a pupil in which the discussion advances from the subject of true statements (those which affirm and those which deny) to the nature of the truth behind them, and concludes (ch. 13) "that there is one Truth in all things that are true."[9] The form of the philosophical dialogue, already familiar, continued to be widely employed throughout the entire Middle Ages, and in due time became a popular vehicle for didactic texts in the vernacular.

A pupil of Lanfranc and Anselm, Abbot Gilbert Crispin of Westminster (died 1117), similarly undertook to apply the methods of medieval dialectic with little appeal to authority in an argument with a Jewish friend, thus trying to convince him of the truth of the Christian belief.[10] The dialogue, which appears to be based on an actual conversation, is remarkable for its tolerant tone, and the vigour with which the author permits his fellow disputant to protest against violence done to the Old Testament by the Christian commentaries on it as an allegorical anticipation of the New, according to the method of four-fold interpretation.[11] It will be recalled that the wandering scientist Adelard of Bath had also tried his hand at a philosophical dialogue early in the 12th century.

It was in the latter part of the century, however, under the reign of Henry II, that medieval Latin culture in England reached one of its highest peaks. Outstanding among the scholars associated with the royal court and the see of Canterbury was John of Salisbury (died 1180), versatile writer and man of affairs who worked for Thomas à Becket. Through John's writings the Platonic tradition received fresh impetus in England, since the author had studied at Chartres in France, then the greatest centre of such derived erudition. Here a number of teachers had embarked on extensive instruction and experimental writing to give a Platonic interpretation of creation as outlined in Genesis. The theme of creation which the Old English poets, both Latin and vernacular, had handled with simpler allegory and in concrete epic style, was now reworked in a different manner to harmonise with the abstractions of Plato. In the first part of the century Thierry of Chartres composed *De Sex Dierum Operibus (The Works of the Six Days)*, treating that theme in terms which can be reconciled with Plato's dialogue *Timaeus* (known then in the Latin translation of Chalcidius). Bernard Silvester of Chartres wrote an imaginative treatment of the same subject in both prose and verse, called *De Mundi Universitate* (between 1145 and 1153). It presents three cardinal principles of the Platonic universe, as allegorised into characters in a story. They are Noys (νοῦς) or Intellect, Physis (φύσις, "that which is or is born") or Nature, and Hyle (ὕλη, literally, "mud") or Primal Matter—that is, matter not yet subject to forms and qualities. The theme is the putting into order (*cosmos*) of the universe. Nature complains that primal matter is in a state of confusion, and asks to have it made orderly as *materies*. As a result, Noys disentangles the four elements, establishes the nine angelic hierarchies (following the writings of the Pseudo-Dionysius), and constructs the firmament with its planets and constellations. Her organisation of the universe is carried out very much as a feudal monarch like William I would perform his task in the world of affairs. As a crowning act, Noys creates man, having requested Urania, Queen of Heaven, to find out the most fitting dwelling-place for him. This is of course the Earthly Paradise, said to be inhabited already by three allegorical ladies: Physis, with her daughters Theory and Practice,[12] damsels unknown to the Biblical Adam.

Thus it was that Bernard applied allegorical personification to his exposition. He was something of a pantheist, but his story makes clear his assumption that a supreme intelligence is primary in both time and importance, as originator of matter in the form known to us. His literary method found many imitators in England as well as France.

John of Salisbury had absorbed the Platonic teachings of his masters at Chartres, and he became a convinced realist (that is, one who believes in the "real" existence of Platonic ideas) under their influence. But his works deal with less abstract subjects than theirs. Some of his writings and correspondence belong to the materials of political history. His *Metalogicon* was something in the nature of a text book, outlining and defending logical methodology as originally taught by the Greeks, notably by Aristotle in his *Organon*. In the *Policraticus* (literally, *The City-Ruler*; better, *The Statesman's Book*),[13] he gives an encyclopedic but rather unoriginal medley of political theory, philosophy, some satire and miscellaneous learning. It constains a vast amount of quotation from classical sources, some of them indirectly known, some fragmentarily preserved in anthologies, some, it must appear, very imperfectly understood. Not everything he quotes about the free citizens of the old city-states, and their struggles against the rise of tyrants, could by any means be applied to the conditions of feudalism. John also wrote a study of church history from 1148 to 1152, called *Historia Pontificalis*, and a rather disjointed poem on a variety of philosophical problems called *Entheticus de Dogmate Philosophorum* (*Insertion on the Philosophers' Dogmas*).

Alexander of Neckam, also called Nequam (1157—1217) composed a handbook describing the universe and the known world, *De Naturis Rerum* (*On the Natures of Things*). Embodying the natural sciences then known, it presents the usual orderly picture of the world with moralising comments and some embroidery of fiction. Alexander covered the same subjects in a verse paraphrase entitled *De Laudibus Divinae Sapientiae* (*The Praise of Divine Wisdom*).

Gerald the Welshman or Giraldus Cambrensis (died about 1220) was one of the most gifted of the Latin prose writers under the Angevins. Archdeacon of St. David's in Wales and court chaplain to Henry II, he accompanied Prince John on the unfortunate expedition to subdue Ireland and he took part in a tour of Wales to preach sermons propagandising a Crusade. Though he served the Norman English court, he was also inclined to the cause of Welsh independence. His experiences resulted in several books: the *Topographia Hiberniae*, a valuable early description of Ireland (1187), a history of the attempt to conquer it (*Expugnatio Hibernica*), and the *Descriptio* and *Itinerarium Cambriae* (1188).[14] In engaging disorder Gerald crams his pages with geography and history both accurate and inaccurate, with folklore, gossip, invective and description. His revealing autobiography, *De Rebus a se Gestis* (*Things I Have Done*), tells about his political intrigues in church and state. The Angevin kings had reason to fear that he would use a bishopric, if he received it, to support political separation for Wales. Many passages in his autobiography are satirical, as for instance his disapproving account of the meal served him by the prosperous monks of Canterbury which (he says) shocked him by its sumptuousness. There is further satire against monks in his *Speculum Ecclesiae* (*Mirror of the Church*). Among his other works is a tract on political theory, *De Principis Instructione* (*The Education of a Prince*), which like John of Salisbury's *Policraticus* draws often and uncritically from classical sources, in a way that shows admiration but not always complete understanding.

Gervase of Tilbury and Walter Map (both living about 1200) also wrote miscellaneous works embodying fact and fancy, history, geography, politics and folklore. Gervase traveled to the court of the German Emperor Otto IV and also visited Southern Italy and Sicily. His *Otia Imperialia* (*Emperor's Leisure*) is a miscellany combining knowledge and ignorance, wisdom and naive credulity, in an abundant variety of diverting materials. Walter Map or Mapes, like Gerald a native of Wales, put down an anthology of sketches and plots and bits of odd information he had picked up from reading and listening to people. His sources were both literary and folkloristic. Since some of the anecdotes and tales justify satire upon courtiers and court life, he calls the book *De Nugis Curialium* (*Courtiers' Trifles*).[15] Some of his materials throw valuable light on the curious primitive ways of thought surviving among people of the countryside. In his invective Map is often violent and unfair (as for instance on the subject of women), but he is never dull.

Among the more scholarly writers of the 12th century, particular mention must be made of the Latin chroniclers. While their work belongs mostly to historiography rather than literature, it contributes directly, of course, to our knowledge of literary backgrounds, and sometimes it transmits literary materials otherwise lost.[16] Thus William of Malmesbury (died 1143) not only helps to bridge the gap in history-writing between Bede and the 12th century; he also paraphrases or translates lost Anglo-Saxon poems dealing with outstanding persons and events. Since he was able to study and write in a rich and well preserved library dating back to the time of Aldhelm, what he tells in his three historical works has great retrospective value.[17] Henry of Huntingdon also used vernacular sources to supplement learned ones in his *Historia Anglorum* (to 1154); he translated the Anglo-Saxon poem on Brunanburh into Latin and inserted it *sub anno* 937. William of Newburgh, one of the most distinguished of the entire group, gave in his *Historia Rerum Anglicarum* a detailed report of events in the latter 12th century, on the whole carefully sifted but not unadorned with anecdote and legend. His words at times reflect stern indignation against feudal lords guilty of lawless violence (for instance, on the occasion of the anti-Jewish riots in York, 1190, fomented by Crusading noblemen in order to get rid of their debts). The protected detachment of monastic chroniclers gave them a certain advantage in criticising abuses by secular authorities.[18]

To these chroniclers, the writing of history was in large part a portrayal of individual political leaders and their doings. They looked for the motive power of history in personalities and in the occasional intervention of supernatural forces. It is no wonder therefore if they devote much space to anecdotes about the private lives of kings, and to reports of visions and miracles. What is more surprising is that despite their restricted viewpoint they give so much precise documentation for the course of political events, so much valuable information for a study of social backgrounds. Without the 12th century Latin chroniclers we should have a much impoverished image of the life being lived then on all levels of society.

A special place must be given to the pseudo-history written by Geoffrey of Monmouth (ca. 1135) under the title of the *Historia Regum Britanniae* (*History of the Kings of Britain*).[19] The Latin text, says the author, is a translation of a "very ancient book in the British (Breton?) tongue" lent to him by Walter, Archdeacon of Oxford. Geoffrey tells us that this borrowed manuscript had satisfied his curiosity concerning the many kings who must have flourished in Britain during the ages before known history began. And so the *Historia* recounts a tale about the fabulous colonisation of England by Trojans (no less) under the leadership of

Brutus, the great-grandson of Aeneas (whence the name Britain). Its early kings are supposed to have included such famous personages as Lear, Cymbeline and Arthur, celebrated in later romance and drama. In part of his work Geoffrey seems to be freely imitating classical models. In other parts he is indebted to known sources such as the Bible, Bede, Gildas, saints' lives and the short composite *Historia Britonum* put together under the name of Nennius from materials of the ninth to the 11th century.[20] The text by Nennius was the first to mention King Arthur as a Celtic leader of the early sixth century and to give a brief account of twelve great battles said to have been fought by him against the Anglo-Saxon invaders. In parts, finally, Geoffrey preserves and transmits fictional accounts taken from Celtic sources, whether exclusively oral (as some argue) or actually written down in an "ancient book" (as others believe).

Scholars have differed vehemently as to Geoffrey's originality, his credibility, and his precise relationship to Welsh and Irish vernacular literatures on the one hand, and to the later cycles of French and English romances on the other. True it is that Geoffrey for the first time presents Arthur as a splendid king, victor over the Saxons, ruler over all of England, successfully challenging the overlordship of the Roman Emperor himself. Many names familiar in later romance do appear beside his: Gawain (as Walganus), Guinevere (as Guenhumara) and Mordred; but there is as yet no Lancelot, no Tristan or Iseult, and no Grail hero. The emphasis is on military deeds, not on the love of the ladies. The fiction is not romantic. Geoffrey claimed to write as an historian and some chroniclers took him seriously, while others—like William of Newburgh and Henry of Huntingdon—denouced him roundly as a liar.

It is probable that French romancers independently used some of the oral sources available to Geoffrey, adapting them to their purposes of entertainment pure and simple, without any pretentions to historicity. Or Geoffrey may actually have had a real book before him and have believed in its historical authenticity. In any event, his pseudo-chronicle quickly became famous and was frequently cited by other writers in all seriousness as an historical document.[21]

4. ANGLO-LATIN POETRY: EPIC, ALLEGORY, SATIRE

Besides writings on history, philosophy and other learned subjects, a number of fairly ambitious poems were also produced in Latin during the 12th century.[22] Some of these likewise dealt with philosophical-theological problems, but they did so under the guise of allegorical tales with literary pretensions. There were also satires and imitations of classical epic. These productions were known only to a limited reading public, of course, and they can not be said to belong to a very high level of artistic creation. Yet they are important in their own right and because their themes affected English satirists later. The Latin satire of this period opened up the field for imaginative works like *Piers Plowman* in the 14th century. Allegorical conventions in satire were taken over by French and English writers. The pseudo-classical epics were also imitated by vernacular writers.

Among the latter, the influence of Virgil was paramount. The most significant imitation of the *Aeneid* was *De Bello Troiano*, about the Trojan war, by Joseph of Exeter (died 1194). The author followed the outline of events transmitted to the Middle Ages in a bare Latin summary of the sixth century, approximately, which goes by the name of Dares Phrygius, for Homer's poems were unknown in the West. Chaucer shows knowledge of both Dares and Joseph in his brilliant handling of the Trojan setting in his *Troilus and Criseyde* (see ch. 11, sec. 4).

A curious verse epic by Geoffrey of Monmouth, the *Vita Merlini*, [23] tells about the life of King Arthur's magician-adviser in a confused tissue of episodes from Welsh tribal history (apparently) and stories imported from the East, where they had been previously told about sages in Sanscrit and Talmudic Hebrew legend. There has been much speculation on how Geoffrey, living in Southwest England in the mid-12th century, could have obtained these Oriental plots for use in imitation of classical epic. The monastic schools fostered imitations of Virgil, of course. An Anglo-Latin text of the early 13th century by Geoffrey of Vinsauf, the *Nova Poetria* (1210), [24] gives interesting precepts about how to go about composing them, and how to adorn them with fitting rhetorical passages.

The Platonic-allegorical type of visionary poem, typical of the school of Chartres as we have seen, was cultivated in England also in the latter part of the same century. An ambitious and rather artificial satire, lively in spots and dull in others, was produced by one John de Hauteville or Hanville, a Norman apparently residing in England, on the general subject of the follies and miseries of mankind. The admonitory theme of his *Architrenius* (for *Archithrenius*, meaning *The Arch-Weeper* or *Lamenter*) [25] was dear to medieval satirists. Contemplation of human woe on a large scale was supposed to lead to a renunciation of the world and resignation from efforts to change it. Those already withdrawn from the world were confirmed in their choice; those living in the midst of it were expected to conclude that nothing would avail to establish a better system: each individual should merely try to conform better to the conditions around him, in a spirit of passive humility.

Malmesbury Abbey, Wiltshire

Hanville's allegory is developed in the form of a quest. It is a pilgrimage by Architrenius to find Nature (again: the hierarchic-Platonic Nature of Bernard Silvester) and ask her for help in his struggle against temptation and vice. On the way he visits allegorical abodes of such personified qualities as Lust (Venus), Gluttony and Ambition, who lives on a terribly steep hill, almost impossible to climb. The symbolic dwellings visited give to the author a chance to denounce many worldly vices, particularly in connection with ambition. He derides the scramble for success at court, the extravagance of courtiers' living, the power of money (pecunia), the pride of worldly monks. En route to Nature, the Lamenter passes through the real city of Paris and describes with incisive realism the cold, hunger and exhausting routine endured by the students there. This digrression is the most memorable passage in the poem. In the end, the narrator finds Nature in the same Earthly Paradise—again, pantheistic rather than Biblical—where the Chartres Platonists loved to place her. She appears as a majestic woman, laurel-crowned, young and at the same time ancient, seated on a throne from which she directs her supremely orderly universe and all her creatures which, save man alone, are obedient to her. The Lamenter begs her for help because he too wishes to obey her but is hampered by temptations and sin. In a long speech of rejoinder she tells about her never-ending solicitude for life in all its forms, and ends by wedding him to Moderation—a very classical virtue—who will help him to live a harmonious life. Conspicuously absent is any emphasis on the role of religion (which one would expect to find playing a decisive part) in promoting the success of the pilgrim's quest.

This 12th-century Latin poem is of a group following the lead of Bernard Silvester, in that they glorify the concept of a Platonic nature by means of an allegorical pilgrimage. John de Hanville's *Architrenius* was also influenced by the poems of a French Latinist, Alanus de Insulis (Alain of Lille), who used the same technique.[26] The *De Planctu Naturae* (*Nature's Lament*) by Alanus had already provided a detailed picture of Nature much as Hanville saw her, and had given her a speech in which she sorrowfully accused man, alone among her creatures, of perverting her laws. The poem *Anticlaudianus* by the same author had described the quest of Nature's messenger Prudence, riding on a symbolic chariot through an allegorical heaven, in order to obtain help in the task of creating, under God's will and guidance, a perfect man. There is more of theology in Alanus than in John de Hanville, but the philosophy is still that of Bernard Silvester. Ratio (reason) is the personified principle which suggests the creation of a perfect man to Nature, but the trip to heaven includes a vision, explained by Theology, with literary perspectives leading onward to Dante, Langland, and the author of *The Pearl.*

All of these Platonic allegories are important, then, for reasons extending far beyond their own literary merits. The allegorical vision became an important instrument in the hands of great vernacular poets of the 13th and 14th centuries. It is hard, in fact, to understand the achievement of Dante in Italian, Jean de Meun in French, Langland or Chaucer in English without some knowledge of these visionary quests composed in Latin in the 12th century. Real life and literary tradition had already collaborated at that time to produce the framework to be adapted for the use of later genius. On the one hand, real life suggested the pilgrimages and adventurous wanderings familiar in medieval experience and obviously applicable as an image for spiritual quest. Classical literature offered models of such wanderings: the long homeward journey of Odysseus, the search of Aeneas for a new homeland; and theological commentators had already transformed these into metaphors of human experience, while medieval philosophers helped to make them into full-fledged allegories. The satiric talent of a John de Hanville, breaking through the pale allegorical conventions, showed (with his interlude of the cold, dirty, exhausted student in Paris) how abstract theses could be driven home effectively by scenes of sharp realism taken from everyday life. In a word, the technique of allegorical satire was already rather well developed among the circle of Latin poet-scholars some time before men of genius arose to use it in the national languages of Europe.

Satire appears in other forms in 12th century Latin verse, some of it telling and incisive, though of course limited in its circulation among a favoured few men of learning. Alexander Neckam, author of the *De Naturis Rerum* (see above, sec. 3) wrote a *De Vita Monachorum* denouncing monks who disgrace their orders by ambition, luxury, gluttony and other vices.[27] The themes are stereotyped but they are treated with animation. Alexander is especially eloquent upon the topics of court life, with its ostentation and intrigues, and all women as a group, whom he accuses of frivolous luxury leading to corruption. He says nothing of the masses of women who lived and died far away from any glimpse of luxury.

Neither of Alexander's topics was new. Much of what he says, even in details, had been anticipated in Roman satire and patristic denunciations, but Alexander repeats the charges with gusto. Typical is his medieval clerical hostility towards woman—that "sweet evil" (*dulce malum*), scapegoat of Adam—who was made to shoulder more than her share of blame for every human weakness. Still, we can read with interest

Alexander's details about lip-sticks, shaped eyebrows, perforated ears, absurd diets and costumes, wondering the while how many details were simply copied from other satirists (as was the frequent practice), and how many came from direct observation.

A contemporary of Alexander's, Nigel Wireker, treated the same themes of court and clergy in his *Tractatus contra Curiales et Officiales Clericos* (*Tract against Courtiers and Churchmen Holding Office*). In describing the unseemly struggle for church benefices he tells about incidents known to himself during the reign of Henry II. More famous and more interesting is Nigel's long poem *Speculum Stultorum* (*Mirror of Fools*), also called *Burnel the Ass*.[28] For this satire he chose, not allegory, but a prolonged animal story of the kind which the Middle Ages well knew from the Roman followers of Aesop. The plot is simple. A foolish ass, representing a stupid but ambitious monk, decides that he will no longer tolerate the humble carrying of burdens which is his proper and "natural" function. As a sign of rebellion he sets out to obtain a long tail, matching his ears, which will presumably change him from one species to another and thus place him outside the class of beasts of burden. His purpose of course runs counter to Nature's plan and is not regarded as righteous and praiseworthy by the author, since it represents a spirit of rebellion condemned by him.

Burnel the Ass journeys through France to Salerno in Italy, then a famous medical centre, and back to his home again, observing and having adventures on the way. These give Nigel his opportunity for satire. A sly merchant of London cheats Burnel of his money; a visit to Paris affords a glimpse at the riotous students drinking when they should be studying—with the English (handsome, talented but frivolous, says the author) outdoing the rest, to shouts of "Wes hail" and "Drinc hail!" The hero visits the houses of several monastic orders and his treatment there causes him to denounce them and the papal curia alike for their sins of avarice. In fact, one of the main themes of Nigel is the ubiquitous practice of bribery, the wrongful giving of rewards (*munera*) in church and court. "Love conquers everything, but itself is conquered by bribes" (*Omnia vincit amor, sed amorem munera vincunt*), he cries.

In the same way, John de Hanville had denounced the power of Queen Cash (Regina Pecunia) as a main source of evil. It may be that the increased use of money under Henry II (after important currency reforms), and the beginnings of money rent to replace goods and labour, called the attention of satirists to this theme with new emphasis. Yet it is hard to see how, so long as they accepted the feudal system, they could object to *munera* in some form or other (land or cash). All of society

was based on the enfeoffment of both lay and clerical parties with property as a reward of some sort. All that the satirists could say was that the
rewards were not made in accordance with abstract principles of justice:
rewarding humility instead of arrogance, let us say, or faithful devotion
instead of selfish ambition. The underlying problem of exploitation was
not perceived by them.

The question of money, bribes and rewards continued to vex serious
thinkers in the later Middle Ages. It is not surprising that some tended
to make the *pecunia* itself responsible for evil, instead of men's use of
it. The allegorical way of thinking, with Pecunia represented as a living,
quasi-human force, gave support to the fallacy. This question was one
seriously and lengthily treated in Langland's *Piers Plowman* (14th century)
under the figure of Lady Meed (i.e., Reward). At many points the later
poem, an outstanding achievement in the history of social satire, shows
indebtedness to the school of pioneer Latin writers of England in the 12th
century.

[1] Detailed but (from a social point of view) not very enlightening information is given by Kate Norgate, *England under the Angevin Kings*, 2 vols. (London, 1887). See also the short study by (Mrs.) J.R. Green, *Henry the Second* (London, 1888).

[2] Amy Kelly, *Eleanor of Aquitaine and the Four Kings* (Harvard University Press, 1950); Curtis H. Walker, *Eleanor of Aquitaine* (University of North Carolina Press, 1950). Still useful is Melrich V. Rosenberg's *Eleanor of Aquitaine* (New York, 1937).

[3] C.H. Haskins, "Henry II as a Patron of Literature," *Tout Essays in Medieval History* (Manchester, 1925). pp. 71—77; William Stubbs, "Learning and Literature at the Court of Henry II," *Seventeen Lectures* (Oxford, 1900), Nos. 6 and 7.

[4] E.g., St. Augustine in his *De Trinitate.*

[5] On this topic see especially Hans H. Glunz, *Die Literarästhetik des europäischen Mittelalters* (Bochum-Langendreer, 1937).

[6] For art, see the abundantly illustrated series of volumes by Emile Mâle, *L'Art religieux en France*, covering the centuries from the 11th to the 15th. The ecclesiastical art and architecture of France are closely associated with theology and philosophy of the times. The same correlation held true in England.

[7] M. Lavarenne, in his edition of *Psychomachia* (Paris, 1933), has traced its influence into the Middle Ages. The vices and virtues of Prudentius do not correspond to the precise list of seven for each which became conventional in later ages. See Morton W. Bloomfield, *The Seven Deadly Sins* (Michigan University Press, 1952), for an historical sketch from ancient writings to the *Faery Queen* of Spenser.

[8] *Pat. Lat.*, CLVIII, cols. 467—86.

[9] *Ibid.*, cols. 141—224.

[10] *Pat. Lat.*, CLIX, cols. 1005 ff.

[11] "Violentiam scripturae infers, et ad fidei vestrae assertionem intorques," *ibid.*, col. 1024.

[12] Bernardus Silvestris, *De Mundi Universitate*, ed. Barch, Bibliotheca Philosophorum Mediae Aetatis, I (Innsbruck, 1876). See Theodore Silverstein, "The Fabulous Cosmography of Bernardus Silvestris," *Modern Philology*, XLVI (1948), 92—116.

[13] Ed. Clemens C.I. Webb, 2 vols. (Oxford, 1909).

[14] Giraldus Cambrensis, *Opera*, ed. J.S. Brewer and others, Rolls Series No. 21, 8 vols. (London, 1861—91).

[15] Ed. M.R. James in *Anecdota Oxoniensa* (London, 1914); translation by F. Tupper and M.B. Ogle (London, 1924).

[16] See Charles Gross, *The Sources and Literature of English History* (London, 1915).

[17] They are: *De Gestis Regum Angliae, Historia Novella* and *De Gestis Pontificum*. These and other chronicles are edited in the Rolls Series.

[18] Hans Lamprecht, *Untersuchungen über einige englische Chronisten des 12. und beginnenden 13. Jahrhunderts* (Breslau Diss., 1937).

[19] Edited by Jacob Hammer for the Medieval Academy of America (Cambridge, 1951).

[20] Ferdinand Lot, *Nennius et l'Historia Britonum* (Paris, 1934).

[21] A short clear account of early Arthurian texts in Latin is given by E.K. Chambers, *Arthur of Britain* (London, 1927). It is still useful, but should be checked with later studies. The main Latin texts are edited with discussion by E. Faral, *La Légende arthurienne*, 3 vols. (Paris, 1929). The recent edition of Geoffrey's *Historia* by Hammer supersedes the one given by Faral. (See note 19.) Both Faral and J.S.P. Tatlock, *The Legendary History of Britain* (University of California Press, 1950) are sceptical about Geoffrey's use of Celtic materials. On the other hand, R.S. Loomis is convinced that he drew on them extensively. See his *Celtic Myth and Arthurian Romance* (New York, 1927), containing arguments later much modified by the author in a number of special articles and in his *Arthurian Tradition and Chrétien de Troyes* (New York, 1949); also Helaine Newstead, *Bran the Blessed in Arthurian Romance* (New York, 1939).

[22] For general discussion see F.J.E. Raby, *A History of Secular Latin Poetry in the Middle Ages*, II (Oxford, 1934).

[23] Ed. by Faral as cited above, note 21; also by J.J. Parry in *University of Illinois Studies*, X (1925).

[24] Ed. E. Faral, *Les Arts poétiques du XIIe et XIIIe siècles* (Paris, 1923).

[25] Ed. Thomas Wright, *Anglo-Latin Satirical Poets*, Rolls Series, No. 59, 2 vols., I, pp. 231 ff.

[26] *Opera, Pat. Lat.*, CCX

[27] Ed. Thomas Wright, *op. cit.*, II, pp. 175 ff.

[28] Both works *ibid.*, I, pp. 146 ff.

CHAPTER VII

ANGLO-FRENCH LITERATURE

1. THE LEARNED WRITERS

The French-speaking circles of court and church also produced literature in England, some of it devotional and learned, some of it worldly and entertaining.[1] The latter was of an international type insofar as it followed a general European fashion in which continental French literature was an acknowledged leader. At the same time it was naturally closer to popular sources in England than was the learned Latin literature we have just been examining. An intimate two-way relationship of borrowing developed between entertainers in both English and French, each side making use of plots and situations known to the other.

The learned writers on both sides also drew on one another almost from the beginning. We moderns must remember, in dealing with medieval literature in general, that originality was not a trait especially prized by either the public at large or those who entertained and instructed them. A good story once told was available to anybody who wanted to try his hand at retelling it or modifying it for fresh purposes. In the realm of science and pseudo-science too, new writers helped themselves verbatim to long passages from the works of their predecessors, very often without acknowledging the debt. Their attitude is explainable when we think that the chief function of many writers in the transition centuries (the fifth to the 11th) had been to salvage parts of classical lore in convenient form, rather than to make additions to it. The writing of compendia was not a task calling for intellectual originality. The point of view of compendia-writers persisted long, fortified by the conservatism of ecclesiastical and lay authority, and in part explains the absence of individual proprietorship in respect to literary materials in the Middle Ages.

Among the types of more learned French literature in England we find Biblical translations, lives of saints and moralised descriptions of nature. For instance, there are two poems of the latter 12th century con-

cerning the life and death of the Anglo-Saxon King Edmund, put to
death by the Danes in 870 and later canonised. One of them (written
ca. 1175 and using English sources) was done by Denis Piramus; the
other is anonymous. Several writers treated various Eastern saints, such
as Thais, Barlaam and Josaphat, and others. Wace, more famous as
a romantic chronicler (see below), wrote lives of Saints Margaret, Nicholas
and George. [2] A certain Beneeit, otherwise unknown, retold in Anglo-
Norman the mythical story of St. Brendan's voyage from Ireland to the
West. Based on a ninth-century Hiberno-Latin text (*Navigatio Sancti
Brendani*) which clearly imitated pagan Celtic tales, this legend described
an earthly paradise and a place of eternal punishment supposed to have
been found by the venturesome saint, along with other picturesque wonders, on mythical islands in the Western Atlantic Ocean. There were
French versions, likewise from a Latin source, of an equally wonderful
trip made to Purgatory by way of an entrance revealed to St. Patrick
in Ireland, and of a vision attributed to St. Paul revealing the sufferings
of the damned in Hell. These lively fictitious excursions into the world
of future castigations were popular, by the way, in many languages
besides French, and they contributed to the stream of visionary literature
which, like the Latin allegories previously discussed, fed the imagination
of Dante.

Among the miscellaneous edifying pieces were the *Bestiary* and
Lapidary of Philippe de Thaon or Thaun (ca. 1125), giving fabulous anecdotes about animals and stones, with moral explanations of their characteristics. Both were written in Norman French verse. The *Bestiary*
is based on the same Graeco-Latin text which inspired the fragments
of an Old English *Physiologus*. Though occasionally echoing more factual
Latin sources like Pliny and Solinus, the two works are anything but
scientific. The *Lapidary* was derived, like other treatments of the same
subject in French, from a moralising Latin poem *De Lapidibus* by Marbod
of Rennes. The bestiaries, with their quaint moralised fantasies about
animals, were popular throughout Europe and their influence can be
traced in the decorative arts as well as literature.

Two church plays written in Norman French are preserved in Anglo-
Norman of the 12th century. One, the *Jus d'Adam* (*Play of Adam*), is
the text of a performance to be given at Christmas, in which various characters of the Old Testament appear to foretell the coming of Christ.
The other is a play on the *Resurrection*, designed for Easter. Both date
from the 12th century, a period from which no English texts of church
plays are extant. [3] For the origins of drama in English we must look to
a much later period.

The Garden of Love in *The Romance of the Rose*
British Museum

Early historiography in French is represented by Geoffrey Gaimar, who wrote an *Estoire des Engleis* (1140) using English written materials such as the Anglo-Saxon Chronicle and also popular romantic legends. It is the only surviving part of a trilogy supposed to trace the origin of the English people from the Trojans to King Arthur and beyond, following the general plan of Geoffrey of Monmouth. The audience for whom Gaimar wrote obviously wanted some spice of fictional entertainment as well as an outline of English history, and he complied with their wishes by interweaving legendary events with historical facts.

The same purpose was served in the chronicles produced by Wace, a prolific author whose work was done in Normandy proper but was dedicated to the Anglo-Norman royal court and exercised an influence on English literature. About the year 1155 he completed an expanded verse translation of Geoffrey of Monmouth's *Historia Regum Britanniae*, under the title of the *Roman de Brut*,[4] in which the previously unadorned pseudo-history is treated with literary amplitude. The scenes are plastically described, conversations are introduced, and there is much colour and movement. Though the form is still that of a chronicle, the style is drawn closer to romance. Some fresh materials are introduced, including the institution of the Round Table, hitherto unknown. There are indications that Wace obtained his supplements independently from oral tradition. The success of the *Roman de Brut* was immediate, and in fact led to a translation into English verse under the title of *Brut*, by an English priest named Layamon or Lawman, living in the Southwestern country. No doubt the success of Wace's effort was due in part to political factors. It was welcome to the author's patrons because it glorified the origins of the Angevin island kingdom in a vernacular text. As a result, Wace was commissioned by King Henry II and Queen Eleanor (1166) to write a versified account of the early history of the Norman dukes from the Scandinavian settlement onwards. The long *Roman de Rou* begins, therefore, with the conquest of Normandy by Vikings under Rou (Hrolf), and deals largely with the period of legend, though Wace made some effort to separate fact from fiction. His poem was never completed.

Among the chroniclers who gave historical information concerning their own times were Jordan Fantosme, a writer directly attached to the court; the anonymous author of *Le Rei Dermot* or *La Conqueste d'Irlande* (which supplements the Latin account by Gerald the Welshman), and the anonymous biographer who composed a long poem, *Guillaume le Maréchal* (dealing with the Earl of Pembroke who was regent during the youth of King Henry III).[5]

Even this brief survey shows how important was patronage in the production of historical writings in French, and how closely it was connected with the limited court circle of the Angevins. The same relationship was true of the first romantic literature in French and Anglo-French, but this eventually reached a much wider public, and it became extremely important for the later versified literature of entertainment in the English language.

2. THE SOCIAL ORIGINS OF ROMANTIC LOVE

When we turn to the lyrics and the verse fiction designed for the feudal aristocracy in France, and later widely imitated in England as well as other countries, we are confronted with a social phenomenon of vast cultural significance. This was the advent, briefly speaking, of a cult of romantic love between the sexes within the ruling class (and only within that class). The cult produced attitudes previously unknown in the cultures of the European peoples. The general term for it is courtly love; in French, *amour courtois*.

The introduction of this cult is intimately related to the social position of women in the feudal aristocracy. Economically, these ladies were of course subordinated to fathers and husbands. Their marriages were determined for them by considerations of property and family prestige; if they were orphaned or widowed heiresses, their overlords were expected to assign them to guardians or husbands who would administer their estates, have the rents collected, organise military protection and discharge the services required by baron or king. In the words of Engels, "For the knight or baron, as for the prince of the land himself, marriage [was] a political act, an opportunity to increase power by new alliances; the interest of the *house* must be decisive, not the wishes of an individual."[6] Still less were the women's inclinations consulted. Wives and daughters were expected to be completely subservient, completely absorbed in the domestic matters under their control. They were often as a matter of fact treated with humiliating harshness, even brutality, by their husbands.

Yet after marriage, if not before, they enjoyed a certain amount of social eminence. They then appeared in public, occupied positions of honour at public banquets, shared with their husbands in the ceremonies at which lower knights and other tenants did homage for land held in fief. Such ceremonies contained an element of personal feeling. The tenant knights not only promised to pay certain kinds of rent and to furnish certain military assistance, but they also expressed devotion to the lord himself, and to his cause, thus pledging to him their valour, fidelity and devotion as well as their economic tribute. The emotional attitude of personal attachment had existed in pre-feudal times. It was not entirely lost in the more complex social relations of the feudal Middle Ages.

The personal devotion to an overlord was extended by courtesy and by practice to his lady, who might (and often did) represent him very effectively during his absences on wars and Crusading expeditions. In Southern France, especially in Provence in the late 11th and early 12th centuries, we find the attitude to the aristocratic lady, the lord's wife, quite suddenly intensified to one of extravagant adulation couched in erotic terms. The chatelaine, being a woman of eminence in the life of the castle, surrounded by knights and men-at-arms in the atmosphere of a military fortress, readily became the focus of whatever softer feelings affected her hardened male entourage. Those with poetic gifts began to write lyrical poems to her in which her beauty and charm were extolled to the skies. It was affirmed that the poet, whether noble amateur or paid professional, owed all his good qualities to her influence; that he lived for her approval; that he worshipped her from afar; that she was his saint, his guide, his inspiration to chivalry, and he was but an unworthy groveller at her feet.

The writers of these lyrics, called troubadours, were connected with the baronial courts of the Southern provinces of France. Their work, though often artificial in the extreme, was at times charmingly lyrical in a simpler way. In their typical love-poems, the troubadours represent themselves as hopelessly fascinated with their lords' wives, endlessly and disinterestedly devoted to them without hope of reward, suffering solitary anguish from a sense of deprivation and unworthiness—especially, of course, in the springtime, when the nightingales sing and the bushes are in flower. The situations are conventional, being largely an aspect of feudal service translated into terms of poetry. We may doubt the genuineness of the passion in many cases, but in some it seems to have been real.

The troubadours' attitude to women was something new. True enough, the world had known poems of intense passion addressed to women before this, and feelings of aspiration, frustration and despair had many times been poured into lyrics in the past. But to elevate a noble lady to the pedestal of something like a saint, to make her sole inspirer of all that was good in her lover, to idealise her as something superior and all but unapproachable—this was the contribution of the Provençal lyricists of the 12th century. It was they who created romantic love as we understand it today, but for them it was essentially an extra-marital tie between men and women. Once more the words of Engels are apt:

"The first historical form of sexual love passion, a passion recognised as natural to human beings (at least if they belonged to the ruling classes)..., this first form of individual sexual love, the chivalrous love of the Middle Ages, was by no means conjugal. Quite the contrary. In its classic form among the Provençals, it heads straight for adultery, and the poets of love celebrated adultery."[7]

Much has been written about the origins of this school of poetry and the influences affecting it. Some have surmised a connection with the heresies which came to Southern France at this time from Asia Minor, ancient centre of pre-Christian cults of goddess-worship; some have looked to the influence of neighbouring Spanish-Arabic poetry, which was also impassioned and erotic (though by no means always heterosexual, nor given to idealising women as superior creatures).[8] The parallels are interesting but not always convincing. Some critics have sought an explanation rather in the doctrines of Platonic love derived from the Greeks and adapted by Arabic philosophers in more speculative writings.[9] Some have suggested that the cult of the Virgin Mary, as exemplified in writers like Bernard of Clairvaux, affected the social attitude to feudal chatelaines. Actually, the influence seems to have gone the other way. The erotic devotion to aristocratic women came earlier, and led to a new, more intense and personal devotion to the Virgin, as a reflection of the more worldly Provençal attitudes already prevalent very early in the 12th century.[10] In any event, both types of devotion became widely prevalent in the century that followed.

Whatever the causes producing courtly love (and they may have been quite various), the cult gave a new tone to life in the castles of Southern France. In this atmosphere Eleanor of Aquitaine had grown up. Her father William of Aquitaine was one of the first troubadours. As a rich feudal heiress she was quite willing to accept the adulation of professional poets as her just due. As one who had witnessed the more refined social life of Byzantium and the cities of Asia Minor, it is quite possible that (as has been suggested in the preceding chapter) she decided deliberately to use the convention of woman-worship in order to improve the manners and attitudes of the uncouth, often ferocious lords who filled the ranks of Western aristocracy.[11] Certain it is that she, her daughter Marie de Champagne (offspring of her first marriage), and a number of other ladies instituted a systematic effort to have the noblemen's behaviour so modified that, formally at least, women were recognised as arbiters of decorum and teachers of chivalrous behaviour through the gentle art of love, romantically conceived. Eleanor's own sons, Geoffrey, Richard and John, were close friends of troubadours and themselves interested in the writing of troubadour lyrics.

Under the patronage of Eleanor a Latin handbook was actually written by a priest, Andreas Capellanus or André the Chaplain, to formulate and explain the rules of the new system of love (ca. 1180).[12] With much learned exegesis—partly burlesque, it would appear—and some illustrative stories, the book purports to lay down serious rules for an ideal lover. He must be faithful, humble, patient, generous in gifts and services, and above all secret in his devotion, since his lady will almost certainly be the wife of someone else. In fact, it is stated as a principle that love and marriage are incompatible, for marriage is a contract precluding the distance and uncertainty necessary for romance. That is to say, romantic love must be adulterous. And it is above all else a strict prerogative of the nobility and the few rich members of the merchant class with money and leisure to play the game properly. Peasants are categorically excluded. Of them it is said that they are moved to the act of love as a horse or mule is moved (*naturaliter sicut equus et mulus ad Veneris opera promoventur*). Courtly love could not apply to them in the conditions of their drudgery in the fields, Andreas insisted frankly, for otherwise crops would not be cared for and people would not be fed. The more refined emotions were the exclusive privilege of the ruling class.

The code of behaviour between the sexes thus enthusiastically propagated by Eleanor and her friends, with the help of the troubadours, found wide acceptance, at least in literature. We may doubt whether it transformed daily life in the castles as profoundly as the poets would have us believe. After the lyrics of the troubadours, it next found expression in long romantic verse narratives composed in Central and Northern France, in the French of England, and later in the English language. The stories were called romances because they were first cultivated in a Romance language as contrasted with Latin. Very soon however the word assumed the sense of unreal fantasy in story form, with love as a main motive and chivalric persons as main characters.

Very many of the medieval love romances use the court of King Arthur as a background. The heroes are knights of the Round Table who expend much time and energy rescuing ladies from dangers such as capture, siege and oppression, attacks by robbers, incursions by monsters or the nefarious doings of magicians. The rescuers go to all sorts of lengths in their services, and patiently endure whatever trials or humiliations the ladies see fit to impose upon them. One of the first writers of extant Arthurian romance, Chrétien de Troyes, composed for Queen Eleanor's daughter Marie de Champagne a story in which Sir Lancelot makes his first literary appearance as Queen Guinevere's lover, and he is just such an abjectly devoted knight as the current vogue demanded.[13] After he has exhausted himself in efforts to rescue her, she treats him with scornful contempt because he once hesitated for a few seconds before taking a distasteful step necessary in order to reach her. The situation between Lancelot and King Arthur's wife is developed entirely in accordance with the rules of Andreas. Countess Marie, the poet tells us, suggested both the plot and the courtly-love interpretation to him. The poem itself resulted thus from the direct dictation of a feudal patroness, and we must assume that she was in sympathy with its ideological trend. Not all of this poet's works conformed so closely, however, to the Provençal patterns of courtly behaviour.

3. FRENCH ROMANCE IN ENGLAND

French romance spread to England and was imitated there as in many other countries. At first it was cultivated in the Anglo-French language, under the direct stimulus of Queen Eleanor. It was for her that a certain cleric named Benoit de Sainte Maure (not a Norman) wrote the long, romanticised account of the Trojan war, *Le Roman de Troye* (ca. 1160),[14] which inserted a new story of a secret, chivalrous love connecting Prince Troilus with a Trojan lady Briseida. This is the first step in the literary evolution leading to Chaucer's famous treatment of the tale. It tells only about the end of the love affair, when Briseida is sent from the besieged city to the camp of the Greeks, and there betrays the memory of her chivalrous Trojan lover by transferring her favour to the persuasive and confident Greek Diomede. Throughout his very long romance, Benoit unrolls a colourful pageant of aristocratic feudal life, describing banquets and costumes, battles, tournaments and love affairs, with a wealth of vivid detail. Despite his prolixity, he manages to impart to his scenes the kind of glamour which a modern cinema director would strive for if he wished to glorify the 12th century as an age of romance.

Queen Eleanor's interest in romanticised history, including the legend of King Arthur, was manifested in her patronage of the French *Roman de Brut* by Wace, and the later English version by Layamon (see ch. 8, sec. 3). The earliest extant version of the Tristan legend was composed, probably about 1160—70, by an Anglo-French poet, Thomas of Britain, who used sources reaching back ultimately to the Celtic prose romances of Ireland. This tale[15] furnishes a classical instance of a courtly love situation, for the hero is a dashing, invincible young Cornish knight, attached to King Arthur's court, who is enamoured of his uncle's young wife Iseult, a princess of Ireland. Their stolen meetings and escapes from detection provide dramatic action, while their periods of separation give occasion for the refined introspective monologues affected by courtly poets. The alternation of exciting action and inner debate seems to have been pleasing to aristocratic listeners.

Another type of romance about Arthurian knights and their ladies was the short *lai* depicting a single adventure or a short, closely connected series of them, focused on a single problem of courtly behaviour. The best-known poems of this type were composed in Anglo-Norman at the court of Henry II and Eleanor, by a certain talented lady called Marie de France, about whose life nothing is known.[16] Marie tells us that she used for plots some of the Breton tales about people and situations already treated by popular lyrical singers. The element of magic is conspicuous in them, but it is subtly adapted by her to the purposes of psychological symbolism. The problems of feeling and action are not those of folk tales, but the kind which might arise among people of her own time and class. Some of the typical characters are: the young wife of an old and jealous nobleman; two adolescents in love; an inexperienced young knight learning from his mistress the necessity for discretion as well as valour; two noble ladies, a wife and a mistress, each generously offering to renounce a beloved knight in favour of the other. In contrast to the usual rambling and amorphous romances, Marie's short *lais* are economical, compactly organised, and very delicately told. The type of narrative was imitated by other writers in French, and later in English also. In addition to her *lais*, Marie also wrote a poem on *St. Patrick's Purgatory*, and a collection of beast fables entitled *Esopet* (from Aesop).

Not all of the romances composed in Anglo-French concern King Arthur and his knights. Many types of subject were handled in the same vein. English materials and English settings appear in *Horn et Rimel* (ca. 1180) and in *Haveloc* (the extant romance post-dates 1190 but appears to be based on a lost earlier version).[17] Both tales deal with princes exiled from their patrimony and regaining it by deeds of arms. They demonstrate the interest of the French-speaking aristocracy in the native milieu and themes. Whatever historical basis may exist for the typical situation in these two plots, it belongs to the age of Viking invasions, but the romances have overlaid it completely with fiction. *Gui de Warewic* (i.e., Warwick) and *Boeve de Haumtone* (Hampton), both of the early 13th century, are quite without historical foundation. They deal mainly with warfare against Saracens, in the spirit of the Crusades but obviously for entertainment. The legend of Alexander's fictitious adventures in the Orient was versified as the *Roman de toute chevalerie* by one Thomas or Eustace of Kent (early 13th century; still unedited). Commonplaces of classical fiction from the tales of Troy and Thebes were woven together with motifs of Arthurian romance by Hue de Rotelande in his *Ipomedon* and its sequel *Prothesilaus* (late 12th century). The scene of this synthetic romance is laid in the Kingdom of the Two Sicilies—that is, the island together with Southern Italy—perhaps because of the marriage of Eleanor's daughter Joanna to the Norman King William then reigning there.[18]

These romantic themes were all treated later in Middle English romances, and will be discussed in connection with them. It should be remarked that in a number of them the interest is concentrated far more on pure adventure than the service of ladies, and the love affairs are not, as in the cases of Lancelot and Tristan, between a single knight and a married lady. More often, as in *Horn, Haveloc, Gui, Boeve* and *Ipomedon*, the heroes' loves and adventures lead them directly to marriage. Of the Anglo-French group, only *Tristan* and the fragmentary early *Amadas et Idoine* (which antedates the complete 13th-century text in Picard French) have a beloved heroine married to someone not the hero; and *Amadas* has strong elements of burlesque openly ridiculing the relationship of illicit courtly love.

The Anglo-French romances were written in several different styles and forms. Some used assonance, some rimed couplets, some identical rime over extended passages. Some, like the *Roman de Rou* by Wace, shifted from one scheme to another. The length of the line varied from octosyllabics to the six-stressed iambic line called alexandrine because it was employed by Gautier de Châtillon in his French romance about Alexander the Great.

The great length and the episodic structure of some of the romances indicate that they were told continuously over a period of several days, with divisions corresponding to the climaxes. The remarks made by poets at the beginnings and at various points throughout the stories suggest that they frequently had trouble in catching attention and making themselves heard in the noisy halls of castles and manor houses. They insert repetitions and reminders for those whose attention has wandered. They also indicate their concern for a due reward, usually at the end of the tale. Style and content of the more refined romances of courtly love clearly reveal their destination for the exclusive upper aristocracy. Such is the *Tristan* of Thomas of Britain; such are the *lais* of Marie de France, with their emphasis on inner conflict and delicate nuances of feeling. Others, more boisterous and full of action, may have reached wider audiences in the courtyards and marketplaces. Such is a second version of the Tristan legend by a continental French writer named Béroul, which contains episodes of exciting suspense and also of vulgar or cruel trickery. Such too are many of the romances with a background of war against the Saracens, where blood flows freely and the enemy are delineated as monstrous creatures somehow improbably endowed with most beautiful daughters. The exaggerations produce a downright comic effect. There are indeed elements of burlesque in these poems, which show a critical, humorous attitude on the part of tellers and' listeners, confirmed, no doubt, by the presence of new middle-class auditors from the towns who had no reason to share the exaggerated attitudes of the castle folk.

The form, style and content of French romance were closely imitated in Middle English, beginning in the latter 13th century. The octosyllabic couplet became the typical verse form (though not the only one) for long romantic narrative. Story-tellers found it appropriate to many kinds of audience, for it was well adapted to the uncomplicated sentence structure of simple narrative, while the riming pairs aided the memory of reciters. Very many anonymous Middle English romances were composed in this form, therefore, and also many of the popular works of instruction and admonition which likewise date from the 13th century. Chaucer used the octosyllabic couplet for a number of his early romantic, visionary tales and allegories composed under French influence. On the other hand, English poets demonstrated considerable skill and independence in the development of various stanzaic forms which they likewise used as vehicles for romantic narrative.

During the time when English story-tellers were imitating French plots and adapting French verse forms, their vocabulary also was receiving more and more loan words from the same source. The structure of the native language remained fundamentally the same, though now simplified, but the influx of new words was very great in the latter 13th and 14th centuries. It can be said that the two vernacular literatures became very close at this period, and it is quite impossible to study the English without some knowledge of the French. At the same time English literature, including the conventional romances, developed traits of its own, marking it off as less narrowly feudal, more frequently popular in its appeal because less exclusively devoted to the cult of courtly love, than the French tended to be. The differences will be pointed out later. It will be seen that despite the cosmopolitanism of romantic medieval literature in general, the English variety attained some degree of independence from the French models with which it was so closely allied.

[1] For general survey see J. Vising, *Anglo-Norman Language and Literature* (London, 1923) and E. Walberg, *Quelques aspects de la littérature Anglo-Normande* (Paris, 1936); both, however, rather schematic.

[2] Willis H. Bowen, "Present Status of Studies in Saints' Lives in Old French," *Symposium*, I (Syracuse, U.S.A., 1947), 82—86, supplementing the author's work in the *Critical Bibliography of Old French Literature* (Syracuse University Press, revised ed., 1952).

[3] *Jus d'Adam*, ed. P. Studer as *Le mystère d'Adam* (Manchester, 1918); *Resurrection*, ed. J.G. Wright (Paris, 1931). For discussion see Grace Frank, *The Medieval French Drama* (Oxford, 1954), chs. 8 and 9.

[4] Ed. Ivor Arnold, SATF (Société des Anciens Textes Français), 2 vols. (Paris, 1938—40); see the introduction for a general discussion. The English *Brut* by Layamon or Lawman was edited by Sir Frederick Madden, 2 vols. (London, 1847).

[5] Brief discussion of all these historical writers will be found in R.M. Wilson, *Early Middle English Literature*, ch. 3; Baugh, *Literary History*, Bk. I, Part ii, ch. 4. For detailed information see Charles Gross, *Sources and Literature of English History* (London, 1915).

[6] F. Engels, *The Origin of the Family, Private Property and the State* (New York, 1942), p. 69.

[7] *Ibid.*, p. 62 (punctuation and orthography slightly modified).

[8] See A.R. Nykl, *Hispano-Arabic Poetry and Its Relations with the Old Provençal Troubadours* (Baltimore, 1946).

[9] This is the source suggested by A.J. Denomy, "An Inquiry into the Origins of Courtly Love," *Mediaeval Studies*, VI (Toronto, 1944), 175—260. The author neglects the social milieu of French feudalism while seeking rather remote philosophical parallels among the Arabs. For critique see Theodore Silverstein, "Andreas, Plato and the Arabs," *Modern Philology*, XLVII (1949—50), 117—26.

[10] Cf. Constance B. West, *Courtoisie in Anglo-Norman Literature* (Oxford, 1938), p. 153.

[11] Amy Kelly, "Eleanor of Aquitaine and Her Courts of Love," *Speculum*, XII (1937), 3—19.

[12] Andreae Capellani *De Amore Libri Tres*, ed. E. Trojel (Copenhagen, 1892); tr. by J.J. Parry with introduction (New York: Columbia University Press, 1941). An adapted version of the text, containing short interpolations in Polish (15th century), is contained in MS. Bibl. Jag. 5230, Cracow. An attempt has been made by D.W. Robertson to prove that Andreas was using irony to denounce the adulterous love he seemed to advocate. See *Modern Philology*, L (1952—53), 145—61.

[13] *Le Chevalier de la charette*, ed. W. Foerster as *Der Karrenritter* (Halle, 1899). On the development of the Lancelot romance see especially T.P. Cross and W.A. Nitze, *Lancelot and Guenevere* (Chicago University Press, 1930) and G.T. Webster, *Guinevere* (Milton, Mass., 1951).

[14] Ed. L. Constans, SATF, 6 vols. See VI (1912) for introduction.

[15] Ed. J. Bédier, SATF, 2 vols. (1902—05).

[16] Marie de France, *Lais*, ed. A. Ewert (Oxford, 1944).

[17] *Haveloc*, ed. A. Bell (Manchester, 1925), is typical of this group.

[18] A romance belonging to the Grail cycle of Arthurian legends was composed by Robert de Boron, a native of Burgundy who settled in England about 1200. But he composed the poem before emigrating, and in the Burgundian, not the Norman dialect. See William Nitze, "Messire Robert de Boron," *Speculum*, XXVIII (1953), 279—96.

CHAPTER VIII

LEARNING AND INSTRUCTION IN THE VERNACULAR
(13TH AND EARLY 14TH CENTURIES)

1. THE FEUDAL STRUCTURE BOTH SOLIDIFIED
AND WEAKENED

The entire 13th century and the first years of the 14th witnessed a development of the struggles already begun in the 12th: that is to say, the burgeoning resistance of the all but unorganised masses of people against exploitation on the land, the first steps in handworkers' organisation and struggle, the rivalries within the ruling class (kings versus barons, ecclestiastical hierarchy against magnates), the fight of minorities against the encroachments of the Anglo-Norman state. On the surface, the structure of society appeared to change little in the course of about 150 years. The feudal forms continued to be observed, the feudal obligations were paid. But beneath the exterior, many transformations were taking place which in due time became clearly apparent in every sphere of life. By the end of the 14th century the conflict between old class interests and new social forces had become revolutionary in the political realm and others as well.

The outstanding economic fact of the 13th century was the state of relative (though not by any means absolute) prosperity maintained by agriculture. Warfare was conducted locally and on a modest scale in England, when viewed in comparison with centuries past and to come. As methods of cultivation improved, the population showed a marked increase, the price levels did not advance over-rapidly, and the general purchasing power was maintained instead of declining.[1] The small farmers, villeins and serfs as well as the large land-owners found it possible to produce more and more food-stuffs and wool for the market. The larger estates belonging to monasteries and the nobility were usually in a position to experiment first with new techniques. Taking adventage of their greater tracts of land, their greater efficiency, and above all their more intensive exploitation of labour forces, they laid the foundations for accumulating wealth which became more and more resented by all the lower orders as time passed. But smaller landowners, free and unfree, also benefited to a certain extent from the expanding market.

The commutation of labour services into rent continued as the money in circulation increased and with it likewise the buying and selling of land (late 13th century). But it must not be thought that the process was one of simple, straightforward evolution.[2] Local conditions varied widely. The new activity of the market did not automatically bring about emancipation of the serfs. In fact, within certain districts where land was productive and located near market centres, but not heavily populated, the new opportunities to obtain cash profits led to a multiplication of the burdens laid on the peasants' backs, and even to re-introduction of labour services that had previously been abandoned. Elsewhere (as for instance in the North, where the market mattered less, and in East Anglia, where the population was great), the lords found desirable the payment of money rent by free peasants, and the occasional hiring of landless free workers for whom the employers were in no way responsible when their services were not needed.

Recent research has brought to light the evidence of many sharp struggles in the 13th century, as the villeins fought against the new demands made upon them, and against the revival of old obligations by both lay and ecclesiastical landowners. Even those who were able to rise somewhat in the social scale through the chance to sell at markets and acquire title to land, were still living in conditions of most primitive discomfort. Their cottages were one- or two-room affairs, with wooden shutters but no glass at the windows, with an open fire in the centre of the dirt floor in lieu of a stove, with a hole in the roof instead of a chimney, and with domestic fowl and animals housed together with the human beings, often without even a partition to separate them from the room in which the family lived. During the autumn and winter they had no light save that of the fire, for candles were too expensive for their use. From about the year 1300, the voices of husbandmen lamenting their hard lives begin to be heard in some of the fragmentary surviving literature of the third estate. Their cries become sharper, and are more frequently embodied in surviving written forms when, in the 14th century, a general depression succeeded the previous boom, and other factors worsened still more the conditions of life for many workers on the land.[3]

In the political world, progress was made towards national unity and the strengthening of central governmental authority despite sporadic opposition by the barons. During the reign of King John (1199—1216), the crown made extreme financial demands upon the latter in order to meet expenses augmented by disastrous foreign wars and maladministration. On this occasion the barons had grievances winning support outside the circle of their own small clique. They compelled John to grant a charter (1215) confirming traditional privileges and rights of the nobility, the church and free towns, defining strictly the limits between royal and baronial courts, the limits of knights' and barons' obligations, and similar matters. A famous clause (No. 39) guaranteed that "no free man shall be taken, or imprisoned, or disseized, or outlawed, or exiled, or in any way destroyed, nor will we go upon him nor will we send upon him, except by the legal judgment of his peers or by the law of the land." As understood at the time, Magna Carta had a restricted class character. It was not concerned at all with serfs or landless workers. Its primary purpose was to preserve one group of the possessing class, there called "freemen," from encroachments by another. Nevertheless its language was general enough to make it a valuable weapon in later struggles leading to the establishment of a bourgeois-democratic parliament. Eventually, in the 17th century, it was turned against the very class which had produced it, and gave legal justification for the revolutionary liquidation of feudalism.[4]

The solidification of government and legal practice was marked under Henry III (1215—72) and his immediate successors. A sign of this was the codifying of law and custom. Important summaries were written in the late 13th century. Noteworthy is the work of Bracton (died 1268) entitled *De Legibus et Consuetudinibus Angliae* (*On the Laws and Customs of England*), and two texts indebted to it: one in French called *Britton*, perhaps from its author's name (ca. 1290), and another in Latin called *Fleta* (same period, author also unknown).[5] At the same time particular statutes enacted in London, especially the two statutes of Westminster (1275 and 1285 respectively), undertook to regulate feudal obligations officially, to formalise local elections, to guard against excessive tolls, lawless fighting, insecure roads, etc.[6] These legal measures helped to achieve and fortify administrative order and unity. It was in this comparatively late period that French became the vernacular language widely used to supplement Latin in the usage of the law, due to special circumstances obtaining in the reign of Henry III.

As an institution, the medieval English church also gained in power, though frequently checked by resistance from the state. Leading prelates were to be found in high governmental posts while continuing to occupy episcopal and archepiscopal sees, which they often neglected. Their dual function threw into sharp relief the political aspect of hierarchical activity, for all to behold clearly. At the same time, the monastic foundations achieved new summits of wealth during the decades of agricultural prosperity. The records give us more and more details of luxury and wordly living in the larger houses, which turned into a mockery the severe rules theoretically imposed upon the monks living in them.

Periodically, indeed, throughout the Middle Ages, the discrepancy became so glaring, the oppression and exploitation of serfs, villeins and poor peasants so obviously contradictory to the official church ideology, that protest movements broke out against the abuses. The cries for reform resulted partly from the pressure of criticism and attacks from the outside, partly from the awareness of danger on the part of those within the institution. Time after time the demand was raised for a return to the idealised practices of early Christianity, when monks and hermits really were poor, austere and hard-working. Various heretical sects, like the Albigensians and the followers of Waldo in Southern France, claimed to have reestablished a purified religion; their temporary success was due to the large measure of social protest embodied in their ideologies. Repeatedly, too, more orthodox reform groups detached themselves from the older monastic orders, or introduced modifications of them, with the avowed purpose of reestablishing a genuine rule of poverty, chastity and obedience, and at least internal social equality. Time after time they failed.

For instance, the Cluniac movement, which strongly affected Aelfric and other late Old English writers, was an attempt to purify the Benedictine order, grown rich and worldly. But Cluny, Fleury and other reformed houses in turn became wealthy, as indeed was to be expected because of the social and economic foundations of the newer institutions as well as the older. In the 12th century, the French order of Cistercian monks, which soon spread to England, similarly attempted to reintroduce ideals and practices of the first Christian centuries, but it too quickly lost the initial zeal for rigours and poverty, and became another chain of rich land-owning abbeys. The pattern was familiar; the instances could be indefinitely multiplied. [7]

Early in the 13th century, two orders of a somewhat new type appeared as a protest against the corruption and decline in influence of the monks. Although eventually following the same pattern of accumulated wealth, power, exploitation and corruption, they still maintained certain distinctive ties with the masses which were important for the development of vernacular literature. The orders in question were those of the preaching friars, the Franciscans and Dominicans, which reached England in the first quarter of the 13th century. Their activity was later shared by the Augustinians and Carmelites. The Franciscans in particular stressed the obligation of poverty, undertook to renounce all possessions, collectively and individually, and to live strictly upon what they could obtain by begging from people. Hence they were called mendicants.

Unlike monks in the older orders, they chose to move about among the population, in the villages and the towns, on the highways and at fairs, instead of remaining cloistered within monasteries. The yield from their begging eventually reached great amounts, wealthy patrons were found to subsidise the new orders by gifts of land and cash, and so in time the houses of the mendicants became quite indistinguishable from the older monasteries in respect to luxury and pretentiousness.

Nevertheless the friars continued to circulate widely among people, to observe and within limits to share in their crises and difficulties. Their preaching brought them to the smallest villages and churchyards, and also into the churches themselves in the role of guest preachers. Their style was popular; they cultivated the gift of appealing to the masses by speaking in their own homely terms. Their success was resented by the regular monks, and likewise by the parish priests. The former objected to the competition offered by the friars, and were vociferous in accusing them of hypocrisy. The priests were disturbed because visiting mendicant preachers, using new and sometimes sensational methods, aroused and played on the feelings of their parishoners, and collected from them what would otherwise have gone to the local church and its pastor. Many polemics were composed against the friars by monks and priests. But the preaching orders retained their popularity for some time, partly by their improved techniques of mass appeal in homiletics. They exercised a stimulating effect on several types of vernacular literature, as we shall see. In addition some of their members developed intellectual activity and became distinguished at the universities.

In the late 12th and early 13th century, the volume of protest and the threat of disunity arising from heretical sects called forth some vigorous efforts at reform within the church itself. Pope Innocent III played a leading role in this internal movement. At the Fourth Lateran Council summoned by him (1215—16), the inner dangers were frankly admitted, the ignorance and corruption of the clergy were stringently criticised, and systematic efforts were made to capture the offensive from critics and heretics. A program of intensive instruction was projected for the benefit of both priests and laity. Fear of sin, death and punishment were stressed as never before. At the same time clergy were called upon to supplement the propaganda of fear by offering better examples themselves in the interests of moral unity. Bishops in the various countries were charged with the task of carrying out the program of education. So that all people might be reached, much more teaching was to be done in the vernacular languages.

The consequences of this campaign were widely felt in literature for laymen. The general program met some of the current demand for the

Cuckoo-Song, about 1250

British Museum

instruction of persons outside the clergy, at least in the fundamentals of doctrine. It opened the way for broader teaching in the vernacular on religious subjects, and this in turn led to some elementary secular learning for the masses. The techniques of admonition, however, playing so greatly on fear of supernatural punishment, set the tone for a vast amount of gloomy moralising which was predominant in Europe until the Renaissance.

2. GENERAL INTELLECTUAL TENDENCIES

Such movements in the church and in secular politics were signs that the structure of medieval society was already being strained by the forces of internal change. The intellectual life of the times, too, showed many signs of internal change. Under the challenge of new knowledge and improved practical techniques, the arts—especially sculpture and architecture—made enormous strides. This was the great century of construction in the Gothic style.

In part the tendencies of the 13th century were, of course, merely a continuation of those already existing, but so strengthened as to lead almost automatically to a qualitative change. The gathering of secondary information into encyclopedic compendia from older sources became more ambitious than ever. Typical of the century, for instance, was the work of a French Dominican friar, Vincent of Beauvais, in a series of three works: *Speculum Naturale, Speculum Historiale, Speculum Morale (Mirrors* or compendia of natural science, history and moral philosophy respectively). In England, a compendious and yet partly original work in history was done by Matthew of Paris in his *Chronica Major*, covering the entire span of time from creation to the year of his death (1259). The reign of Henry III is described in rich detail, some of the characters and scenes being delineated from the author's own knowledge and experience.

In the field of philosophy the Platonic influence continued, but was combined with a fresh impulse drawn indirectly from ancient Greek thought: namely the intensive study of certain works by Aristotle hitherto not generally known in Western Europe. The learned Arabs of Spain had translated and commented upon his *Physics, Metaphysics, Natural History, Ethics* and *Psychology (De Anima)*, besides the texts in logic already current in Christian-Latin translations. These Arabic versions got into French, English and other university circles by way of Hebrew translations later put into Latin. The results were, of course, a rather transmogrified Aristotle. The Arabs had engrafted upon his thought certain elements of pantheism and fatalism which they, like the Chartres philosophers in France, took from Neo-Platonic sources. But the orientation towards problems of natural science was perceptible; the emphasis in these Aristotelian works was on fact and reason rather than vision and intuition. One effect of the new interest was to diminish the Platonic element in speculative philosophy, though by no means to reject it entirely. And the Platonic influence continued to be strong in the literary allegorical forms used to dress up theological and philosophical exposition.

For its method, scholasticism made intensified use of the logic of Aristotle, and thus, within certain limits, placed more emphasis on reason than had the mystically inclined patristic writers previously. Nevertheless, the *a priori* assumption was that logic and "dialectical" reasoning (in the scholastic sense) would, if not demonstrate, at least not contravert the dogmas of revelation. St. Augustine, still close to the philosophy of classical antiquity, had said: "I believe in order to understand, and I understand in order to believe" (*credo ut intelligam*; *intelligo ut credam*). St. Anselm, more the mystic, had claimed that the first statement alone sufficed (*neque enim quaero intelligere ut credam, sed credo ut intelligam*). The scholastics now once again placed more emphasis on the second thesis, but at no time was any serious challenge raised against the requirement of unconditional faith in the fundamental Christian mysteries.

Scholastic instruction was carried out by lengthy exposition on Aristotle's texts in relation to others. The meanings were expounded, definitions were formulated, possible objections were raised and answered. Frequently, two or more texts in seeming contradiction were opposed to each other and a solution was found, either by showing that the contradiction was not real, or by demonstrating that one text had to be rejected as inconsistant with a higher authority. Abelard in his *Sic et Non* (early 12th century) had anticipated this method by his confrontation of texts from the Bible alone, but he left the contradictions unsolved. Now St. Thomas Aquinas (1225—74) subjected the Arabianised texts of Aristotle to an elaborate scrutiny (in *Summa contra Gentiles*), in order to sift out the discordant elements which made them unacceptable to Christian thought. The procedure was ambitious; it required a mastery of the knowledge then available, and an incisive ability in the formulating of distinctions. It deferred the appeal to revelation, *a priori* principles and authority to a later stage in the argument—but that appeal had necessarily to be made in the end.

Thus there was no basic conflict between the scholastics and their predecessors as to the ultimate purpose of philosophical disputation. In both cases the argument was obliged to lead to a justification of the same theory of the universe, the same view of man and society. Scholasticism in and of itself did not favour a direct scientific investigation of nature any more than Christianised Platonism and Neo-Platonism had done, despite its greater formal use of reason in the shape of syllogistic argument. After the initial stimulus of discovery, the new learning quickly degenerated into arid commentary and debate. [8]

Still, the vogue of Aristotelianism was in its day a considerable innovation. The university faculties such as Paris and Oxford (organised early in the 13th century) were divided on the value of the new orientation towards logic, physics, and metaphysics; church and state authorities at first condemned the Aristotelian texts to public burning. [9] Even the ambitious critique embodied in the *Summa Theologica* of Thomas Aquinas — since accepted as the citadel of orthodoxy — was regarded with suspicion by some contemporary authorities, who found its method too rationalistic for safety.

The Aristotelian texts, after being duly reconciled with orthodoxy, were actively defended by the preaching friars who were university teachers, and their cause eventually won the day. European universities became absorbed in repetitious commentaries on these textbooks. Question and answer, confrontation of discrepancies and solution by purely logical procedures (plus appeals to authority) continued to be the sole method of advanced instruction. In this way the *Summae* of the 13th and 14th centuries were written by the leading scholastics. Their methods affected the manuals of instruction for laymen which began to appear in the vernacular languages especially after the mid-14th century.

In a few instances the stimulus of recovered Greek scientific texts, combined with favourable social circumstances, led to bold speculation and independent inquiry. The Hohenstaufen Emperor Frederick II (1194—1250), ruler over the Arabo-Graeco-Italianate island of Sicily, profited by the instruction of Mohammedan teachers and developed a strong vein of rationalist thinking which in some ways anticipated the scepticism of French materialist philosophers in the 18th century. His versatile gifts were celebrated in England by Matthew of Paris, who called him *stupor mundi* (wonder of the world). Less unconventional as a thinker but more productive as a scholar was his English contemporary Robert Grosseteste, Bishop of Lincoln (died 1253), who lectured at Oxford on mathematics and science (especially optics), and during his sojourn there encouraged the study of Greek and Hebrew for purposes of Biblical and scientific scholarship. [10] The fresh zeal for compiling scientific information — albeit still unoriginal and quite unverified, in the manner of most writers at the time — is apparent in the ambitious encyclopedia by the Franciscan known as Bartholomew the Englishman, *On the Properties of Things* (Bartholomaeus Anglicus, *De Proprietatibus Rerum*, completed about 1250).

The one scientific writer who towers over all others of the age, both in England and on the continent, was another Franciscan: Roger Bacon (died about 1292). His devotion to science and linguistic studies was first stimulated at Oxford by teachers like Robert Grosseteste, whom he never wearied of praising in his own works. Bacon's conflict with church authorities over the orthodoxy of his studies and beliefs is well known. It led to penalties of long-term confinement which he twice endured at the hands of his order (1257—67 and 1278—92) because of suspected innovations on his part (*propter novitates suspectas*). His interest in the possible advent of a new golden age of human goodness, happiness and equality —an interest stimulated by the confused prophetical writings of Joachim de Flore in Italy—may have contributed to the suspicion with which he was regarded, for the followers of Joachim were denounced as subversive elements in society. Actually Bacon never abandoned any essential religious dogma, nor did he ever go so far as to make reason a higher arbiter than faith. He was one of those who felt confident that reason was an ally of faith. Nor did he attack the reliance upon authority *per se*, but insisted rather that the authorities be good ones, and that they include not only the church Fathers, but also non-Christian scientific writers: Aristotle, Avicenna (whom he called leader and prince of the philosophers after Aristotle) and the Arabs. He not only insisted that such scholars should be read in the original languages, but he mastered the art himself and showed the way to do so for others willing to learn.

But beyond the authorities, Bacon constantly demanded verification by experiment. This, and his attacks upon mere verbalising speculation, were his great contributions to the history of science.[11] Here lay his threat to authority, and perhaps in a tendency to social utopianism, rather than in anything specific he said about religious doctrine. He constantly denounced the intellectual otiosity which permitted lecturers and writers to repeat previous statements blindly, without any attempt to verify them:

It is commonly said [on the basis of a statement by Pliny] that a diamond can not be broken except through the agency of the blood of a goat; and the philosophers and theologicans go on misusing this statement. But there has never been a verification of such breaking by means of blood of this kind, when worked out for this purpose; and without that blood it can easily be broken. For I have seen this with my own eyes *(hoc enim vidi oculis meis)*, and it is necessarily so, for jewels can not be cut save by fragments of this stone.

Such a drive towards experimental science had never before found expression in medieval Europe. Combined with Bacon's wide knowledge of previous scientific lore, and his devotion to mathematics as an instrument

of physical research, it made him an outstanding original thinker and
a contributor, somewhat in the manner of his later namesake, to the
advancement of learning. Bacon's true significance was not appreciated,
however, until modern times, when his works began to appear in scholarly
editions (18th and 19th centuries).

3. TEXTS OF VERNACULAR INSTRUCTION, CHIEFLY RELIGIOUS

Protests and threats of division within the church led to more than
the efforts at institutional reform made early in the 13th century. At
the Fourth Lateran Council Pope Innocent III had also demanded greater
efforts towards educating both the clergy and the laity. As in the times
of Alfred attention was called once again to the shocking ignorance
of people and priests, and of many holding rank above them, concerning
the fundamentals of creed and sacramental services. All bishops of the
several countries represented at the Council were instructed to carry
out education and reform according to the canons of the Council. Part
of the program was a dissemination of knowledge about the seven sacraments, which had been officially recognised by the mid-12th century.

In England, Archbishop Stephen Langton (King John's opponent)
was one of the chief promoters of the Lateran program, as was Bishop
Robert Grosseteste, Bacon's admired teacher. Their reforms made no
attempt to separate the church from the system of feudal exploitation,
but its ministers were required (not for the first time) to raise the level
of their information and their *mores,* and particularly to pass on what
they knew to their parishioners.

The campaign was important because it explicitly stressed teaching
in the vernacular. Robert Grosseteste, for instance, in 1238 enjoined
a program of simple indoctrination embracing the creed, the decalogue,
and the seven sacraments. Especial attention was given to the sacrament
of penance, and connected with it were discussions of the seven major
sins and preparations for confession. All this was to be carried out in
the native tongue (*doceant frequenter laicos in idiomate communi*).[12]
Simultaneously, greater care was to be expended on the preparation
of sermons. The average priest, it was admitted, knew too little and
had too few materials to compose homilies independently. He normally
depended on collections of much older texts made by others. Hence,
the first step was to make a larger number of models available to him:
whole sermons, and illustrative legends and moral tales. He had been
accustomed to memorise mechanically selected sermons from the church
Fathers and others; now the number of models was increased. In this

connection too the use of the vernacular was stressed. In the words of the Bishop of Coventry, sermons were to be prepared *non solum in idiomate Latino, immo in proprio idiomate*.[13] Priests were frequently exhorted to address their congregations simply, too, without any "fantastic texture of subtlety."[14]

The drive to multiply sermons, and to make them more interesting to ordinary people, was greatly intensified by the friars of the preaching orders who were devoting much of their attention especially to the art of homiletics. Out of their activity developed a new interest in improving the techniques of preaching, as is testified in a number of rhetorical hand-books on the subject called *artes praedicandi*.[15] The efforts to teach and to engage popular interest more effectively were in fact very general. They may well have been a response to new demands for education and improvement resulting from the increased prosperity of the 13th century.

Such are the conditions which form the background for the Middle English texts of religious instruction. The impulse spread to instruction not exclusively religious as well.

One of the earliest lengthy texts of the sort is a curious work by an Augustinian canon named Orm. Though numbering about 10,000 lines, his work is incongruously called by the diminutive term *Ormulum* (composed early in the 13th century).[16] It is a verse paraphrase of the Gospels in the mass-book for the whole year, with explanations. The unifying theme is the life of Christ. It is carried out in a set of 32 homilies based on these Gospel texts. The lines of verse are seven-stressed (four feet before the caesura, three afterwards), as in the medieval Latin line called the septenarius. The effect is monotonous and the work as a whole is uninspired, but it has a particular interest for students of the English language. Perhaps as a guide to preachers reading aloud these versified sermons,[17] Orm devised a system of indicating short vowels in closed syllables by doubling the consonants following them:

> For wha-se mot to læwedd follc larspell off goddspell tellenn,
> He mot wel ekenn maniʒ word amang goddspelless wordess.

The very form of this poem, then, bears witness to the interest in popularising homiletic materials in the vernacular.

Ancren Riwle (*Rule of Anchoresses*) is a prose work of much higher literary merit. Its date is a matter of dispute, with some arguments being advanced in favour of the mid-12th century; but a more likely surmise is that it was composed about the same time as the *Ormulum*, but—as its dialect reveals—in the Southwest of England.[18] The purpose was to provide for three women dedicating themselves to solitary religious lives, a combined rule and manual of general advice, in the absence of a traditional rule to live by. The unknown author of the *Riwle* produced much more than a conventional work enjoining strict discipline and denouncing the pleasures of the world. His admonitions, expressed in a spirited colloquial style, are exceptionally liberal when contrasted with the more extreme tracts being written at this time on the misery of worldly life and the need to hold it in contempt [19]. He advises moderation in watching, fasting and other ascetic practices; he urges wide reading to supplement prayer, and gives vivid, detailed and sensible instructions on household arrangements. The three women were of the upper class and were to be attended by servants. Their abnegations were therefore by no means extreme. The passages on religious services, sins, confession and penance are enlivened by allegorical comparisons, anecdotes about animals, proverbs, and many shrewd comments on human foibles which seem to spring from wide experience and observation. The women are warned, for instance, against garrulous autobiography at confession as a form of egoistic display. The author's greatest originality is shown in his treatment of the domestic vices to which women are particularly prone as a result of their environment. The examples he gives throughout are vivid with impressions of kitchen and garden, field and forest. For instance, Eve chattering fatefully to Adam about the forbidden apple is compared to a heedless hen cackling over an egg and thus advertising her presence to a marauding fox:

> ʒe, mine leove sustren, voleweð ure Lefdi and nout þe kakele Eve...
> þe hen, hwon heo haveð ileid, ne con buten kakelen. And hwat biʒit heo
> þerof? Kumeð þe cove [thief] anon riht and reved hire hire eiren, and
> fret al þet of hwat heo schulde vorð bringen hire cwike briddes.

The language, the style, and the outstanding common-sense of *Ancren Riwle* earned it unusual popularity. It not only exists in several later modified forms, but was translated from English into both Latin and French. [20]

Poema Morale is another work of admonition, but shorter and of more general application. It is written in 396 long verse lines resembling Orm's. The dialect is Southern. [21] The opening lines are personal in tone and have a certain lyrical quality:

> Ich em nu alder þene ich wes, a wintre ent a lare,
> Ich welde mare þene ich dede, mi wit ahte bon mare.
> Wel lonʒe ich habbe child i-bon, a worde ent a dede,
> Pah ich bo a wintre ald, to ʒung ich em on rede.

[Ich = I; welde = have strength; bon = be, been; rede = good counsel]

—but very soon the theme becomes just another denunciation of the world and its sinfulness, in very general terms. The poem is not specifically didactic on the subjects of creed and commandments, confession and penance then being intensively taught in the vernacular. It may in fact antedate the other works here being discussed. It has been assigned to ca. 1200, but may have been composed in the latter 12th century.

Genesis and Exodus, [22] a paraphrase of about 4000 lines, was written in Norfolk, ca. 1250 in its present version, and it represents an attempt to disseminate the Biblical narrative in a popular form. It makes use of extra-Biblical texts such as the *Historia Scholastica* of Petrus Comestor. The *Bestiary* is a versified paraphrase of a text already treated in Anglo-Saxon and Anglo-Norman. The edifying unscientific anecdotes and morals about animals and their imagined habits are here put into about 800 lines of East Midland English. The verses combine old traditional alliteration and the newer use of rime. *Body and Soul*, a theme also known in Old English, had meantime been developed into a more ambitious argument in Latin, and was now adapted in English stanzaic verse as a *disputisoun* or disputation on the familiar topic. [23]

Layamon's *Brut* (ca. 1200) has already been mentioned (ch. 7, sec. 1) as an expanded English version of Wace's poem in Norman French on the legendary history of Britain. The English poem is a curious example of native verse narrative whose four-stress lines with caesura and plentiful alliteration suggest a survival of Old English epic techniques in a freer, less rigid form. The author, otherwise unknown, at times achieves exceptional vividness of style, especially in the parts about King Arthur. Layamon's purpose may well have been to popularise historical knowledge in an agreeable form (fictional verse chronicle).

Another form used for instruction was the debate, already long since familiar in Latin exercises of the schools. It was at this time beginning to be cultivated in vernacular languages for many purposes. It became more and more popular in the next age.

The Owl and the Nightingale is an ambitious debate, far superior to its conventional predecessors in both style and originality of theme. Ostensibly it is a discussion between two birds, who are delightfully and satirically humanised as two types of human beings: the one gloomy, studious, carpingly critical and night-loving; the other gracious, gallant, and tolerant towards the human passions if only they are disciplined by rules of courtly behaviour. The date of composition is not known. It has been surmised to be of the late 12th or early 13th century according to internal evidence: almost certainly after the death of Henry II and very probably during the reign of King John. [24] The dialect is of the central South; [25] the name of a certain Nicholas of Guildford appearing at the end as a possible arbiter of the birds' dispute has been thought to refer to the author, but of this also we are unsure.

The Bestiary: Perindes arbor

Bodleian Library

The underlying meaning of the poem has been variously interpreted. It has been said to represent the contrast between asceticism and pleasure, age and youth, wrath and love, philosophy and art, or even between two styles of singing. Preeminently, however, it appears to be the characterisation of two social orders in upper-class feudal society: the clergy (Owl) and nobility (Nightingale). The poet shows no rancour, no deep-going criticism of either, but rather a good-humoured jesting at the extremes of both ways of life. The Owl is accused of needlessly frightening people by his ominous croaking and ungracious discourse; the Nightingale is accused of leading men's souls astray by frivolous songs luring to wordly pleasure. Examples of the latter, cited by the Owl, reveal direct acquaintance with romantic *lais* like those of Marie de France. One curious and important passage (1. 509 ff.) closely echoes the doctrine of Andreas Capellanus in declaring that peasants are incapable of refined love, being subject merely to a transitory physical desire quite different from *amour courtois*:

511   Hit nys for luue nopeles,
        Ac is þeos cherles wode res.

        'Tis not for love, though, none the less,
        It is but this churl's maddened impulse.

If the author is inclined to favour nobility over clergy in his characterisation, the preference is but slight compared with his despairing reference——no doubt justified by the evidence as he saw it—to the brutish ignorance and neglected squalor of the masses. These conditions he attributes to perverse sinfulness, which he of course condemns. His social point of view is clear. But what he writes, within the framework chosen by him, is executed with great skill, lightness of touch, and a masterly command of various sources dealing with the lore of birds.

Lyrics composed in the English language in the 13th century indicate another source of inspiration which affected the author of the *Owl and the Nightingale*. Poetry intended for song has not survived in great quantity from this period, but there is enough to reveal a sense of nature already highly developed, and considerable literary mastery in the expression of personal feeling. The popular and the courtly styles are both represented in these anonymous verses. The love poems —the Nightingale's preferred genre—are generally far more simple and unaffected than those written in French or Provençal, and they appear to spring from broader social strata. A fresh, direct view of flowering fields and singing birds and even wintry landscapes animates even those traditional forms like dialogue and elegy and versified prayer which were clearly imitated from the Latin. The conversation of a Thrush and Nightingale,[26] for instance,

12

is an attractive modest effort in the style more elaborately worked up in *Owl and Nightingale*. A number of the religious lyrics have strong didactic elements, others are adaptations of erotic themes to sacred subjects (love-songs addressed to Christ and Mary), and some are unadorned presentations of intense moments of experience, very powerful in their stark pictorial effect. The following four lines, called "Sunset on Calvary" by their modern editor, achieve force by the choice of images and economy in lyrical expression:

> Nou goth sonne vnder wod[e],—
> me reweth, Marie, þi faire rode.
> Nou goth sonne vnder tre,—
> me reweþ, Marie, þi sone and þe.
>
> Now sets the sun beneath the wood:—
> I sorrow, Mary, for thy fair hue;
> Now sets the sun beneath the tree:—
> I sorrow, Mary, for thy Son and thee.

[rode = face (now sorrow-stained); tre = cross]

The popular elements everywhere conspicuous in these varied songs lead us to suppose that many more of them were composed and lived on people's lips than the limited number that have come down to us in surviving manuscripts. In all of the vernacular poetry of this period, it will be observed, the number of French words is still relatively small.

4. LATIN FABLES AND *EXEMPLA*: THEIR POPULAR APPLICATIONS

While the fairly ambitious efforts at moral and religious instruction were being made in the English language, and technical skill was being developed in lyrics and poems like *Owl and Nightingale*, there was no less activity in the writing of Latin for similar purposes. In fact large collections of material were gathered in order to help make sermons more lively and attractive. The preaching orders were leaders in this activity, but it was not limited to them. Among the types of entertaining illustrations recommended for use in sermons which were to be delivered in translation, one of the most popular was the fable or short story about animals and birds, which also contributed to the creation of the *Owl and Nightingale*. A number of these witty, pointed and frequently satirical tales can be traced back to classical Latin sources (for instance, to Phaedrus and Cornelius Nepos), and to a later collection attributed to an unknown fabulist called Romulus. *The Bestiary*, now available in English as well as French and Latin, added further material. The collections of animal stories were expanded throughout the Middle Ages. [27] Additions were made from time to time

out of the anonymous resources of folklore. Latin tales of the greedy
wolf, the sly and hypocritical fox, the timorous mouse and others had
been adapted to contemporary satire within the monastic schools and
later developed on the continent into a full-fledged mock epic, *Isen-grimus*, with these animals as characters representing familiar types
in medieval society. The fables enlivening sermons were of course very
short. They also contained elements of satire, specifically medieval in
character, and often reflecting feudal conditions.

Especially interesting is the Latin collection of animal stories made
in the early 13th century by Odo of Cheriton, expressly for adaptation
in preparing English sermons. [28] The writer's sympathy is clearly with
the villeins in his congregation, and against the landlords. The popularity
of his fables, indicated by the number of manuscript copies of them
still extant, is thus readily understood. For instance, one fable tells about
a wolf who nearly strangled on a bone until his servants thought of fetch-ing a long-billed stork to pull it out. But instead of rewarding his
benefactor, the wolf shouts harshly: "It's enough that I didn't kill you
when your head was in may maw!" And Odo comments: "Thus the poor
people and the countrymen, when they serve their lords, can obtain no
reward. For the lord says: Thou art my man; is it not enough that I do
not have thy skin stripped off, but let thee live?" Greedy monks and
friars are subjected to similar gibes in the characters of animals.

But it was the preaching friars themselves, not the beneficed priests
like Odo, who did most to enliven sermons by illustrative tales and
anecdotes. Such materials, called *exempla*, were gathered by them and put
down in Latin in the 13th and early 14th centuries; later, in the 14th
and 15th, came the compilations in English. [29] The friars welcomed the
most heterogenous and seemingly inappropriate anecdotes, provided only
they were entertaining and could be given a perfunctory moral twist
at the end, after they had aroused the listeners' attention. Not only the
more lively episodes from the Bible and saints' lives, from classical and
medieval history were exploited to this end, but also fiction, fairy tales,
jokes, bits of gossip, folklore and real events in the district which preachers
mention as "seen and heard by myself" (*visa et audita*).

Since the aim was mass appeal, and to an exceptional degree the
friars identified themselves with the masses, many of the anecdotes
are laden with bitter satire against the vices inherent in rich people,
and detailed descriptions are sometimes given of their sufferings after
death. In a Latin collection made in England by a Franciscan, *The Laymen's
Mirror (Speculum Laicorum, [30] ca. 1280), we read a startling accounf
of the torments visited upon a rich lord's cruel bailiff in hell because
of the "calumnies and accusations, robberies and extortions, imprison-

ments and tortures" he had inflicted on the peasants. After death he appeared to one of the poor tenants "in a black tunic, sticking out his tongue and with his own hand cutting it in little bits by means of a razor, and then casting those same pieces into his mouth and once more thrusting out his tongue, all whole again, and cutting it, and so on continually... He said that he had undergone this suffering because of the burdensome expenditures he had so often imposed on the poor folk, and lifting up his tunic, he showed his body glowing like red-hot iron." Another Latin collection made at the same time in England, *A Book of Exempla for Preachers* (*Liber Exemplorum in Usum Praedicantium*,[31] ca. 1270), is notable because it records customs and superstitions observed by friars abroad in Ireland and Denmark, and cited for sermons at home. It is one of a number of collections using an alphabetical system to classify the tales according to the sins denounced, from sloth (*accidia*) to the taking of interest on money (*usuria*). Many anecdotes are told about the vanity, extravagance and unseemly dress of women. Since these too are largely directed against the vices of idle, wealthy ladies, the class angle is often clearly apparent.

Later, in the 14th century, a collection of stories was put together from both literary and oral sources: classical, feudal-romantic and Oriental, with much less reference to contemporary conditions. It was called the *Gesta Romanorum* (*Deeds of the Romans*). The plots are often quite worldly, even occasionally vulgar, but a moral explanation is always solemnly attached. In this way, somewhat distorted to be sure, many famous plots and myths were first introduced to popular audiences in Western Europe, including the story of the Three Caskets later adapted by Shakespeare in *The Merchant of Venice* and the motif of the Three Rings appearing in Lessing's *Nathan der Weise*. Sometimes the stories were told to illustrate elaborate systems of the vices and sins, classified and subdivided in detail. Not only in England but elsewhere the passion for collecting Latin *exempla* was general in the 13th century. A collection by the French Dominican named Etienne de Bourbon, the *Tractatus de Diversis Materiis Praedicantibus* (ca. 1250) exists in one manuscript version containing no less than 2857 *exempla*.[32] We shall see how, in the next century, English writers made use of such collected plots for many different literary purposes.

5. ANGLO-FRENCH DIDACTIC LITERATURE; EXPANSION OF ALLEGORY

The social stimuli which produced longer didactic works in Middle English similarly affected French writers in England. Robert Grosseteste, already several times mentioned for his educational and scientific activities (above, sec. 1 and 2), composed an Anglo-Norman allegory embodying essentials of religious doctrine for laymen. His *Chateau d'Amour* (*Castle of Divine Love*) recounts in outline the story of man's fall and his redemption, in terms of a rebellious serf who is nevertheless succoured by a wise and benevolent master after he has forfeited his legal right to help. The allegorical castle in this poem is the Virgin Mary who prepared the way for redemption. Robert's purpose in using French is made clear in the opening lines:

15 Tuz avum mestier d'aie, Of help do all men stand in need
  Mes trestuz ne poüm mie But all of us can not indeed
  Saver le langage en fin Acquire the Hebrew tongue nor eke
  D'ebreu de griu ne de latin, Read in Latin or in Greek
  Pur loer sun creatur... To give to their Creator praise...

26 En romanz comenz ma reson This fable I have now begun
  Pur ceus ki ne sevent mie To tell you in the Romance tongue
  Ne lettreüre ne clergie. For folk that learning lack and letters.

This text was later translated into English.[33] Robert Grosseteste also showed concern for the improvement of men's physical well-being, for he translated into French the *Manual of Husbandry* by Walter of Henley (mid-13th century)—a very important document in the history of English agriculture.

In France proper, the use of allegory for didactic purposes was greatly expanded at this time. In fact, a broad school of writing developed in this genre, which supplied models for imitation and translation in English, as in other tongues, for two centuries to come. One very important device was worked out by a number of poets: the combination of a vision of the other world (as in the *Visio Pauli* and other 12th century Latin poems) with the narrative form of a pilgrimage peopled by the allegorical vices and virtues so frequently imitated since Prudentius. Thus the French poet Raoul de Houdenc (early 13th century) dreams of a pilgrimage from one inn or court of hell to the next,[34] watching the followers of allegorised sins and beholding the horrible torments inflicted on the human perpetrators of those sins: notably on the "Bulgars" or Manichean heretics, who are having their tongues roasted. Rutebeuf (latter 13th century), in *La Voie de Paradis* (*Road to Paradise*)[35] also dreams of the strongholds on the road to hell, against which he is warned by Pity, at great length, and of the narrower path to heaven which lies beyond the city of repentance.

Most ambitious of these edifying dream-visions in French were three written by Guillaume de Déguileville, a monk of Valois in France (first half of the 14th century). In an extensive allegory, *Le Pèlerinage de la Vie humaine* (1330),[36] the poet recounts his dream-adventures in trying to reach the heavenly Jerusalem, which he had seen reflected in a mirror. He is strengthened by the virtues, tempted by various sins, and endlessly lectured at by such characters as Reason, Nature, Grace-Dieu, Penance, Labour, Idleness, and many others. In the author's revised version, this text numbered no less than 24,832 lines. It was not only translated into English verse in the 15th century by John Lydgate (see ch. 13, sec. 3), but was put into several prose translations, one of which (an abbreviated form) dating from the 17th century,[37] may actually have been seen by John Bunyan and have affected the composition of his *Pilgrim's Progress*. Guillaume de Déguileville composed two other ambitious allegories: *Le Pèlerinage de l'Ame* and *Le Pèlerinage de Jesu-Christ*. His work represents the high point of religious didactic allegory in French. In many ways it foreshadows the English 14th-century visions like *Piers Plowman* (see ch. 10, sec 4), though Guillaume was far more prolix and repetitious than the English writers. The generic resemblance to Dante's *Divina Commedia* is much clearer in the French visions than in the 12th-century Latin ones which preceded them.

Even more influential for English literature was a didactic allegorical dream-vision in French which treated a theme ostensibly romantic, not religious. This was the *Romance of the Rose* (*Roman de la Rose*), begun in the middle years of the 13th century by Guillaume de Lorris, and completed on an enlarged scale by Jean de Meun (died ca. 1303) towards its end.[38] The plan, as narrative, is very simple. The poet dreams that he is walking by a clear stream on a lovely spring day. It leads him to an enclosed garden surrounded by a decorated wall. Figures carved on the outside of this portray the characteristics most inimical to love: Old Age, Poverty, Hatred, Avarice, Envy, Villainy, etc. These must forever remain excluded from the garden, for it is love's domain, where dwell such personages as Youth, Courtesy, Mirth, Fair Welcome (Bel Acueil) and Generosity. The gate to the garden is opened to the dreamer by Idleness (Oiseuse), for as Andreas Capellanus himself would have said, none can enjoy the society within the walls unless he has much time at his disposal, as well as money, social position and youth, to dedicate to the amorous art.

Inside the garden, the dreamer soon espies a beautiful rose bush reflected in a crystal spring. One half-opened blossom, obviously representing a young girl, attracts his admiration. While he gazes upon it, the God of Love (Cupid) wounds him with an arrow. Smitten with desire, and encouraged by his ally Fair Welcome at the instance of Venus, the dreamer rashly tries to steal a kiss from the Rose. But his hasty gesture, result of an undisciplined natural impulse, violates the code of courtly behaviour between the sexes. Allegorical figures like Shame, Jealousy and Danger (here meaning feminine pride, apparently) surround the rose-bud, and a wall of opposition cuts him off from it. Fair Welcome, who alone had made possible his abrupt approach to the Rose, is imprisoned in a tower, over which these negative forces stand guard. A vigilant old women, a Duenna (La Vieille), is put in charge of him. Obviously the lover must learn to discipline his natural desire with courtly behaviour before he can again approach the Rose.

So far Guillaume de Lorris developed his rather charming allegory of a lover's induction into the system of courtly love. When he left it unfinished he must have been near the end of his planned work. Nothing remained but to describe the lover's second, more circumspect campaign to win the Rose, and his ultimate success. But no more of his work is known to have been written, beyond the 4282 lines now extant.

When Jean de Meun took up the allegory to conclude it, forty or fifty years later, he quite transformed its character. The lover's efforts and victory became a mere framework upon which the second poet attached long satirical digressions, philosophical reflections, and passages containing scientific and historical lore, moral instruction and the like. He made use of Guillaume's attractive scheme, no doubt already known to many readers, in order to popularize in the vernacular a whole miscellany of philosophy and general information among secular readers.

The rest of the story itself, now a matter of secondary interest (though totalling 18,326 additional lines) is easily told. Despite an appeal by Reason to abandon his entire plan, the lover calls upon the god of love to help him in the storming of the tower where Fair Welcome languishes. An army of allegorical "barons" is mustered for the attack. It includes, Riches, Gallantry, Courtesy—and especially False-Seeming or Social Hypocrisy (which enables a lover to appear harmless while he is actually planning seduction). These undertake to deal with their opposites defending the Rose, in a kind of courtly Psychomachia. At a critical moment the god of love summons his mother Venus (sensual passion) who in turn impels Nature to activity. Nature's priest, called Genius, is sent to harangue the army of love and to direct it in the final successful assault upon the defenses surrounding the Rose.

Jean de Meun's digressions usually take the form of long speeches delivered by leading allegorical characters. The old Duenna, for instance, though employed to keep Fair Welcome from the Rose, chatters amiably and garrulously with him about women and their wiles, frequently citing her own wide experiences in handling lovers during her very active youth. The tone is satirical, much of the substance being imitated from the Latin patristic and medieval denunciations of woman's vanity, frivolity and lust. But the form and technique are brilliantly original.

The Duenna evokes vivid scenes in polite society, gives lifelike and detailed accounts of table manners, flirtations, clothing, cosmetics, food and drink, fragments of conversation. She pours out advice on the management of several lovers simultaneously, the concealment of natural defects (bad breath, scanty hair, undeveloped bust), the effective use of tears and laughter. One does not soon forget the picture of an overdressed dame, bent on amorous conquest, sailing down a muddy street like a proud ship, lifting her full skirts fore and aft to display a well-turned ankle, or flourishing a delicate hand for all to admire. The whole discourse is spiced with anecdotes, *exempla*, and heart-felt exclamations of regret for past joys or opportunities neglected. This figure, though in one sense an allegorical abstraction, is a literary forerunner of Chaucer's unforgettable Wife of Bath (who owes much to her), and of the Nurse in Shakespeare's *Romeo and Juliet*. The zestful portrayals by Jean de Meun, enlivening the course of an abstract allegory, seem to reveal a strong inner sympathy with the very types of people he is supposed to be satirising.

Many other subjects arouse Jean to satire, but none more bitterly than the hypocrisy which he finds prevalent among the friars. When False-Seeming is enlisted to help break down the defenses of the Rose, he puts on the garb of a friar. Jean thereupon denounces the mendicants for greed, laziness, and the shirking of duties arising from a normal life: labour and the rearing of children. It is all very well, he says, for the few chosen persons with a calling for religious lives—for saintliness or learning— to withdraw from the world and become celibates, but most of the friars and the monks too are merely lazy men looking for an easy life. They are abhorrent to Nature, who denounces them roundly, because they frustrate her efforts to replenish mankind biologically; they hamper her in the age-long war conducted by her against Death, eternally depleting her ranks. Nature's complaint, and her confession to the priest Genius, echo many of the concepts of the Latin Platonists of Chartres in the 12th century. Jean's Nature, speaking French instead of Latin, inclines to be pantheistic like the similar characters in earlier poems, though in all these cases she admits her subordination to the Christian God.

The figure of Nature dominates the last part of the *Romance of the Rose*. She permits the poet to talk at length about geography and meteorology, animal lore and cosmology. The newer learning is reflected in the long digression on mirrors, lenses and optics, which engaged the attention of Robert Grosseteste and Roger Bacon. The contemporary compendia of history and mythology are plundered by Jean for numerous *exempla* to illustrate both main plot and digressions. The philosophical problems of fate and free will, the rival claims of reason and natural impulse, are presented fluently, clearly and with charm, so that any moderately educated reader of the time could grasp and also enjoy the exposition.

The popularity of the *Romance of the Rose* is very easy to understand. Its importance for English literature can only be measured after a detailed study of the many allegories of entertainment and instruction modeled upon it from the 14th to the end of the 15th century, and even later, spanning the periods of time between Jean de Meun and Edmund Spenser.

[1] A.R. Myers, *England in the Late Middle Ages* (London, 1952), Part i, ch. 3; J.E.T. Rogers, *Six Centuries of Work and Wages* (London, 1912), ch. 2.

[2] This was the erroneous assumption of English bourgeois-liberal historians in the 19th century, in large part due to their failure to recognise the character and role of revolutionary forces in successive phases of medieval history. For critique and corrections see Е. А. Косминский, *Исследования аграрной истории Англии XII века* (Москва, 1947), English translation (Oxford, 1956),

[3] Rogers, *loc. cit.*, especially p. 67 f.; see also the general studies by G.G. Coulton, *The Medieval Village* (Cambridge, 1925); H.S. Bennett, *Life on the English Manor* (Cambridge, 1938); G.C. Homans, *English Villagers in the Thirteenth Century* (Harvard University Press, 1942).

[4] Compare the discussion of Magna Carta in William Stubbs, *The Constitutional History of England*, I (Oxford, 6th ed., 1897), pp. 569—79 with the article "Великая Карта Вольностей," *Большая Советская Енсиклопедия*, IX (1928); 2nd. ed. VII (1951), p. 212.

[5] On the jurists see Charles Gross, *Sources and Literature of English History* (London, 1915), pp. 312—14; A.J. Carlyle, *A History of Medieval Political Theory in the West*, III (Edinburgh, 1928). Bracton, *De Legibus et Consuetudinibus Angliae* has been edited by George E. Woodbine, 3 vols, (Yale University Press, 1915—40)

[6] Kenneth Vickers, *England in the Later Middle Ages* (London, 1919).

[7] For a detailed history, see G.G. Coulton, *Five Centuries of Religion*, I—II (Cambridge, 1927—29).

[8] Hastings Rashdall, revised by F.M. Powicke and A.B. Emden, *The Universities of Europe*, III (Oxford, 1936).

[9] In 1210 a Council of Paris forbade the teaching of Aristotle and ordered his works burnt. In 1231 the texts on physics and metaphysics were excluded from teaching by Pope Gregory IX; the decree was reaffirmed by a legate in 1265.

[10] Francis Seymour Stevenson, *Robert Grosseteste, Bishop of Lincoln* (London, 1899).

[11] Roger Bacon, *Opus Majus*, ed. John Henry Bridges, 3 vols. (London, 1900) For references see George Sarton, *Introduction to the History of Science*, II, Part i (London, 1931). Stewart Easton has collected facts and bibliography in *Roger Bacon and his Search for a Universal Science* (Oxford, 1952); the biographical interpretations are however often very speculative.

[12] E.J. Arnould, *Le Manuel des Péchés: Étude de littérature religieuse Anglo-Normande* (Paris, 1940), quotation on p. 20.

[13] Quotation from · C.R. Cheney, *English Synodalia* (London, 1941), p. 150 in D.W. Robertson, Jr., "Frequency of Preaching in Thirteenth-Century England," *Speculum*, XXIV (1949), 376 — 88, especially p. 383. The orthography is here normalised.

[14] In the words of Archbishop Peckham (1281): "Vulgariter absque cujuslibet subtilitatis textura fantastica." See D.W. Robertson, *loc. cit.*

[15] See. H. Caplan, *Medieval Artes Praedicandi*: *A Handlist* (Cornell University Press, 1934); Th. M. Charland, *Artes Praedicandi*: *Contribution a l'histoire de la rhétorique du moyen âge* (Ottawa, 1936).

[16] *Ormulum*, ed. R.M. White and R. Holt (Oxford, 1878). For discussion see Heinrich C. Matthes, *Die Einheitlichkeit des Ormulum* (Heidelberg, 1933); Hans H. Glunz, *Die Literarästhetik des europäischen Mittelalters* (Bochum-Langendreer, 1937), pp. 311 — 29 (containing some debatable suggestions).

[17] The suggestion is made by R.M. Wilson, *op. cit.*, p. 175 f.

[18] Hope Emily Allen, "The Origin of the Ancren Riwle," *PMLA*, XXXIII (1918), 474 — 546, XLIV (1929), 635 — 80, and L (1935), 899 — 902, has tried to identify the three anchoresses in question with three noble-born ladies resident in a hermitage Kilburn under Westminster Abbey, between 1127 and 1135. Most scholars are doubtful about this very early date, especially since the dialect does not accord with the location of the hermitage. A.C. Baugh, *Literary History of England*, argues for a date ca. 1200. Miss Allen's articles have general value, however, for the light they throw on female monasticism in the 12th century, before the founding of the orders for women. For a survey of theories and problems see R. W. Chambers, "Recent Research upon Ancren Riwle," *Review of English Studies*, I (1925), 4 — 23.

[19] Typical of the gloomy view are *De Contemptu Mundi* written by Pope Innocent III, ca. 1200, and the poem by Bernard of Morlaix on the same subject, beginning: "Hora novissima, tempora pessima sunt: vigilemus."

[20] Charlotte D'Evelyn, *The Latin Text of the Ancren Riwle*, EETS, OS, No. 216 (1944); J.R. Hulbert, *The French Text of the Ancren Riwle, ibid.*, No. 219 (1944). Recent studies leave no doubt that the English was the original, not either of these two. The English text was first edited by J. Morton for the Camden Society (1853). a new edition edited by Mabel Day has appeared in the EETS, OS, No. 225 (1952). *Ancren Wisse* was a revised form of the *Riwle* adapted about 1230 for a larger community. A 14th-century revision called *The Recluse* has interpolations showing Lollard influence; see Eric Colledge in *Review of English Studies*, XV (1939), 1 — 15 and 129 — 45. On the later influence of the text see John Fisher, "Continental Associations for the Ancren Riwle," *PMLA*, XLIV (1949), 1180 — 89.

[21] Ed. H. Marcus, *Das frühmittelenglische "Poema Morale"* (Leipzig, 1934). J. Hall, *Selections from Early Middle English*, I (Oxford, 1920).

[22] *Genesis and Exodus*, ed. R. Morris, EETS, OS, No. 7 (1865).

[23] Ed. R. Morris in *An Old English Miscellany*, EETS, OS, No. 49 (1872). For the *Debate between Body and Soul* see J. Hall, *Selections from Early Middle English*.

[24] *The Owl and the Nightingale*, ed. J.W.H. Atkins (Cambridge, 1922); diplomatic print of the two 13th-century MSS, by J.H.G. Grattan and G.F. Sykes, EETS, ES, No. 119 (1935). Henry B. Hinkley has argued for a date before the death of Henry II in *PMLA* XLIV (1929), 329 — 59, as has Kathryn Huganir (but for different reasson) in *The Owl and the Nightingale* (Philadelphia, 1931). Strong arguments for a later date (between 1189 and 1216) are given by Frederick Tupper, *PMLA*, XLIX (1934),

406 ff. A.C. Cawley, "Astrology in *The Owl and the Nightingale*," *Modern Language Review*, XLVI (1951), 161—74, finds internal evidence for composition after 1186, probably after 1189.

[25] Bertil Sundby, *The Dialect and Provenance of the Middle English Poem* The Owl and the Nightingale (Lund, 1950) has not been accessible to me.

[26] Carleton Brown, ed., *English Lyrics of the XIIIth Century* (Oxford, 1923).

[27] See E. Moll, "Zur Geschichte der mittelalterlichen Fabelliteratur," *Zeitschrift für romanische Philologie*, IX (1885), 161—203; L. Hervieux, *Les Fabulistes latins depuis le siècle d'Augustus jusqu'à la fin du moyen âge*, I (Paris, 1893). For the use in Middle English, see F.R. Whitesell, "Fables in Mediaeval Exempla," *Journal of English and Germanic Philology*, XLVI (1947), 348—66 (a systematic tabulation).

[28] L. Hervieux, *Les Fabulistes latins*, IV (Paris, 1896); Albert C. Friend, "Master Odo of Cheriton," *Speculum*, XXIII (1948), 641—58. The fables are edited by E. Voigt, *Liber Parabolarum* in *Quellen und Forschungen*, XXV (1878). The English *Bestiary* has been edited by M.R. James for the Roxburghe Club (1936). For general discussion see Beatrice White, "Medieval Animal Lore," *Anglia*, LXXII (1954), 21—30.

[29] On the general type see Joseph Albert Mosher, *The Exemplum in the Early Religious and Didactic Literature of England* (Columbia University Press, 1911); J.-Th. Welter, *L'Exemplum dans la littérature religieuse et didactique du moyen âge* (Paris, 1927). Especially valuable is G.R. Owst, *Literature and Pulpit in Medieval England* (Cambridge, 1933).

[30] *Speculum Laicorum*, ed. J.-Th. Welter (Paris, 1914), cap. 11, p. 17 f.

[31] Ed. A.G. Little (Aberdeen, 1908).

[32] J.-Th. Welter, *L'Exemplum*, p. 215 n.

[33] French text, ed. J. Murray (Paris, 1918); there are several Middle English translations. For references see John Edwin Wells, *A Manual of the Writings in Middle English* (Yale University Press, 1916), p. 820 f.

[34] Raoul de Houdenc, *Le Songe d'Enfer*, ed. A. Jubinal, *Mystères inédites*, II (Paris, 1837), pp. 384—403.

[35] Rutebeuf, *Oeuvres complètes*, ed. A. Jubinal (Paris, 1847), pp. 169—203.

[36] Two recensions were made by the poet, the latter ca. 1355. See the edition for the Roxburghe Club, vol. 124.

[37] MS. Cambridge Library Ff.6.30; see K.B. Locock, introduction to Lydgate's translation, EETS, ES, No. 92 (1904).

[38] On the authors of the poem see Ernst Langlois, *Le Roman de la Rose*, I, SATF (Paris, 1914). A general discussion in relation to English literature is given by C.S. Lewis, *The Allegory of Love* (Oxford, 2nd. ed. 1938).

PART III

LATER MIDDLE ENGLISH

CHAPTER IX

THE FLOURISHING OF ROMANCE AND DIDACTIC LITERATURE IN ENGLISH

1. ROMANCES OF ADVENTURE: ENGLISH AND GERMANIC THEMES

The literature intended to entertain aristocratic listeners in England of the later Middle Ages followed much the same pattern as that produced for the like purpose in France. In many instances the same plots were used. The same ingredients went into the literary mixture: warlike adventure, whether in the form of internal feuds, crusades against Saracens or encounters with supernatural foes; love and chivalrous service performed for noble ladies; complications of personal relations such as false accusations, the separation and reuniting of families, quests for information, for revenge, for magic talismans. English romancers handled many types of plots. French writers supplied the greatest number of them, whether directly or indirectly, from sources ultimately classical, Oriental, Celtic and Germanic. Here was an international literature (if one may apply a contemporary term to the past), of varied origins, appropriate to the age preceding modern nationhood. The institutions of feudalism, being in some senses supra-national, made use of a supra-national fund of romantic fiction.

Nevertheless the English treatments achieved a characteristic emphasis and a transformed atmosphere of their own.[1] In brief, it may be said that English poets treating of the international love romances avoid the over-refined analyses of sentiment and behaviour which were characteristic, for instance, of predecessors like Chrétien de Troyes in French. Instead, they more often stress action and adventure; they also concentrate less often on elegant adultery and more often have the stories culminate in the "happy ending" of a conventional marriage. Courtly love plays a role here, but not an overwhelming one.

In the earlier part of the period being considered (ca. 1250 to 1400), the long romances were evidently composed for direct oral delivery by poet-entertainers in the halls of noble patrons. By the end of that period, the mode of production and consumption had, so to speak, undergone an economic transformation. The English aristocracy had grown in numbers, in wealth, and in literacy. Its representatives no longer depended exclusively on oral entertainment; they began to aspire to ownership of romance texts for private reading. Manuscripts of the late 14th century and the 15th were executed for such purchasers with careful attention to beauty of appearance. With their fine lettering and glowing illustrations done on parchment or superior paper, they differ strikingly from the undecorated, much-worn, hastily written texts for the practical use of ordinary minstrels, samples of which have also come down to us. By the end of the 14th century the demand for chivalrous fiction in verse had become so great that something of an attempt was made to "rationalise" its production. Not only the copying but also the very composition of romances was organised in a kind of elementary system of manufacture. We have evidence of at least one commercial enterprise of the sort in London which gave out piece work to be done on the romances in popular demand, by hack writers who received apportioned jobs of translation and adaptation. In this fashion, it appears, the famous Auchinleck manuscript collection of romances was put together. [2]

A rather small group of romances deals with heroes represented as English in origin or residence [3]. These include some of the oldest representatives of the literary type in England. They are also among the least amorous or sentimental in tone.

King Horn (early 13th century)[4] is a lively tale of a prince abducted from his homeland of "Suddene" (probably South Dean, Scotland) as a tender youth, when it is invaded by the "Saracens" (i.e., the pagan Vikings). He twice enters the service of a foreign king, once in Westerness (England), and once in Ireland; twice he performs valorous deeds for the king being served, and on both occasions he wins the love of the king's daughter. He is the victim of treachery, which he punishes; he tactfully avoids marriage with the second princess, in order to return to the first, named Rimenhild, who has been waiting for him in England for seven years. In the end he returns to Suddene and reclaims the country from the usurping Saracens. The fundamental theme of the story is thus a formula of a hero's expulsion and return, with intervening adventures: a very popular structure of epic fiction in feudal and pre-feudal times.

Though its setting is English, this tale was first treated in Anglo-Norman as *Horn et Rimel* (ca. 1180; see ch. 7, sec. 3). The English adaptation has a certain forceful directness of style and a lively movement in its action, which is rapidly depicted in short verses riming in pairs. The heroine Rimenhild is remarkable for her direct action and speech, for

Knights Jousting

Walters Gallery, Baltimore

it is she who does the wooing, while Horr, the stranger, is reluctant to accept her love. Uncomplicated in plot and psychology, the tale was probably an effective item in the repertoire of a professional minstrel earning his living by oral recitation. A later version in English, on the other hand, one of the Auchinleck romances called *Horn Childe and Maiden Rimnild*, reduces the simplicity to banality, and the language to stereotyped artificiality.

Havelok the Dane (latter 13th century),[5] is another tale of exile and return, also preceded by a Norman French romance of the late 12th century.[6] (The latter is, however, not the direct source of the English.) Havelok, son of Birkabein, is heir to the Danish throne, but a wicked usurper threatens his life and he is forced to flee to England accompanied by a kindly fisherman named Grim. Here he and his protector do manual labour to earn their living. By his prowess in sports Havelok wins the daughter of King Athelwold as his bride, for she too has become the victim of a usurping guardian after her father's death. This man had planned to get rid of her by declassing her socially:

> 1091   For he wende, þat Hauelok wore
> Sum cherles sone, and no more.

[wende = supposed;   wore = were]

Of course Havelok overthrows the usupers in both Denmark and England and reigns happily over both realms, together with his wife.

The names of these personages are Germanic. Birkabein is a genuine Scandinavian epithet, famous in the 12th century, and Havelok has been identified tentatively with Olaf or Anlaf Cuaran, the Viking ruler of Ireland who fought with King Athelstan at Brunanburh in 937. The plot, however, is pure fiction, and that of the simplest kind. Connection with historical personages, if any, is most tenuous. The least stereotyped character is Grim the fisherman, a common worker idealised for upper-class audiences because of his devotion to the hero. His presence no doubt aided the popular reception of the romance among wider groups of the population than the aristocracy. It is Grim whose integrity and skill shine clearest in the realm of practical affairs. With reason the poet honours him by making him the eponymous founder of the city of Grimsby in Lincolnshire. His figure dominates the poem as it does the Great Seal of Grimsby, on which Havelok and his wife appear as pigmies sheltered under his arms. The popularity of *Havelok* is indicated by the fact that Robert Manning of Brunne (see below, sec. 5) mentioned it as current among "lewd" (i.e., lay) folk in English, and a later interpolator inserted a condensed account of it into Robert's translation of Peter Langtoft's chronicle.

Guy of Warwick and *Beves of Hamtoun* are also popular romances which, though featuring English persons and localities, closely followed previous French treatments of the same themes. In both, the events are commonplaces of European romantic fiction, lacking any foundation in specifically English conditions. Yet the English versions, as usual, achieved a quality of their own, through characteristic traits of expression. Both romances are among the texts preserved in the Auchinleck manuscript.

Sir Beves of Hamtoun (ca. 1300),[7] originating in an Anglo-Norman romance of the 13th century, starts its hero on his career of exile and adventure by having him persecuted at the hands of his stepfather and his own mother, who had previously incited her present husband to kill her first. In the fabulous East of medieval fiction, Beves later wins the love of a Saracen princess named Josiane, but narrowly escapes death at the instigation of her father. While he performs prodigies of valour against adversaries both human and monstrous, the princess employs both magic and homicide to keep herself unmarried until his return. Having rescued her from imminent execution for hanging an unwanted husband, Beves carries her off, promptly converts her to Christianity, returns with her to England, and there defeats and kills his stepfather. Here the story should end, but an appendix to it sends Beves into exile once more, separates him from his wife and small sons, and provides him with further adventures before the family is reunited and the parents retire to the East together.

Because two of Beves's adventures vaguely recall the plot of *Hamlet* as told by Saxo Grammaticus (ca. 1200)—that is, the hero's conflict with a stepfather guilty of his father's death, and the device of a sealed letter ordering the hero's execution, which he unwittingly carries from one king to another—an attempt has been made to connect the two plots. There has also been speculation on the generic relations between Beves and the exiled hero Havelok.[8] But all these motifs, like others in *Beves*, are commonplaces of romance and folklore. What the entertainers did in concocting such a tale as *Beves* was to draw upon a popular treasury of well-known themes, some of them originating in the revenge feuds of the Viking age and some much older, and to put them together somehow, obtaining variety and some measure of originality by the varying of combinations in the plots and characters. The language and versification also offered some opportunity for the display of individual skill. In none of these respects is *Sir Beves* a work of outstanding literary merit. In fact, it displays some of the conspicuous weaknesses of made-to-order epic narrative at its least inspired. These were the defects which lent themselves to satire in a later and more sophisticated period.

Guy of Warwick (oldest version ca. 1300, French sources of ca. 1200 or earlier),[9] shows the same characteristics. It is built on the perennial theme of a youthful champion sprung from the minor aristocracy (Guy is the son of the Earl of Warwick's steward) who aspires to the love of a high-born lady (the Earl's daughter), and finally wins her in marriage by distinguishing himself in a series of adventures at home and abroad. There is the usual quota of single combats against natural and supernatural enemies. The romance is vaguely associated with King Athelstan and the Danish invasions under someone called Anlaf (Scandinavian Olaf), but the enemies encountered abroad are Saracens. *Guy of Warwick* is exceptional in permitting the hero to become an old man, to turn devout, and to end his days as a hermit. A sequel of *Guy of Warwick*, named *Reinbrun*, tells of the adventures of the hero's son after being stolen and presented to an African king. The plot is a tissue of quests and rescues. It testifies to the appetite for continuations to such adventure stories as Guy's. Mere wordiness and repetition of incidents were no deterrent to the popularity of these patch-work narratives, if the hero had once established himself in general favour. The theme of patriotic service in time of invasion, though not strongly emphasised, may have been a factor in making Guy a popular hero.

Athelston (written ca. 1350; no French source known)[10] differs from *Beves* and *Guy* in treating themes close to home with a certain harsh and convincing reality. It is based on a motif of court intrigue and violent action which reflects contemporary *mores* with some fidelity, as we can surmise from analogous incidents recounted in historical sources. Yet the plot itself has no basis in any actual events connected with King Athelstan. It tells how that King readily gives credence to slanderous reports of a treacherous plot against himself, presumably being organised by the Queen and an eminent feudal subject. The accuser is impelled by pure envy of the accused. The King, convinced without evidence, furiously kicks his pregnant wife and thus destroys his unborn child. Intervention by the Archbishop merely provokes a royal threat of dismissal, but the Archibshop counters with excommunication and interdict, the people prepare to revolt, the Archbishop establishes the innocence of the accused Queen and her supposed confederate, by having the latter undergo an ordeal. The accuser's guilt is thereupon revealed, also by ordeal, and so obedience is restored and justice is vindicated.

Here the underlying motif is a combination of false accusation and exculpation by ordeal. Medieval fiction abounds in such situations. Usually the victim is a beautiful and innocent queen charged with adultery or (as here) treasonable conspiracy or (in plots closer to primitive folklore) with witchcraft, infanticide and the like.[11] She may be vindicated by a personal ordeal such as lifting a red-hot iron with impunity, or by a champion's victory, or the discovery (usually years later) of evidence decisively clearing her good name. Thus in *Emaré* (latter 14th century),[12] a fairly close analogue of Chaucer's Man of Law's Tale, the Queen suffers persecution and long exile because her mother-in-law accuses her of giving birth to a monster; in *Le Bone Florence de Rome* (ca. 1400),[13] a less close analogue, she suffers a like fate because her brother-in-law charges her with adultery during her husband's absence. The use of an ordeal by combat to clear the accused party is best exemplified in the well-told *Erl of Toulous* (after 1350; probably 15th century),[14] marked by unusual ethical sensitivity.

Like other stories of accused queens, *Athelston* has touches of pathos easily degenerating by way of exaggeration into the sentimental; it has interest for us because it shows the severe treatment no doubt often meted out to the victims of court intrigue in real life.[15]

Richard Coeur de Lion (early 14th century)[16] like *Athelston* is attached to the name of an historical personage, and indeed it more or less follows the course of Richard's carreer, though embellished by much exaggeration, including elements of the supernatural. The hero shows traits of wanton brutality outdoing even the attested performances of his historical prototype. He is for instance represented as zestfully feeding off the boiled heads of captured Saracens, in the presence of messengers who are their countrymen. Gory descriptions were of course not uncommon in crusading tales, both French and English, but Richard's cannibalism is exceptional.

Gamelyn (ca. 1350),[17] unlike some of these others, is a truly English story in both setting and style. Simpler than they, it is however constructed on the ubiquitous theme of exile and return so often used in them. The youngest of three brothers, a champion at wrestling, is cheated of his inheritance by the eldest and cast into chains. He is thence rescued by a faithful servant named Adam: faithful, that is, but not quite disinterested:

> 417   He vnlokked Gamelyn   boþe hand and feet
>   In hope of auauncement   þat he him byheet [promised].

These two join a band of outlaws. With their aid and that of the loyal second brother, summary if not legal justice is executed on the oldest, together with his corrupt judge. The poet comments with bitter satisfaction: "He was hanged by the neck and not by the purse!" This rough-and-ready narrative was at times most improbably attributed to Chaucer under the title of The Cook's Tale of Gamelyn. It is noteworthy because,

by way of Lodge's *Rosalynde*, it contributed characters and situations
to Shakespeare's *As You Like It*, where the atmosphere is of course
tempered into something far more gracious and idyllic.

2. THE CLASSICAL AND CAROLINGIAN THEMES

When Benoit de Sainte Maure wrote his long and elaborate *Roman
de Troye* in French in the 12th century (see ch. 7, sec. 3), he initiated a wide
European vogue for telling the heroic legends of classical antiquity in
terms of medieval chivalry. Further impetus was given by the composition of a handy Latin compendium based on his romance and including
summaries of important myths anterior to the Troy story. The *Historia
Destructionis Troiae* written by a Sicilian, Guido delle Colonne (1287),[18]
was used directly or indirectly by Middle English poets treating the grand
cycle of Homer—for Homer himself was unknown to them.

An alliterative verse paraphrase of Guido's version was made by an
anonymous Northern poet of the latter 14th century, under the title of
the *Gest Historiale of the Destruction of Troy*.[19] Although about 14,000
lines long, it contrives to remain vigorous and is at times even impressive
in its phraseology. Thus it tells us that when Helen of Sparta heard of
Paris and his beauty, "Sho was lappit in longyng þat louely to se";
when Prince Troilus realises that his beloved Briseida must leave the
city "He was tourment with tene, tynt [i.e., lost] was his hew"; and it
is thus that Hector receives his death-blow:

> 8656   Achilles grippit a gret speire with a grim wille,
> Vnpersayuit of the prince, prikit him to,
> Woundit him wickedly as he away loked,
> Thurgh the body with the bit of the bright end
> That he gird to the ground and the gost yeld.

[vnpersayuit = unperceived;   bit = sharp point;   gird = fell]

The Seege of Troye, a short and comparatively undistinguished
summary, dates from the same period. On the other hand the Laud *Troy
Book* (so called because it is preserved in a Laud manuscript at the Bodleian Library in Oxford), composed about 1400,[20] is another example of
lengthy paraphrase. The style is rather monotonous and very impersonal,
but the irregular short couplets sometimes achieve an unhackneyed,
even poignant effect, as when Medea says to Jason, questing for the
Golden Fleece,

> 714   And I haue gret pyte
> Off thi manhede and beute,
> That thou thus foule schalt be spilt
> For a schepis skin that is ouer-gilt.

Legends about the historical Alexander the Great were also treated, if less extensively, in the form of medieval romances. Most accounts are derived from a fabulous report of the conqueror's adventures, purporting to be by his contemporary Callisthenes. A Roman writer, Julius Valerius, reworked the text of the Pseudo-Callisthenes in the fourth century, and his version circulated widely in abbreviated form. [21] To this epitome were added fictitious letters—actually of the ninth century—supposed to have been exchanged between Alexander and his erstwhile tutor Aristotle. As we have seen, the Latin Letters were known in Anglo-Saxon England (see ch. 4, sec. 5) and treated in the vernacular. The first romantic presentation of Alexander after the Conquest was done in French: the *Roman de toute Chevalarie* (13th century), assigned variously to Eustace or Thomas of Kent. The text is still unpublished. On it is based the 14th-century *King Alisaundre*, a Northern poem in short couplets derived from the South. Most of the content is warlike, but the element of fantasy appears in the non-historical account of Alexander's birth and the wonders he encountered in the East.

King Alisaunder (ca. 1300), [22] preserved in the Auchinleck manuscript and elsewhere, is a spirited adaptation of the entire French narrative, conveying well the sense of strangeness, even terror, in far-off places, and diversified by passages of lyrical nature description. An alliterative *Romance of Alexander* survives in two fragments (14th century), the first telling about the hero's parentage and youth, the second about his dealings with King Dindimus of India. A third alliterative fragment, independent of the other two, called *The Wars of Alexander* (15th century), is devoted to martial exploits. [23] Of these three, the second is the most interesting. It shows the proud conqueror being morally reproved by the Gymnosophists, a tribe of unclothed pacifists who jeer at his pretensions as conqueror, and it includes his correspondence with the ruler of the "Bragmans" (Brahmans), who lead lives of virtuous simplicity. Though distorted and indirectly conveyed, this impression of Indian wisdom and the Indian doctrine of non-resistance was the first to be reflected in English literature.

The great cycle of French epics and romances about Charlemagne and his family was not extensively adapted in English. Most of the surviving texts deal with fabulous exploits against Saracens who are unhistorically represented as destroying Rome and ravaging Italy until defeated by Charlemagne and his intrepid champions. The many *chansons de geste* telling of bitter civil war between Carolingian monarchs and rebellious feudal vassals did not evoke the interest of English poets. Significantly, these writers preferred themes of united struggle against outsiders. In a number of cases, the poem reaches its climax with the single combat of a Christian knight against a gigantic representative of the Saracens. There are two possible outcomes to these naive epic struggles: (1) either the heathen champion is killed and his co-religionists are routed, or (2) he is converted to Christianity by a combination of force and persuasion, and himself aids in the rout. Sometimes the physical combat is interrupted by an elementary discussion of theology by the two parties. Such passages reveal the influence of Latin dialogues used for instructional purposes, especially the *Elucidarius* (*Elucidator*), a widely copied and widely imitated didactic text attributed to Honorius d'Autun.

Roland and Vernagu, [24] preserved in the Auchinleck manuscript (ca. 1340), describes such a typical encounter. After telling of Charlemagne's quite unhistorical journey to aid the Emperor of Constantinople, this poem surveys his warfare in Spain, during which Roland fights and kills the Saracen giant Vernagu. The theological disquisitions addressed to his adversary during an intermission are unavailing; the giant is killed. The source is a Latin chronicle text called the *Pseudo-Turpin* — actually a literary forgery claiming to have been written by Charlemagne's Bishop Turpin, slain in the battle of Roncevalles (A.D. 778) together with Roland.

Otuel, [25] preserved in two different versions, tells how Vernagu's nephew, serving the pagan King of Lombardy, undertook to avenge the slain giant but was himself converted and became a Christian champion. The same subject was treated another time in *Duke Roland and Sir Otuel of Spain* (ca. 1400), [26] with more elaboration of chivalric conventions. Here even the Saracen characters adhere to the tenets of courtly love.

The Siege of Milan (latter 14th century) [27] describes the quite fictitious campaign of Charlemagne in Italy during which he defeated the Saracen King Arabas of Lombardy. It tells of a sharp difference of opinion between the Frankish Emperor and Bishop Turpin, during which the two almost engage in civil war on the soil of Italy. All of these poems derive ultimately from a French cycle dealing with Charlemagne and his nephew Roland.

Sir Firumbras (latter 14th century) [28] is based on a lively French *chanson de geste* entitled *Fierabras*. Here Oliver is the Christian knight who fights a gigantic heathen adversary. The latter, Firumbras himself, is converted after a series of combats and colloquies, but Oliver is captured, together with Roland and others who have gone to rescue him. However, all of the Christian knights are aided by the Saracen Princess Floripas, who had long been in love with one of them. She is a harsh and forthright young lady, quite ready to defy her father and commit murder in order to gain her desire. Her rudeness, her amorous aggressiveness and her unhindered brutal conduct are of course anything but typical of the segregated Mohammedan women of real life, just as the Saracen princes who appear in the Carolingian epics are also untypical. The Saracens as a whole are represented as primitive, ignorant, polytheistic, and often drunk, whereas they were in fact sober, abstemious, strictly monotheistic and very often more cultured than their opponents. These deliberate distortions of Mohammedan customs have been traced to the crusading propaganda of Peter the Venerable and others in the 12th century.[29]

The Sowdon of Babylon (ca. 1400)[30] covers the same action more briefly. It is supposed to have been taken from a different French version called *Balan*, from the name of the father of Fierabras and Floripas.

The Song of Roland itself, the first and the greatest of the French *chansons de geste*, was adapted into English verse late in the 14th century or early in the 15th.[31] It describes the much-celebrated ambush of Charlemagne's rear guard, led by Roland, in the passes of the Pyranees mountains; the slaughter of the army at the hands of the Saracens, and Charlemagne's revenge. The end of the English version is missing. The verse is unskilfully handled and the expression is weak. The theme was perhaps too specifically French, too alien to English experience, to attract the attention of a really gifted poet.

3. THE ARTHURIAN CYCLE

The cycle of tales most typical of feudal-aristocratic verse for entertainment is undoubtedly the famous one devoted to legends of King Arthur. Here the knightly class found the mirror in which it liked to believe its best traits were reflected: personal loyalty, idealisation of women belonging to the same class, unmercenary adventurousness, bravery in defense of the weak. The less admirable traits also appear from time to time: trickery, brutality, glorification of bloodshed, contempt for women not noble or fair, contempt for the lower classes, contempt and hatred of non-Christians, and above all an unceasing rivalry for the possession of landed estates; but these traits are less obvious here than in the *chansons de geste*. The greater atmosphere of fantasy served to modify reality more flatteringly in the Arthurian romances.

The first literary stage of development has already been traced in connection with the romanticised chronicle narratives of Geoffrey of Monmouth, Wace, and Layamon, and the beginnings of the French romances proper with Chrétien de Troyes (ch. 7). Earlier stages belonging to oral tradition can only be surmised on the basis of the written texts.

In Middle English, a few of the romances stand close to the chronicle tradition in that they outline King Arthur's career with emphasis on his wars and conquests. Such is *Arthour and Merlin*,[32] existing in two versions, the earlier of which is extant in the Auchinleck manuscript and was composed about 1300 or before. The ultimate source is Robert de Boron's 12th-century poem about the magician-sage, as retold in intermediate prose redactions. The versification in four-stress couplets is pleasant and easy, if not greatly varied.

The alliterative *Morte Arthure* (latter 14th century)[33] is a very vigorous treatment of Arthur's career, rising to real distinction in the account of the King's last battle against his traitor-nephew Mordred. The words and rhythms echo with resemblances to Old English heroic verse, still perceptible after the lapse of centuries. Various historical works also embody fairly ample accounts of Arthur's life and death, the substance of this poem, sometimes giving them in metrical form.

A stanzaic *Morte Arthur*,[34] on the other hand (late 14th century), deals with the more romantic complications attending Arthur's downfall. Here for the first time we meet Sir Lancelot in a full-scale English treatment. The poet recounts the episode of a young maid's loving devotion for the famous knight, which caused her death and Queen Guinevere's jealousy. Thence he passes on to a false accusation levelled against the Queen and to Lancelot's rescue of her. This action is followed by the plot which reveals their guilty love to King Arthur; Lancelot's second rescue of the Queen, which costs the life or Gawain's brother; the ensuing bitter feud between Lancelot and Gawain, who had once been close friends; the betrayal of Arthur by his nephew Mordred; the return of Arthur to England and his fatal battle with the traitor; the slaughter of all but a handful of his followers, and his own departure on a mysterious vessel, guided by three queens, for the land of Avalon which promises healing and peace after the tumults of this world.

Based on an early 13th-century French prose romance of unusual merit (the *Mort Artu*), this Middle English stanzaic poem also reaches exceptional heights of literary effectiveness. The action marches from one dramatic scene to another, driven by the force of inner human conflicts: loyalty against loyalty, love against fidelity, friendship at odds with the demands of revenge. The mood is sombre and portentous, and from the beginning the reader senses that not merely personal destinies are involved but the fate of a whole order. Lancelot, having fought his way out of the ambush set for him in the Queen's chamber by his enemies, says ominously:

1886   "We haue be-gonne thys ilke nyght
       That shall bring many a man full colde."
          Bors then spake with drery mode:
       "Syr," he sayd, "sithe it is so,

> We shalle be of hertis good
> Aftyr the wele to take the wo."

[ilke = same; sithe = since]

The poem, like Malory's prose handling of the same theme a century later, seems to pronounce a lamentation and a eulogy upon an ideal order which, though never realised in the grim world of actuality, represented a desire to see the feudal system ameliorated by elevating the responsible role of individual noblemen within its framework—while in no way, of course, challenging the foundations on which it was built.

A few Middle English romances are devoted to the exploits of individual Arthurian knights. *Yvain and Gawain*,[35] for instance (ca. 1350), is a condensed treatment of Chrétien de Troyes' poem *Yvain*, stressing the adventures and reducing the love passages. *Sir Percyvelle of Galles* (latter 14th century)[36] is a much abbreviated and naively simplified retelling of the long *Perceval, ou le Conte del Graal*, another of Chrétien's works. In the French, Perceval had traditionally been a leading knight questing for the Grail: that is, the chalice from which Jesus supposedly drank at the Last Supper. In the English poem, however, the Grail is omitted entirely and the story thus becomes a short, uncomplicated set of very conventional exploits. The absurdities of the much-padded verses with tail rime were burlesqued by Chaucer in his *Sir Thopas*, which also contains verbal echoes of the poem.

Joseph of Arimathie,[37] composed in the same period, is an alliterative fragment dealing with the legendary peregrinations of the Grail while it was being transported from Jerusalem to Britain, and the miracles wrought by it on the way. The poem is derived from a long French romance in prose, *Le grand Saint-Graal*, which in turn was expanded from Robert de Boron's *Joseph* (12th century; see ch. 7, sec. 3). *Sir Tristrem* (early 14th century),[38] like *Sir Perceval*, is a short and unimpressive romance which has magnificent analogues in Old French and Middle High German. The tragic plot about King Mark, his nephew Tristan, and Iseult the Princess of Ireland, failed to appeal to any English poet of the calibre of Gottfried von Strassburg or the French Thomas of Britain or even Béroul, perhaps because the situation was too typical of courtly love, with its cult of high-class adultery, to be popular in England. The same may well be true of the story of Lancelot and Guinevere, which apart from the stanzaic *Morte Arthur* mentioned above, survives in only one independent verse treatment, the Lowland Scots *Lancelot of the Laik*[39] of a much later period (late 15th century). Neither of these romantic tales enjoyed the success they achieved in France.

If Yvain, Perceval, Tristram and Lancelot failed to attract the Mid-

dle English romancers in any considerable number, Arthur's nephew
Sir Gawain compensated by attaining far greater popularity than he had
enjoyed in France. It was Gawain the fearless champion and devoted
friend (as in *Yvain and Gawain*), rather than Gawain the lover of the
ladies, who appealed to the English poets. In the former capacity he
became the centre of a number of plots originally independent of the
Arthurian cycle. The poems about him were written in the 14th and 15th
centuries.[40] The best of them, *Sir Gawain and the Green Knight*, will be
discussed in the next chapter, as the work of one of Chaucer's outstanding
contemporaries. Several of the less famous poems, as well as this one,
were composed in the Northern districts of England (the Northwest
Midlands), and use alliteration abundantly.

The *Awntyrs* (i.e., *Adventures*) *of Arthur at the Terne Wathelyn* (Tarn
Wadling) (mid-14th century) contains two adventures in which Gawain
figures prominently. First, he escorts Queen Guinevere during a stormy
hunting party that takes place near the haunted Tarn, not far from
Carlisle. Here the Queen's dead mother appears to her in horrific guise —
"ȝollande ȝamyrly, with many lowde ȝelle," and suggesting a combination
of Medusa and Grendel's dam—to warn her daughter against adultery,
to prophesy the downfall of Arthur, and to beg masses for the repose
of her own sinful soul. The second episode hinges on Gawain's combat
with another knight who claims lands recently awarded to him. The
solution is amicable. *The Avowing of Arthur* (latter 14th century)[41] is
also localised near the Tarn Wadling. Here Arthur, Gawain and several
other knights make boasting promises to undertake certain adventures,
and sally forth to accomplish them. Sir Kay, as usual, is worsted, while
Gawain is covered with glory. Such a series of boasts was more than once
employed in early Celtic (Irish), Icelandic and Anglo-Saxon traditional
tales to begin the telling of concatenated adventures. The plot thus gives
evidence for the survival of a more primitive genre in story-telling down
into Middle English literature.

In *Sir Gawain and the Carl of Carlisle* (14th or 15th century),[42] Arthur's
nephew is faced with a dilemma of courtesy, for his host demands as
recompense for hospitality, the performance of acts which appear to violate
the very code of a chivalrous guest: to cast a spear at the Carl, to make
love to the Carl's wife, and similar deeds. This strange behaviour is due
to an irrational vow taken by the host many years previously. Gawain
tactfully shows him the error of his ways and he repents. The background
of the tale is primitive: there are many tales in Old Irish, for instance,
about a magic spell or *geis* which compels a man to behave thus irration-
ally. But the point of this story is not at all primitive. It glorifies Gawain
as a knight of courtesy because his tactful behaviour enables him to

extricate himself from the situation without damage to any of the proprieties.

Some later romances about Gawain add to his fame for courtesy and prowess, but not all are interesting in substance or execution. *Golagrus and Gawain* (15th century) shows the hero dealing with a rebellious vassal who has hitherto denied homage to any overlord; *The Green Knight* and *The Turk and Gawain* are belated analogues of *Sir Gawain and the Green Knight*. *The Geste of Sir Gawain* is founded on adventures attributed to the hero in continuations, of Chrétien's *Perceval*. *The Wedding of Sir Gawain and Dame Ragnell* (also 15th century) is a later analogue of the tale told by Chaucer's Wife of Bath (see ch. 12).

Libeaus Desconnus (meaning *The Fair Unknown*, ca. 1350)[43] concerns an illegitimate son of Gawain, Sir Gingelain, who wins glory for himself by very conventional exploits. His adventures are so stereotyped and his attitude so far from practical that he is made to appear like a burlesque on knighthood. The purpose of his quest is to rescue a certain Lady of Sinadoune, the victim of foul enchantments; but he also rescues other damsels on the way. His comment on being engaged in a secondary job of rescue is typical of his insouciant attitude throughout, and could be put into the mouth of many other knights errant:

> 1759　Libeaus saide, "Sikirly,
> 　　Fiȝte I schall for þy lady,
> 　　　Be heste of king Arthour;
> 　　But I not, wher fore ne why
> 　　Ne who her doþ þat vilany
> 　　　Ne what is her dolour."

[sikirly = certainly;　not = ne wot, do not know]

Here an unknown romancer inadvertently put his finger on the kind of literary absurdity which evoked Chaucer's dainty burlesque in *Sir Thopas*, and much later the magnificent satire of Cervantes in *Don Quixote*.

4. MISCELLANEOUS ROMANCES AND "LAYS"

Outside of the main cycles, a number of individual romances also gained popularity in English. Their plots are constructed out of the same familiar materials. Many are localised in the Orient, Eastern Europe, Sicily and other exotic regions. Indirect Greek influence appears in the proper names of some. A few have a marked didactic purpose, but most are for pure entertainment, relying much on the stuff of fairy-tales for their plots.

Floris and Blanchefleur (mid-13th century, derived from the French),[44] for instance, begins in Saracen Spain and ends in Babylon. The boy prince of Spain having fallen in love with a high-born girl, a Christian captive, his parents sell her into slavery and inform him that she is dead. But Floris does not believe them. He traces Blanchefleur to the East and finds that she has been confined in a tower preparatory to marriage with the Sultan of Babylon. He is smuggled into her room in a basket of roses, and when discovered, he gallantly vindicates his first claim to her in combat. The Sultan eventually blesses and unites the pair of adolescent lovers. Analogous situations have been pointed out in *The Arabian Nights*,[45] and it is probable that the plot originated in the Orient. It is one of the best-told of the non-cyclic romances, employing supple octosyllabic couplets in its easy course, and it enjoyed considerable popularity.

Ipomadon (ca. 1350),[46] a stanzaic romance based on the Anglo-French tale of the same name by Hue de Rotelande in the 12th century (see ch. 7, sec. 3), preserves its Greek names and South Italian setting in Calabria and Sicily. Two later versions of the tale were made in the 14th century. The main action centres on the hero's anonymous exploits at a tournament on three successive days, in three different suits of armour (a popular motif known as the Three Days' Tournament). The alliterative *William of Palerne* (also mid-14th century)[47] is another tale of Southern Italy, likewise founded on a French source. The central theme is here the folkloristic motif of the werwolf—a man bespelled into a wolf—who befriends the orphaned and persecuted hero William and is later unspelled with his aid. *Parthenope of Blois*,[48] still another romance from the French, was twice treated in English (15th century). It represents a variant of the widespread folklore theme of a supernatural marriage like that of Cupid and Psyche, but with the roles reversed (as is not unusual): here the bride is the other-world person, and the hero is the one who is under a tabu not to look upon his mate. He does so, of course, is separated from her, but reunited to her after sundry tests and adventures which prove his mettle. *Sir Gowther* (ca. 1400)[49] combines the story of a child born of a devil—like Merlin—and later redeemed, with the motif of a three-days' tournament.

Generydes,[50] extant in two different treatments (earlier 15th century) is a composite of numerous chivalric themes: the illegitimate son of a hero reared by his mother, war service and an amour at a foreign court, eventual recognition by his father and belated marriage between his parents—with all villains punished and all virtuous folk rewarded. The action occurs in India, Persia and Tharse. The last-named country is probably the Tabriz in Iran which is the scene of *The King of Tars* (early 14th century),[51] a story of a Christian princess wedded to a Saracen, who brings about his conversion. There are historical personages in this romance, but they are obscured behind the fictitious element of miracles.

Several romances use false accusations against innocent people as the motif which starts a series of adventures in exile. Conspicuous in the social situation is the thoughtless credulity often attached to the grossest charges. *Athelston*, among the English romances, has already been mentioned as belonging to this type, and together with it *Emaré*, *Florence de Rome* and *The Erl of Toulouse* (above, sec. 1). *Octavian*,[52] existing in two separate treatments (both ca. 1350) of a French source, is another story in which the victim is a young queen forced into exile with two small children because of a lying accusation by her mother-in-law. In *Emaré*, the heroine had first been obliged to flee from an incestuous father, and later from a spiteful mother-in-law; in *Florence de Rome* the accuser had been her brother-in-law; in *Sir Triamour* (early 14th century)[53] he is an ambitious steward. In some cases, the heroine suffers persecution and exile because her father is reluctant or downright opposed to having her married; hence he places great difficulties in the way of any suitor, and, if she becomes pregnant through a secret love affair, he tries to destroy the girl and her son or sons. This situation appears in early mythology—the legend of Danaë and her son Perseus is typical—and in fairy tales. In both *Sir Eglamour of Artois* (latter 14th century) and *Sir Torrent of Portyngale* (early 15th century)[54] the heroine is set adrift with her illegitimate offspring at her father's command, but in the end she is recovered and married to her lover, and her father is punished. *Sir Degaré* (early 14th century)[55] complicates the plot by motifs recalling *Sohrab and Rustem* and the Oedipus story. The father's fear of his daughter's marriage is a widespread theme in folklore, and may reflect family relations long antedating feudal society.

In a few romantic tales the exiles and sufferings are visited upon hero and heroine, not because of a false accusation or a fearsome parent, but by divine interference, in order to test the victims' steadfastness. The type is as old as the Biblical Book of Job. It was developed in the legend of St. Eustace (also called Placidas), who was said to have suffered loss of property and dispersal of his family under the Emperor Trajan. But Eustace was reunited with his family by a series of fortunate accidents and recognition scenes recalling late Greek romances like *Apollonius of Tyre*. In the same way, the hero of *Sir Isumbras* (late 15th century)[56] endures the test of fate. Here the didactic purpose is so obvious that the story might be classified as a pious tale almost as readily as a romance. The same is true of other miracle stories in chivalrous settings, such as *Amis and Amiloun*, *Sir Amadace*, *King Robert of Sicily* and *Sir Cleges*.[57]

The term "Breton lays" is given to a few of the miscellaneous romances by their composers. Such are *Emaré*, *Sir Degaré*, *Sir Gowther* and *The*

Erl of Toulous. There is no direct connection of these, however, with any of the short French narratives called *lais*, written by Marie de France or her imitators (ch. 7, sec. 3). On the other hand, *The Lay of the Ash Tree* (*Lai le Freine*,—early 14th century) and *Sir Launfal* (two versions of the French *Lai de Lanval*) are close to the French models.[58] The *Lay of Orfeo*,[59] based on the classical myth of Orpheus and Euridyce, is transformed in the spirit of Marie's *lais*, with their touches of fairy lore and symbolic meaning. It is a gem of its kind.

As a whole, medieval romances have a limited appeal, as can be inferred even from this rapid survey. Escape from reality or an idealisation of it were the chief values desired of the romancers. Much of the action has its mainspring in an enchanted world where everyday reckonings do not have to be made. Only occasionally does a hero in trouble—like Havelok during his exile—establish a kind of contact with reality by engaging in useful labour. Even when the plot itself depends but little on magic and the supernatural, the tone and the motivation remove it from reality. At their best the romances may charm us by their quaint appeal to the imagination, which is intended to ennoble human conduct; at their worst they bore us with a tasteless series of incredible adventures constructed on trite formulas. A few are content to delineate life in castles and manor-houses with a certain fidelity to truth (as then understood). Such for instance is *Sir Degrevant* (latter 14th century),[60] telling about the feud between a peppery Earl and the young knight who is desirous of marrying his daughter. *The Squire of Low Degree* (15th century),[61] a simple and otherwise commonplace tale about the winning of a princess by a low-born suitor, is redeemed by its vivid and convincing pictures of court life. Both texts indicate a desire to appeal beyond the narrow circle of the higher aristocracy to what might be called the average landed gentry.

The best and liveliest of all the anonymous romances, including all the types here analysed, were as a matter of fact able to attain currency among wider groups in the population than the top layer of the aristocracy. After the invention of printing, many of the romances were revamped and put into fresh circulation, thus beginning a new career of popularity extending far beyond the aristocratic circles in which they took their first social origin.

5. WORKS OF INSTRUCTION (CHIEFLY RELIGIOUS)

While romantic literature was proliferating in the domain of entertainment, works of religious instruction were also multiplying in the vernacular. In the latter 13th and throughout the 14th century they were more and more often represented by English texts which—like the Latin and French ones before them—were sometimes carried out on a very large scale.

Collections of homilies and saints' lives became more inclusive than ever. The treatment of certain themes, both Biblical and hagiographic, reveals a desire to appeal to popular lay audiences far beyond the cloistered walls where this literature took its origin in Latin. The narrative at times becomes dramatic in a manner suggesting a close kinship with the religious plays then taking shape in the vernacular (see ch. 14, sec. 2).

The *South English Legendary* (late 13th century)[62] is one of the large collections of this sort, containing versified stories of the saints and events of the New Testament. In scope it resembles the contemporary *Legenda Aurea* or *Golden Legend*, put together in Italy by Jacobus de Voragine (died 1298), to which it was at least partly indebted. Many of the legends are flatly told, in a style earnest rather than inspired; others attain a certain dignified eloquence in the scenes of trial and martyrdom. The account of the Crucifixion[63] is given with a simple restraint and sincerity elevating it above the naive thaumaturgy of most of the other sections. Direct speeches are few, dignified in tone, and close to the Biblical text. Neither Mary nor Jesus pronounces a formal lament during the final scene. After Christ's farewell to the Apostles, the author tells us tersely:

58   Oure lord ne spak to ham namore   þat we owher rede
Ak þo he was overcome ney   and his lymes mey alle dede
Wiþ dreori chere wel pytouslich   "A-þurst ich am," he sede.

[owher =anywhere;   ak = but;   þo. = when;   ney = nearly]

The *Northern Homily Cycle* (early 14th century, perhaps from the region of Durham), though similar in scope to the Southern, is more dramatic in its handling of the traditional materials. The difference appears strikingly in the Passion scenes, which are based on an Anglo-Norman source. Here (in contrast to the Southern cycle) the speeches are developed in a style not unlike that of the early plays:

1755   Pan spak ihesus ful mildely
Vnto þe puple þat past him by:
"3e folk that passes by þe strete,
Lukes vp and se my wondes wete
And whatkin turmendes I here take,
And suffers sorows for 3owre sake;
Bihaldes if any oþer pine
May be likkind vnto myne,
Or if any oþer thing
Sufferd euer so hard pineing."

[puple =people;   pine = pain;   likkind = likened]

Imagined Portrait of Sir John Mandeville

Late in the 14th century a collection of legends was made in Scotland also. [64]

A number of the saints' lives were treated at some length, separately, in a style recalling the romances. This was true of the fictitious legend of St. Gregory, a curious combination of an intensified Oedipus situation (the hero who marries his own mother being himself the offspring of an incestuous union), with a typical medieval resolution by penance and forgiveness miraculously assured. [65]

The campaign for simplified moral and doctrinal instruction in the vernacular, begun by the authorities in the 13th century, produced in the 14th a number of lengthy didactic works in English. In the North, an ambitious encyclopedic work was composed in verse, called *Cursor Mundi* (*Runner of the World,*—ca. 1300 — 25), [66] which undertook a twofold task of instruction. First, it gave laymen a panorama of world history from the ecclesiastical point of view, divided into seven ages. Second, it added disquisitions on a variety of subjects including those stressed in Latin and French during the Lateran reform movement of the preceding century: the Creed, Lord's Prayer, and the meaning of penance. The author or group of authors, while drawing on a wide variety of learned sources, remain true to the aim of popularisation throughout the enormous work (almost 30,000 lines in its most complete form). The *Handlyng Synne* (*Manual of Sins*) [67] by Robert Manning of Brunne, also designed for popular consumption, is an expanded paraphrase of William of Wadington's Anglo-Norman work of moral instruction, *Le Manuel des Péchiez*, composed in the 13th century. The method of instructing in such matters as the Ten Commandments, Seven Deadly Sins, Seven Sacraments, and so on, was by illustrative stories: most taken from written sources, some from current folklore, many told in a style effectively appealing to the interests of simple men and women.

William of Shoreham, a Kentish priest (early 14th century) also wrote on these topics in a series of separate poems. [68] A fellow-countryman, Dan Michel of Northgate, put a French penitential work by Friar Lorens, *La Somme des Vices et des Vertues*, into prose under the title of *The Azenbit of Inwit* (*Remorse of Conscience*, 1340). [69] He explicitly states that he used the local Kentish dialect in order the more effectively to reach the simple people of the district. From this period there are also many individual paraphrases and explanatory pieces devoted to the elements of religious instruction. Titles such as *The Lay Folk's Mass Book, The Lay Folk's Catechism, The Lay Folk's Prayer Book*, reveal their scope. Early in the 15th century, John Mirk, a priest living in the Southwest, wrote some versified *Instructions for Parish Priests*, and a prose *Festial* embodying saints' lives and other topics for sermons. [70]

Allegory, already highly developed in Latin and French during the preceding century, was also widely applied to didactic ends in the English language of this period. Robert Grosseteste's allegory, *Le Chateau d'Amour* (see ch. 8, sec. 5), was done into Middle English at least three times as *The Castle of Love*. A short prose text called *The Abbey of the Holy Ghost* follows the tradition of *Sawles Warde*; and another treatise, *Ghostly Battle*, presents the individual's struggle against evil under the metaphor of chivalrous combat, in a tradition stemming from both the Bible and the *Psychomachia* of Prudentius.[71] There are others of the same type. *The Quatrefoil of Love*[72] is somewhat unusual in that it adapts a courtly situation—the plaint by an aristocratic lady about her failure to find a faithful lover—to religious didacticism. The lady is advised to turn her desire towards a heavenly lover, since the earthly ones have so clearly failed her.

These didactic tracts and allegories are of very uneven merit from the literary point of view. Dan Michel's *Azenbit*, for instance, is a dreary classified catalogue of the vices, elaborated into seemingly endless subdivisions. The work of Manning is on the other hand constantly vivified by his scenes and conversations taken from ordinary life. The allegories are for the most part unpretentious. Not until the next century were the long allegories of Guillaume de Déguileville put into English, quite successfully, by John Lydgate (see ch. 13). Meantime the dialogue form was also used as a favourite framework for instruction, carrying on the fashion set earlier in Latin texts like the *Elucidarius*.[73] When one of the parties arguing is a devil, he is of course triumphantly refuted by his human antagonist. The interchange becomes livelier without diminishing the didactic purpose.

In secular education no such impressive labour was done as in the moral and religious sphere. Scientific knowledge—both the traditional compilations and the work of the isolated innovators like Roger Bacon—remained far from the masses. Not until the invention of printing did any significant change occur in this regard. However, English was now used more and more for historical writing, along with Latin and French. The latter 14th century produced quite a galaxy of chroniclers whose work was so broad in scope that they deserve the title of historians. It is true that they still wrote mostly in terms of personalities: good kings and bad, saints and sinners, prideful and humble folk, without any conception of mass movements as we understand them, nor the economic transformations conditioning them. But they have left us a wealth of detailed information on the leading figures of the age, and indirectly on their background. With the help of these sources a modern historian can penetrate far into the then hidden causes of change.

Among the less original writers was Robert of Gloucester (latter 13th century), an innovator in establishing the use of English for chronicles. Robert Manning, author of the *Handlyng Synne*, put together a riming verse history of England from various sources which, though less original than many others, is exceptional in being designed for simple, unlearned readers. John Trevisa (ca. 1360) translated into English prose the Latin *Polychronicon* written by the Benedictine Ralph Higden. The work is unoriginal; but Trevisa prefixed to his version an interesting tract on medieval political theory, a dialogue between a knight and a clerk, [74] based on one by William Ockham (see next chapter). It tried to define the limits of church and state in order to prevent encroachments by the former on the latter. *The Brut of England*, a prose compilation drawing from various sources, circulated widely in three versions: French, Latin and English.

Some chronicle writers of the latter 14th century went far, however, beyond mere compilations. A group of monastic writers in Latin, such as Knighton and the author of *Chronicon Angliae*, contribute abundant and generally trustworthy details on the events of their own time and the immediate past. They seem to have had access to primary documents and other reliable sources. In the vernacular, a striking contribution was made by John Barbour of Scotland, who told in the riming verse *Bruce* [75] about the struggle of his nationality for independence under the leadership of a brave and resourceful chieftain. The story is vividly presented, and despite some legendary elements and inaccuracies of detail it gives an authentic picture of the events covered. The text is a pioneer effort in the writing of Middle Scots.

In French, a monumental contribution to both historiography and literature was made by Jean Froissart, long resident in England and personally known to many of the royal and noble personages and representatives of the wealthy merchant class about whom he wrote. Naturally Froissart's prose *Chroniques d'Angleterre* reveal the limitations of his age and class. He sees history primarily as a sequence of glittering individuals and dramatic events, thrown into relief against a slow-moving background of unappreciated importance. He held the views of his age about the nature of historical causation. His prejudices in respect to popular movements of protest are obvious. Nevertheless he gives such an abundance of living detail—for instance, in describing the struggle of pro-English and anti-English factions in the Flemish towns—that underlying causes are revealed almost, it might be said, against his own will and intention. The style is of a high literary order. The finely executed decorations and pictures in the best manuscripts of the *Chroniques*, brilliant in colours and gold-leaf, unroll the pageant of people and events as Froissart saw them, with the eyes of a courtier. Thus his work transmits to us more of the social reality of his time than he himself could be aware of.

In conclusion it may be appropriate to mention an odd text, neither fictional nor scientific but important for both fiction and science, which had a certain importance in stimulating contemporary interest in geography. This was the enormously popular *Travels of Sir John Mandeville*, [76] a work (originally composed in French) purporting to describe an Englishman's experiences in journeying about the world. The itinerary is continous in an Easterly direction, and the world is represented as spherical. Actually the book is a clever amalgamation of known sources, from Pliny and Solinus down to recent factual reports of travels in the Mongol Empire of the Great Khan. The author likewise mixed in some fictitious accounts of a fabulously wealthy India that was supposed to contain, among other *mirabilia*, a Fountain of Youth and rivers with sands of gold. Though expressed in a style of straight-faced sobriety, the extravagances of the *Travels* have an effect of delightfully humorous exaggeration. The descriptions of religious observances in Eastern lands often read like deliberate burlesques of practices in contemporary Europe. The reading public eagerly absorbed the fantastic adventures and the descriptions of equally fantastic creatures supposed to inhabit Asia and Africa: the one-legged Monopodes who leap rapidly over the sands and in the heat of the day lie down with their single feet raised aloft as anatomical umbrellas; the Monoculi or one-eyed folk; the hermaphrodites and headless humans with features planed on their chests. Old maps show drawings of these weird creatures roaming about in the still barely known areas South and East of the Mediterranean. Descriptions of them are echoed down to the time of Shakespeare, who through the mouth of Othello speaks of

> .... the Cannibals that did each other eat,
> The Anthropophagi, and men whose heads
> Do grow beneath their shoulders.

Grotesque as these fables may have been, they had a beguiling air of probability for the readers of Sir John. His Fountain of Youth, his treasures of India, his intriguing monsters played some part in inflaming the imagination of Europe, turning the interest of men towards exploration and discovery. When the technology, experience and daring were historically matured, a hundred years later, many explorers set out with their heads full of these fictitious reports, eager to seek the continents and seas that lay still unsuspected by Western man, far to the East of the Red Sea, and below the horizons of the uncharted Atlantic Ocean to the West.

[1] A general appraisal is given by George Kane, *Middle English Literature* (London, 1951), but from the literary point of view exclusively, disregarding chronology, sources and social foundations. For factual information see J.E. Wells, *Manual*, ch. 1, with bibliography and supplements. For literary problems see also Dorothy Everett, *Essays on Middle English Literature* (Oxford, 1955).

[2] The Auchinleck MS. is now in the Advocates' Library, Edinburgh. Its origin as part of a commercial enterprise for turning out romances has been suggested by Laura Hibbard Loomis in *PMLA*, LVII (1942), 595—627. This article contains full bibliography on the arts of book production in the Middle Ages.

[3] Max Deutschbein, *Studien zur Sagengeschichte Englands* (Cöthen, 1906).

[4] *King Horn*, ed. Joseph Hall (Oxford, 1901); discussion by Walter Hoyt French, *Essays on King Horn* (Cornell University Press, 1940). Suddene was identified by Walter Oliver, *PMLA*, XLVI (1931), 102—14.

[5] *Havelok*, ed. W.W. Skeat, revised by K. Sisam (Oxford, 1923).

[6] *Le Lai d'Haveloc*, ed. A. Bell (Manchester, 1925). Gaimar included the summary of an earlier form of the story in his *Estiore des Engleis* (ca. 1150).

[7] *Beves of Hamtoun*, ed. E. Kölbing, EETS, ES, Nos. 46, 48, 65 (1885—94).

[8] Rudolf Zenker, *Boeve-Amlethus* (Berlin, 1905).

[9] *Guy of Warwick*, ed. J. Zupitza, EETS, ES, Nos. 25 and 26 (1875—76).

[10] *Athelston*, ed. W.H. French and C.B. Hale, *Middle English Metrical Romances* (New York, 1930).

[11] On the general type see M. Schlauch, *Chaucer's Constance and Accused Queens* (New York University Press, 1927).

[12] *Emaré*, ed. Edith Rickert, EETS, ES, No. 99 (1906).

[13] *Le Bone Florence de Rome*, ed. Victor and Knobbe (Marburg, 1893).

[14] *The Erl of Toulous*, ed. G. Lüdtke (Berlin, 1881) and French and Hale, *op. cit.*

[15] A.C. Baugh has suggested a source of *Athelston* in Walter Map, *De Nugis Curialium*, I, cap. 12. See *PMLA*, XLIV (1929), 377 ff.

[16] *Der mittelenglische Versroman Richard Löwenherz*, ed. Karl Brunner (Vienna, 1913).

[17] *Gamelyn*, ed. W.W. Skeat in Chaucer's *Works*, V (Oxford, 1893); French and Hale, *op. cit.* On the connection with *As You Like It* see E.C. Petlet, *Shakespeare and the Romance Tradition* (London, 1949).

[18] Guido delle Colonne, *Historia Destructionis Troiae*, ed. Nathaniel Griffin (Mediaeval Academy of America, 1936).

[19] *The Gest Historiale,* ed. G.A. Panton and D. Donaldson, EETS, OS, Nos. 39 and 56 (1869 and 1874).

[20] *The Seege of Troy,* ed. Mary Elizabeth Barnicle, EETS, OS, No. 172 (1927). See also G. Hofstrand's edition (Lund, 1936). The *Laud Troy Book,* ed. J.E. Wülfing, EETS, OS, Nos. 121 and 122 (1902—03).

[21] Paul Meyer, *Alexandre le Grand dans la littérature française du moyen âge* (Paris, 1886).

[22] *King Alisaunder* has not been edited since H. Weber's *Metrical Romances,* I (1810).

[23] These fragments ed. F.P. Magoun, Jr., *The Gests of Alexander of Macedon* (Harvard University Press, 1929).

[24] *Roland and Vernagu,* ed. S.J. Herrtage, EETS, ES, No. 39 (1889). See H.M. Smyser, "Charlemagne and Roland and the Auchinleck MS.," *Speculum,* XXI (1946), 275—88.

[25] *Otuel,* ed. Herrtage, *op. cit.*; second version ed. Mary Isabelle O'Sullivan, EETS, OS, No. 198 (1935). See R.N. Walpole, "*Charlemagne and Roland,*" University of California *Publications in Modern Philology,* XXI (1944), No. 6, pp. 385—452; also R.N. Walpole in *Medium Aevum,* XX (1951), 40—47.

[26] *Duke Roland,* ed. S.J. Herrtage, EETS, ES, No. 35 (1880).

[27] *The Siege of Milan, ibid.*

[28] *Sir Firumbras,* ed. Herrtage, EETS, ES, No. 34 (1879).

[29] See C. Meredith Jones, "The Conventional Saracen of the Songs of Geste," *Speculum,* XVII (1942), 201—25; also W.W. Comfort, "The Literary Role of the Saracens in the French Epic," *PMLA,* LV (1940), 628—59.

[30] *The Sowdan of Babylon,* ed. E. Hausknecht, EETS, ES, No. 38 (1881).

[31] *The Song of Roland,* ed. Herrtage, EETS, ES, N. 35 (1880).

[32] *Arthour and Merlin nach der Auchinleck-HS.,* ed. E. Kölbing (Leipzig, 1890).

[33] Allit. *Morte Arthure,* ed. Erik Björkmann (Heidelberg, 1915).

[34] Stanzaic *Morte Arthur,* ed. James Douglas Bruce, EETS, ES, No. 88 (1903) and S.B. Hemingway (Boston, 1912).

[35] *Yvain and Gawain,* ed. Gustav Schleich (Oppeln and Leipzig, 1887).

[36] *Sir Perceval,* ed. J. Campion and F. Holthausen (Heidelberg, 1913).

[37] *Joseph of Arimathie,* ed. W.W. Skeat, EETS, ES, No. 44 (1871).

[38] *Sir Tristrem,* ed. E. Kölbing (Heilbronn, 1878—82), with other versions.

[39] *Lancelot of the Laik,* ed. M.M. Gray, Scottish Text Society, N.S., No. 2 (1911).

[40] The group of romances about Gawain has been edited together by Sir Frederick Madden, Bannatyne Club Series (1839).

[41] *The Avowing of Arthur* ed. separately by French and Hale, *op. cit.*

[42] *Sir Gawain and the Carl of Carlyle* ed. A. Kurvinen (Helsinki, 1951).

[43] *Libeaus Desconus,* ed. Max Kaluza (Leipzig, 1890).

[44] *Floris and Blanchefleur,* ed. A.B. Taylor (Oxford, 1927).

[45] See Samuel Singer, "Arabische und europäische Poesie im Mittelalter," *Zeitschrift für deutsches Altertum,* LII (1927), 77 ff.

[46] *Ipomadon,* ed. E. Kölbing (Breslau, 1899).

[47] *William of Palerne*, ed. W.W. Skeat, EETS, ES, No. 1 (1867).

[48] *Parthenope of Blois*, ed. A.T. Bödtker, EETS, ES, No. 109 (1911).

[49] *Sir Gowther*, ed. Breul (Oppeln, 1886).

[50] *Generides*, ed. W.A. Wright, EETS, OS, Nos. 55 and 70 (1873 and 1878).

[51] *The King of Tars*, ed. F. Krause in *Englische Studien*, XI (1888). See Lillian Hornstein, "The Historical Background of *The King of Tars*," *Speculum*, XVI (1941), 404—14.

[52] *Octavian*, ed. Gregor Sarrazin, both versions (Heilbronn, 1885).

[53] *Sir Triamour*, ed. F.J. Furnivall in The Percy Folio MS. (London, 1867—69).

[54] *Sir Eglamour*, ed. G. Schleich in *Palaestra*, LIII (1906); *Sir Torrent*, ed. E. Adam, EETS, ES, No. 51 (1887).

[55] *Sir Degare*, ed. G. Schleich (Heidelberg, 1929) and French and Hale, *op. cit.*; see the study of the romance under the same title by G.P. Faust (Princeton University Press, 1935).

[56] *Isumbras*, ed. G. Schleich, *Palaestra*, XV (Berlin, 1901).

[57] *Amis and Amiloun*, ed. E. Kölbing (Heilbronn, 1884), with analogues; *Sir Amadace*, ed. H. Weber, *Metrical Romances*, I (1810); *Sir Cleges*, ed. French and Hale, *op. cit.*; *Robert of Sicily*, ed. C. Horstmann, *Altenglische Legenden* (Heilbronn, 1878).

[58] *Sir Launfal* (earlier version) in French and Hale, *op. cit.*

[59] *Sir Orfeo, ibid.*; also in K. Sisam, *Fourteenth Century Verse and Prose* (Oxford, 1921).

[60] *Sir Degrevant*, ed. L.F. Casson, EETS, OS, No, 221 (1949). See the appreciation by George Kane, *op. cit.*, pp. 90—94.

[61] *The Squire of Low Degree*, ed. French and Hale and separately by W.E. Mead (Boston, 1904).

[62] *South English Legendary*, ed. Carl Horstmann, EETS, OS, No. 87 (1887). On its development see Minnie E. Wells in *PMLA*, LI (1936), 337—60 and *Journal of English and Germanic Philology*, XLI (1942), 320—44.

[63] *The Southern Passion*, ed. separately by Beatrice Daw Brown, EETS, OS, No. 169 (1927). *The Northern Passion*, ed. Frances Foster, EETS, OS, Nos. 145, 147 (1913—16).

[64] The Scottish collection, ed. C. Horstmann (Heilbronn, 1881—82), also by W.M. Metcalfe, Scottish Text Society, 3 vols. (1896).

[65] *Gregorius*, ed. Keller, *Die mittelenglische Gregoriuslegende* (Heidelberg, 1914).

[66] *Cursor Mundi*, ed. R. Morris, EETS, OS, Nos. 57, 62, 66, 68, 99, 101 (1874—92).

[67] *Handlyng Synne*, ed. F.J. Furnivall, EETS, OS, Nos. 119 and 123 (1901—03), with the French source. On the author see Ruth Crosby in *PMLA*, LVII (1942), 15—28.

[58] William of Shoreham's poems ed. in EETS, ES, No. 86.

[69] *Aʒenbit of Inwit*, ed. R. Morris, EETS, OS, No. 23 (1866).

[70] John Mirk, *Instructions*, ed. E. Peacock, EETS, OS, No. 31 (revised 1902); *Festial*, ed. T. Erbe, EETS, ES, No. 96 (1905).

[71] *Abbey of the Holy Ghost*, ed. G.G. Perry, EETS, OS, No. 26; *Ghostly Battle*, ed. C. Horstmann, *Yorkshire Writers*, 2 vols. (London, 1895—96).

[72] *Quatrefoil of Love*, ed. in *Furnivall Miscellany* (Oxford, 1901).

[73] Fr. Schmitt, *Die mittelenglischen Versionen des Elucidarius* (Würzburg diss., 1909). Another popular dialogue of instruction was *Ypotis*, ed. C. Horstmann, *Alt englische Legenden*, Neue Folge, I (1881). See *ibid.*, Erste Folge I (1878), for a dispute between a Christian and a Jew. Horstmann has edited a "Dialogue between a Good Man and the Devil," EETS, OS, No. 98. (1892)

[74] John Trevisa, *Dialogus inter Militem et Clericum*, ed. A.J. Perry, EETS, OS, No. 167 (1925).

[75] Barbour's *Bruce*, ed. W.W. Skeat, EETS, ES, Nos. 11, 21, 29, 55 (1870—79).

[76] *The Travels*, ed. P. Hamelius, EETS, OS, No. 153 (1919). See the recent study by Josephine Bennett, *The Rediscovery of Sir John Mandeville* (New York: Modern Language Association, 1954).

THE CONTEMPORARIES OF CHAUCER

1. THE LATTER 14TH CENTURY: ECONOMIC AND POLITICAL DEVELOPMENTS

The second half of the 14th century was an age of dramatic events and conspicuous transformation affecting all of society. Whereas the conditions of the 13th century had been relatively stable, and a certain prosperity had developed—albeit on a low level—, the following age was one of crises, shifts in economic status and violent upheavals. The causes of most of these changes had long been present, but they now gained momentum, and new factors were also added. The result was the beginning of an essential change which first emerged with entire clarity in the 16th century. The political history of the times can only be understood in the light of these factors, old and new.

The population of England had been increasing steadily from the 11th century—the time of the last invasions—until 1340. And within that increased population, a larger and larger proportion lived in the towns.[1] Trade between town and country assumed greater importance, and in this period international trade also became very considerable. The merchants of England began to play an important role in European economy. At home, they became a force in politics and in upper-class society. The basis of their affluence was the wool trade. English sheep-raising was so successfully developed, and on such a broad scale, that raw wool of superior quality became available in large quantities for export. The Low Countries became the chief importer of this commodity. In the Flemish towns, where the crafts of spinning, dyeing and weaving were far advanced, fine textiles and tapestries were produced for the European market, a part of which were sent to England. Thus some of the English wool returned home in a new shape. On the basis of wool chiefly, trade expanded in the direction of Southern France, Spain, the Mediterranean, and also the Scandinavian and Baltic areas. The feudal families holding lands devoted to sheep-raising began to enjoy a luxury unknown to their ancestors. Other landlords, producing foodstuffs principally, shared in the new sources of wealth by provisioning the towns engaged directly or indirectly in the lucrative wool trade.

There was a conflict of interests, however, between two types of producers: those handling foodstuffs and those dealing in raw materials for textiles. The two were known as the victuallers and non-victuallers respectively. The former, including groups like millers, grocers, bakers, fishmongers, etc., were naturally concerned to sell food products at high prices. Their wares were perishable, their interests generally local. They favoured protective toll barriers around their limited areas, and other special privileges to save them from neighbouring competitors in the same field. Thus their point of view was particularist and limited rather than broadly national or international. The shipwrights and wool merchants, on the other hand, were necessarily concerned with international relations, and could more easily conceive of England as a national unit in the economic as well as the political sense. Self-interest led them to forward-looking policies such as reduction of tolls and taxes, free trade and the like. [2] Those who controlled manufacturing, such as the master drapers, also wished to keep the prices of food down, in order to reduce their labour costs. Hence they too came into conflict with the victuallers. The struggle between the two groups was sometimes noisily reflected in the municipal politics of London, and it had repercussions affecting the entire country.

It was the non-victuallers, especially the wool-producers, who largely shaped the foreign policy of England during the 14th century. They built up a decisive influence on the internal economy of Flanders, since the prosperity of the towns there depended on supplies of raw materials from England, and an embargo could reduce its people to mass unemployment and misery. The textile guilds and merchants—the very important middle class generaly—thus formed the heart of the pro-English faction predominating in the towns. On the other hand, the feudal lords, together with their adherents and provisioners, tended as in England to adhere to the old system of local autarchy. They favoured alliance with the French monarchy in opposition to England (although they were divided among themselves on a number of more immediate issues).

The French government was of course eager to hamper or if possible to terminate the Anglo-Flemish trade. In addition, certain of the English wool interests, for reasons of their own, wished to have the dyeing and weaving industry taken over by England. To obtain it at the expense of Flanders they pressed for and put through export taxes and even temporary embargos on wool, to the consternation of shippers and others engaged in the foreign trade. [3]

Despite the many complexities and contradictions in the situation, the contest over control of Flanders was one of the main causes of the long, unhappy Hundred Years' War (1337—1453), initiated during the reign of Edward III (1327—77). The King's dynastic pretensions to the French throne were a surface phenomenon.[4] More urgent was the English desire to retain suzerainty over the feudal duchy of Gascony, so important for trade with the South, including Spain. The early victories won by English arms at Crécy (1346) and Poitiers (1356) were followed by a period of defeat. The English army on French soil was profoundly hated, the Black Prince and other English overlords imposed upon the French people proved themselves to be oppressive and wantonly destructive. The ensuing defeats were made more bitter for the English people by a growing awareness that corruption was rampant in the ruling class. To the feudal lords on both sides, the warfare often tended to become a game of jousting and gentlemanly ransoms, rather than the grim reality experienced by the ordinary soldiers. By the end of the reign of Edward III the English forces had been driven back to the coastal region between Calais and Bordeaux. Under Richard II (1377—99) they were unable to regain their former advantages. There were times when a French invasion of England seemed imminent. Periods of truce and negotiations alternated with periods of desultory warfare.

Other questions of policy hinged very largely on the alignments of this war, foreign and domestic. Within England, the victuallers in general looked upon the struggle as wasteful and irrelevant, though not until defeats threatened their prosperity. They became the core of the anti-war party. The non-victuallers supported the war, determined to defeat France in order to maintain control over Gascony and Flanders. Outside of England, the papacy became an instrument in the struggle. The French kings had captured the Holy See for a time and used it obviously as a political weapon. They actually compelled the popes to transfer residence from Rome to Avignon, in Southern France. In 1376 Pope Gregory XI returned to Rome, but was murdered in 1378. In that year the Anglo-French split among the cardinals was so deep that two popes emerged from the election, each claiming to be the sole head of Christendom. Urban VI, in Rome, represented the English party, while Clement VII in Avignon represented the French. Throughout Western Europe the church authorities received bulls and encyclicals from these two rivals, in an unseemly contest which did much to undermine the prestige of the papacy everywhere. Outside of the church, English ties with Italy were strengthened at this time by the loans and trade agreements negotiated between the English crown and Italian bankers and shipping interests.

Other countries were involved in the Anglo-French contest. The claimants for the throne of Aragon—King Pedro called the Cruel and his half-brother Enrrique—were supported by the English and the French respectively. The latter were actuated by the hope of ending England's naval power with Spanish cooperation. When Pedro met his end by assassination, the English tried unsuccessfully to place an English nobleman—John of Gaunt, who was then Pedro's son-in-law—on the throne of Spain. The Portugese government was drawn to the side of the English. In Eastern Europe, a marriage between Richard II and Anne of Bohemia was part of the strategy of foreign alliances aimed at the encirclement of France.

2. SOCIAL CHANGES AND THE DECLINE OF FEUDALISM

The expansion of trade brought much prosperity to certain sections of English society and lifted a new group, the middle class, to a position of affluence and prestige between the hereditary nobility and the lower commons. The merchants gave financial and political support to the King, but used it to strengthen their new advantages at the expense of nobility and royalty alike. Edward III himself aided a group of wool-exporters in a monopoly arrangement which controlied the foreign export, enriched the big producers and ruined the smaller ones.[5] Royal privileges made possible the buying up of supplies and the creation of an artificial scarcity, at fixed prices; in return the King obtained a share in the profits for his private income. Typical of the wealthy mercantile class now rising was the family of Sir William de la Pole, a merchant of Hull, whose son Michael became a guardian of the young Richard II; and played a conspicuous part in the court intrigues surrounding the King. Chaucer and his friend Gower were members of this new social group.

Wherever royalty and aristocracy and church hierarchy were able to augment their rent incomes from the golden profits of foreign trade, luxury increased to an unprecedented degree. For some it was further augmented through booty and ransoms obtained in the French wars. Contemporary satirical descriptions, as well as works of plastic art, portray for us the extravagant costumes and the richly furnished houses of leading members of the court circle. The very clothing they wore expressed their opulent parasitism, both in the materials and the styles. The men appeared (when out of armour) in absurdly short fur-trimmed tunics of brocade, with pinched-in waists and dangling pointed sleeves guaranteed to prevent any useful physical activity on the part of the wearer. Court ladies moved about clad in voluminous robes, stiff with gold thread, and surmounted by elaborate headgear of fine textiles. The full, high-waisted skirts emphasised the fashionable low-cut bodices above them; the headgear framed elongated faces made sophisticated by plucked eyebrows and artificially heightened foreheads. The vogue for jewels was great. Alice Perrers, the grasping mistress of Edward III in his later years, was an ardent collector of pearls, conspicuous even among the circle of court ladies sharing her expensive tastes. Wives of merchants and other commoners imitated these modes as far as possible.

The glitter and extravagance may have given an impression of prosperity within certain privileged circles, but in many ways the country's economy was unsound, and a feeling of insecurity was widespread. As the war bogged down in defeats and stalemate, more and more taxes were demanded for unfruitful military expenditures. The burden, as usual, fell on the poorest agricultural workers, who became more and more restive under them. The food supply was often inadequate, as land was shifted from farming to sheep-raising. Moreover, many landlords now began to lease out farmland to others, as a purely commercial venture; the sub-landlords exacted even more from the peasants. As early as the 14th century, the landlords had also begun appropriating free common land for their private pasturage. The separation of peasants from their land, and the beginning of absentee landlordism, can be traced to this period.

A new and horrible threat was added in the 14th century to the old dangers surrounding human life. Several times in the decades between 1340 and 1380 England was devastated by nightmare visitations of the Great Plague. Striking and killing with mysterious suddenness among people still ignorant, naturally, of its biological causes, this terrible disease is said to have reduced the population of England by one-third in the middle of the century. [6] Villages were reduced to ghostly settlements, farms lay untilled, the lords' manors functioned partially if at all. Town life was paralysed while the disease took its dreadful toll. The social consequences were, at least for short periods, a loosening of normal ties and an opportunity for free and unfree labourers to improve their status. With sheep and cattle dying and crops unharvested, the landlords were willing to employ farm workers at relatively high wages, and they did not inquire too strictly whether those they hired were runaway serfs. During these unsettled times, too, a number of serfs made good their flight to the cities where they automatically became free men if they remained undetected for a year.

The ruling class tried to check the sharp rise in wages and prices, and to hold back escaping serfs. The Parliament of 1349—50 passed a Statute of Labourers, repeatedly violated and repeatedly reenacted, which attempted to maintain the previous low wages, to confirm a long working

day, to penalise men fleeing or refusing to work, and even to inflict severe
fines on landlords offering wage increases in order to obtain sorely needed
workers. All this was in vain while conditions were difficult. Yet when
the crisis passed, most of those who had not made good their escape were
thrust back into their old positions of misery and servitude. The ruling
class had in effect used the crises as pretexts, for as Marx points out they
kept the oppressive wages-and-hours laws in effect for centuries afterwards, and repeatedly tried to enforce them, despite resistance and
the lessons of their own experience. [7] The Black Death had accelerated
tendencies already existing as the result of developments beginning
about 1300; it was not itself the revolutionary ecconomic factor which
some historians have seen in it. [8]

In the towns, class divisions and conflicts were becoming more marked.
Whereas the guild organisations of the 13th century had been founded
on principles of inner equality, and the social distinctions among free
burghers had not been great, the later development of trade and craft
production brought about sharp differentiations and antagonisms. The
masters in the more powerful guilds, and the wealthy merchants, gathered
into their hands a tight control over production. By means of special
rules and fees they kept down the number of apprentices and journeymen
who could rise to the rank of master. Many qualified workers were thus
forced to remain permanently on the lower level. The wealthy merchants
began to treat the poorer craft guilds as organisations for sweated labour.
The drapers, for instance, were able to buy up raw wool and give it out
for spinning, weaving, dyeing, etc., to craftsmen working for them.
They alone could market the final product; others were forbidden to do
any trading in cloth. The city populations thus became more and more
differentiated into extremes of wealth and poverty, dominance and
subservience.

All of these developments were a fruitful source of grievances. During
the 1370's they were aggravated by a more and more crushing burden
of war taxes, some of which were obviously being diverted from military
purposes, to maintain an inefficient government and a wantonly luxu-
rious court. Resentment at treason in high places was added to the age-
long grievances of expropriation and exploitation. It became apparent
that any further economic strain on the producers of England's wealth—
the actual workers of town and country—might well rupture the confines of the feudal system under which they lived. Yet the Parliament
of 1380 voted to impose just such a strain in the form of the notorious
Poll Tax, as unwise as it was unjust. This tax was simply uncollectable.
It provoked a movement of social revolution, the Rising of 1381 (erro-
neously called the Peasants' Revolt), which for the space of about a week

seized control of the state apparatus and with amazing singleness of purpose attempted to terminate the feudal system throughout England.

The story of those eventful days has often been told and need not be rehearsed here. [9] How the resistance broke out in Kent, an area of relative freedom; how it developed into a well organised campaign with strategic plan and clearly formulated program; how it embraced widely disparate social ranks with grievances against the feudal order; how it ripened into a provisional revolutionary government established in London and all but captured the unwilling boy King, Richard II, as its nominal head—all these events have been told many times. The striking self-discipline of the revolutionary army, its abstention from looting even when it executed the chiefs of those named traitors and destroyed their sumptuous dwellings, its clearly defined objectives, have been acknowledged even by hostile writers both medieval and modern. The program called for the following reforms: all men were to be free and equal in England, all titles and ranks were to be abolished, save for the king's; all feudal labour services, all taxes, tolls and rents were to be ended, save for a flat tax-rent of four pence per acre; all political prisoners and victims of the Statute of Labourers were to be released. Considering the rebels' inexperience, the predominantly peasant character of the revolution (which pre-doomed it to failure in any bid for lasting state power), and the forces arrayed against it, its brief period of success remains an astonishing achievement, unparalleled in all medieval history elsewhere.

Several points concerning the Rising are important for a grasp of the social factors reflected in contemporary literature. First, the revolt was a broad one. It included not only serfs and villeins and free peasants (though these were in the majority); it also numbered in its ranks many craftsmen of the towns, poor priests (like John Ball, the ideological exponent of the movement), small tradesmen and scattered members of the gentry, who had their own grievances against the barons and the court. In London, it was three members of the City Council, belonging to victuallers' guilds, who opened the gates of the city to the rebels. This broad support shows how widely was felt the need for drastic social changes.

Second, the rebels were very clear as to who were their enemies, and why. They were especially bitter against lawyers, for they saw in them the architects of the system which oppressed them. Besides, they were much aware that their own ancient title to the soil of England, reaching back to Anglo-Saxon times, had been violated by feudal law. That is why they repeatedly demanded, at the castles and abbeys they captured, the "charters of their liberties" which they claimed had been stolen from them. That is why in the Temple area of London they burnt the lawyers' records which stipulated their fees and obligations under feudalism.

A second main objective of the rebels' hatred was the clique of powerful barons who held large tracts of England as their private property, and swayed domestic and foreign policies under Richard II. Chief of these was John of Gaunt, Duke of Lancaster, uncle of the King and pretender to the Spanish throne. Resentment at his power led to the burning of his London residence, the Savoy House, during which treasures of inestimable value were systematically destroyed but not a single act of looting was permitted to go unpunished by the rebel army itself. Finally, state officials known for their class policy of oppression were marked out for summary judgment, which in some cases terminated in execution. Such were Archbishop Simon Sudbury, the King's Chancellor, and Robert Hales, his Treasurer, declared traitors by the rebels. It is obvious that popular anger was felt against the former, not as churchman, but as mundane politician, one of a familiar and widely hated type. When abbies were sacked, like wealthy St. Alban's, it was because they had acted as oppressive landlords, not because they were religious houses *per se.*

The Rising failed. Its forces were cleverly divided by the enemy, its leaders were seized and put to death. The old services and obligations were reestablished—if not everywhere, at least wherever the landlords were able to enforce them. But the feudal system had received a blow never forgotten on either side. Its weakness, and the demoralisation of its leaders, had been revealed for all to see. The pattern of future change was established. From then on the currents leading to the Reformation and (in the 17th century) to the successful social revolution took their course with gathering strength and clarity.

3. RELIGIOUS WRITERS: THE REFORMERS AND MYSTICS

Protest against the political role of the church, which contributed to the Rising of 1381, was also expressed in more theoretical ways by reformist writers using both Latin and English. The Franciscan William of Ockham (died ca. 1350) had already formulated elaborate refutations to the popes' claim of supreme temporal power, but his Latin polemics were phrased in terms of the old controversy between Guelfs and Ghibellines, between papacy and empire. They did not bear primarily on the specific situation in England.

Closer to home was the criticism of John Wycliff (1324—84), which contained strong elements of social protest. Wycliff's background was academic, for he was a doctor of theology at Oxford, but he was drawn into practical politics by his concern with the limitation of church power in relation to the state. This was the theme of his works *De Dominio*

Christine de Pisan and Three Allegorical Virtues from *La Cité des Dames*

Bibliothèque Nationale, Paris

Civili, *De Officio Regis*, and *De Ecclesia* (*On Civil Power*, *On the King's Office* and *On the Church*), among others. His attacks on the political ambitions of prelates suited the purposes of John of Gaunt, and so that mighty baron, together with others at court, extended protection to Wycliff when he was charged with heresy in these matters. More significant is the support he received from wide sections of the community outside of the court. The citizens of London (most of whom were hostile to John of Gaunt) supported the reformer, and so did his colleagues at Oxford. When charges of heresy against him reached the University, its chancellor and doctors attached no great importance to them.

The source of his strength among the masses was his practical work affecting their daily lives. Wycliff saw that many of the people were deprived of adequate spiritual care by a system of absentee priests or "provisors" who drew revenues from the parishes and left poor and ill-qualified vicars to do the work. He saw too that many of the hierarchy were no more than worldly politicians making careers for themselves, without any interest in the welfare of the masses. A glaring example was offered by the career of Henry Despenser, Bishop of Norwich. He had received his bishopric while still a youth, in return for purely military service to Urban VI in Italy. He continued to dedicate himself to warfare thereafter. He personally led a bloody charge against the rebels of 1381, slaughtering many with his own hand, and he was later called upon by the Pope to lead a military campaign in Flanders against the adherents of the anti-Pope Clement: a campaign which Urban tried to dignify by the name of crusade, enlisting the friars to preach for it, and promising indulgences to those who participated in it. This pseudo-crusade was an object of sharp denunciation by Wycliff, and it fortified the vigour of his attacks on the papacy as a whole.

To make good the lack of a true people's clergy in England, Wycliff organised a group of "Poor Priests" who, like the early Franciscans, agitated for a return to the primitive Christian ideals of simplicity, equality and humility. They and their followers were generally called Lollards. The Poor Priests were blamed for some of the revolutionary ardour of 1381, though their doctrines were not actually revolutionary in the political sense. Long after the Rising had been suppressed, they were persecuted as dangerous to the church and state.

The theoretical basis of Wycliff's program was the thesis that no lord or other official, whether secular or ecclesiastical—not even the pope—has a right to demand obedience if he is himself in a state of mortal sin. In other words, he claimed that dominion must be founded on a state of grace. Without this, the bonds of feudal authority were declared by him to be dissolved, so far as ordinary people were concerned. Much of

15

Wycliff's invective was turned against the upper hierarchy, who obviously did not meet his requirements for priesthood. He denounced the wholesale use of excommunication and interdict as political weapons, arguing that no one can be cut off from the Christian community unless it is by his own acts. No wonder the organised church took alarm. The state authorities were at first more tolerant, although his program threatened them too, because they saw in it a justification for the aggrandisement of secular rulers at the expense of ecclesiastical. Only after Wycliff's death did the state perceive how these doctrines would undermine its own power. Self-disqualification from secular lordship because of a state of mortal sin would have left few in the royal or chief noble families of the time (according to their own chroniclers) with a right to govern England. Realisation of this implication led to the persecution of the Lollards in the early 15th century.

In the 1380's Wycliff reached the conclusion that, for theoretical reasons, he must reject the teachings of the church on the subject of the eucharist. He now maintained that the bread and wine of the sacrament were not, in actual fact, changed into the flesh and blood of Jesus Christ by the intercessionary words of the officiating priest. His denial meant that he was rejecting the cornerstone of Catholic philosophical doctrine, and substituting a heretical interpretation. Those who supported him for purely political reasons did not share it. They could not accompany him when his teachings began to militate against the very advantages previously gained from his attacks on church rule, for he was now endangering the entire order which gave them privileged status. His dual challenge, both practical and theoretical, had far-reaching international results in the 15th century, especially in Bohemia and Poland. One of the earliest poems written in the Polish vernacular of that period is a eulogy of Wycliff by Andrzej Gałka, combined with an anti-papal philippic adapted from Wycliff's theses. [10]

So far as the English language and literature are concerned, Wycliff is chiefly important because of the sermons and tracts he composed in the vernacular, [11] and his great project of a translation which for the first time gave the English poeple a full text of the Bible in their own tongue. His tracts and sermons about true repentance and a state of grace, about the hypocrisy and greed of prelates and friars, were disseminated through the agency of his Poor Priests. In writing English, Wycliff used an admirably simple style, very easy for untutored listeners to understand. In these terms, for instance, he deplored the Great Schism which split Werstern Christendom:

For al oure west lond is wiþ þat oo [one] pope or þat oþir; and he þat is wiþ þat oon, hatiþ þe oþir, wiþ alle hise, and ȝit ipocritis feynen þat al þis is for charite, and þis ypocrisie is worse þan þat oþer synne bifore, for þis world growiþ in synne fro yvel to worse.

Wycliff often took the opportunity to defend the use of the vernacular in religious services, as here in his explanation of the origin of the Lord's Prayer:

And so he [Jesus] tauȝte hem oute þis prayer; bot be þou syker [sure], noþer in Latyn noþer in Frensche bot in þe langage þat þey usede to speke, for þat þey knewe best. And here is a reule to Cristen men, of what langage evere þey be, þat it is an heye sacrifice to God to kunne here Pater Noster, þe gospel, and oþer poyntes of holy writ nedeful to here soules, and þey to do þer-after, wheþer it be ytolde to him or wryten in Latyn, or in Englysshe, or in Frensche, or in Duchyssche, oþer in eny oþer langage....12

The Biblical translation was done by Wycliff and a group of associates. He himself probably translated the New Testament only, while Nicholas Hereford did the Old, with assistance, and John Purvey revised the whole. The work was finished by 1388.

In many ways Wycliff anticipated the Reformation of the 16th century, and the teachings of the Puritans who in the 17th put an end to the last relics of feudal servitude. His emphasis on the individual conscience, his appeal to the Bible rather than to the traditions of the Latin church; his insistence on qualification by a state of grace, itself contingent upon predestination; his disapproval of the excessive cult of the saints (though he did not deny their sainthood); his non-institutional definition of the church as the sum total of those destined from eternity for salvation[13]—all these elements in his thinking pointed clearly to the rise of Protestantism in England. It is likely that he himself was unaware of their historical significance. Any one of these doctrines, if accepted, was a lever powerful enough to unsettle the entire feudal state, as well as the unified medieval church. But his sense of the betrayal and injustice committed by these institutions under the cloak of Christianity moved him to undertake his reform movement before he could have been aware of the mass following it would win. His steadfastness and principled courage under harassment revealed how essentially he differed from those who supported him from motives of mere political advantage.[14]

Less directly than Wycliff, the mystical writers of the age also represented a kind of challenge to the unified Western church. As Engels has pointed out in connection with Thomas Münzer,[15] the mystics of the 14th and 15th centuries were non-conformists of a sort, since they sought a direct, personal and independent contact with God, apart from the official channels provided by the church. They were privately cutting through the barriers of ecclesiastical formalities at the very time when organised masses of the people were trying to cut through the network of tolls, rents, services and other restrictions hampering their economic lives. In belief the mystics were usually quite orthodox, not seeing the institutional consequences of what they were trying to do. Engels has pointed out the kinship between late medieval mysticism and the rebellious plebeian movements of the cities. It is probably no accident, historically, that the tendency developed strongly in the Low Countries which had a flourishing commercial life, essentially anti-feudal, and that it appeared in England in the areas tied to Flanders by trade (Norfolk and Yorkshire). Flemish hermits were already established in Yorkshire early in the 14th century.

Richard Rolle of Hampole (ca. 1300—49) was the most celebrated of the 14th century mystics. [16] After an uncompleted education at Oxford, he retired to a hermit's retreat on a patron's Yorkshire estate. His writings in Latin and English include some emotional prayers, meditations on the Passion, paraphrases of the Psalms, and expositions of the mystical experience in its three stages. Curiously, Rolle's writings, even when most charged with personal feeling, were composed in an elaborate, even artificial style suggesting much polishing and working-over by the author. The Latin is often decorative in a tortuous way. In English, Rolle experimented with carefully constructed sentences, studded with alliteration, assonance and occasional rime. The units are of similar length, and their ends are marked by cadence (called *cursus* [17] in medieval Latin usage): that is, rhythmical effects obtained from certain well-defined stress patterns terminating clauses and sentences. Typical are these sentences from "Gastly Gladnesse" (i.e., "Spiritual Joy"), which are crammed with alliteration, inversion, paradox and *cursus*:

It war na wonder if dede [death] war dere, þat I myght se him þat I seke. But now it es lenthed [separated by distance] fra me, and me behoves lyf here, til he wil me lese [release]. Lyst and lere of this lare [listen and learn of this lore], and þe sal noght myslike. Lufe makes me to melle [be confused], and joy gars me jangell [causes me to speak janglingly]. Loke þow lede þi lyf in lyghtsummnes; and hevynes, holde it away. Sarynes, lat it noght sytt wyth þe; bot in gladnes of God evermare make þow þi gle. *Amen.*

Very different was the emotional outpouring of Juliana of Norwich, whose *Revelations of Divine Love* [18] was composed in 1373. Her visions and meditations on sin and redemption are expressed in an artless language, often confused, but also at times gruesomely concrete. With her *Revelations*, mystical writing becomes what we should today call hysterical. Her brooding on the physical anguish connected with redemption reminds us of the art of certain early Flemish painters who concentrated on details of blood and suffering against grotesque backgrounds of dream-like horror.

Walter Hilton (died 1395) is sometimes classified with the mystics, but his religious works are didactic without being extremely emotional, and his prose style lacks Rolle's elaboration. *The Scale of Perfection* describes the familiar problems of sin and temptation, prayer and repentance, in relation to the active and the contemplative life. *An Epistle on the Mixed Life* explains how a combination of these two types of living is under certain circumstances to be recommended for secular and ecclesiastical lords, in view of their practical responsibilities. [19]

4. PIERS PLOWMAN

The most important literary document picturing the social and religious agitation of the 14th century is *Piers Plowman*. This is a lengthy allegorical poem in alliterative long lines, a form already used in two earlier moral satires, *Winner and Waster* and *The Parlement of the Three Ages* (ca. 1350). *Piers Plowman* has come down to us in 47 manuscripts representing three quite different versions. They are commonly designated as A, B and C respectively. In all versions the text is divided into sections of unequal length called *passus*. Like many of its predecessors in Latin and French, the poem is told as a visionary experience on the part of the author. [20] The name of the poet is unknown. But a Latin note in one of the manuscripts (Dublin D. 4, 1), together with the wording of line B xv, 148:

I haue lyued in *londe*, quod I, my name is *longe Wille,*

(and other probable puns in the text) have led many scholars to assume that the author was named William Langland. [21] Some critics have argued that more than one writer produced the several versions of *Piers Plowman*; that the B and C forms are revisions of A which the poet could not have made, since they show blundering misapprehensions of the original meaning. [22] But other critics have refuted the cases cited, and variously explained away the discrepancies. [23] For the purposes of general discussion it will be simplest to follow traditional practice and call the author or set of authors William Langland, referring to one name while recognising that it may cover a complex situation.

The dating of the poem is also a matter of controversy. The editor of the first complete modern edition, W.W. Skeat, [24] placed the three version at periods separated by intervals of almost fifteen years: A in 1362,

B in 1376—77, C about 1392. But his evidence was limited to internal allusions whose significance has been challenged. Recent studies have tended to reduce the gaps between versions, and to place all three in the 1370's, during the end of the reign of Edward III, and the beginning of Richard's. This contraction of the span in dating probably strengthens the claim for single authorship of the versions. [25]

In its broad outlines, at least, we can discuss the contents and the significance of this great poem without reference to the knotty problems of dating and authorship.

The B version may be taken as a basis for summary of the main points of the poem. It is much fuller than A, while the C-text reveals changes chiefly in matters of emphasis and detail. In the Prologue the author tells us that he fell asleep and dreamed that he beheld a "field full of folk"—a vision of humanity, engaged in its many activities within the space between a Tower of Truth and Valley of Evil. He notices the deceitful ways of many groups in society, such as friars, merchants and pardoners, and he recounts the fable of a rats' parliament engaged in discussing how to get rid of a tyrannical old cat (i.e., the king?) that plagues them. They wonder whether a kitten (Richard II?) might not be worse. [26]

In Passus i of the text proper, Langland asks Holy Church for instruction, especially in the art of recognising falsehood and its works. In reply, she points to the allegorical figures of Falsehood and his companion Lady Meed (Reward or Bribery), surrounded by such personages as Flattery, Simony and Guile. Meed is to be wedded to Falsehood, but Theology objects, and so the entire crew of deceivers appeal to the King in London. Here threats of punishment frighten some of them, but Meed—a familiar of popes and princes—makes a hypocritical defense before Conscience. Impressed by it, the King bids Conscience give a kiss to Meed, but he refuses and admonishes the King on the proper use of his royal power.

A second vision begins with Passus v. It is devoted to a sermon preached by Reason to the Seven Deadly Sins, who are in turn moved to repentance. Each Sin is described as a vividly particular person, living, breathing, roistering, weeping and repenting, though each at the same time represents an abstract character. Joined by a multitude of people, the reformed Sins now resolve to go on a pilgrimage in quest of Truth. Piers Plowman, the humble but enlightened worker who stands for an idealised clergy, suddenly appears and says he will guide them, but first every man has work to do in the world, each according to his station in society. This section ends (Passus vii) with a not entirely clear discussion about the role of good deeds—as opposed to prayer and penance—in winning salvation (the "pardon" sent by Truth). [27]

Up to this point the plot of the story is known as the *Visio* of Piers Plowman. Its sense is fairly clear. It deals primarily with the "social" sins such as avarice, public corruption and falsehood in human relations, and the need to cure them. The rest of the poem in all versions carries forward the quest by showing in contrast three forms of the good life which may be sought under the names of Do-Wel, Do-Bet and Do-Best. Hence this section is entitled the *Vita* of Piers Plowman. In A, it is a mere sketch of three *passus*; in B it is increased to ten (with three prologues), and in C to thirteen.

In the *Vita*-section the emphasis becomes more subjective and the allegory more learned and complex. Not only are the allegorical figures multiplied, but their meanings do not seem to remain the same throughout. It is quite consistent with medieval aesthetic usage, of course, for one and the same character to have many meanings, literal and figurative; but the *Vita* in Piers Plowman is especially baffling, and critics have differed widely in their interpretations of it. One suggestion is that the forms of the good life may stand for the active life, the contemplative life and a combination of the two in the life of an ideal prelate. [28] Certain it is that the figure of Piers or Peter Plowman himself shifts and expands in meaning. At one moment he appears to represent the simple plowman readily exemplifying the ordinary secular priest guiding his parishioners; later he suggests a member of the upper hierarchy. His office is compared to St. Peter's and to the idealised papacy, and he is even in a shadowy way identified with Jesus Christ. [29] There is an impressive if not too clear metaphorical section in which the Passion is described as a chivalrous jousting against Satan for the rescue of man's soul (B xvi—xvii). Throughout, the author is deeply concerned about the corruption of an institution supposed to have been founded, through St. Peter, for the spiritual care of humanity. [30]

The author of *Piers Plowman* was essentially conservative in his social-political theories. He endorsed without reservation the doctrine that men and women should remain in the classes of society into wich they were born. His denunciation of friars and pardoners, absentee priests and worldly bishops, did not mean a frontal attack on the church from without, but rather a plea for reform from within. Langland was no Lollard. In B xv, 207, for instance, Anima states that charity does not reside in "lollerns ne in land leperes [i.e., vagabond] hermytes." Similarly, the poet's denunciation of bribery and corruption at court embodied no real challenge to feudal kingship and overlordship. Even the thesis (put into the mouth of Conscience, B iv, 182) that a king can not rightly rule without assent of the "comure wil" has a narrower significance than progressive modern readers might suppose: no one would have dreamed of consulting the will of serfs and villeins as part of the commons. The poem also contains warnings against the desire to penetrate too deeply into science, for this caused the downfall of Adam and Eve (B xv 60 f.).

But if Langland was no democrat in political theory as we understand it today, he was democratic on his broad human sympathies. In his religion he constantly stressed the principle of spiritual democracy: the equal preciousness of all souls before God, and their equal responsibility for their neighbours (within the medieval class system, of course). The idealised figure of the Good Samaritan, the type of a good neighbour, is merged with that of Jesus (B xvii). Langland's keen eye and sympathetic heart recorded in living colours a pageant of scenes depicting the people's misery, in town and country. Thus the entire poem is a unique and invaluable social document. One of the most moving passages, an addition to the C-text, takes us into the cottage of a harassed serf or villein, causing us to share the cold, the hunger, the crying of the children and the endless worry about rent:

C x, 71   The most needy aren our neighebores   and we nyme good hede,
    As prisones in puttes   and poure folke in cotes,
    Charged with children   and chef lordes rente,
    That thei with spynnynge may spare   spenen hit on hous-hyre
    Bothe in mylk and in mele   to make with papelotes
    To a-glotye here gurles   that greden after fode.
    Al-so hem-selue   suffren muche hunger
    And wo in winter-tyme   with wakynge a nyghtes
    To ryse to the ruel   to rocke the cradel,
    Bothe to karde and to kembe   to clouten and to wasche
    To rubbe and rely   russches to pilie
    That reuthe is to rede   othere in ryme shewe
    The wo of these women   that wonyth in cotes
    And of meny other men   that muche wo suffren...

[nyme = take;   puttes = pits;   spenen = spend;   papelotes = porridge;   a-glotye = satisfy;   greden = cry;   to the ruel = regularly;   clouten = patch;   rely = rewind; pilie = peel;   wonyth = dwell]

As a satirist, Langland strove to concentrate his denunciations upon matters of general principles: principles accepted in advance from his religion. On this foundation he constructed a work of hope and triumph. There is no trace in him of that hostility to humanity which has corroded the work of other gifted satirists like Jonathan Swift. On the other hand, his positive conclusion is reached in an atmosphere of increasing mysticism which becomes more obscure as it becomes more rapturous; the future victory is abstract and visionary, being expressed in terms of the defeat of Anti-Christ and the ultimate triumph of the purified church

The Dreamer of the *Pearl*-poem

"Fro spot my spyryt þer sprang in space"

in an age beyond ordinary human experience. Despite much learned commentary, it is difficult to be sure of the author's message in these latter parts, the more so as the commentators themselves disagree about the author's intentions, his orthodoxy and the extent of his learning. [31]

In the earlier part of the poem, however, the *Visio*, the message is usually fairly clear, and the artistic method is one of the most successful to be applied to medieval allegory. A very effective type of genre-realism is employed to supply a running commentary, as it were, on the abstract meanings. For instance, the Seven Sins who listen to the sermon of Reason and repent, are not only moral-theological concepts; they are also pictured as real people, with the sensuous details of their physical appearances sharply defined. Avarice, as an example, is beetle-browed, thick-lipped and blear-eyed,

B v, 192   And as a letheren purs   lolled his chekes
            Wel sydder than his chyn   thei chiueled for elde...

[sydder = wider; chiueled = shivered]

Gluttony, after his repentance, starts for the church to confess his sins. But Betty the brewer lures him into the inn to drink her good ale; he joins his village cronies there, swilling, laughing and quarreling. By evensong he is so drunk that he can not walk home straight: "He myȝte neither steppe ne stonde, er he his staffe hadde." He staggers and falls over his threshold, and his wife and servant have the sorry task of putting him to bed:

B v, 355   And whan he drowgh to the dore   thanne dymmed his eighen,
            He stumbled on the thresshewolde   an threwe to the erthe.
            Clement the cobelere   cauȝte him bi the myddel
            For to lifte hym alofte   and lyede him on his knowes.
            With al the wo of this worlde   his wyf and his wenche
            Baren hym home to his bedde   and brouȝte hym therinne.

[eighen = eyes;   knowes = knees]

Once again we are reminded of the technique of 14th and 15th-century painting, in which scenes of tactile realism surround the personages representing abstract ideas — the divine and saintly ones — and provide a commentary on them, often by way of contrast. In Poland, the work of Wit Stwosz illustrates this method of juxtaposition. Medieval art introduced its most effective realism as illustration of pre-conceived abstract principles, whereas modern art tends to make the generalised meanings grow out of the typicality inherent in specific concrete instances, when conceived and interpreted against a broad social background.

5. THE *PEARL*-POET AND HIS SCHOOL

Contemporary with *Piers Plowman* is another poem (ca. 1370), also an allegorical dream-vision but shorter and more lyrical in tone, which is devoted to the exposition of religious doctrine by means of a personal mystical experience. This is the *Pearl*,[32] which appears on the surface to be an elegy for the death of a two-year-old girl, possibly the daughter of the poet. He tells about a visionary colloquy with the lost child which brought comfort to him in his grief. The conversation occurs across a clear glittering stream which separates the living from the felicitous inhabitants of heaven. The child is the precious pearl that had slipped away from the poet and been lost under the sod. She is now clad in dazzling white, pearl-adorned, and wearing a pearl-encrusted crown. She discourses to him of the bliss in heaven and explains the celestial economy, very different from the terrestrial, which permits a creature so young and inexperienced to enjoy bliss in the highest ranks of the elect. (The orthodoxy of this part has been questioned.[33]) The poet is allowed to behold from afar the indescribable splendour of the New Jerusalem, resplendent with a light far exceeding the sun's. Here in the throng of the blessed he once more glimpses his "little queen" from afar. Consumed with longing, he tries to plunge across the forbidden stream, but with that vain effort he awakes.

The linguistic virtuosity of this poem is remarkable. On a minor scale, it achieves the kind of difficult perfection realised with vaster amplitude in Dante's *Paradiso*. The enriched alliterative vocabulary forms a shining mosaic of words drawn from many sources into Middle English. They are wrought into the text with careful skill, and so aptly that the effect of emotional sincerity is in no way diminished. No less striking is the poet's sense of literary form. The organisation of the 101 stanzas into subdivisions, the interlinking of lines between stanzas, the use of a refrain echoing the last line of one in the first line or the next, are details of a poetic architecture again suggesting the gifts of a Dante *in parvo*. There is even the possibility of direct influence from Dante.

The dialect of *Pearl* is that of the Northwest Midlands, which at this time was being used in an impressive amount of distinguished alliterative verse, written by anonymous poets. Though *Pearl* is unique in quality, it does not stand isolated.[34]

The precise meaning of the poem is not clear. Once again, the ambiguities of medieval technique suggest a multiplicity of possible interpretations, not necessarily mutually exclusive. The elegy may be a personal one[35] (though not all critics agree on this), and it may be indebted to *Olympia*, a Latin elegy by Boccaccio, also lamenting the death of a little

daughter. (The possible debt to Boccaccio would explain, by the way, a generic similarity to the last of the *Threnodies* written by the 16th century
Polish poet Jan Kochanowski on the death of his daughter Ursula. [36]) But
the theme may not be personal at all. It has been interpreted in several
different ways as a purely theological allegory; the pearl lost and recovered through a vision has been identified with spiritual purity, or with
man's primal innocence. [37] However, medieval poetic experience was quite
often valid on two or more levels. It could simultaneously treat of an
actual experience, and an abstract (allegorical) or doctrinal thesis, just
as Dante's Beatrice may at one and the same time represent a real woman,
a moral quality, and the allegorical figure of Theology. There is no reason
why *The Pearl* should not likewise be valid on two or even more levels
of interpretation. [38]

Sir Gawain and the Green Knight, best of all Arthurian romances
(see ch. 9, sec. 3), is uniquely preserved in the same manuscript (Cotton
A. x. 4) containing our sole copy of *Pearl.* [39] Here too we find a brilliant
polychromatic vocabulary and fluent alliterative verse masterfully organised in the rime-scheme of a difficult stanzaic form. In this text groups
of long lines are tied up just before the final one by clusters of short
riming lines; the pattern is called the "tail-rime" stanza. The narrative
technique is heightened by unobtrusive use of devices made familiar
by Virgil. [40]

The plot of the romance combines two themes about the testing
of a hero in order to glorify further the already popular figure of Sir
Gawain. The main story tells how Gawain accepts and carries out the
challenge offered to him in the winter season by a grim supernatural
adversary, the Green Knight. It is in the form of a test called the Beheading Game. The challenger says: You may cut off my head now, and
later I (a self-restoring magician) will have the right to cut off yours.
The odds appear overwhelmingly unfavourable to a mere ordinary mortal,
be he never so brave, but Gawain emerges from the test alive and only
slightly scathed. Interwoven with this plot is a secondary test of Gawain's
knightly qualities: at the abode of the Green Knight (unrecognised at
the time, for the Knight is now in ordinary mortal guise), Gawain is
obliged to resist the amorous advances of his hostess. Conforming to an
agreement with her husband, he must yield up to the latter at the end
of each day any gifts he has received as guest. He thus surrenders several
kisses (though gallantly refusing to reveal their origin), but he disho-
nestly retains a girdle which is supposed to make him immune to any
enemy's blows. Considering the decapitation he expects shortly to face,
it is no wonder that he succumbs to this one temptation. Later, when
he re-encounters his host in the form of the Green Knight, he is twice

completely spared from a threatened death-blow and then the third time only slightly nicked in retribution for his one deception in the matter of the girdle. The Green Knight reveals his identity, explains the aim of the test and his wife's planned role in it, and congratulates Gawain on his behaviour. The single lapse from perfection has, we feel, not only heightened the interest of the story but made its hero more credibly human than he would otherwise be.

The materials for the plot can be traced back to Celtic sources.[41] A strikingly close analogue to the Beheading Game—in a more primitive setting—is to be found in the Irish prose tale *Fled Bricrend* (*The Feast of Bricriu*), dealing with pre-Christian heroes and composed well before 1000 A.D. This early treatment has overtones suggesting associations with some sort of nature-myth, such as the passing of the old year (under the guise of a hero or divinity) to be replaced by a new. These overtones echo through intermediary French romances and can still be faintly heard in the Middle English.[42] The colour of the Green Knight, the holly branch he carries, the occurrence of his magic beheading at the time of mid-winter, the very nature of the hero's test, do indeed invoke thoughts of primitive custom and belief. But these memories are already deeply buried. The poet tones down the wild and supernatural elements of the traditional plot. Instead, he stresses the rich settings, the refined manners and the humanity of the characters in the style of chivalrous romance. Especially delightful are the conversations in which Gawain tactfully parries the advances of his hostess, contriving at the same time to spare her feelings and protect his own integrity. These passages sparkle with the subtlety of high comedy.

But the most striking and original gift of this author is his superb command of nature description. Before him, the medieval poets had limited themselves, almost exclusively, to the conventional and monotonous celebrations of spring: always a spring of mild sunshine and flowers, never a season of rain and belated frosts. The *Gawain*-poet, unlike them, responded deeply and with fine perception to all the seasons of the year. He creates for us summer's heavy heat, the dusty wind-storms and driving rains of autumn, the icy sleet and low dark clouds of winter. When he introduces a hunting scene he evokes the frosty air, the barking dogs, the low red sun. He helps us to hear and see, to touch and taste by proxy. By the same gift he makes us share a knight's weariness under cold wet armour, and the glow of welcome felt upon entering a warmly hospitable hall. The individual details are convincingly concrete, and they are even touched at times with humour. Yet they are carefully selected and disposed in such a way that they heighten rather than disturb the atmosphere of romance. Throughout, the postulates of chivalry are as uncritically accepted as in the 12th-century works of Chrétien de Troyes. Rarely however have they been incorporated in art of so high an order.

Two other poems in the same dialect (but not regularly stanzaic in form) are contained in the *Pearl-Gawain* manuscript. These are the didactic religious pieces *Patience* and *Purity*.[43] Both inculcate the lessons suggested by their titles, through the use of *exempla* from the Bible. The former gives lively treatment to the story of Jonah; the latter, among other warning illustrations, recounts the story of Noah and the Flood. The long, unrimed alliterative lines are vigorous and even impressive. Because of the high literary quality of all four poems contained in this same manuscript, and the identity of the dialect throughout, it is widely assumed that all are by the same author. Nevertheless internal evidence of style and vocabulary,[44] and even subjective impressions on the part of critics, have been cited as evidence that two or more authors created this cluster of unusual works. If so, they must have been closely associated in locality, in training, and in the possession of a like order of talent.

Saint Erkenwald[45] is a separately preserved poem which can be compared with the preceding four in respect to language, dialect, use of alliteration and even literary skill, but it is almost certainly by a different writer. It rises above the ordinary run of saints' lives, with their stereotyped miracles, because it worthily treats a problem of serious concern to medieval thinkers: the eternal damnation assigned to all heathen, even the most virtuous of those who lived under the Old Law, according to the teachings of the church Fathers. Dante had shown his uneasiness at this severe judgment; he tells with satisfaction about the special intercession by Pope Gregory the Great which was supposed to have saved the good Emperor Trajan and won him a place in heaven, despite theological disqualifications (*Purgatorio*, x, 73—93). *Piers Plowman* also refers to the salvation of Trajan. In the present poem, St. Erkenwald intercedes for the salvation of an ancient Briton, a virtuous and upright judge with whose undecayed body he holds miraculous converse. The poem excels the average of its type by its strong sense of sympathy and justice, surmounting the limits of creed and conventional doctrine.

6. THE WORK OF JOHN GOWER

A famous contemporary of Chaucer, and his close associate, was John Gower (1330—1408).[46] He is an important figure because of the scope of his work and the languages in which he wrote. A member of the well-to-do commons now achieving social eminence, he was the last writer of note to employ with equal readiness the three traditional languages familiar to intellectuals: French, Latin and English. In his lifetime, English was receiving official recognition as the national language, and the use of the others became more and more restricted. [47] Gower subsumes many results of medieval literary culture without stepping beyond them, as Chaucer did, into a democratic realism and a bolder scepticism prophetic of the Renaissance. [48] It is likely that he was well known in the royal court. King Richard himself, he says, proposed the composition of the *Confessio Amantis*.

The first of Gower's three major works, the *Miroir de l'homme* (*The Mirror of Mankind*, composed ca. 1376—79) is a long didactic piece in French denouncing the crimes and follies of humanity under the headings of the seven major vices, elaborately subdivided. Though nearly 30,000 lines long, the poem has been left unfinished. There is an element of pale allegory in the introduction, for the seven vices are represented as daughters of Sin itself by the Devil. Death also is the result of that alliance, and the Devil begets further offspring by his seven daughters. The subdivisions correspond to these progenies. As in *Piers Plowman*, Reason and Conscience give aid to man in his fight against the Satanic brood. Gower surveys the effects of the several vices in the three estates of society: nobility, clergy and commons. This threefold social division is in turn subdivided many times over. Gower's plan provides, for instance, for detailed invective against simony among curates, greed, lechery and love of venery among monks, commercial brokerage and usury at the papal court, malicious gossip among nuns. The other orders are dissected with the same minute attention. [49] There is a concrete reality to be sensed behind the most general statements. Expressed in abstract terms, the topics often run very close to those indirectly treated by Chaucer through the medium of his created personalities. Particularly interesting is Gower's denunciation of luxury at the courts of kings, and the deleterious effect of the new wealth upon the ladies of royal households. The work is broadly eclectic in its borrowings, but Gower has produced from them a unified social document. [50]

Vox Clamantis (revised soon after 1381), a poem in Latin elegiacs, was also planned as a moralist's view of human society, but the events of the great Rising caused Gower to prefix a long allegorical account of that event which is more interesting than the remainder. The Rising filled him, naturally, with horror and fear. He recounts its course metaphorically as a revolt of animals against the harmonious rule of Nature:

217　　Magnos magna decent, et paruos parva, set illi,
　　　　Qui sunt de minimis, grandia ferre volunt.

> Great things befit the great ones, little the little folk; but these
> Men of the lowest estate, wish to bear them as grandees.

Asses, the normally patient beasts of burden, try to act like lions; the oxen throw off their yokes and assume the paws of bears and the tails of dragons, abandoning the cultivation of the fields; the swine run amok, led by a wild Boar of Kent (John Ball). To Gower the dissipation of the rebellion seemed of course like the merciful intervention of providence. His allegorical account, animated by his fear, gives a valuable insight into the emotions felt by many others like him. Supplemented by his more factual sequel the *Chronica Tripertita*, it likewise indicates the widespread dissatisfaction felt even by conservatives at the policies of Richard II, and the reasons why the King eventually lost the support of anti-reform as well as reform groups on the middle class.

The *Confessio Amantis* (*Lover's Confession*, completed in three different versions between 1390 and 1393) is, despite its Latin title, the long English work upon which Gower's fame chiefly rests. It begins with a Prologue of moral lamentation upon the corruption of the three estates,[51] much in the vein of Gower's preceding works. But the framework of the whole belongs rather to the courtly school than the satirical. The poet, being love-sick, appeals to Venus, who tells him to confess his sins against love to her priest named Genius. (This character derives from the *Romance of the Rose*.) The rest of the eight books consist of the colloquy between the Lover and Genius, abundantly illustrated by appropriate stories. The entire work is thus a long series of *exempla* put into an allegorical narrative setting. Compared to Chaucer's *Canterbury Tales*, that setting is of course static and lifeless, but the project was no less ambitious. Gower carefully divides and subdivides the sins against love as he had subdivided the vices of society in the *Miroir*. The subject is ostensibly lighter, but the tone remains incorrigibly glum. The situation—a priest-like figure solemnly teaching the amorous art by examples—might have been treated as light-hearted burlesque, but it is not. As narrator for entertainment Gower still retains the style of a moral satirist, and he does not extend his approval to the fashionable adultery of courtly love. The end is unconventional. Venus cures the lover (Gower) of love by showing him his own face in a mirror. He accepts the unpalatable truth that he is too old for her ministrations, and resigns all hope of success in the erotic art.

The stories in the *Confessio* come from the many springs which fed medieval collections of *exempla* and romance in general, with particular emphasis on Biblical and classical history and Ovidian mythology. Among the medieval plots, two are important because they are close analogues to tales in Chaucer's *Canterbury* group. Gower's story of Constance (ii, 587—1612) parallels the Man of Law's Tale, and that of Florent (i, 1407—1861) parallels the Wife of Bath's Tale. Gower shows no signs of influence by Chaucer's superior treatments; the resemblances are due rather to the use of common sources. The digressions in the *Confessio Amantis* touching on science, pseudo-science, education, political theory and the like are often more interesting to us than the familiar tales which prompted them.

As a versifier, Gower is smooth and competent, neither disturbing nor inspiring. This holds true of his shorter lyrical poems as its does of his narratives. He often achieves pathos, but never rises to grandeur. He employs dialogue, description, action and reflection as one who is both instructed and experienced in the art of story-telling. Had he not been a contemporary of Chaucer, his ability would probably stand out with greater brilliance. As it is, he suffers the diminution resulting from a juxtaposition with genius.

Gower's writing, no matter what his subject, is that of a social monitor deeply concerned about the welfare of mankind. Because of his concern for didactic interpretations he well earned Chaucer's epithet "moral Gower"—though in a somewhat different sense than our own use of the word. The admonition "Praise of Peace," addressed to Henry IV in English, reflects his hatred of war—a theme to which he returned more than once. He also stressed frequently the responsibility of princes to the peoples ruled by them. His learning was wide for the times; his interest in science was unusual for one concerned primarily with the arts.[52] On more than one issue we find him occupying a progressive position for *a priori* reasons that are moralistic rather than scientific in the modern sense. Thus he opposed astrology, not because he anticipated the genuine science of astronomy, but because he opposed determinism and wished to vindicate man's free will. He, like Jean de Meun, denounced celibacy for those without a genuine calling to an austere life; he, like Alanus de Insulis, regarded Nature's plan for procreation as fundamentally good when not corrupted by men; he saw through the social sham of courtly love. His convictions looked backward, of course, to an unreal past that never existed; not forward to the Renaissance. But despite himself he called attention to the glaring discrepancies which marked the period of late feudalism, already clearly announcing its end.[53]

[1] The increase in urban population between the latter 11th and latter 14th century was from five per cent to 12 per cent of the total population. See Алексеев, *История Английской Литературы,* p. 95.

[2] George Unwin. *The Gilds and Companies of London* (London, 1938 ed.) p. 132 ff.

[3] George Unwin, *Finance and Trade under Edward III* (Manchester, 1918).

[4] A.L. Morton, *A People's History of England* (London, 1938), p. 107 ff.

[5] Unwin, *Finance and Trade,* p. 190 ff.; also George M. Trevelyan, *England in the Age of Wycliffe* (London, 1899), ch. 1 (on the merchant princes).

[6] J.E.T. Rogers, *Six Centuries of Work and Wages,* p. 223.

[7] Karl Marx, *Capital,* I, Part iii, ch. 10, sec. 5; Moore and Aveling translation, I, p. 297 f.

[8] Maurice Dobb, *Studies in the Rise of Capitalism* (New York, 1947), p. 51; A.R. Myers, *op. cit.,* p. 47. On urban democracy before 1300, see p. 84.

[9] H. Fagan and R.H. Hilton, *The English Rising of 1381* (London, 1950), gives the story vividly, with consistent sympathy for the rebels. Abundant detail and full documentation are provided by Д. М. Петрушевский, *Востание Уота Таилера* (Moscow, 1937). Valuable source materials were also collected by André Réville, *Le Soulèvement des travailleurs d'Angleterre en 1381* (Paris, 1898), with introduction by Charles Petit Dutaillis. English bourgeois histories give mostly hostile accounts of the Rising: G.M. Trevelyan, *op. cit.,* Edgar Powell, *The Rising in East Anglia* (Cambridge, 1896), Charles Oman, *The Great Revolt of 1381* (Oxford, 1906). Important articles are those by George Kriehn, "Studies in the Sources of the Social Revolt of 1381," *American Historical Review,* VII (1901—02), 254—85; B. Wilkinson, "The Peasants' Revolt of 1381," *Speculum,* XV (1940), 12—35. On the evidence for later outbreaks see Powell and Trevelyan, *The Peasants' Rising and the Lollards* (London, 1899).

[10] Gałka's "Cantilena Vulgaris" in praise of Wycliff is printed in the *Codex Diplomaticus Universitatis Studii Generalis Cracoviensis,* II (1873), 116—18; also in Stefan Vrtel-Wierczyński, *Wybór Tekstów Staropolskich* (Warsaw, 2nd ed., 1950).

[11] Wycliff, *Select English Works,* ed. Thomas Arnold, 3 vols. (Oxford, 1869—71); also *English Works Hitherto Unprinted,* EETS, OS, No. 74 (1880); H.E. Winn, *Select English Writings* (Oxford, 1929).

[12] Wycliff, *English Works,* citations from II, p. 401 and III, p. 100.

[13] Wycliff, *Tractatus de Ecclesia,* ed. J. Loserth (London, 1886).

[14] Joseph H. Dahmus, *The Prosecution of John Wyclif* (Yale University Press, 1952) has attempted to diminish Wycliff's stature by a detailed examination of the papal bulls and trial documents in his case. The interpretation by H.B. Workman

in his standard biography (Oxford, 1926) is however essentially sound; see S. Harrison Thomson's review of Dahmus in *Speculum*, XXVIII (1953), 563—66.

15 Fr. Engels, *The Peasant War in Germany* (New York, 1934). See also M. Smirin, *Reformacja Ludowa Tomasza Münzera*, tr. from the Russian, 2 vols. (Warsaw, 1951), I, 96 ff.

16 See Hope Emily Allen, *Writings Ascribed to Richard Rolle* (Oxford University Press, 1927), for discussion of the canon. English prose treatises are edited by G.G. Perry, EETS, OS, No. 20 (1866, revised 1920). See also Carl Horstmann, *Yorkshire Writers* (London, 1895—96).

17 This term was applied to the patterns of stress appearing at the ends of clauses and sentences in Latin rhythmical prose. For instance, *cursus planus* was a cadence ′xx′x. The same pattern, or a choriamb ′xx′, was often used in English rhythmical prose, e.g., *jóy gars me jángell*; *him pat I séke*; *pou máke pi glé*. Rolle may have been influenced by the Anglo-Norman rhythmical prose of Edmund Rich, Archbishop of Canterbury (1233—40). See H.W. Robbins, *Saint Edmund's "Merure de Seinte Eglise": An Example of Rhythmical Prose* (University of Minnesota diss., 1927).

18 Juliana of Norwich, *Revelations* modernised and edited by Grace Warrack (London, 1901).

19 For Hilton's writings see C. Horstmann, *Yorkshire Writers*, I; G.G. Perry as in note 16.

20 Dorothy Owen, *Piers Plowman: A Comparison with Earlier and Contemporary French Allegories* (London, 1912).

21 The Latin note suggests that he may have been named Robert, but this is less likely. Oscar Cargill, "The Langland Myth," *PMLA*, L (1935), 36—56, proposes a William de Rokayle who might be the son of Eustace de Rokayle mentioned as the author's father in the Dublin note. Morton W. Bloomfield, "Was William Langland a Benedictine Monk?" *Modern Language Quarterly*, IV (1943), 57—61, supports a suggestion originally made by Allan Bright that his real name was William Colewell or Colvill. Neither proposal has obtained currency.

22 This thesis was propounded by J.M. Manly, *Piers Plowman and its Sequence*, EETS, OS, No. 135B (1908), and aroused much controversy at the time. The consensus of opinion eventually shifted back to the theory of single authorship. See Allan H. Bright, *New Light on Piers Plowman*, preface by R.W. Chambers (Oxford, 1928). The theory of multiple authorship has been argued afresh by J.R. Hulbert, "*Piers the Plowman* after Forty Years," *Modern Philology*, XLV (1947—48), 215—25, and by C.D. Fowler, *ibid.*, L (1952—53), 5—22. See also Fowler's *Critical Edition of the "A" Version of Piers Plowman* (Johns Hopkins Press, 1952) and the reply to Fowler by A.G. Mitchell and G.H. Russell, *Journal of English and Germanic Philology*, LII (1953), 445—56.

23 A lengthy point-by-point refutation is given by B.F. Huppé, "The Authorship of the A and B Texts of *Piers Plowman*," *Speculum*, XXII (1947), 578—620. E. Talbot Donaldson, in his study *Piers Plowman: The C-Text and its Poet* (Yale University Press, 1949), finds no stylistic discrepancies between C and A or B to warrant the assumption of different authors; but he leaves the question open.

24 *The Vision of William Concerning Piers Plowman*, three parallel texts ed. W.W. Skeat (Oxford, 1924; first ed. 1886).

25 For arguments moving the A-text close to B in the period of the Good Parliament, see Oscar Cargill in *PMLA*, XLVII (1932), 354—62 and B.F. Huppé, *ibid.*,

LIV (1939) 37 ff. For the delay of B to ca. 1377—79 see J.A.W. Bennett in *Medium. Aevum*, XI (1943), 55—64 and Huppé in *Studies in Philology*, XLVI (1949), 6—18. An unpublished dissertation by Sister Mary Aquinas Devlin (University of Chicago) places the C-text at the time of 1381 or earlier.

[26] The fable does not appear in A; its political references seem to point to a date before the death of Edward III in 1377.

[27] R.W. Frank, Jr., "The Conclusion of *Piers Plowman*," *Journal of English and Germanic Philology*, XLIX (1950), 309—16 and "The Pardon Scene in *Piers Plowman*," *Speculum*, XXVI (1951), 317—31.

[28] See H.W. Wells, "The Construction of *Piers Plowman*," *PMLA*, XLIV (1929), 123 ff. and "The Philosophy of *Piers Plowman*," *ibid.*, LIII (1938), 339 ff.; also T.P. Dunning, *Piers Plowman: An Interpretation of the A-Text* (London, 1937). The combination of active and contemplative life by Do-Best corresponds to what Walter Hilton called the "mixed life." See R.W. Chambers, *Man's Unconquerable Mind* (London, 1939), essays on *Piers Plowman*, pp. 88—171.

[29] H.W. Troyer, "Who is *Piers Plowman*?" *PMLA*, XLVII (1932), 368—84

[30] D.W. Robertson, Jr., and B.F. Huppé, *Piers Plowman and Scriptural Tradition* (Princeton University Press, 1951). The authors draw extensively on Biblical commentaries to illustrate the theological doctrines in *Piers Plowman*; they are not primarily interested in the sociological aspects of the poem. For them, the narrator Will is the human will allegorised. The philosophy and theology of the poem are further analysed by W. Erzgräber in *Anglia*, LXXIII (1955), 127—48.

[31] Greta Hort, *Piers Plowman and Contemporary Religious Learning* (London, 1937), has tried to estimate the extent of his theological knowledge. Robertson and Huppé give the poet credit for a more detailed acquaintance with patristic and scholastic thought.

[32] *Pearl*, ed. Charles G. Osgood (Boston, 1906); I. Gollancz (London, 4th ed., 1921); E.V. Gordon (Oxford, 1953) with an introduction conveniently summarising previous discussions.

[33] By Carleton Brown in *PMLA*, XIX (1904), 115—53, but others have defended the orthodoxy of the poem.

[34] J.P. Oakden, *Alliterative Poetry in Middle-English* (Manchester, 1930).

[35] I. Gollancz assumes that the loss is personal and attempts to construct a biography of the poet on the basis of internal evidence.

[36] Juliusz Krzyżanowski, "Olympia-Perła-Urszula," *Sprawozdania Polskiej Akademii Umiejętności*, L (1949), No. 7, 388—92.

[37] Basic studies on the symbolic meanings were made by W.H. Schofield in *PMLA*, XIX (1904), 154—215 and XXIV (1909), 585—676; also by J.B. Fletcher, "The Allegory of the *Pearl*," *Journal of English and Germanic Philology*, XX (1921), 1—21 and further by Sister Mary Madeleva, *Pearl: A Study in Spiritual Dryness* (New York, 1925). Marie Hamilton identifies Pearl with man's lost innocence in *PMLA*, LXX (1955), 805—24.

[28] Both literal and allegorical meaning are assumed by O. Cargill and M. Schlauch, "The *Pearl* and its Jeweller," *PMLA*, XLIII (1928), 105 ff. The authors suggest identities for both the child and the poet, but the evidence is not decisive.

[39] Ed. Mabel Day and Mary Serjeantson, EETS, OS, No. 210 (1940). Photographic copy of the entire manuscript by I. Gollancz, *ibid.*, No. 162 (1922). There is a separate edition by T.R. Tolkien and E.V. Gordon (Oxford, 1925).

[40] Coolidge Otis Chapman, "Virgil and the *Gawain*-Poet," *PMLA*, LX (1945), 16—24.

[41] G.L. Kittredge, *Gawain and the Green Knight* (Harvard University Press, 1916).

[42] Alice Buchanan, "The Irish Framework of *Gawain and the Green Knight*," *PMLA*, XLVII (1932), 315 ff.; R.S. Loomis, "More Celtic Elements in *Gawain and the Green Knight*," *Journal of English and Germanic Philology*, XLII (1943), 194—84. E.K. Chambers, in his *Medieval Stage* (Oxford, 1903), had identified the Green Knight with "vegetation spirits" personified in folk plays. This interpretation has been reaffirmed in a somewhat modified form by William Nitze, "Is the Green Knight a Vegetation Myth?" *Modern Philology*, XXXIII (1935—36), 351—66. But the theories of Wilhelm Mannhardt in *Wald- und Feldkulte* (Berlin, 1905) and Sir James Frazer, on which the "vegetation myth" is based, have been essentially revised. See W. Luingman, *Traditions-wanderungen Euphrat-Rhein*, Folklore Fellows Communications, Nos. 118—19 (Helsinki, 1937—38). A.H. Krappe dissents from other critics in identifying the Green Knight with Death, *Speculum*, XIII (1938), 206 ff,

[43] *Patience*, ed. I. Gollancz (London, 1913) and by H. Bateson (Manchester, 1912 and 1918); *Purity*, ed. J. Menner (Yale University Press, 1920) and I. Gollancz (London, 1912 and 1933).

[44] The most recent challenge to advocates of unified authorship is advanced in refutation of Oakden, *op. cit.*, by John W. Clark, in *Philological Quarterly*, XXVIII (1949), 261—73 and *Modern Language Quarterly*, XII (1951), 387—98. The basis of argument here is the vocabulary of the four poems.

[45] *Erkenwald*, ed. H.L. Savage (Yale University Press, 1926).

[46] John Gower, *Works*, ed. G.C. Macaulay, 4 vols. (Oxford, 1899—1902).

[47] In 1362 English was made the language of the law courts; in 1363 the Chancellor used it for the first time to open Parliament. In 1387 the first known will in English was attested. See A.R. Myers, *op. cit.*, p. 80.

[48] М. П. Алексеев, *op. cit.*, pp. 130—40.

[49] For the application to Gower's times see Gardiner Stillwell, "John Gower and the Last Years of Edward III," *Studies in Philology*, XLV (1948), 454—71.

[50] J.B. Dwyer, "Gower's *Mirour* and its French Sources," *ibid.*, XLVIII (1951), 482—505. This article is a partial refutation of claims made by R. Elfreda Fowler, *Une Source française des poèmes de Gower* (Paris diss., Macon, 1905).

[51] On the general type see Ruth Mohl, *The Three Estates in Medieval and Renaissance Literature* (Columbia University Press, 1933).

[52] George G. Fox, *The Medieval Sciences in the Works of John Gower* (Princeton University Press, 1930).

[53] An appreciative study of Gower has been made by George Coffman in his articles "John Gower and his Most Significant Role," University of Colorado *Studies in Language and Literature*, Series B, II, iv (1945), 52—61 and "John Gower, Mentor for Royalty," *PMLA*, LXIX (1954), 953—64.

Chapter XI

GEOFFREY CHAUCER: LIFE AND EARLIER WORKS

1. THE CAREER OF CHAUCER

Incomparably the greatest poet of the English Middle Ages, one of the three or four supremely great in all English literature, Geoffrey Chaucer lived in the second half of the 14th century and died on the first year of the 15th (1340—1400).[1] He resembles Shakespeare in his abundant creativeness and in the range and depth of his human sympathies. Like Milton, he managed to combine two careers in one lifetime, serving both art and the affairs of state. Chaucer, however, did this longer and more consistently than Milton, for his activities as politician, civil servant and diplomat cover his entire adult life, not merely a limited section of it. Far from holding himself aloof from the turbulent developments in the society of his time, he was immersed in them from the beginning to the end of his career. Unlike Milton, on the other hand, Chaucer identified himself with the old established order, so far as his official services were concerned.

Like Gower, Chaucer came from the type of recently enriched mercantile family which was beginning to contribute outstanding personalities to English public life. His biography is an index of the transformations marking the decline of feudalism, for it would be difficult to imagine such a career two hundred years previously. His father was a wholesale wine merchant, engaged in a trade which at that time contributed significantly to the economy of the country. The women of his family too included a number who were independently successful in business, for the guilds accepted them on a basis of equality when they carried on handicrafts and trade as *femmes soles*.[2] Shipmen and merchants, apprentices and active guildswomen must have been familiar types in Chaucer's early experience, and their personalities left vivid traces in his memory, from which he obviously drew for the delineation of his unforgettable Canterbury pilgrims.

But Chaucer's middle-class family stood high enough to have access to court connections too. His father was able to have him received in the household of Elizabeth of Ulster, wife of Duke Lionel of Clarence who was one of the sons of Edward III.[3] After serving briefly in the French war (1359—60), Chaucer is next found attached directly to the royal court by the latter 1360's. His function may have been secretarial. Recipient of an annuity from the King, he is one of many persons equipped with mourning apparell on the death of Queen Philippa in 1369. By this time he had married Philippa Roet, sister of Katherine Swynford who was for many years the mistress and finally the wife of John of Gaunt, the powerful Duke of Lancaster. Chaucer appears to have been a member of the circle surrounding the Duke: a brilliant if heterogeneous group which at various times included persons as widely different as the notorious Alice Perrers, mistress to the King, and John Wycliff, the puritanical reformer.[4] Chaucer was not, however, primarily dependent upon the Duke. His advancement came directly from the royal household of Edward III and later that of Richard II. Chaucer's wife, who entered service in the Duke's household (1372), did however obtain a pension from John of Gaunt, and both she and Chaucer received many gifts from him.

By 1370 Chaucer's skill in practical politics had won him substantial recognition. He began to be sent abroad on missions of considerable importance to England's foreign policy. In 1372, for instance, he was commissioned to treat with the Doge of Venice and the city government of Genoa on matters connected with Italian-English trade. Since his report mentions a visit to Florence, probably concerned with credits for the English crown, it is very likely that he also visited the celebrated poet Petrarch, then living not far away in Padua. In 1376 and 1377 he was sent several times to Flanders and France on secret negotiations having to do with peace and a possible marital alliance between a French princess and the young Prince Richard. In 1378 he visited Northern Italy again, this time seeking help from the wealthy "tyrants" of Milan for the financing of the war against France.

Northern Italy was at this time a centre of wealth, splendour and enormous artistic activity. The cultural movement which is traditionally designated as the Renaissance was here in its first full tide, to the accompaniment of unprecedented material prosperity. The merchant-bankers of the Italian city-states were in a position to act as creditors for the crowned heads of Europe. The opulent prosperity of the trading oligarchies and the wealthier guild manufacturers was of course founded upon the ruthless exploitation of lower orders, including the minor guilds, apprentices, workers and peasants generally. Not long before Chaucer's visit, Florence had been rocked to its foundations by a social revolution—swiftly suppressed—which on a smaller scale closely anticipated the course of events in the English Rising of 1381. Nevertheless the spectacle of luxury, of refinement and high artistic achievement must have dazzled a visitor from England. The homeland had a court of no mean splendour itself, marked like the local Italian ones by both violence and decadence as well as polished formality, but neither France nor England could show anything to Chaucer such as he found in Italy. Here he encountered not only the wealth upon which England wished to draw, but also the enormous intellectual and artistic stimulus to which a man of his genius could effectively respond. When he returned home he brought with him not only vivid memories of beauty seen, but also copies of literary texts which fructified his own writing.

Between his two Italian journeys Chaucer had been appointed (1374) controller of customs for wools, hides and wool-fells passing through the port of London. It was his function to collect taxes on these products being exported from England, an important and well-paid job. The income from it was supplemented by various other duties and missions. By 1381 he was living in the house built above Aldgate, a portal of the city through which the army of rebels entered London. In 1385—86 he was a justice of the peace for Kent, and in 1386 he represented that county in Parliament as knight of the shire.[5] For a time his fortunes apparently suffered eclipse when a court faction including some of his associates was temporarily shorn of power at the hands of a baronial clique. At this time, late in 1386, Chaucer lost or resigned his customs employment. But a turn of intrigue and fortune brought his friends back into favour. In 1389 Chaucer received from Richard II the lucrative and demanding post of clerk of the works for all the royal residences. This means that he was responsible for construction and repair work, for temporary undertakings such as the building of lists for tournaments, and also for handling the wages of hired free workers. Later he resigned this exacting job and lived upon a modest royal pension plus the income from a quasi-sinecure (as agent and sub-forester on an estate of Roger Mortimer, Earl of March), and from occasional gifts that must have come to him as a very successful poet. His last years may have entailed some financial restrictions, but he was by no means destitute. Late in 1399 Chaucer leased a residence within the precincts of the Abbey of Westminster, a normally peaceful place which was no doubt congenial to his tastes in retirement. Here he died in 1400 and was buried in the Abbey, which has since become the resting place of many other distinguished writers.

The poet's life had been a varied one. He had many opportunities to view many ranks of society, both at home and abroad. His ability to capture the intricate truths of human nature, to grasp the type in the individual and the individual against the class or group conditioning him, to sympathise or denounce or condemn with a passion tempered by humour—all these gifts qualified him to extract the utmost from his experiences for literary ends. Even when he is handling traditional plots and adapting conventional forms, he makes us feel beyond them to the authentic world of living, breathing, suffering and rejoicing people in which he moved.

2. THE EARLY IMITATIVE WORKS

Histories of literature conventionally divide Chaucer's work into three periods designated as the French, the Italian and the English, according to the main sources of the their inspiration. This is in general a valid division, but it is also somewhat misleading. The first period, it is true, was predominantly French, but it is also true that French literature never ceased to affect Chaucer even when he fell under the spell of Italian, or even when he gained artistic independence of either in the period of the *Canterbury Tales*. A degree of Italian influence appeared during the first period, when he was writing dream visions in the French manner. There is no sharp boundary separating the phases of his work from one another.

It is natural that French literature should have influenced Chaucer's earliest attempts, in respect to both themes and attitudes, and have moulded the literary forms adopted by him for expression. [6] Nowhere between Iceland and Spain was the prestige of French culture higher than at the English court where (in contrast with the country as a whole) the language was still current and its fashions were sedulously imitated. The love lyrics and romances of French chivalry and the allegorical dream visions inspired by the *Roman de la Rose* still held undisputed sway there, being read in the original by many who also read and composed in English.

It was the *Roman de la Rose* [7] which first attracted Chaucer to an apprentice's literary effort. He himself tells us in a later work (the Prologue to the *Legend of Good Women*) that he translated it, but whether he ever finished the task is not known. Of three surviving fragments of such a translation, one at least—covering the first section of the part by Guillaume de Lorris—is very probably Chaucer's. The English octosyllabic couplets move forward in an unrippled if not very original style, much as in the French; the work was a rewarding exercise for one mastering the resources of Middle English for fluid narrative.

To the same period belongs a conventional lyrical poem called "Compleint to Pity," and the stanzaic translation of a prayer to the Virgin, taken from Guillaume de Déguileville's *Pèlerinage de la Vie Humaine* (see ch. 8, sec. 5). Chaucer chose words to open the succeeding lines of the poem in such a way that they come in alphabetical sequence. Hence the title "An ABC." The result is naturally formalistic. It is a beginner's *étude* for the exercise of his skill.

With *The Book of the Duchess* (1369—70) Chaucer began his career of independent composition, although still closely conforming to admired models and the precepts of rhetoric. The poem, in octosyllabic couplets, is cast in the form of a dream vision serving as an elegy on the death of a young and beautiful court lady—almost beyond doubt, Blanche of Lancaster, the first wife of John of Gaunt. The experience is recounted in the first person. The narrator represents himself as first reading himself asleep with the help of Ovid's sad tale of drowned Ceyx and his wife Alcyone (that is, Halcyone). The ghostly cry of Ceyx still rings in his ears — "To lytel while oure blysse lasteth" [8]—when he dreams that he encounters a sorrowful Black Knight who is lamenting the loss of a lady near and dear to him. By tactful questions the dreamer (whose personality is not to be completely identified with Chaucer's [9]) leads the bereaved man to relive his first acquaintance with the lost beloved, and his happiness with her. This brings solace for the time being. Gradually the Knight's glowing tribute merges into a renewed expression of grief, and he is finally forced to blurt out the stark fact which he had already indicated in advance: "She ys ded!" To this the dreamer can only reply with a heartfelt if not very articulate phrase: "Is that youre los? By God, hyt ys routhe," and with the striking of a bell in a nearby castle, the dream is over.

For this combined eulogy and elegy Chaucer drew heavily on three other poets. Ovid gave him the introductory legend about Ceyx and his devoted wife, known to Chaucer in a French verse paraphrase with moral commentary (the *Ovide Moralisé* [10]). The opening lines of the poem are taken directly from the autobiographical *Paradys d'Amours* by Jean Froissart, for the famous chronicler whom Chaucer probably knew was also a gifted lyricist. The encounter with the Black Knight is indebted to a lyric, "Le Jugement dou Roy de Behaigne" (The Judgment of the King of Bohemia) by another contemporary of Chaucer's, Guillaume de Machault. The French poem contains lamentations by both a bereaved lady and a betrayed knight who contend with each other concerning the measure of their sorrows, each claiming to have suffered the more.

Other lyrics by Machault have also contributed to the *Book of the Duchess*.
Yet despite Chaucer's use of these sources, he already shows a distinct
independence in the organising of his materials. The dream atmosphere
is evoked far more successfully than in the improbably lucid and coherent
French works of this genre. The nature descriptions and the tribute to
the dead lady, though faithful to established conventions, achieve their
own qualities of freshness and charm.

The next two works, *The Parlement of Fowles* and the *Hous of Fame*
(probably written between 1374 and 1382) mark a great advance on
Chaucer's part. The order of composition is a matter of dispute. It has
been proposed that the former may have been composed in anticipation
of a betrothal at one time projected between Richard II and a child princess of France, Marie (died 1377), [11] but it has also been plausibly argued
that the occasion was the marriage of Richard to Anne of Bohemia in
1382. The *Hous of Fame* belongs to the same period and it too has been
thought to be connected with the same royal marriage. There is no external evidence determining the date or purpose of either. The *Hous* is in
octosyllabic couplets, the traditional French form, while the *Parlement*
is written in the stanzaic pentameter form (riming *ababbcc*) so brilliantly
employed, somewhat later, in the *Troilus and Criseyde*. This does not
mean necessarily, however, that the stanzaic composition came later.
The question of chronological order has not up to the present time been
definitively decided. [12]

The Parlement of Fowles is cast in a framework resembling *The Book
of the Duchess*. It too is introduced by the summary of a book being read
by the narrator before sleeping: in this case, Cicero's *Somnium Scipionis*
(*Dream of Scipio*). The text was preserved for the Middle Ages in the
verbose commentary by Macrobius (fifth century). Its substance is
a report of a vision of the heavens and the spirits of departed virtuous
folk which was vouchsafed to the Roman patriot Scipio on the night
before his death. In the original by Cicero, emphasis is placed on civic
(rather than personal) virtue as a qualification for happiness after death.
The *Somnium* sets the tone for a rather solemn poem, but Chaucer soon
changes the initial mood, and introduces us to the bright vernal landscape
setting typical of a Guillaume de Lorris. He depicts Dame Nature seated
on a hill of flowers within a grassy lawn, and engaged in assigning birds
to their mates. Her favourite, a royal female eagle, is the subject of
contention by three male tercel eagles. Nature asks the female to choose;
she coyly asks to be excused from decision, and Nature—after letting
the other birds express an opinion—permits her to wait for another year.
If the poem is not complete as it stands, it is nearly so. The action, obviously, is very slight. The real interest lies in the unexpected humorous

enlivening of the over-familiar theme and setting, and the undercurrent
of light satire in the treatment of courtly love.

The birds represent the several classes of society, and they chatter
self-importantly in their respective roles, much as human beings might

Chaucer's *Parlement of Fowles*. A woodcut

do in a real parliament. The birds of prey fittingly represent the nobility,
and they are all for the strict code of courtly love, with its demands of
bravery, discreet devotion and fidelity maintained for indefinite periods
of time. The lower orders have a much more practical, down-to-earth
view. A spokesman of the geese says, "If she won't love him—let him
love another!" To this a "gentle" sparrow-hawk replies scornfully: "the
perfect reasoning of a goose!" A duck argues: what is the sense in loving
eternally without a reward? There are more than a pair of stars in the
sky! But the tercel eagle condemns the duck no less sharply:

597   "Out of the donghill cam that word ful right!...
601   Thy kynde is of so low a wrechednesse
       That what love is, thow canst nat seen ne gesse."

[kynde = nature]

The cuckoo, finally, shows impatience with the entire problem. Just let me have domestic peace with my mate, he says, and I don't care how long these aristocrats quarrel. This view also annoys the gentry. The cuckoo is called "worms' corruption" for his pains, but the effect of the satiric contrast is certainly to invest the aristocrats' pretensions with absurdity. *The Parlement of Fowles* is important because it reveals a critical attitude to courtly love from the earliest period of Chaucer's work. And it shows, too, that Chaucer had already read widely, for we find here the traces of his indebtedness to Cicero (through Macrobius), the Roman poet Claudian, Alanus de Insulis, Dante and others. His Nature is indebted to the conceptions of 12th-century Platonists. As is usual with him, however, Chaucer carries off his borrowings with graceful ease. They belong organically in his work; they live in it, and are never pedantically used. [13]

The Hous of Fame [14] is unfinished; it ends before telling us the "tidings" which it was presumably composed to convey. But the three books or cantos which survive have abundant interest. Once more employing the setting of a dream vision, Chaucer first describes his solitary inspection of a temple of glass which is decorated with scenes from classical mythology and the *Aeneid*. They furnish a pretext for summarising the story of Dido at some length. Emerging from the temple, Chaucer (for here he is himself the dreamer, beyond doubt) is suddenly carried aloft by a Golden Eagle, who whirls him into another region, the abode of the capricious goddess of Fame. The suggestion for this allegorical figure is of course to be found in the *Aeneid*. In her temple Chaucer watches for a time while she arbitrarily apportions good fame or bad or none at all to her various suppliants, regardless of their wishes. Then he wanders farther. He has just encountered a mysterious old man dispatched apparently to impart weighty news of love to him, when the fragmentary text is broken off.

Here again we find a combination of indebtedness and independence on Chaucer's part. Besides considerable borrowings from the *Aeneid*, [15] there are numerous shorter ones from Dante and Ovid and Macrobius once more. By all odds the most original and amusing part is the depiction of Chaucer's sudden breath-taking journey through the upper regions of the heavens. The poet, clutched in the Eagle's claws, is frightened and breathless. The bird himself is a kindly and loquacious creature, pluming himself on his knowledge of astronomy, physics (the nature of sound), music, and other lore. He is eager to converse and instruct, but "Geoffrey" confines his answers chiefly to gasped monosyllabes. Having lectured lengthily at his half-conscious victim, the Eagle asks whether he does not have a truly remarkable gift for untechnical exposition. Upon

receiving Chaucer's laconic "Yis" in reply, he offers to discourse in detail
upon the stars, but Chaucer begs off, saying that he is too old for such
instruction. Regretfully the Eagle yields, agreeing that the poet can find
in books any specific information he may need for literary work. If, as
some have thought, the Eagle is an allegorical character representing
Philosophy, he sounds at the same time like a good-humoured caricature
of a human type: the talkative professor, for instance, eagerly dispensing
information and full of innocent pride in his "popular style." He also
recalls the verbose Macrobius, Cicero's commentator. Chaucer shows
no less skill in depicting himself, for he includes many touches of the
humorous self-depreciation which was characteristic of him throughout
his entire career as an artist.

Concerning the many classical and medieval Latin writers to whom
Chaucer refers, here and elsewhere, a word of warning is needed. In view
of the rarity of medieval books and the very modest number of those
in private collections, we can not imagine Chaucer having easy access
to the full works of those whom he cites.[16] It has been demonstrated,
indeed, that in many cases he used miscellanies and anthologies which
gave him selections rather than complete texts. Nevertheless his reading
was amazingly wide. In an earlier century it would have been incon-
ceivable on the part of a layman.

3. THE BOETHIUS TRANSLATION AND THE LYRICS

Among the literary allusions occurring to the Chaucer of the *Hous
of Fame* during his swift flight aloft, there is one (11. 972—78) paraphrasing Boethius, whose *Consolation of Philosophy* had long previously
attracted King Alfred as a translator (see ch. 4, sec. 3). To this period
in Chaucer's work we can assign his similar undertaking. The poet made
use of a prose translation by Jean de Meun[17] which embodied glosses
on the original, for Chaucer often leaned on French versions when dealing with Latin texts. In this way he rendered the entire *Consolation*
(including the *metra*) into English prose. The tone is appropriate to the
serious and dignified subject. Chaucer clearly expended special care on
the style of his translation, availing himself of the known patterns of
prose rhythm already employed by mystics like Richard Rolle.[18] Ana-
phora, parallel constructions and balanced sentence parts heighten the
rhythmical effects.

The problems of fate, predestination and free will apparently occupied Chaucer's reflective thought during all periods of his literary activity. There are echoes of this preoccupation in *Troilus and Criseyde* and
some of the *Canterbury Tales*. If we may interpret from allusions through-

out his works, Chaucer was always deeply troubled by the problem
of divine justice in relation to human misery. He did not, to be sure,
look upon that misery quite as did the stern moralist who wrote *Piers
Plowman*, nor did it arouse him to revolutionary protest. Instead of
stressing aspects of guilt and responsibility, he tempered his judgments
with humour and an inclusive understanding of human nature. His professional activities taught him the art of compromise. Yet beneath his
lighter commentary on deeds and destiny, he meditated upon the question:
how could an omnipotent and presumably benevolent God permit injustice to have such broad dominion on the earth? To this searching
question the 14th century could offer no answer differing essentially from
that of Boethius in the sixth century. The *Consolatio* had been the work
of a man gifted with literary talents, an earnest (if not very original)
thinker in philosophy, a writer who was also a diplomat and—within
limits — a statesman. In short, there were analogies between the careers
and interests of Boethius and Chaucer, which made the translation of
the *Consolatio* a very congenial task for the English poet.

To the problem of fate and free will, the Boethian figure of Philosophy offered an evasion rather than a solution. Moreover, the combination of Epicureanism, Platonism and Christianity in the *Consolation*
would not tend to encourage vigorous protest against the misery which
it recognised. It would not lead a man in Chaucer's position to reject
the overbearing and immoral masters (both politically and personally
so) for whom he worked. But it would remind him of their weakness
and transitoriness, and it would open up to him the more serene world
of philosophical speculation into which tyrants are not qualified to
enter.

But yif the liketh thanne [Philosophy had said to Boethius] to
looken on the derknesse of the erthe that thou hast forleten, thanne shaltow
seen that these felounous tirantz, that the wrecchide peple dredeth now,
schullen ben exiled fro thilke faire contre (Book iv, Metre 1).

The lyrical pieces which Chaucer wrote from this period to the end
of his life bear strong marks of the philosophical reflectiveness encouraged
in him by both Boethius and Dante. Like these and others of his predecessors, he liked to let his mind dwell on the felicity of the hypothetical
"Former Age," before men developed the arts of oppression and destruction along with civilisation, and to contrast that imagined period with
his own times:

> For in oure dayes nis but covetyse,
> Doublenesse, and tresoun, and envye,
> Poyson, manslauhtre, and mordre in sondry wise.

In a ballade of ten stanzas entitled "Fortune," the poet laments "this wrecched worldes transmutacioun," recalls man's source of strength — the light of his reason — in sustaining misfortune, and ends with a graceful plea for more solid aid from royal patrons. A shorter ballade on "Truth" exhorts the reader to renounce ambition, leave the world as it is, but hold to the highway of Truth. In "Gentilesse" Chaucer concisely restates the conventional thesis, familiar in medieval theory if not in practice, that true nobility is founded on virtuous behaviour, not on inherited rank. In "Lak of Stedfastnesse," on the other hand, addressed to King Richard, he gave unusually fervid expression to sentiments of his own on the falsity and ruthlessness he saw in the world about him. We do not know the date of this poem, nor any specific event with which it may be connected, for the admonition to the King to "cherish thy folk and hate extorcioun" would have been apt at any time during the reign of that monarch.

In several of his later lyrics Chaucer reveals the delightfully humorous bent which came to full expression in the *Canterbury Tales*. A ballade addressed to Henry Scogan jestingly accuses his friend of angering the gods and causing calamitous floods — because he has impatiently abandoned a mistress who would not listen to his pleas. Such rashness, says the poet, will bring Cupid's vengeance on all grey-haired and plump-waisted lovers, who would otherwise (the ironical reference is no doubt to himself) be likely to succeed in love! Another ballade, addressed to Bukton, counsels the recipient to think twice before giving up his freedom and marrying; if he consults the sayings of Chaucer's own Wife of Bath (see ch. 12, sec. 1) he may change his mind. A ballade composed in the last year of Chaucer's life is a humorous plea to King Henry IV to grant him financial aid. The first three stanzas appeal "To his Empty Purse", according to the title, in terms which a lover might use to his mistress, begging it to recover its radiant yellow complexion like the sun's. The envoy shifts the appeal to the new monarch, begging him to have mind upon the poet's need and supplication.

Closely connected with Chaucer's interest in Boethian philosophy was his curiosity about the physical heavens and the stars appearing in them. He studied the astronomy known to his age, together with the astrology then inseparably connected with it. The scientific and technological interest is revealed in his *Tretis (Treatise) of the Astrolabe*, an adapted translation of a Latin text originally composed in Arabic (eighth century). The work describes an instrument used to determine the sun's altitude, and other problems in astronomy. The text is shortened and revised in such a way as to make it understandable to a boy of ten, the "lyte Lowys my sone" mentioned in the opening sentence. The exposition has been made "under full light reules and naked wordes in English," says Chaucer, "for Latyn ne canst thou yit but small, my litel sone."

The book on the astrolabe was done towards the end of Chaucer's life. Elswhere too he showed keen interest in the zodiac, both as subject of scientific description and as source of influences presumably exercised by the planets, in their various positions, upon human destiny. [19] Here again the problem of fate and freewill was involved. If the conjunctions of Mars, Venus and the rest really could exercise a measureable influence on people's lives and temperaments, what became of the free choice that human beings were supposed to exercise, and their moral responsibility for its consequences? It was the problem which Boethius posed to Philosophy, stated in a cruder form. Chaucer pondered on this dilemma, without proposing a solution for it.

In lighter vein he has adapted lore of the zodiac to the framework of courtly love poetry in a "Compleynt of Mars." Ostensibly the poem gives merely a conventional lament by a lover (here, the Ovidian god of war) upon being obliged to quit his lady (Venus) in the early morning. In form it thus belongs to the type of *aubade* or dawn song of parting lovers, first developed in Provence (12th century). It is in fact however an allegory of the astrological situation arising when Mars approaches the "house" of Venus in the zodiac, in a manner regarded as friendly or auspicious. There is a "Compleynt of Venus" which may in a sense be regarded as a companion piece, but it is actually no more than a translation of three ballades written by Oton de Graunson, a French knight of Savoy who was in Chaucer's time a refugee at the English court. There is evidence that the French poems referred to an illicit love affair of John of Gaunt's stepdaughter, the Princess Isabella of Spain, who later became Duchess of York. A late tradition attempts to connect Chaucer's previous "Compleynt of Mars" likewise with this rather scandalous affair in high society, but with less likelihood. [20]

4. *TROILUS AND CRISEYDE*

Among the Italian texts acquired by Chaucer in Italy was a copy of *Il Filostrato* by Boccaccio, a lyrically passionate narrative in verse about a young man's love affair with an experienced widow—at first tempestuously happy because of her ready compliance with his desires, later wretched and heart-sick because of her infidelity. Chaucer appears to have been under a misapprehension concerning the author's identity, for he refers to him constantly as "Lollius." [21] The setting of the Italian story is the medieval version of the Trojan War (see ch. 9, sec. 2). Boccaccio

xerat: ratio
nifcp curfu ad
alia quedam
tractanda atcp
expediendda uer
tebat. B. Tū
ego recta qui/
dem incp exhor
tacio tua cp precelus auctoritate dig
niflima. Sed cp tu dudum de prouti/
tecia questionem pluribs alijs im
plicitam esse dixisti re experior. Que

we enim an esse aliquid omino · et cp
nam esse casum arbitrere · P ·
Du hadde vulseit ende
irkeerde de cours van
harer redene omme ee
nigh andre zake te ha
delene est ghere idene ·
B · Doe zeidic rechtuerdich eq ze
ker disn vermanen est met alle weir
dich vsi ghelouene. Naer datta wij
len eer zeids de questie der woedach
tichteit met wle meer andre te wijm/

The Consolation of Philosophy
Boethius being taught by Philosophy

prince. In Boccaccio the heroine's short and rather hypocritical resistance sprang chiefly from anxiety about her reputation. Chaucer emphasises far more the reluctance of a high-born widow, enjoying a tranquil and cultural, independent life among sympathetic Trojan matrons, to become

Caxton's edition of Chaucer's
Troylus and Creseyde

involved emotionally in any love relationship. In feudal society, a widow of the ruling class was in a far more enviable position than a young unmarried girl. Having been passively assigned in marriage once, at her father's command, she now enjoyed economic security and a certain freedom of choice in her future relationships (even though an overlord might put pressure on her to take one of his vassals as second husband). If she did not wish to marry, but to form a romantic liaison in the fashion so prevalent in high society, she could do so with considerably less risk than was incurred by her married friends.

All this means that a widowed lady like Criseyde had a certain freedom of decision in matters of a personal emotional nature. Without that freedom in relationship, that limited approximation to equality between the sexes within the privileged group, it is impossible to develop literary situations of refined comedy. Compulsive relations precluding choice may be used to produce an effect of tragedy or pathetic sentimentalism or protest, but not to create a comedy of manners, as the genre was later to be called in English literature. Criseyde, exercising her privileged faculty of choice, decides at once that she does not want another husband: they are (she says) either jealous, or masterful, or given to seeking novelty elsewhere (ii, 754—56). About a lover she hesitates long, fearing for her reputation and reluctant to subject her own feelings to another's. Pandarus, a skilful stage-manager, finds it necessary to work up many scenes preparatory to the climax in which she finally succumbs. Yet at this moment she is frank enough to admit that she had long since yielded to Troilus in her thoughts, otherwise she would not then be present in Pandarus' house late on a stormy night, with the young prince not far away:

iii, 1210   "Ne hadde I er now, my swete herte deere,
              Ben yold, ywis, I were now nought here!"
[er = ere, before;   yold = yielded]

It was Criseyde's desertion of Troilus, of course, not her yielding to him, which made her reprehensible according to the standards of romantic love. And her own intention was, Chaucer assures us (iv, 1415 ff.), to remain loyal. Her protestations to her lover and speech of praise for him on the eve of their separation bear the accents of conviction and sincerity—insofar as she understands herself, at that moment. One gets the impression that events are serving to lift veil after veil of the covering which originally concealed the real person inside of a demure, correct, well-contented society lady, and are showing her more and more completely to herself and us. It has been well said that her character does not change so much as it is progressively revealed.[23] Until her departure from Troy for the camp of the Greeks, no circumstance had indicated that she was a person dependent on the proximity of a loved one to maintain her devotion to him; a direct and sensual woman instead of the reserved and self-controlled heroine of ordinary romance. Separated from Troilus, Criseyde tries hard to evoke his image, to vivify it by recalling the scene of their love. She does so with insufficient effect (v, 715—21). When she transfers her love to Diomede, it is once more—though now more readily—because of pity and proximity, and she tries to assure herself that this time at least she will be faithful ("To Diomede algate I wol be trewe," v, 1071). But the very words show a new insight on her part, and the doubts engendered by it.

Diomede, the dashing Greek warrior, brings about Criseyde's self-revelation. Chaucer's character is even more prompt and urgent in his wooing than Boccaccio's; instead of waiting, he begins his overtures at once, on the way to the Greek camp, and this although he has glimpsed heart-break in the eyes of both lovers, and understood it. Within a few moments he is telling Criseyde that he never before loved any woman in his whole life; he visits her in her father's tent and persuades her to admit him under her improbable stipulation that "he will not speak of such matters" as love (v, 951); he makes her admit that she would give her favour to him if any Greek could win it (v, 1000 f.). He finally obtains from her the very brooch she had received from Troilus. There was little need of that particular act of infidelity, remarks Chaucer. Sketched in bold strokes and utterly convincing as a certain type of male charmer, Diomede exists mostly as a foil to Troilus and as a source of illumination on Criseyde's personality.

Pandarus is a character almost as life-like and fascinating as Criseyde. Much of his personality is revealed by linguistic means, for he is witty, loquacious, subtle of speech, a master of genial conversational English studded with apt proverbs and short penetrating comments. Hearing him, we can imagine that we are listening to a kindly and worldly-wise courtier in Chaucer's own circle—humorous, tolerant, cultured, and quite uncritical of the *mores* of his society. As Criseyde's uncle (not her youthful cousin, as in Boccaccio), he is exempt from illusions about her. He never believed his niece to be the inaccessible heavenly creature imagined by her lover in the style of courtly love ("It sit hire naught to ben celestial," i, 983). When the imminent departure of Criseyde is causing heartbreak for Troilus, the older (though not necessarily elderly) man suggests that he look elsewhere for consolation ("This town is ful of ladys al aboute/ And, to my doom, fairer than swiche twelve / As evere she was," iv, 401—03). He tries to distract Troilus from his sorrow by entertainment, and hints that the waiting is in vain ("Ye, fare wel al the snow of ferne yere!" v, 1176). He sees through his niece's protestations of reluctance at the begininng better than she does herself, and he is a past master in the gradual breaking down of her psychological resistance.

In connection with the character of Pandarus, it is important for the modern reader to keep one point clearly in mind. The help given by this older man to the young lovers is completely non-mercenary. He is a member of their own social class, playing the role of the traditional disinterested friend. [24] Whatever satisfaction he receives for his services is the pleasure of witnessing a joy which, as he tells us, he never was able to experience for himself. It was only in a later age, an age when commercial relations had replaced feudal ones in decisive sectors of the upper class, that the name of this typical character deteriorated (in the form *pander* or *pandar*) to become synonymous with *bawd*. For a medieval reader his conduct would appear quite acceptable because it sprang from friendship unconcerned with pay.

Troilus is the most conventional of the persons in the story.[25] He represents the tradition of courtly love more simply and clearly than do any of the others. His doubts and anguish, both at the beginning and the end, are portrayed in relatively close dependence on the Italian text. To Boccaccio he is also indebted for the very beautiful passage lyrically expressing his joy in consummated love.

The entire narrative is permeated with a sense of destiny. There are references at almost every turn of events to the power of the stars over human destiny, and the futility of trying to oppose what they—or the "gods"—have decided. The element of determinism is so strong, indeed, that some have seen in it the inner meaning of the whole poem. Very significant is the passage, unknown to Boccaccio's version, in which the unhappy Troilus retires to a temple upon hearing of the decision to send Criseyde away, and indulges in a closely-reasoned meditation upon fate and free will (iv, 946—1078). The argument is taken from Boethius, whose *Consolation of Philosophy* was dominant in Chaucer's thinking at the time.[26] Manuscript evidence[27] indicates that this passage was inserted in an already completed draft of Book iv. Troilus uses the logical device of Boethius in order to salvage free will for man, while still affirming God's omnipotence; but the total effect of all references to this theme is a sense of inevitability in the development of situations and relations among all the characters.

This unorthodox effect is somewhat counteracted by the epilogue of the poem, paraphrased from another poem of Boccaccio's,[28] in which Chaucer depicts the soul of Troilus ascending to the heavens after death. He looks down on the little spot of earth where he had suffered the pangs of love and betrayal; he beholds the weeping of the Trojans for his death, and he is suddenly moved to a fit of celestial merriment—so different have his values become, so incomprehensible the values of earth. After this Chaucer appeals to his readers to reject the type of love portrayed in his poem, to turn their thoughts away from wordly vanity, and to seek refuge in the only kind of love which can endure: the love of God. He concludes with a short but impressive prayer paraphrased from Dante, asking for protection against foes visible and invisible, and for divine mercy.

This conclusion is strikingly out of tone with the attitude pervading the rest of the poem. The reversal is expressed with solemn fervour but it comes so abruptly as to disturb the otherwise unified effect of the entire work. We must assume that Chaucer himself felt divided in his attitude to the code of love. Here the final rejection is expressed in religious terms. Later, as we shall see, his rejection came to be expressed in terms of social morality (see ch. 12, sec. 5 and 7).

The realism of characterisation in *Troilus and Criseyde* has been highly praised, and with justice. One must however define the kind of realism meant. It is the realism of fidelity to the special setting and to the emotional and psychological processes of individuals within a limited and protected circle. The skilful observation and delineation of them by the author make us see and hear as if we were ourselves present, to share in the plausible thoughts and feelings of the people. We hear Pandarus cover his hesitation with a polite cough, we listen to his easy colloquial chat about the neighbours living opposite Criseyde's house; we feel the knowing assurance with which he thrusts Troilus's love-letter into the bodice of her dress even though she protests that she will certainly not read such a message so delivered; we lean out of the window with the two of them to watch Troilus ride by, flushed and battered from recent combat; we are almost physically present on the windy rainy night when the lovers are united under Pandarus's roof. All this however is a realism of faithful reflection and keen perception, not what we call critical realism today. The critical element was to appear with increasing effect in Chaucer's later work, the stories of the *Canterbury Tales*.

Within the framework given by Boccaccio, Chaucer was at pains to elevate the story above the level of facile intrigue which he had found in it. Hence he went so far as to strengthen certain romantic aspects which would refine the atmosphere and make for delay. To this end he added material from other sources, notably songs by Petrarch, and he introduced such new factors of romance as a nightingale's singing, moonlight, and a love lyric sung by one of Criseyde's maids, all for the purpose of playing upon the heroine's feelings. [29] The result of such additions and modifications was, it is true, to reduce the elements of sensuality and passion found in the original, and to heighten a certain effect of remoteness, but they did not therefore produce a throw-back to the old unreal romances of chivalry. Their purpose, we may surmise, is to let Chaucer place his psychological realism upon a plane of subtler observation with regard to motives and influences affecting his characters. In this general effort he was indisputably successful. His *Troilus and Criseyde* is a supreme achievement in the realm of medieval storytelling.

5. AFTER *TROILUS AND CRISEYDE*

The reversal of attitude which we find in the epilogue of *Troilus and Criseyde* is not the only one to which Chaucer gave expression in relation to it. The epilogue was probably due to his own genuine subjective doubts about the courtly ideology of the romance. In addition he was, as he tells us, also challenged later by criticism from without. Certain ladies of the royal court apparently objected to his portrayal of an aristocratic lady-love (Criseyde) who was fickle. Despite what history tells us of the frequently shifting amours in high life, such ladies liked to think of themselves as models of dignity and decorum. So pressure was brought to bear on Chaucer to make amends, whether seriously or not, in a work celebrating women's constancy in contrast to the fickleness of men.

The Legend of Good Women (ca. 1385[30]) was Chaucer's reply to the request. This is an unfinished collection of tales, chiefly from Ovid, about classical ladies of fiction who remained faithful despite death or desertion by heroes such as Paris, Jason, Theseus, Aeneas, and others. The stories succeed from time to time in evoking pathos, but for the most part they are quite conventional. As in Ovid, the expression is often rhetorical to the point of artificiality. The collection has no conclusion, and the impression is strong that Chaucer wearied of his task imposed from without. There is a humorous touch, amounting to burlesque, in his designation of the separate tales as *legenda* or legends, thus comparing the deserted nymphs, victims of love, to saints who died as martyrs. In fact, he later referred to this work (in the Prologue to the Man of Law's Tale) as "the Seintes Legends of Cupide." To call Queen Cleopatra a "martyr," as he does in the heading to her tale, is surely to invite merriment.

The Prologue to the *Legend of Good Women* represents writing of a much higher order. In this long introduction, extant in two versions (called F and G), Chaucer tells us of a vision he experienced on a benign evening in May, after a day spent in delighted contemplation of daisies in the green meadows. Having fallen asleep "in a lityl herber [garden] that I have," he dreamed that the god of love appeared before him and sternly reproached him for causing rebellion among otherwise devoted lovers:

F 332   "And of Creseyde thou hast seyd as the lyste,
     That maketh men to wommen lasse triste,
     That ben as trewe as ever was any steel."

[as the lyste = as you pleased]

Queen Alcestis, represented as Love's consort, is clad in dazzling garments of white, green and gold fretted with pearls which show her as an incarnation of the daisy beloved of Chaucer. She intercedes with the angry god and persuades him to accept a new work by Chaucer, praising women's fidelity, in exculpation of his fault. The figure of Alcestis, whether or not modeled on an historical personage,[31] is indebted to the contemporary French vogue for glorifying women under the name of the flower called the marguerite, which can also mean a pearl. In this spirit Froissart had written "La Dittie de la Fleur de la Margherite" and Guillaume de Machault his "Dit de la Marguerite" and "Lai de Franchise."[32] The French lyrics probably also influenced *The Pearl*, which in turn may have been known to Chaucer. Though the Prologue is thus part of a well-established tradition, Chaucer succeds in infusing it with a vital freshness. His joy in the floral season of spring seems to radiate from his own experiences while walking in the meadows, not—as in the case of minor poets—from the reading of others' sentiments in books.

A secondary theme in the Prologue shows Chaucer's interest in political theory. When Alcestis is interceding with the god of love to temper his anger against Chaucer, she pleads for mercy somewhat as did royal ladies known to Chaucer: Richard's Queen Anne, Edward's Philippa, and Joan of Kent, the widow of the Black Prince—on occasions reported by contemporary chroniclers. Moreover, she reminds him that a king should be mild to his people, give ready ear to their grievances, keep his lieges and vassals within the bounds of justice, "and han of pore folk compassion." In short,

G 357   Hym oughte nat be tyraunt and crewel,
         As is a fermour, to don the harm he can.

[fermour = farmer of taxes]

This passage (G 353 ff. gives the longer version of it), like some of the lyrics already discussed, offers further evidence that, although Chaucer did not speak out directly on the burning issues of his day, he was by no means indifferent to them, and that the burdensome taxes and expropriations from which poor people suffered were very present to his mind and heart.

To this period (the earlier 1380's) may be assigned an unfinished poem, *Anelida and Arcite*, embodying another complaint by a lady deserted by her faithless lover. There is some indebtedness to Statius and to the *Teseide* of Boccaccio, which tells the story of Palamon and Arcite later adapted into the Knight's Tale, but most of the material is original. Attempts to identify this deserted lady with someone in contemporary English society lack adequate foundation. The emphasis on women's loyalty and men's infidelity suggests that the poem may have been intended, like the *Legend of Good Women*, to serve as a palinode or retraction for the *Troilus and Criseyde*. The impression is strengthened by certain verbal parallelisms between the poem and the romance.[33] What is most interesting about *Anelida* is the variety of stanzaic and metrical patterns in which it is composed. The fragment suggests a kind of exercise through which Chaucer strove for a surer mastery of his linguistic and metrical medium.

By the end of this period he had certainly attained that mastery. The Prologue to the *Legend of Good Women* was written freely and smoothly in the riming pentameter couplets which he was to employ so masterfully in the Prologue to the *Canterbury Tales*. He was ready, indeed, to work on that great panorama of English life and English types which is the supreme achievement of his creative art.

[1] No attempt will here be made to refer explicitly to all of the important Chaucer research of recent decades. For useful surveys see A.C. Baugh, "Fifty Years of Chaucer Scholarship," *Speculum*, XXVI (1951), 659—77; Robert Roy Purdy, "Chaucer Scholarship in England and America," *Anglia*, LXX (1952), 345—81. Basic is the *Bibliography of Chaucer, 1908—1953*, by D.D. Griffith (University of Washington, Seattle, 1955).

[2] The background of Chaucer's family is well depicted by Marchette Chute, *Geoffrey Chaucer of England* (London, 1946). The short biography by J.L. Lowes stresses the intellectual background (Boston, 1934).

[3] Documentation of these and other events will be found in *Life Records of Chaucer*, published by R.E.G. Kirk and others for the Chaucer Society (1900).

[4] Haldeen Braddy, "Chaucer and Dame Alice Perrers," *Speculum*, XXI (1946)· 222—28.

[5] Margaret Galway, "Geoffrey Chaucer, J.P. and M.P.," *Modern Language Review*, XXXV (1941), 1—36; Florence Scott, "Chaucer and the Parliament of 1386," *Speculum* XVIII (1943), 80—86.

[6] The early period of Chaucer's work has been treated by W. Clemen, *Der junge Chaucer* in *Kölner anglistische Arbeiten*, XXIII (1938).

[7] Dean Fansler, *Chaucer and the* Roman de la Rose (Columbia University Press, 1914).

[8] All citations from the texts are taken from the edition by F.N. Robinson (Boston, 1933).

[9] J.R. Kreuzer, "The Dreamer in *The Book of the Duchess*," *PMLA*, LXVI (1951), 543—47.

[10] *Ovide moralisé*, ed. de Boer (Amsterdam, 1915).

[11] Haldeen Braddy on *The Parlement of Fowles* in *Three Chaucer Studies* (New York: Oxford University Press, 1932).

[12] Some striking likenesses are to be found between the *Parlement* and a satirical Latin poem, the *Pavo* of Jordan of Osnabruch, ed. F.W.E. Roth, *Romanische Forschungen*, VI (1894). Phillip W. Damon has proposed this as a source of Chaucer's poem in *Modern Language Notes*, LXVII (1952), 520—24.

[13] For an appreciative study see Gardiner Stillwell, "Unity and Comedy in Chaucer's *Parlement of Fowles*," *Journal of English and Germanic Philology*, XLIX (1950), 470—97. Charles O. McDonald sees in the poem a contrast between natural and artificial love, *Speculum* XXX (1955), 455—57.

[14] The basic study on the *Hous of Fame* is that by W.O. Sypherd (London: Chaucer Society, 1907 for 1904), still valuable for an understanding of the literary background.

[15] Chaucer's summary varies from Virgil's treatment in plan and details which are shared by the 12th-century Latin *Ilias* of Simon Chèvre d'Or (Aurea Capra). It may well have been known to Chaucer. See A.C. Friend, "Chaucer's Version of the *Aeneid*," *Speculum*, XXVIII (1953), 317—23. For a general study see E.F. Shannon, *Chaucer and the Roman Poets* (Harvard University Press, 1929).

[16] See particularly Robert A. Pratt, "Chaucer's Claudian," *Speculum*, XXII (1947), 419—29, and the same author's essay "The Importance of Manuscripts for the Study of Medieval Education," *Bulletin* published on the Progress of Medieval and Renaissance Studies in the United States and Canada, XX (1949). The *caveat* should be kept in mind in reading older studies such as T.R. Lounsbury's *Studies in Chaucer*, 3 vols. (New York, 1892).

[17] Definite proof has been given by V. L. Dedeck-Héry, "Jean de Meun et Chaucer, Traducteurs de la *Consolation* de Boèce," *PMLA*, LII (1937), 967—91.

[18] See M. Schlauch, "Chaucer's Prose Rhythms," *PMLA*, LXV (1950), 568—89. Others have tended to judge Chaucer's prose style more severely, e.g., B.L. Jefferson, *Chaucer and the* Consolation of Philosophy *of Boethius* (Princeton University Press, 1917) and George Philip Krapp, *The Rise of English Literary Prose* (New York: Oxford University Press, 1915).

[19] It appears that Chaucer composed the newly discovered *Equatorie of the Planetis*, now in the library of Peterhouse, Cambridge, and recently edited by D.T. Price for the Cambridge University Press (1955). For general discussion, see Walter Clyde Curry, *Chaucer and the Medieval Sciences* (London and New York, 1926).

[20] Haldeen Braddy, "Chaucer and Graunson," *PMLA*, LIV (1939), 359 ff.

[21] This may be due to Chaucer's misreading of two lines in Horace's *Epistles*, ii, 2; cf. R.A. Pratt, "A Note on Chaucer's Lollius," *Modern Language Notes*, LXV (1950), 183—87. For argument identifying Lollius with the Italian humanist Laelius Pietri Stephani de Tosettis, see Lillian H. Hornstein in *PMLA*, LXIII (1948), 64—84.

[22] For detailed study see H.M. Cummings, *The Indebtedness of Chaucer's Works to the Italian Works of Boccaccio* (University of Cincinnati Press, 1916).

[23] Arthur Mizener, "Character and Action in the Case of Criseyde," *PMLA*, LIV (1939), 65—82.

[24] Eugene E. Slaughter, "Chaucer's Pandarus: Virtuous Uncle and Friend," *Journal of English and Germanic Philology*, XLVIII (1949), 186—95.

[25] J.S.P. Tatlock, "The People in Chaucer's *Troilus*," *PMLA*, LVI (1941), 85—104, emphasises the divergences of the characters, not only from Boccaccio's treatment of them, but from the formal tradition of courtly love.

[26] Theodore A. Stroud, "Boethius' Influence on Chaucer's *Troilus*," *Modern Philology*, XLIX (1951—52), 1—9.

[27] Robert Kilburn Root, *The Textual Tradition of Chaucer's* Troilus (Chaucer Society, 1916 for 1912), pp. 216 ff.

[28] Boccaccio, *Teseide*, xi, 1—3, describes the soul of Arcita after death. Chaucer used this epic for his Knight's Tale in the *Canterbury Tales*. There is some influence from Dante as well. See John W. Clark, "Dante and the Epilogue of *Troilus*," *Journal of English and Germanic Philology*, L (1951), 1—10.

[29] See Thomas A. Kirby, *Chaucer's Troilus: A Study in Courtly Love* (Louisiana State University Press, 1940); also Karl Young, "Chaucer's *Troilus and Criseyde* as Romance," *PMLA*, LIII (1938), 38—63. This valuable article fails however to distinguish sharply enough the difference between the old type of romance and the new psychological romance here initiated by Chaucer.

[30] This date has been based on the assumption that Chaucer was indebted to Machault's "Lai de Franchise" (1385) as primary source for his Prologue to the *Legend*. That assumption has been refuted by Marian Lossing, "The Prologue to the *Legend of Good Women* and the 'Lai de Franchise'," *Studies in Philology*, XXIX (1942), 15 ff. The work nevertheless belongs to the general period indicated. Robert M. Estrich has suggested that Chaucer was indebted to another poem of Machault's rather than the "Lai de Franchise"; see his "Chaucer's Prologue to the *Legend of Good Women*" in *Studies in Philology*, XXXVI (1939), 20—40.

[31] Alcestis is usually identified with Queen Anne, but Margaret Galway argues for Joan of Kent, King Richard's mother, in "Chaucer's Sovereign Lady," *Modern Language Review*, XXXII (1938), 145—99. Objections are raised by W.E. Weese, "Alceste and Joan of Kent," *Modern Language Notes*, LXIII (1948), 477—80.

[32] Jean Froissart, *Poésies*, ed. J.A. Bouchon (Paris, 1829), pp. 124—30; Eustache Deschamps, *Oeuvres complètes*, ed. de Queux de Saint-Hilaire (Paris, 1880), pp. 203—14. The debt of Chaucer to this school of writing was pointed out long since by J.L. Lowes in *PMLA*, XIX (1904), 593—683 and XX (1905), 749—864.

[33] Compare 1. 20 with *Troilus*, ii, 3 f.; 1. 81 f. with v, 1718; 11. 120 and 126 with ii, 755 f.; 1. 147 with v, 1053; 11. 169 ff. with iv, 736 ff., and ii, 771 ff.

CHAPTER XII

CHAUCER'S CANTERBURY TALES

1. THE PROLOGUE AND ITS PEOPLE

Chaucer's *Canterbury Tales* is not only the masterpiece among the poet's own works; it is the high point of all English medieval literature. Yet the work as it has come down to us is a fragment. The scheme was planned to embrace a collection of stories to be told by a group of pilgrims journeying from London to Canterbury and back again, each individual to tell two stories going and two returning. Since the company consists of 30 people besides the narrator,[1] this would provide for 120 or 124 tales. Instead, we have only 21 complete tales and three unfinished ones. No pilgrim has succeeded in telling more than a single story.

What was realised of the original plan is nevertheless enough to establish Chaucer's commanding position as narrator and creative artist. With respect to general scheme and individual tales, Chaucer was not so much an innovator as a great transformer, using inherited plots and forms in order to create a living microcosm of people and society in his own times.

The device of putting stories within a framework which is itself a story was not, of course, an invention of Chaucer's. We have seen how Gower put his *Confessio Amantis* (ch. 10, sec. 6) into the framework of a lover's confession. The stories used as *exempla* in *The Seven Sages of Rome*[2] were embodied in a narrative situation of an amorous stepmother trying to ruin the stepson who had rejected her illicit love. This diverting collection had reached Europe from the Orient, which (for example in India, Egypt and Arabia) produced many complicated specimens of the type.[3] In Italy, the device of framing stories within a story setting was tried several times in the 14th century. Most famous is Boccaccio's *Decamerone,* in which some wealthy Florentines, fugitives from the plague, entertain one another with *novelle* in a salubrious mountain resort. However, there is no certain evidence that Chaucer knew this collection. Another writer, Sercambi, placed his tales or *Novelle* (1374) in a setting which comes closer to Chaucer's, for he has his narrators go on a journey while entertaining one another. Again, however, there is no direct evidence that Chaucer was indebted to Sercambi either.

By setting his narrators into motion along the route to Canterbury, Chaucer provided the interest of a changing background, and he opened up many possibilities for by-play and conflicts of personality among the pilgrims. As the frame itself moves, it is as if a third dimension had been added to the traditional flat technique. The characters are chosen from all ranks of English society, and they are delineated in the Prologue by a combination of typical traits and vivid, individual details, recalling the methods of portrait painters in the later Middle Ages. Just as an artist in colours took care to indicate a knight's status by some detail like a hawk on his wrist, and clerics or craftsmen by costumes and objects held in their hands, so Chaucer first presents his pilgrims against the background of rank and profession, with remarks about their places in these. Then however—again like the portrait painters—he proceeds to give the vivid details making each figure unforgettably distinct from all others of his group. We see the black wide nostrils of the Miller, and the hairy wart on his nose; we catch a glimpse of the Wife of Bath's red stockings; we hear the sentimental exclamations of the Prioress over her pet dogs, and the singing of the young Squire; we guess Chaucer's shrewd surmises about the Pardoner's falsetto voice, the Cook's sores and the Friar's helpfulness in marrying off poor village girls. The quiet irony and indirect statements sometimes convey very harsh facts, as when Chaucer lets us know that his Shipman or sea-captain is really a merciless privateer. The poet does this, not by forthright statement, but by telling us that upon capturing war prisoners in his armed vessel, the Shipman is accustomed to "send them home by water"—that is, to cast them into the sea.

The metrical form of the Prologue—iambic pentameter couplets skilfully varied—is a fine elastic medium for the smooth and subtle portraiture.

The various orders of society are represented by corresponding groups of people.[4] To the upper classes (though not to the most powerful groups in them) belongs first of all the Knight, who has fought in Lithuania and Russia with the Teutonic Order of Prussian Knights.[5] Close to him is his son the Squire; also the Man of Law (holding a very high position in the legal profession). There are, further, the prosperous Merchant, the Franklin (representative of the landed gentry), and the Physician, a trained professional man—although his practice was in those days grounded more on magic than on science, as Chaucer himself indicates.

To the clergy belong pilgrims of various ranks and types. The higher and more prosperous ones include an aristocratic and rather affected Prioress, a Monk addicted to horses and "venery" (hunting), a Friar adept in persuasion and seduction, a Canon of religion who joins the party en route with an attendant yeoman, and a Pardoner who makes a good living by selling indulgences and fake relics of saints. Humbler members of the clergy are a nun and at least one priest journeying with the Prioress, and a country Parson who—in contrast to the Monk, Friar and Pardoner —represents the type of unmercenary, hard-working priest of humble origin obviously admired by Chaucer. The Clerk of Oxford, still a student, is also a sincere devotee of his profession.

There are a number of folk who represent various types of manual labour. The hearty, talkative Wife of Bath is a skilled weaver, surpassing even the world-renowned Flemings ("hem of Ypres and of Gaunt") in her craft; the Miller and Plowman (brother of the Priest) and Yeoman work in the countryside; the Cook sells his wares in the city streets. He has been employed by five guildmen: a Haberdasher, a Carpenter, a Weaver, a Dyer and a Tapestry-maker. These wear the same livery, indicating membership in the same "fraternity"; their clothing shows that they are prosperous. Three pilgrims are employed in activities not directly productive. The Manciple is a kind of major-domo waiting upon a group of students at a university. The Reeve is an overseer on a wealthy lord's estate, a man both feared and hated by the peasants, partly because of his very office, and partly because of his irascible nature. The Summoner serves notices issued by an ecclesiastical court to persons charged with crimes falling under its jurisdiction. He is hated because he abuses his office to extort, bribe and inform on prospective victims and even lead them to commit the sins for which he will then denounce them. He is a thoroughly nasty person.

Striking indeed is the amount of satire, sharp in effect if mildly expressed, which is introduced into the character descriptions of the Prologue. Many of the pilgrims are shown as abusing their jobs or offices. Three of the clerics are charged with types of racketeering and corruption, widespread in Chaucer's day, [6] which was the more reprehensible since the agents were men of some education and pretended to be spiritual guides of the laity. The Physician is thirsty for gold. The Cook sells and re-sells stale pies, just as the Pardoner later confesses that he sells sheep's bones as relics of saints. The wealth of concrete detail deftly woven into these accounts serves to evoke the whole 14th-century social world of Geoffrey Chaucer. Some of the pilgrims may in fact be modeled on living people, as has been argued. Whether or not, he has made them real for us. And one of the most living persons in the group is that born master

of ceremonies, Harry Bailly, host at the Tabard Inn: he who shepherds
the pilgrims on their journey, directs the storytelling, comments unabashed on the performances, praises and admonishes and generally infuses
into the whole undertaking his own gusty, down-to-earth plebeian humour.
It was the confident, pushing Harry Baillys, active in many towns, who
were thrusting aside old class inhibitions and preparing the way for the
middle-class culture later to become predominant in England.

2. PLAN AND ORDER OF THE TALES; THE ACTION
WITHIN THE FRAME STORY

It was a master-stroke of Chaucer's original genius that he not only
presented his story-tellers in a many-coloured living group at the beginning,
but also put their personalities into activity during the journey, and
caused them to act and react upon one another like characters in a play.
They are made to quarrel and drink, praise and jeer as living people
do, in the intervals between stories. Thus new side-lights are cast upon
their natures. Moreover, the sudden irruption of a new pair of characters,
the Canon and his Yeoman, at Boughton-under-Blee provides fresh
interest and a new conflict of personalities after the original group has
grown familiar. The marked element of drama in Chaucer's frame story
distinguishes it from all others of its kind.

Certain groups of tales are bound together by sequences of narrative
in the frame story, called links. These contain remarks by the Host and
other pilgrims on the tale just told, and a request for the next one to be
contributed. Within the links too, as well as in the separate prologues,
epilogues and occasional interruptions to the tales, there occur the arguments among the pilgrims which remind us constantly of the setting.
But some stories end without any such interlude or any indication of what
is to follow. These mark the conclusion of a block of tales. There are nine
such separate blocks according to the majority of manuscripts; ten
blocks in some, where a certain link is missing. [7]

Artistically the links are on as high a level as any passages in the
tales themselves, and represent the finest flower of Chaucer's creative art.
After the Knight has told his long and dignified tale of chivalry, the
Host shows that he had intended to ask the Monk to follow suit (the
hierarchy thus appropriately following the nobility), but the Miller,
already drunk to the point of pallor, obstinately insists on intruding
his ribald tale here, in spite of the objections by his enemy the Reeve.
Next, the latter needs must cap it with a like ribald tale having a miller
as its butt. The Cook, in an ecstasy at the Reeve's performance, can not

Front Page of the *Canterbury Tales*
British Museum

his attendant Yeoman. The master, embarrassed by the revelation, hastily flees from the company. The Yeoman's Tale ends this block. Another which, like it, lacks any introduction is the one initiated by the Physician's Tale of Virginia. The sad conclusion of the story moves Harry Bailly to a fit of sympathetic swearing, after which he begs the Pardoner to provide some merry entertainment, presumably ribald, for relief. When the "gentle" folk protest at the prospect of vulgarity, the Pardoner smooths things over by suggesting an interval for refreshment at an inn. Fortified by draughts of ale, he then begins—not his tale, but a most wittily cynical account of his own methods in fleecing poor simple people under the pretext of religion. There is no more devastating revelation of religious charlatanry in all medieval literature, yet the usual moralistic commentary is entirely lacking. The reader is expected to draw his own conclusions; Chaucer does not draw them for him.

During the pilgrimage the Friar and Summoner, as rivals in deception, develop hostility towards each other and tell stories at each other's expense. On another occasion, the Host intervenes actively to interrupt Chaucer's own attempt at a burlesque of medieval romance entitled *Sir Thopas*, the point of which quite escapes him; and he comments with frank favour or disfavour on the tales that follow. Even when he is wrong, his remarks are refreshingly honest.

Towards the end of the pilgrimage the Manciple takes advantage of the Cook's inebriation in order to insert his own contribution. After him, the Host suggests a fable of some sort from the Parson. But the latter, being a sober and rather puritanical cleric, suspected by the Host of lollard tendencies, rejects the opportunity for entertainment and concludes the series of extant blocks with something more in his own vein: a tract on penance and the seven deadly sins.

Most lively of all the conflicts among the pilgrims are the ones centring on the Wife of Bath. Alisoun herself is one of the most original of Chaucer's creations. Though he has taken many hints for her personality out of traditional satire against women, notably from the *Miroir de Mariage* by Eustace Deschamps,[8] he has made her a rounded individual such as no previous satirist had conceived of. The Wife of Bath is a hearty and sensual creature who proclaims openly her inability to grasp ascetic ideals. The Prologue to her tale is a disarmingly frank account of her five marriages, revealing the tricks and devices by which she had ensnared her husbands and maintained control or "maistrie" over them. Not until the 20th century, in writers like D.H. Lawrence, for instance, is there to be found so searching a fictional document on marriage, recounted from the woman's point of view. Its unconventionality has shocked

some critics, and it shocked the Pardoner, who is represented as inter-
rupting to protest its thesis about women's indirect domination over
men in the marital relationship. Her discourse and her tale precipitate
a discussion on marriage by several other pilgrims. Not in uninterrupted
sequence, to be sure, but in close proximity, a number of them keep
coming back to the subject of marriage and "maistrie." [9] The Clerk,
after telling about a heroine who exemplified unbounded submission
to her husband, appeals directly to the ·Wife of Bath in disclaiming
any desire to have women in real life imitate so unnaturally docile a spouse.
The Merchant, on the other hand, wishes his own wife were more like
the Clerk's long-suffering heroine, and he passes on to tell a very amusing
and satirical story of women's wiles in deceiving husbands. It is the
Franklin who offers a balance between the extremes of male and female
domination in marriage through the medium of his tale.

About Chaucer's intentions in -finally ordering the blocks of tales
we can not be sure. Quite possibly he had not decided about the order
at the moment of his death. The 57 complete or nearly complete manuscripts, together with the early printed versions, can be classified in four
groups according to their arrangements of the blocks. [10] None appears
to have final authority.

Another problem arises when we try to place the blocks in order
geographically, according to the route to Canterbury (or to Canterbury
and back [11]). All manuscripts agree in the contents of their first block
(the tales of the Knight, Miller, Reeve and Cook). All of them follow this
with a second block initiated by the Man of Law. After his tale discrepancies appear. Many manuscripts [12] place the Squire's Tale after that
of the Man of Law, with a link pointing to it as next in order; one group
of manuscripts [13] puts the Wife of Bath's Prologue and Tale next without
an introduction. But all main groups of manuscripts place a series of tales
(begun by the Shipman) rather late in the journey, although it contains
a reference to the town of Rochester which ought obviously to precede
a reference to the more distant Sittingbourne in the earlier Wife of Bath's
Tale. To avoid this geographical contradiction, the editor of the first
great modern edition of Chaucer, W.W. Skeat, [14] decided to reject the
order found in all main manusripts and to take that of a relatively poor one (MS. Selden Arch. B. 14) having the advantage of geographical plausibility. Skeat designated the blocks of tales by letters.
The second one, B, may be subdivided into two parts at the point where
certain manuscripts lack any link. [15]

Keeping Skeat's system of designation for the for the tales, but
indicating the division occuring within group B, we may thus list the
entire series as he presented it, with arrows to show links:

18*

A   Prologue → Knight's Tale → Miller's Tale → Reeve's Tale → Cook's Fragment

B1   Man of Law's Tale → (this link lacking in a number of MSS.)

B2   Shipman's → Prioress's Tales → Chaucer's (unfinished) *Tale of Sir Thopas* → Chaucer's *Melibeus* → Monk's Tale → Nun's Priest's Tale

C   Physician's → and Pardoner's Tales

D   Wife of Bath's → Friar's → Summoner's Tales

E   Clerk's → Merchant's Tales

F   Squire's Fragment → Franklin's Tale

G   Second Nun's → Canon's Yeoman's Tales

H   Manciple's Tale

I   Parson's Tale; Chaucer's Retraction[16]

Another editorial policy was followed by F.N. Robinson[17] in his one-volume edition. Here an outstanding early manuscript was chosen on the basis of date, legibility, accuracy in transcription, and similar advantages, though like many others it contains the geographical inconsistency already mentioned and also lacks the clearly authentic Man of Law's end-link.[18] The manuscript in question, called the Ellesmere, places the Wife of Bath's Tale (the first of D) after the Man of Law's (B[1]).

There is evidence that Chaucer several times changed his intentions regarding the assignment of tales to narrators, as is shown by inconsistencies between references in links and in tales.[19] Much ingenious speculation has been devoted to the attempted reconstruction of various stages in Chaucer's work, and surmises about the best arrangement to be followed. But it must be admitted that difficulties arise in connection with every proposal made thus far.[20] For the reader mainly interested in Chaucer's work, not as material for editing but for artistic appreciation, it is perhaps enough to say that we have a set of brilliantly executed groups of stories, linked by passages of dramatic interchange among the narrators, unsurpassed for realistic verisimilitude in medieval literature, and that we need not devote further time to speculation about the stages in the evolution of the author's unifinished project. The links alone form a separate and imposing testimonial to Chaucer's gifts as a realist in art.

For present purposes it will be desirable to discuss the separate tales in groups, not as they occur in any manuscript or group of manuscripts, but according to the literary genres they represent.[21]

3. ROMANCES, LONG AND SHORT

For his Knight, Chaucer appropriately selected a long romance, or rather romantic epic, written by Boccaccio. It is based on a classical theme. The Italian *Teseide*, as its name indicates, was loosely attached to the story of Theseus of Athens, while its main plot concerned the loves of two captive Theban knights for the fair Emilia, sister-in-law of Theseus. These last three characters are unknown to classical mythology. The rivalry of Palamone and Arcita, their tournament, and the death of Arcita, as told by Boccaccio, furnished a slight framework upon which the Italian poet hung his splendid and rhetorical speeches and glowing descriptions. [22] The whole is something of a *tour de force*, a superb, much expanded literary exercise. In adapting it, Chaucer has reduced the original poem by three-quarters and has inserted some fine new passages of his own. He has also illuminated the conventional tale with touches of humour. [23] Nevertheless, for all its merits, the Knight's Tale remains a somewhat formal affair. Since Chaucer had mentioned a work of his dealing with Palamon and Arcite in the Prologue to his *Legend of Good Women* (ch. 11, sec. 5), this condensed and somewhat independent version of the Italian poem was apparently done, at least in first draft, by the mid-1380's. Thus Chaucer must have taken a work already prepared and attributed it to his Knight with not too much care for plausibility. Fitting though the theme may be, a poem of over 2200 iambic pentameter lines is far less adapted to recitation by the road than are any of the other tales.

Other romances told on the pilgrimage fit their narrators in scope as well as character. The Squire begins—but leaves unfinished—a colourful Eastern fantasy about a Tartar Prince Cambuscan and his beautiful daughter Canace. The Princess was wooed by a suitor arriving on a magic steed of brass, bearing gifts of a supernatural power. The Princess is turned against him by listening to a female falcon in the royal gardens denouncing male infidelity. The rest of the story would very probably have told of the adventurous exploits of this wooer, designed to win the favour of the Princess, interwoven with exploits of her brothers Algarsife and Cambalo. The atmosphere is redolent of the Arabian *Thousand and One Nights*, in which several analogous situations are to be found. These were not directly known to Chaucer, but an abundance of similar material is to be found in the 13th-century French romance *Cléomadès* (probably drawn out of the Arabic from a Spanish source), which was accessible to him. King Cambuscan is to be identified with the historical Ghengis Khan, and the fabulously wealthy kingdom attributed to him is like that reported of the mythical Prester John in India. What is remarkable about Chaucer's fragment is its success in evoking the sense of exotic opulence, the magic of little-known lands beckoning beyond the Eastern horizon. The theme has a certain relevance, too, to the discussion of "maistrie" in marriage, [24] since the wooer is obliged to overcome Canace's resistance to it.

The Wife of Bath's Tale is a miniature Arthurian romance. Its unnamed hero is under sentence to find out within a year's time what it is that women most desire—or lose his life. An ugly witch-woman tells him the answer: they desire most to have sovereignty in marriage. He buys the information with a promise to marry the loathly lady who gave it. On their marriage night she suddenly becomes a beautiful young

Canterbury Tales: The Yonge Squyer. A woodcut by Pynson

woman, and she asks him: Would you rather have me ugly, old and faithful to you, or beautiful and of uncertain fidelity? Having learned his lesson about maistrie, the knight dutifully leaves the choice to his wife, and she thereupon becomes both beautiful and loyal, to his great and lasting delight.

At the basis of this tale, which was also told by Gower (ch. 10, sec. 6) there lies an old fairy tale of a woman unspelled from the curse of being a monstrous creature by day and a lovely human being by night. By changing the subject of the knight's quest, and also the dilemma placed before him at his wedding,[25] Chaucer has ingeniously adapted the theme to the Wife's overwhelming interest in husbands and their subjection to women's will. After an interval, however, the tables are turned on her. The Clerk's Tale of Griselda, closely paraphrased from a Latin prose story by Petrarch,[26] celebrates the invincible humility and patience of a wife when her subservience is cruelly tested by her husband. This tale, cast in the stanzaic form of the *Troilus*, exploits fully all the pathos

inherent in the situation, but even its narrator finds Griselda's yielding
to her husband's maistrie an excessive virtue, and he concludes ironically with a direct reference to the Wife of Bath—by urging other
wives to behave in a precisely opposite manner. The gratuitous cruelty
exhibited by the husband of Griselda has disturbed most commentators
on this tale. [27]

Canterbury Tales: The Wife of Bath

A romance told by the Franklin offers a balance between the two
extremes of domination in marriage. Chaucer calls this tale a Breton *lai*.
During the absence of her knightly husband, a lady rashly promises to
grant her love to an amorous squire if he will perform a seemingly impossible act: remove from the Breton coast those rocks on which, according
to her brooding fears, her husband's ship may be wrecked upon his
voyage home. Wth a magician's aid the squire performs the miracle. The
lady, in great distress of spirit, confides her predicament to her returned
husband, her partner in a marriage of equality. Much moved, the knight
controls his feelings and with simple directness asks merely for assurance: "Is ther oght elles, Dorigen, but this?" (F 1479)—and then breaks
off, overmastered by tears. He bids her keep her pledge. When the young
squire learns of the husband's decision he is himself moved to generosity,
and frees the lady from her promise. The story can be traced back to
Oriental sources, but Chaucer has adapted the plot to exemplify an ideal
for the marriage relations of his own time—an ideal which, as many

of his other tales indicate, was far from realisation under normal conditions.

All of Chaucer's romances are conspicuously unified and (with the exception of the Knight's Tale) concise. Quite alien to his genius for form were the long-drawn, amorphous adventure stories of the past age. In the part of a tale attributed to himself, he in fact satirised them with a fine sense of their ridiculousness. This is *Sir Thopas*, a burlesque of the contemporary English verse romances like *Libeaus Desconnus, Horn Childe, Beves of Hamtoun* and others. It has been pointed out that a number of the specific romances humorously echoed in *Sir Thopas* are to be found in the famous Auchinleck manuscript (see ch. 9, sec. 3), which Chaucer probably handled. Out of the absurdities of the genre the poet has constructed his delicately comic picture of a dauntless knight, intent on finding himself a fairy mistress somewhere or other, who rides through a forest full of dangerous creatures—such as deer and hare; who goes seeking adventure—but neglects to don his armour; who encounters a giant—and begs the favour of deferring combat until he is properly equipped for it. The humour of the satirical narrative is lost on Bailly, who interrupts with a cry "Namoore of this, for Goddes dignitee!" What we have of *Sir Thopas*, however, though a mere 917 lines in tail-rime verse, is an embryonic anticipation of the immortal *Don Quixote*. It is acute literary criticism by exemplification. It forecasts, though it does not yet mark, the end of chivalrous romance: that most typical secular product of literature under feudalism.

4. SAINTS' LIVES AND PIOUS TALES

Narrative for edification included, as we have seen, the very popular domain of hagiography. It is represented in the *Canterbury Tales* by the stanzaic life of St. Cecilia, told by the Second Nun accompanying the Prioress. Chaucer's mention of a completed work on this subject in the Prologue to the *Legend of Good Women* indicates that it was composed earlier and then placed in the Canterbury framework. The treatment follows the version contained in the well-known *Legenda Aurea* by Jacobus de Voragine, with supplementation from other versions. Little of Chaucer's originality is evident in this conventional tale of worldly joys renounced, of persecution endured and martyrdom achieved, yet it is marked by qualities of unaffected sincerity which place it far above the numerous uninspired examples of the type being circulated in his time.

The Prioress's Tale is a miracle story connected with the cult of the Virgin and belonging to an ugly type of Christian medieval folklore. It purports to tell of a little boy, devoted to the service of the Virgin, who was done to death by Jews out of pure hatred, but continued miraculously to sing "Alma Redemptoris Mater" even after his throat was cut. The miracle is recounted in a number of versions outside of Chaucer's, some ending (unlike his) with the restoration of the child to life. The poet has fully exploited the pathos inherent in the picture of an innocent child meeting a dreadful death. His literary skill is not enough, however, to obscure the sinister context of this plot in medieval culture. It was in fact one of the instruments used to arouse and direct violence against peaceful communities of Jews throughout Europe; it must be considered in relation to the anti-Jewish pogroms which in both medieval and modern times have formed some of the blackest episodes of European history. Chaucer himself merely accepted uncritically a piece of slanderous fiction. He did not create it. Yet even the most ardent of Chaucer's admirers must regret that he was so limited by the prejudices of his environment as to contribute to this fictional legacy of hatred.

Two shorter tales offer pious edification without belonging to religious literature in the strict sense. One is the Physician's Tale of the Roman maiden Virginia, killed by her father to save her from the lecherous grasp of the tyrant Appius Claudius. Jean de Meun had included this bit of historal lore in his part of the *Roman de la Rose*, with details of heightened sensationalism; but besides this version, Chaucer also made use of the classical source in Livy's history (*Ab Urbe Condita*, iii, 44—58). The story, though dealing with pagans, was readily adapted to serve as an *exemplum* (see below) for Christian moralists. The Friar's Tale, openly directed against the Summoner, describes just such another corrupt servant of the ecclesiastical courts, and relates how he lost his soul to the Devil. The rash bargain by which he forfeited it is made to hinge directly on the unsavoury means he uses to terrorise and extort fees from innocent people. No wonder that the real Summoner protests at the Friar's skilful satire of his practices. This story too may be regarded as an *exemplum*; the Friar's art in handling it is due, we may surmise, to his experience in popular preaching.

The Man of Law's Tale follows the familiar pattern of romances about innocent accused queens finally vindicated and restored to happiness. In tone it recalls the more romantic of saints' lives. [28] In plot it is close to Gower's treatment of the same theme in his story of Constance (*Confessio Amantis*, ii, 587—1612), except that Chaucer has exploited even more fully its potentialities for sentimental pathos. Despite the absurd improbabilities in the plot, we are carried along by the poet's sheer power to arouse human sympathy. The stanza comparing his long-suffering heroine to a pale-faced victim being led to the scaffold (B 465—51) is a metaphor of unusual emotional impact.

5. *EXEMPLA* LONG AND SHORT

More obviously didactic in their intention than these last tales are the *exempla* directly used to illustrate a sermon, thesis or argument. The Monk's stanzaic Tale is in fact merely a collection of melancholy anecdotes—Biblical, historical, mythological and contemporary—illustrating the downfall of eminent persons from prosperity to a miserable death. Such a downfall constitutes a "tragedy" in the medieval sense of the word, which had no necessary connection with drama. The Monk's collection, drawn from various sources, is a miniature *De Casibus Virorum Illustrium* such as Boccacccio had previously written. The high point in it is the example of Ugolino of Pisa, translated from Dante (*Inferno*, xxxiii). The horror is somewhat reduced by Chaucer; nevertheless the passage is one of great power.[29] To the Middle Ages, unaware of the laws of historical causality, such personal calmities seemed to be the result of capricious forces operating (paradoxically enough) under God's will.

Anecdotal also is the Summoner's Tale, which is really a loosely organised diatribe against friars, with a number of vivid if malodorous illustrations of their greed in trying to obtain legacies for the orders. The Canon's Yeoman's Tale, similarly, is an account of the tricks and deceptions of alchemists, playing on the credulity and greed of their victims to enrich themselves. The Yeoman tells of incidents he has seen with his own eyes, reporting them from the servant's point of view with pictorial detail. Chaucer's own references indicate that he had read some text books on this medieval pseudo-science, which claimed to "multiply" or transmute base metals into gold. His condemnation of it in this Tale is so very strong and circumstantial that some critics have surmised that an unlucky personal experience of his own deception was the motive for the polemic. Nevertheless, accounts by others would probably have sufficed to stir his interest in the problem. His scepticism was shared by such contemporaries as Petrarch.[30] It is not impossible that his curiosity and condemnation alike resulted from contacts made during his sojourn in Italy. Both the Summoner's Tale and that of the Canon's Yeoman are outstanding for their realistic portrayal of imposters and their methods. The versification too is that of Chaucer's maturest years.

The short Manciple's Tale is the kind which would fit into a collection meant to illustrate women's depravity, in familiar clerical style. In fact a close analogue to it is to be found in *The Seven Sages of Rome*. Drawn ultimately from the *Metamorphoses* of Ovid (ii, 534—632), perhaps through the *Ovide Moralisé* or a similar paraphrase, this fable tells of a white crow which revealed to Phoebus the adultery of his wife. The bird was punished for its pains, according to the myth, by being deprived of its song and being changed into a black-feathered bird of ill omen. The simple plot is less interesting than the digressions and comments by the author. Speaking through the mouth of the "boystous" Manciple, who does not believe in mincing words about adultery, Chaucer here strips from courtly love its pretense of immunity from the standards of ordinary simple people. These lines (H 203—22) indicate that Chaucer was writing for an audience far wider than the restricted circle which had delighted in his *Troilus and Criseyde*. He now puts forward the wider view, socially, and lets the Manciple, representative of the common man, condemn the snobbish exclusiveness, the actual immorality, of courtly love.

The Pardoner's Tale and the Nun's Priest's Tale, though simple in plot and serving the purposes of exemplification, are handled in an unusually complex and subtle manner.

The former begins with an invective against swearing[31] but shifts to a denunciation of the love of gold. To illustrate that vice, the Pardoner tells a story which he localises in Flanders although (once more) it is actually derived from the great reservoir of transmitted Oriental fiction. The background is a Flemish town where the plague is raging. From the start we are made to feel the ubiquitous presence of death, the eerie instability of daily life. Three drunken revellers in a tavern, insensed that Death should have played such havoc with their companions, set out to find this dreadful executor of mankind. They encounter a mysterious Wanderer who proclaims his weariness with life, his vain desire for death. Their interlocutor bids them seek under a certain tree. Here they find a treasure of gold, and in delight at their discovery they forget their quest. But the gold becomes their death in sober truth, for all three perish in the intrigues of each against the others to possess it solely. Unforgettable is Chaucer's handling of this traditional plot. The mysterious Wanderer and his speech (brilliantly adapting part of an elegy by the late Roman poet Maximian) suggest Death himself and also the legendary figure of the Wandering Jew. The apothecary from whom one of the companions buys poison is a garrulous, self-important person, realistically delineated in striking contrast to the symbolic Wanderer. Once the Pardoner is launched on this gripping tale, he throws into it all his experienced art in narration. At the end he is quite able (as is his custom) to turn its stunning effect to account—in order to try to press his fake relics on the pilgrims for sale. Perhaps, carried away by his own eloquence, he has forgotten his previous revelation of their falsity.[32] Harry Bailly, however, has not forgotten, and he rejects the Pardoner's sales talk in language as tonic as it is earthy. The Tale is an amazing performance; but it does not lead any pilgrim to buy a sheep's bone in place of a saint's.

The Nun's Priest's Tale is also simple in plot and yet artistically complicated in expression. In essence it is the straightforward fable of a cock, a hen and a fox: the narrow escape of the rooster from the fox, and the moral attached to the incident by the story-teller. In short, it belongs to the type of moralised anecdote about animals made famous by Aesop, Phaedrus and Cornelius Nepos, and adapted by Marie de France in the 12th-century *Esopet*. Fables like these were often used as *exempla* by

Canterbury Tales: The Friar, printed by W. Caxton

preachers. (Cf. Odo of Cheriton as discussed in ch. 8, sec. 4.) Many of them, like the one basic to the Nun's Priest's Tale, were woven into the animal epics of unknown authorship, written in Latin and Old French, which effectively satirised types of human society in the form of mock-epics with animals as actors. Thus Chaucer's plot was taken by him from a type of literature already well known and widely circulated. An independent borrowing from the same cycle had already been made in the clever short text entitled *The Fox and the Wolf*.[33] Chaucer's transmutation of a similar incident is, however, a work of much higher order. The simple framework of the fable is used by him as the occasion to depict a poor medieval cottager's farmyard, alive with sound and colour. In the colloquy between cock and hen he embodies a burlesque of chivalry and courtly love, a humorous insight into the ways of human wives deflating their husband's egos, and a mock-solemn disquisition on the nature of dreams. The conversation betweenn fox and rooster also embodies much humorous comment on male vanity. The capture of the proud bird, the cackling and confusion in the barnyard, the pursuit by the mistress and her maids, are described in deliberately inflated style producing a riotous burlesque of formal epics. Wide borrowings from medieval science, pseudo-science and literature are unobtrusively interwoven into this mature satire, heightening its subtle effectiveness by the art that conceals art. Pleasure and instruction here achieve that delicate balance often desired and seldom realised by the best of literary craftsmen.[34]

6. EDIFYING PROSE TRACTS

Two prose "tales" in the Canterbury collection are really not stories but didactic essays. The first, *Melibeus,* is Chaucer's contribution in his own person. It does at least have a story framework for the debate which preaches its lesson. The source was a Latin work of the 13th century, the *Liber Consolationis et Consilii* by an Italian jurist, Albertano of Brescia. A number of vernacular translations exist, and once again we find Chaucer using an abridged one in French, this time quite without reference to the Latin original. Albertano's theme is an important one. He tells of a wealthy but headstrong landlord named Melibeus, married to an allegorical wife Prudence (a woman clearly akin to the Boethian figure of Philosophy), whose household is subjected to violent assault and robbery during the master's absence. Furious at the injury, Melibeus wishes to take the law into his own hands, encouraged by certain hot-heads among his supporters. But the saner element oppose such action. Prudence, his wife, conducts a philosophical argument with him on the need to follow legal procedure, on the futility of private warfare (indeed, of most warfare), on the higher wisdom of peace and forgiveness. Her persuasion is successful and the ending is a happy one.

This piece may well have been prepared in advance of the Canterbury framework, and perhaps first intended for the Man of Law to "speke in prose," as he himself announces. Appropriate it would have been for an eminent lawyer, with its insistence on due legal process as opposed to lynching. In assigning it to himself, however, Chaucer gave it a still greater prominence. This tale has been condemned in the past as a dull work, the reverse of entertaining for Chaucer's imaginary pilgrims. Such strictures ignore the vast appetite of the medieval public, including the laity, for didactic fiction and non-fiction. Recent critics[35] stress this fact, and also point to the intrinsic merits of the piece. It has a renewed importance for our times. The defense of peace and order against lawless violence is no less vital now than during the 14th century. Chaucer's rendering of the vital debate in *Melibeus* is truly eloquent. There are signs that

he expended much care on its language, its prose rhythms, the architecture
of its sentences. It deserves the position it holds as Chaucer's serious
tale, placed in contrast with the delightful spoofing of *Sir Thopas* which
the Host had interrupted.

The Parson's Tale lacks any pretensions to narrative. In substance
it is a conflation of two didactic types widely current since the 13th cer-
tury: the penitential, and the treatise on the seven deadly sins. The latter
theme is interpolated by Chaucer in a general discussion of penance.
His Latin sources (which he much reduced and adapted) belong to the
age when such writing was first being fostered on a wide scale (see ch.
8, sec. 1.) Today the form and the themes appear quaintly archaic, and
it must be admitted that the Parson's Tale is least fitted of all to the
purpose set forth by Harry Bailly in organising the pilgrims' entertainment. Nevertheless there are points of interest in the disquisition on
sins. Under Superbia or Pride, for instance, a concrete and vigorous diatribe is made against extravagant fashions in clothing, which throws
light on one curious aspect of medieval culture.

The Parson's Tale, which is last in all arragements of blocks in the
collection, is followed by a Retraction on the part of Chaucer. It is a short
passage, present in all manuscripts not lacking the final folio entirely.
Here Chaucer revokes all works of his pen not explicitly designed to inculcate virtue by means of religion. Such an appendix fits well enough
with the general tone of the Parson's tract, but it is startling as coming
from the poet himself, since it disavows many of the greatest efforts
of his varied genius. Its significance will be discussed below (sec. 8).

7. THE *FABLIAUX*

During the age when romances flourished as chief entertainment
of the European aristocracy, a different type of story-telling was developed for the diversion of city traders, guildsmen and their associates.
It consisted of short, versified tales designed to evoke merriment and
called in French *fabliaux*.[36] They are comic and irreverent and even
sadistic at times, frequently satirising women and clergy and tricksters
of various sorts. They often hinge on brutal practical jokes. Many of the
more ingenious plots can be traced to Oriental sources; others appear
to have sprung up spontaneously within the plebeian culture of medieval
European towns. Relatively few of the type survive in English,[37] and
of these most are to be found in collections of *exempla*.

The *fabliaux* were essentially anti-romantic, but this does not mean
that they were therefore automatically realistic. The plots are often as

wildly improbable as those of the romances. Most of the situations in which husbands are victimised or thieves and adulterers punished could not by any stretch of the imagination be conceived as occurring in real life. When Boccaccio includes *fabliaux* in his *Decamerone*, they are usually stories with analogues widely current elsewhere, and he relies on the ingeniuty of the traditional plot, his language and his explicit satire to gain his effect. The settings may be sharply realised, but the characters are the most shadowy types. His lascivious matrons and eager wooers and bawds are cut to single patterns little varied. None is a three-dimensional being.

Chaucer's *fabliaux* are basically as improbable in plotting as are Boccaccio's or any other. Most of those included in the *Canterbury Tales* have more or less close analogues in the *Decamerone*. But mere plots are of secondary importance. The enormous difference is that Chaucer's characters live; their social environment is real, their conversation is conducted in the easy colloquial style that is supremely right for them. Because they are conceived with this deep fidelity to real life, they not only convince as literary creations; they imply and convey a critical social commentary while not ostensibly aiming to do more than entertain. [38]

The Reeve's Tale, for instance, is developed out of a schematic, unlikely situation in which two visitors ingeniously take advantage of a man's wife and daughter, to his humiliation, as a result of confusion in the sleeeping arrangements. Here the husband is a tricky and prosperous miller who cheats some university students, his clients, while grinding their corn into flour. The man and his setting are realised before our eyes with the loving accuracy of a Flemish painter's brush-strokes. His wife and his heavy-set daughter, too, might well appear in a village scene by Breughel, complete with broad buttocks and upturned noses. The respectfully jovial speech of the miller, concealing his guile, has the true ring of everyday colloquialism, and that of the students is further distinguished by being convincingly put into the Northern dialect. [39] It is the living stream of such realistic detail which wins our credence for the nocturnal farce enacted in the miller's one-roomed dwelling. The farce itself is not pure unmotivated deviltry; it is revenge for an abuse by the miller which, according to contemporary satire, was typical of many in his trade. Although indirect, Chaucer's satire is here by no means incidental.

The Miller's Tale similarly embodies a farcical plot laid against a setting of highest realism. The action hinges on a double deception practised by Alisoun, the young wife of a prosperous elderly carpenter, with the aid of her lover, a student of Cambridge who lodges with the family.

The two young people not only hoodwink the husband by an elaborate, most unlikely pretense, but also cruelly turn the tables on another wooer of Alison's, the parish clerk. Humour is here directed against the husband's superstitious credulity and the affected manners of the second lover. Again, the veracious details of the characterisations are reinforced by the supremely appropriate language of the dialogues. Short as they are, their colloquial manner, adapted carefully to the individual speakers, contributes greatly to the enrichment of realism in the tale.

The Cook's Tale exists only as an initial desription of its leading character, a young apprentice in a victualers' guild, a youth given over to revelry, gambling and rioting. The poet's intention appears to have been to give a glimpse into the street life of London's underworld, and it is a pity that he did not complete the sketch. The extant lines are a valuable exemplification of what we know about unruly apprentices from historical sources.

The Shipman's Tale and the Merchant's Tale are *fabliaux* dealing with upper strata in bourgeois society, and the satire implied in them is expressed rather subtly, with less of the exuberant vulgarity found in the Miller's and Reeve's farces. The Shipman describes the solidly affluent household of a French merchant living in St. Denis. He is a self-important man who takes his business very seriously. An affable young monk who is a frequent visitor in the household takes advantage of the young wife's financial difficulties—which she wants to keep secret—in order to obtain from her the satisfaction of his amorous desires. His device is borrowed from a well-known motif of folklore. The humour of the story lies in the fact that the husband unwittingly supplies the money the monk uses as a bribe and the wife uses to pay her debts. Moreover the monk ingeniously contrives to avoid repayment to the husband. We are here introduced to the merchant patriciate of the late medieval towns, when cash economy was gradually yet powerfully undermining the very basis of medieval social relations. Once again, the characters of the traditional marital triangle are made sharply individual while remaining validly typical. The monk is suave and worldly and quick to grasp a psychological advantage in conversing with the wife. She, for her part, is a volatile and empty-headed creature, ready with tears and hyperbole. "Myn housbonde is to me the worste man / That evere was sith that the world bigan," she exclaims (B 1350 f.). She is just as ready with her gaity a moment later when her problem has been solved—by whatever means. The merchant himself, ponderously at work on the reckonings in his counting-house, or discoursing solemnly on the hazards of his business ventures, is both an individual and a type, like the merchants depicted in medieval portraits.

Still more ambitious is the satirical integument surrounding the Merchant's Tale. Here too the plot is both simple and improbable. An elderly knight named January, foolish to the point of senility, marries a young girl and attempts to keep a jealous unremitting watch over her actions. When he becomes blind he increases his demands upon her time and attention. Yet she and his young squire Damian contrive to outwit him and satisfy their desire in his very presence. His sight being supernaturally restored at this juncture, his wife May nevertheless extricates herself skilfully from the predicament and even persuades him that she acted thus expressly to restore his sight to him. In the end, the doting husband is reduced to thanking her for her very act of infidelity.[40]

Historically this plot of Oriental origin was designed as just one more illustration of women's quick-witted depravity. Such, however, is not Chaucer's main point (although it is still a conspicuous one). He has converted the banal triangle of adultery into a mordant satire on courtly love. Externally, the situation follows its accepted pattern. The young squire Damian loves his feudal lady, he falls ill and sighs for her presence, the lady visits him to comfort him. The relations are ostensibly those of a 12th-century French romance. But the tone and the attitudes belong rather to urban jesters at the expense of aristocratic refinements in love. Like Troilus, Damian manages to convey a letter to his mistress, but her reading of it (unlike Criseyde's) is placed in circumstances which unsparingly suggest her unromantic physiological aspect. No quasi-disembodied saint of love is she:

E 1950   She feyned hire as that she moste gon
          Ther as ye woot that every wight moot neede;
          And whan she of this bille had taken heede,
          She rente it al to cloutes atte laste,
          And in the pryvee softely it caste.

[wight moot neede = everyone must needs;   bille = letter;   cloutes = pieces]

The unloved husband here occupies a position corresponding to that of King Mark in the Tristan legend. But with what a difference! There is no courtly reticence. concerning the physical distastefulness of January: the cough that wakes him (and her) in the morning, the scrawny neck, the slack skin about his jaws that shakes when he sings. The passionate young wife has been caught in an unsavoury trap. She does succeed, it is true, in obtaining a kind of revenge for the condition of indignity into which she has been sold under the guise of marriage, but her method is no more admirable than the motives of those who betrayed her into it. Here again Chaucer has charged a slight and seemingly frivolous tale with an enormous weight of satirical judgment.

Since his method is indirect, many critics have overlooked what Chaucer was saying beneath the surface of this *fabliau* and the others like it. There has been a tendency to dismiss those tales with distaste because of their element of tonic vulgarity, though the technical skill evinced in narrating them has been admitted. Actually they deserve far more serious and appreciative commentary than they have hitherto received. The realism in them must be carefully distinguished from other literary elements. Such as is present belongs to a very high order and it transcends many limitations of the earlier medieval heritage.

8. CHAUCER'S PLACE AS WRITER AND THINKER

Even so cursory a discussion as the preceding must have indicated something of Chaucer's versatility, the wide range of his interests and of the literary forms which he employed for the purposes of an exceptionally vital art. Like other writers of genius, he accepted current forms and materials with no very striking change in their external aspects. His greatness lay in the freshness of his interpretation, directly related to the life around him, rather than in innovations in the mode of expression. Chaucer closely followed the models available to him, at least throughout much of his career, though from the beginning he introduced profound qualitative changes in the handling of them. Therefore it is usual to see in him (and from one point of view, rightly so) the culmination of medieval culture, representing the best of its more positive aspects.[41] Literary histories and monographs tend to stress his conformity, the absence of revolutionary fervour in his social views, even when he is effectively pointing out contemporary abuses. His humorous detachment has been hailed as his outstanding trait, and he has been described, though not by all, as indifferent to issues of progress and reaction.[42] He has been regarded as a culmination of the past rather than a prophet of the future, since the stress in literary research has been upon his models and his sources.

It must be admitted that Chaucer was a conformist in his personal career. And it can not be denied that he shared the dominant intellectual limitations of his time. For all his abundant zest in life, so variously reflected in his poetic works, Chaucer was deeply imbued with the pessimistic medieval world view inculcating a fear or distrust of human joy. That attitude, uncompromisingly enunciated by Innocent III (ca. 1200), found a sympathetic echo in one part of Chaucer's personality.[43] If admittedly no revolutionary, he was at least always poignantly aware, under his jesting, of the vast hostile forces, natural and man-made, which threatened humanity's security and happiness. Like many endowed with the gift of satirical humour (like Mark Twain, for instance), he was also somber in his deepest reflections. Personal observation in an age of war and pestilence and political upheaval would serve to confirm the attitudes officially disseminated by influential church writers.

Thus one side of his nature, which by over-simplification we may call the conformist-medieval, harmonised with the ascetic other-worldliness which had dominated European intellectual life since the westward diffusion of early monasticism. If questioned about this, Chaucer could have pointed to the panorama of fear and suffering so conspicuous in the 14th century world, the products of ignorance, exploitation and greedy competition, and have claimed an ample justification for his attitude. In his time, plagues and warfare made death an omnipresent factor in life. When he was himself close to death, Chaucer expressed his negative mood in the Retraction appended to the Parson's Tale. Here, where he personally revokes all his worldly writings, including the most brilliant of them, he specifically excepts "the translaccion of Boece de Consolacione, and othere books of legendes of seintes, and omelies, and moralitee, and devocioun..."—those which from the literary point of view were inferior. Admirers of his work have occasionally expressed some doubt on the authenticity of this passage, but there is neither internal nor external reason for rejecting it. Moreover, it merely accentuates the mood in which Chaucer had much earlier concluded his *Troilus and Criseyde*, abruptly reversing the human and world-centred viewpoint of the romance proper into one of stern religious condemnation, climaxed by a prayer of mystical fervour. The Boethius translation, certain of the lyrics, and scattered passages in the *Canterbury Tales* reflect his desire to escape into an unknown absolute existence cleansed from the painful imperfections of our own world.

When all this is duly recognised, however, it accounts for but one mood, one literary aspect of his writing. The contrasting mood, which is by far the more conspicuous, permeates the greater part of his work with an abounding love of life and of people. His affection for humanity is conditioned on both humorous understanding and pity, and it extends to all sorts and conditions of folk. He sees them as both types and individuals. He finds them in all ranks of society. When he condemns, he softens judgment with a vast comprehension of the personal and social causes of their vices. He grasps with intuitive insight the comedy and tragedy of an individual pinioned on an institution with which his own nature clashes: the Wife of Bath, generous sensualist, in conflict with social prejudice against a widow's remarrying; the restless, virile monk misfit in a celibate order and expending his superfluous energy in the hunt; the elegant and courtly Prioress removed from the environment most pleasing to her temperament. Above all he viewed the people around him with the eye of a national poet, the first of whom this can be said in a truly broad sense. Limited neither by the aristocratic clique which he served politically, nor even by the vigorous new class from which he sprang, he gradually widened his sympathetic vision to embrace all levels of English society, with an especial fellow-feeling—unprecedented in medieval literature—for the humbler orders of peasants, craftsmen, village workers and other labourers, whose hands were creating the material basis of England's wealth, the material expression of it plastic arts.[44] His instinctive perception of women's plight in medieval society was also exceptional. The greater amount of his best poetry is oriented squarely towards the masses of the people and the problems of this world.

There are certain aspects of his work, too, which make Chaucer appear less as a medieval synthesis than as a herald of the Renaissance. From Italy he brought away much more than that heightened love of form and colour and sound which has enriched the equipment of more than one English poet through the centuries. He was also stimulated, it would appear, by the intellectual ferment of Petrarch's age, aside from its art, and this fortified in him the tendency to question and to doubt. Though his scepticism never pushed him beyond the limits of orthodoxy,[45] it led to many a tentative inquiry on matters currently accepted without question. He read widely in the literature of science and pseudo-science; he was beyond many of his day in perceiving (as with alchemy and medieval medicine) how much of hocuspocus and chicanery was involved in its pursuit. Jesting references to scholastic philosophy indicate that, if his interests and associations had turned his attention in that direction, he might have followed Pertrarch in challenging its very methodology. Through his creation of people and his ability to share imaginatively in all the concerns of all of them—high and low, rich and poor, petty and great—he not only produced a microcosm of medieval culture. He did far more. Like other men in the first rank of genius, he laid bare, better than he himself knew, the social origins and the complex psychological momenta of the forces actuating the people of his time. After him there is no such revelation to be found in the realm of literature until Shakespeare.

NOTES TO CHAPTER XII

[1] Chaucer says "nyne and twenty," but including himself as one there are actually 31. It is possible that the reading "preestes three" at 1. A 164 of the Prologue is the result of tampering with a line left unfinished by Chaucer.

[2] *Seven Sages of Rome*, ed. Karl Brunner, EETS, OS, No. 191 (1933).

[3] C.B. Hinkley, "The Framing Tale," *Modern Language Notes*, XLIX (1934), 69 ff.

[4] Detailed discussion by Muriel Bowden, *A Commentary on the General Prologue to the* Canterbury Tales (New York, 1948); on the general plan and portraits see among others J.R. Hulbert, "Chaucer's Pilgrims," *PMLA*, LXIV (1949), 823—28; J. Swart, "The Construction of Chaucer's General Prologue," *Neophilologus*, XXXVIII (1954), 127—36.

[5] W. Borowy, "English Visitors to Prussia, Lithuania and Poland in the 14th Century," *Baltic Countries*, Sept., 1936.

[6] There have been attempts to weaken the effect of Chaucer's satire against clerical abuses and the implied criticism of church authorities for conniving at them. Apologies are offered by Arnold Williams, "Chaucer and the Friars," *Speculum*, XXVIII (1953), 499—512 and A.L. Kellogg and L.A. Haselmeyer, "Chaucer's Satire of the Pardoner," *PMLA*, LXVI (1951), 251—77. But there is much evidence of the wide prevalence of abuses satirised by Chaucer. His figures appear to be typical, not exceptional, in view of the materials gathered by G.G. Coulton, *Five Centuries of Religion*, IV: *The Last Days of Medieval Monasticism* (Cambridge University Press, 1950).

[7] This is the link following the Man of Law's Tale. See Robinson edition, p. 90 for text; consult textual notes for the manuscript situation.

[8] Eustache Deschamps, *Miroir de Mariage* in *Oeuvres complètes*, ed. Gaston Paris, SATF, IX (1894) and XI (1903).

[9] G.L. Kittredge first suggested that a "Marriage Group" of tales exists within the Canterbury roster. His argument is summarised in his volume *Chaucer and his Poetry* (Harvard University Press, 1915).

[10] These are designated as *a, b, c, d,* by J.M. Manly and Edith Rickert in their eight-volume edition, giving a wealth of detail on manuscripts, variant readings, etc.: *The Canterbury Tales* (Chicago, 1940). A shorter introduction to the manuscript situation is given by W.S. McCormick, *The Manuscripts of Chaucer's Canterbury Tales* (Oxford, 1933), in a clear and succinct account.

[11] Charles A. Owen, Jr., "The Plan of the Canterbury Pilgrimage," *PMLA*, LXVI (1951), 820—26, is alone in trying to distribute the tales over both journeys.

[12] Those belonging to groups *b, c,* and *d* in Manly and Rickert's terminology.

[13] Group *a* in the system of Manly and Rickert.

[14] *The Complete Works of Geoffrey Chaucer,* ed. W.W. Skeat, 6 vols. (Oxford, 1894—97).

[15] Most manuscripts place B² before G.

[16] New reasons for reverting to the Skeat order are given by Robert A. Pratt, "The Order of the Canterbury Tales," *PMLA,* LXVI (1951), 1141—67.

[17] See ch. 11, n. 8. F.N. Robinson's edition, which contains the scholarly apparatus of textual and literary notes, should be supplemented by more recent studies. Supplements to J.E. Wells, *Manual of the Writings in Middle English,* the annual bibliographies of the Modern Humanities Research Association, and the *Year's Work in English Studies* are helpful, as well as bibliographies appearing in *PMLA, Speculum, Neophilologus* and other journals. An admirably clear account of the whole problem of the *Canterbury Tales* is given by W.W. Lawrence in his *Chaucer and the Canterbury Tales* (Columbia University Press, 1950).

[18] Robinson's order, according to Skeat's terminology, is: A B¹ D E F C B² G H I. Some manuscripts split E and/or F into sub-groups, separated by other tales; but not so the group of manuscripts to which Ellesmere belongs.

[19] The Shipman speaks once as if he were a woman (B 1202 ff.), and the Second Nun refers to herself as an "unworthy son of Eve" (G 62). The Shipman's Tale (considering its plot) may well have been assigned at an early stage to the Wife of Bath, to whom it would be appropriate; and the Second Nun's Tale to a male ecclesiastic. Another change in plan is indicated when the Man of Law first announces that he will "speke in prose" (B 96), and then tells a rimed tale. Perhaps his contribution was to have been the *Melibeus,* a prose story dealing with a basic theory of law. Attempts have been made by Carleton Brown to trace Chaucer's revisions and changes in plan, in articles in *Studies in Philology,* XXXIV (1937), 8—35; *Modern Language Notes,* LV (1940), 613—19, and *PMLA,* LVII (1942), 29—50.

[20] J.S.P. Tatlock, "The Canterbury Tales in 1400," *PMLA,* L (1935), 100—39, has argued that no arrangement of blocks in any group of MSS. has any authority, but that all are the work of editors trying to arrange the tales for circulation after the poet's death. Much ingenious speculation and close reasoning have been expended in an effort to establish the procedure of scribes and literary executors responsible for the various arrangements achieved. See especially a series of articles by Germaine Dempster in *PMLA,* LXI (1946), 379—415; LXIV (1949), 1123—42; LXVIII (1953), 1142—59.

[21] Material on Chaucer's immediate sources is conveniently gathered in Bryan and Dempster's *Sources and Analogues of Chaucer's Canterbury Tales* (University of Chicago Press, 1941). Only studies appearing since this volume will be referred to below in notes dealing with sources.

[22] The classical inspiration came to Boccaccio from the *Thebaid* of Statius. See Robert A. Pratt, "Chaucer's Use of the *Teseide*," *PMLA,* LXII (1947), 598—621.

[23] For general appreciation see Charles Muscatine, "Form, Texture and Meaning in Chaucer's Knight's Tale," *PMLA,* LXV (1950), 911—29; P. Mroczkowski in *Życie i Myśl* (1950), No. 5/6.

[24] Cf. Marie Neville, "The Function of the Squire's Tale in the Canterbury Scheme," *Journal of English and Germanic Philology,* L (1951), 167—79.

[25] See M. Schlauch, "The Marital Dilemma in Chaucer's Wife of Bath's Tale," *PMLA*, LXI (1946), 416—30; F.G. Townsend, "Chaucer's Nameless Knight," *Modern Language Review*, XLIX (1954), 1—4.

[26] Chaucer made use of a French redaction. See J. Burke Severs, *The Literary Relations of Chaucer's Clerk's Tale* (Yale University Press, 1942).

[27] Genetically, the cruelty in this plot may be explained by ultimate origin in a fairy tale, where the husband is a non-human creature testing a mortal. As adapted by Petrarch the story no longer shows this factor. An attempt has been made to justify the plot *in toto*: James Sledd, "The Clerk's Tale," *Modern Philology*, LI (1953—54), 73—82.

[28] On historical elements embodied in the Constance cycle of tales see M. Schlauch in *Philological Quarterly*, XXIX (1950), 402—12.

[29] E.M. Socola finds a developing pattern in Chaucer's treatment of fortune in these *exempla*; see *Journal of English and Germanic Philology*, XLIX (1950), 159—71.

[30] In Dialogue iii of *De Remediis Utriusque Fortunae*. Another Italian sharing Petrarch's scepticism was Thomas of Pisa, father of the gifted French poetess Christine de Pisan. See George Sarton, *Introduction to the History of Science*, III (1948), p. 1480 f.

[31] See the separate edition of the Pardoner's Tale by Carleton Brown (Oxford University Press, 1935), introduction. This passage on swearing would be fitting for the Parson. A.C. Friend has shown similarities in theme between the tale and Odo of Cheriton's *exempla*, *Journal of English and Germanic Philology*, LIII (1954), 383—38.

[32] The point is discussed by R.M. Lumiansky, "A Conjecture concerning Chaucer's Pardoner," *Tulane Studies in English*, I (1949), 1—30; G.H. Gerould, *Chaucerian Essays* (Princeton University Press, 1952), pp. 55—71.

[33] *The Fox and the Wolf*, edited with the text of the Old French source in Brandl and Zippel, *Mittelenglische Sprach- und Literaturproben* (Berlin, 1927).

[34] Recent appreciative studies include J. Burke Severs, "Chaucer's Originality in the Nun's Priest's Tale", *Studies in Philology*, XLIII (1946), 22—41 and R.M. Lumiansky, "The Nun's Priest in the *Canterbury Tales*," *PMLA*, LXVIII (1953), 896—906. Mortimer J. Donovan has tried, not very convincingly, to give a religious allegorical significance to the tale, "The Moralité of the Nun's Priest's Sermon," *Journal of English and Germanic Philology*, LII (1953), 498—509. Donovan is supported by Charles Dahlberg, who in addition claims that the tale reflects controversies between secular clergy and the friars, *ibid.*, LIII (1954), 277—90.

[35] W.W. Lawrence, "The Tale of Melibeus," in *Essays and Studies* in honor of Carleton Brown (New York University Press, 1940), pp. 100—10; Gardiner Stillwell "The Political Meaning of Chaucer's Tale of Melibeus," *Speculum*, XIX (1944), 433—44.

[36] The pioneer study is *Les Fabliaux* by Joseph Bédier (Paris, 3rd ed. 1912). The author tends to minimise the Oriental element in these French tales. More recent work in numerous monographs (especially those published by the Folklore Fellows in Helsinki) compels the modification of some of Bédier's arguments. His interpretation of the French social milieu is however still valuable.

[37] The best example outside of Chaucer is *Dame Siriz*, ed. G. McKnight in *Middle English Humorous Tales* (Boston, 1913).

[38] See especially И. Кашкин, "Реализм Чосера" *Литературный Критик* (1940, No. 9/10), pp. 73—136; also Louis Haselmeyer, "The Portraits in Chaucer's Fabliaux," *Review of English Studies*, XIV (July, 1938; digest of a dissertation), 310 ff.

[39] The effect of popular speech in the tales is discussed by M. Schlauch, "Chaucer's Colloquial English," *PMLA*, LXVII (1952), 1103—16 and by Michio Masui in *Anglica* (Hiroshima, 1954), 425—37.

[40] A study of broader literary relations is made by John C. Galliard, "Chaucerian Comedy: The Merchant's Tale, Jonson, and Molière," *Philological Quarterly* XXV (1946), 343—70.

[41] Thus for instance the studies on Chaucer by Lounsbury, Coulton, Canon Looten and the recent useful if much simplified account by Nevill Coghill, *The Poet Chaucer* (London, 1949).

[42] This viewpoint has been vigorously opposed by R.S. Loomis, "Was Chaucer a Laodicean?" Carleton Brown *Essays and Studies* (see above, n. 35), pp 129—48.

[43] Innocent's *De Contemptu Mundi* was used by Chaucer in the Prologue to the Man of Law's Tale and in the Pardoner's Tale. In the Prologue to the *Legend of Good Women* he tells us that he had translated this work under the title "Of the Wretched Engendering of Mankind" (G 414), based probably on an intermediary version.

[44] Chaucer's role as national poet is well defined by Дживелегов in *История Английской Литературы*, I (1943), p. 165. His sympathy for the common people has often been remarked, e.g. by Hans Marcus, "Chaucer, der Freund des einfachen Mannes," *Archiv*, CLXXI and CLXXII (1937), 174—87 and 28—41.

[45] See Edith Mary Thomas, *Medieval Scepticism and Chaucer* (New York, 1950).

Part IV

TOWARDS THE NEW AGE

Chapter XIII

THE DECLINE OF FEUDAL LITERATURE

1. NEW FORCES BEHIND OLDER SOCIAL FORMS

After the galaxy of writers that illuminated the latter half of the 14th century in England, the literary culture of the next period offers a spectacle of decline. There were more writers producing literature than ever before, some in considerable quantities, but the level remained lower throughout the century. The best of these writers remained conspicuously imitative. Yet great transformations were going on in the social sphere, and the foundations were being extended for a much broader national culture than England had ever known before. The shifts in power in the ruling class and the rise of new elements within it were for some time, however, unreflected in any marked corresponding change in reading matter.

The main shift took the form already forecast in the previous century: the rise of a newly enriched element from among the large-scale traders, strong enough to displace a majority of the old feudal families and to assume a predominant role in government as well as commerce. Merchant adventurers, as they were called, leaders in the international wool trade, fortified their economic position by maintaining close combinations among themselves, together with control over the channels of export. Financial dealings with the crown enabled them to obtain substantial recompense in the form of monopoly privileges and immunities, their first charter being granted by Henry IV in 1407.[1] In Flanders, where their body established a whole community to conduct and control the wool trade through exclusive ports ("staples"), they obtained privileges that made them practically autonomous. The new merchant plutocracy ruled London—a city now more prosperous than ever—through its body of Aldermen, most of whom were wealthy guildsmen. They exerted a strong influence counterbalancing the divisive struggles of baronial families and favouring a consolidated national government. Their policy was of course to foster domestic peace and foreign trade. By the end of the century[2] they were making use of kings who turned to them for profitable alliance against their feudal rivals: Edward IV (1468—83) was the first to adopt such an alliance as a major policy, and after him the Tudors (beginning with Henry VII, 1485—1509) developed it further. An increase in power tending to absolutism was the benefit exacted by the kings for their collaboration with the commons. Yet there were rivalries within the alliance, too, for the kings continued to depend on members of the agriculture-based baronial group, opponents of the merchants, for military and economic support and for social security against the lower classes.

The barons and other large land-holders of England went through a critical period in the 15th century preliminary to their complete eclipse. Politically they were rent by a factional struggle known as the War of the Roses, in which two cliques, headed by the houses of York and Lancaster respectively, carried on civil war. Both families were descended from sons of Edward III (John of Gaunt, Duke of Lancaster, and Edmund Duke of York). Their rivalry first took the form of competition for influence at court during the incapacity of Henry VI through madness (he was deposed in 1461). A decisive part in the military struggle was played by the Duke of Warwick, who first succeeded in having the Yorkist Edward IV made king after Henry, but later—alienated by his protégé's cultivation of the merchant class at the expense of the baronial—switched his allegiance to the Lancastrians. Upon the defeat of Edward's brother Richard III (1483—85), the last male survivor of the family, undisputed succession was achieved by the Tudor Henry VII, husband of Edward's daughter Elizabeth and himself a Lancastrian.

Political historians relatively little concerned with economic and leading social factors have given exaggerated importance to this domestic struggle among feudal rivals. In districts such as Norfolk, at certain times, the loss and disorder may have been quite serious, but the country as a whole remained relatively undisturbed. Even for those days the battles were fought on a relatively small scale,[3] and interested the masses of the people very little. The most important result, in the long run, was the depletion of the baronial families in numbers, wealth and prestige, thus facilitating the substitution of new landlord elements from the ranks of wealthy commoners.

More serious for the national economy had been the attempt, begun earlier in the century under Henry V (1413—22) to renew the war in France and regain the old feudal holdings claimed by Edward III. The brutal campaigns and temporary successes were enough to reduce that unhappy country to a state of political and economic chaos. They ended (1453) in complete catastrophe for the English, who were obliged to abandon all territory save a small section including the port of Calais. The constant levies of men, the taxes, the waste of resources, had been a most irksome burden in the first half of the century, and what popularity the war may have had in its period of success (the victory of Agincourt, 1415) was quickly dissipated as reverses set in. Trade declined, and with it the national prosperity, during these decades. The combination of defeats abroad, heavy taxes, and poor harvests produced an agrarian rebellion led by Jack Cade in Kent which resembled the more successful uprising of 1381 in many ways.

The situation in agriculture and land ownership was being gradually transformed in the 15th century. As population increased again after the visitations of plagues, the greater supply of labour led once again to a relaxation of the efforts to enforce a declining serfdom. Landlords who now leased out their property for others to farm cared much less about maintaining stable relations among tenants. Liveried attendants on the nobility began to replace the old tenant followers. Peasant farmers were able to rise in the social scale as class relations became more fluid. More and more the work of the village became specialised, being performed by craftsmen (weavers, blacksmiths, carpenters, and so on) like those in the towns. Ties of subservience to the old feudal system were further weakened as wealthy merchants bought over the great estates of extinguished or ruined families. Nevertheless the new families tried to take over the prestige, the manners and way of life of their predecessors as far as possible. Maurice Dobb has well characterised such new owners:

These new men had to be ingratiating as well as crafty: they had to temper extortion with fawning, combining avarice with flattery, and clothe a usurer's hardness in the vestments of chivalry.... To acquire political privilege was their first ambition, their second that as few as possible should enjoy it. Since they were essentially parasites on the old economic order, while they might bleed and weaken it, their fortune was in the last analysis associated with that of their host. Hence the upper strata of these bourgeois *nouveaux-riches* took to country mansions and to falconing and cut capers like a gentleman without embarrassment, and what remained of the old baronial families took these upstarts into partnership with a fairly cheerful grace.[4]

The social position which led to such sedulous aping of their predecessors explains, among other things, the conservative tastes in reading matter shown by the newly enriched and newly ennobled families. At the same time, the extension of education, increasingly secular, was preparing the way for a qualitative change in the culture of the rising class.[5]

The latter part of the 15th century has been depicted as an age of prosperity, the "golden age" of English agriculture.[6] It may well be that the condition of the peasants was far better in England than on the continent, especially in France, and it was happy by contrast with the mass misery which was to afflict it in the next period, as a result of dispossession and enclosures. The foundations of prosperity, such as it was, were however insecure. No advance of importance was made in the techniques of producing or preserving food during this era, and as population increased once more, the ever-present threat of famine could all too readily become a reality through failure of crops.

The economic situation had its effects on wealthy landowning institutions of religion. Mismanagement, badly financed expenditures, personal enrichment in defiance of monastic rules, and similar internal factors sometimes led to bankruptcies in difficult times. These in turn led to investigation and intervention by state commissions.[7] Moreover, the diverting of very large sections of the national income to the monasteries caused difficulties, not only for the economy of the state, but also for other branches of church administration. Wealth was inevitably causing more and more corruption: not a new phenomenon, to be sure, but now obviously rampant on a very wide scale. Some quite orthodox leaders saw the need for fiscal reform at least: Henry V, for instance, who dissolved many foreign priories (i.e., branches of orders founded from abroad) which were diverting rents and other funds out of England, and Chancellor Gascoigne of Oxford University, who recommended transferring monastic incomes to the use of parish churches, where the religious lives of the common people were centred. The orders themselves, however, obstinately resisted investigations by the state, and rejected the attempts to have their affairs scrutinised from without. They constantly made appeals to Rome to obtain exemptions from control. The economic imbalance between church and state was already prophetic of the drastic change to come under Henry VIII.

In the sphere of morals, too, the decay of monasticism was so flagrant as to cause great bitterness and disaffection among the lay masses. Lollardy was extremely widespread early in the century; the influence of Wycliff long outlasted his death. To combat the resulting spread of heresy, the Parliament under Henry IV enacted the statute *De Haeretico Comburendo* (On the Burning of Heretics, 1401), which drove a number of victims to death at the stake. One of them was Sir John Oldcastle, who had been a correspondent of Hussites in Prague.[8] The English movement continued in fact to influence reformation movements in Bohemia and Poland during the period of the Councils of Constance and of Basle, and it was at this time that a Polish professor of theology at Cracow

University[9] composed (ca. 1450) a vernacular poem in honour of the great English reformer. The violent suppression of heresy in England checked its spread for the time being, but critical dissatisfaction was obviously unabated throughout the century, as the satirical literature clearly indicates.

Intellectually, the learning of the church produced nothing signally new in the 15th century. Mysticism continued to attract certain less conventional religious spirits: for instance, Margery Kempe, who (in contrast to earlier mystics) was an uneducated member of the laity.[10] An ambitious attempt was made by Reginald Pecock (died. ca. 1461) to refute Lollardy by logic alone or the "doom of reason," as he called it, for he claimed that this method would have a force beyond that of heaven's angels, if disagreement were to arise between the two. Pecock evolved a curious special language for his ponderous arguments in English, full of neologisms (loan translations, hybrid compounds and the like).[11] Though his purpose was the refutation of heresy, his use of reason to that end was highly suspect, and he himself, ironically enough, was charged with heresy, removed from his bishopric, and compelled to spend his last years in monastic retirement. Aside from Pecock's ambitious apologetics, other religious writings continued to be produced in the form of conventional allegory, saints' lives and material for sermons very much in the manner of the 14th century (to be discussed below). Ecclestiacal art too flourished and continued to treat the old themes in painting, sculpture and coloured windows. What changes occurred in literary and plastic arts were to be found rather in heightened mannerisms, greatly elaborated decoration, and increasing naturalism in detail, rather than in matters of major techniques. As for general intellectual and artistic life in England, it may be said that preoccupation with wars foreign and domestic was enough to check temporarily the influence of the Italian Renaissance which had begun so auspiciously in Chaucer's generation.

2. SOCIAL SATIRE: THE SCHOOL
OF *PIERS PLOWMAN*

New forms were not devised for the expression of social satire in the 15th century, but the example of *Piers Plowman* inspired some gifted imitators who continued the denunciation of the abuses signalised in the model. *Pierce the Plowman's Crede*,[12] though probably written before 1400, post-dates the death of Wycliff, to whom it refers admiringly (11. 528—30). The author speaks of himself in the first person, as a simple ignorant man who has grown up without learning the creed. He undertakes a quest to each of the orders of friars (Franciscans, Dominicans, Carmelites and Augustinians) in order to ask for instruction. All four are pictured as being housed magnificently—lazy and double-chinned from soft living, quite unwilling to instruct the petitioner. Each denounces the members of the other orders; they all tell him not to concern himself with this matter of the creed. Instead, he may buy a pardon from them (if he has money) and leave praying and creed-saying to them. In the end he obtains the desired instruction from Piers Plowman, who with his wife's aid is toiling in desperate poverty to cultivate the land. The physical appearance of these two is described with realistic detail; nevertheless the figures are allegorical. The social philosophy of the author is as conservative as Langland's. Despite his championship of the poor and hard-working folk who seek enlightenment, he denounces those sons of lowly workers who wish to rise in the social scale:

744   Now mot ich soutere his sone   setten to schole,
And ich a beggars brol   on þe booke lerne,
And worþ to a writere   & wiþ a lord dwell,
Oþer falsly to a frere   þe fend for to seruen.

[ich soutere = each cobbler;   brol = offspring;   worþ = become; oþer = or;   fend = fiend]

Mum and the Sothsegger (*Mum and the Truth-Teller*, ca. 1405) is a vigorously written if somewhat obscure and incomplete poem also inspired by *Piers Plowman*. It is an ambitious satire, to which the fragmentary *Richard the Redeless* (dealing with evils during the reign of Richard II) is to be attached.[13] The author of *Mum* first reports the arrival of Henry IV in England with the purpose of deposing Richard II, and then reproaches the latter monarch for the misrule which has alienated his subjects from him. The extravagance of upstart favourites has led to heavy taxes, he says, and is a great burden to the people. No one had dared to tell truth at Richard's court, and the same conspiracy of silence exists at Henry's. "Mum" rules all officials, urging people to keep quiet about abuses. The poet himself goes on a quest to find a truth-teller. Instead he finds Mum supreme with the four orders of friars, with the mayor, in Parliament, and throughout the three estates. During a dream-vision he wanders into a beautiful valley where the bee-keeper on a flourishing estate instructs him and fortifies his courage.

Though the example of conformist communities among the bees is not a hopeful choice by the author, the political theory expressed in his poem belongs to the more progressive tradition of the Middle Ages. Kings are not regarded as irresponsible absolutists, but as executors of the people's collective will on a contractual basis. The legal right to

depose tyrannts is defended. Thus the theme of the vision is directly connected with the events which had occurred in 1399 with the removal
of Richard II from the throne on charges of tyrannical rule. [14]

Less striking and in a vein different from *Mum* is the stanzaic *Plowman's Tale* by an anonymous Lollard, sometimes attributed to Chaucer
and included in the *Canterbury Tales* by early editors. [15] In form the poem
is a dialogue between a Griffon (representing the worldly upper hierarchy)
and the humble Pelican (the voice of Lollardy). The former makes charges
of envy and heresy; the latter counters them by protesting its orthodoxy
and detailing the familiar abuses of which the clergy are guilty. It makes
the interesting point that whereas the king may impose no taxes without
the commons' consent, the bishops do so arbitrarily and irresponsibly.
The Pelican's last word is a threat of burnings and hangings to extirpate
heresy: a very real instrument of religious repression under Henry IV.

God Speed the Plow [16] (ca. 1500), coming at the end of the century,
also belongs to the *Piers Plowman* tradition and testifies to its vitality.
It is a stanzaic lamentation, spoken by a ploughman, on the extortionate
tithes demanded by the church. The plough sorely needs a blessing, exclaims
the weary husbandman:

> And so shulde of right the parson praye,
> That hath the tithe shefe of the londe;
> For our sarvauntys we moste nedis paye,
> Or elles ful still the plough maye stonde.
> Than cometh the clerk anon at hande,
> To haue a shef of corn there it groweth;
> And the sexton somwhate in his hande;
> "I praye to God, spede wele the plough."

The alliterative tracts which go under the name of *Jack Upland* [17] contain
a scathing attack on the friars, notable for their popular and homely if
crude style of expression. The *Reply of Friar Law Topias* is supposed
to be a defense against "Jack Upland's" attacks, but it merely provides
the occasion for his lively *Rejoinder*.

A dramatic text which actually falls within the ensuing period—
Ane Plesant Satyre of the Thrie Estaitis [18] (1540) by the Scots writer Sir
David Lyndsay (tutor to King James V)—may be discussed here, because
its style and technique are closely related to those of medieval satire.
The play, which was acted at the Scottish court, is an allegorical denun-
ciation of government and church, written as a warning. The King,
Rex Humanitas, deserts the principles of just rule when he takes Sensual-
ity as concubine on the urging of Wantonness. Characters such
as Flattery and Deceit become his Counsellors. The grievances of a typical
Poor Man are presented, and the abuses are exemplified by a cynical

Pardoner selling his wares much as Chaucer's Pardoner had done. Reform begins however with the appearance of Divine Correction, who liberates the imprisoned virtues. A Parliament of the Three Estates—nobility, clergy, mercantile commons—is called, at which a personified Commonwealth of Scotland gives voice to the country's general complaints. Sensuality is sent packing to Rome, where it belongs, and all is well again in Scotland.

The tone and specific contents are directly connected of course with the Reformation ferment of the 16th century. There are passages of very daring realism in the play, but technically that realism still manifests itself in the medieval way: as concrete detail embroidering or illustrating theses propounded in abstract allegory. Social satire is focused on abuses already made familiar by all the authors of the *Piers Plowman* school.

3. THE CHAUCERIAN EPIGONES, ENGLISH AND SCOTTISH

Most of the outstanding individual writers of the 15th century were direct imitators of Chaucer. Under the stimulus of his genius some lesser men did estimable work which however remained on a level distinctly below that of their master.

John Lydgate (ca. 1370—1451?) was by far the most prolific of the English Chaucerians. His adult life was spent as a monk at Bury St. Edmund's. Despite his monastic status he was occasionally at court and traveled in France on state business. He found encouragement and subsidy from a variety of patrons outside the cloister. Commissions came not only from noble and royal lords (Henry V and Henry VI among them) but—typically for his times—from patrons of the middle class, such as the London Companies of Mercers and Goldsmiths.[19] His writings fall within the medieval traditions established for lengthy romances, allegories, courtly dream-visions, moralised *exempla*, hagiography and lyrics. His productivity was enormous; his mimetic earnestness is usually of the plodding type, lit now and then with flashes of fortunate phraseology or independent insight.

The Temple of Glas [20] (1403) is a Chaucerian dream vision from beginning to end, indebted especially to the *Hous of Fame, Parlement of Fowles* and the Prologue to the *Legend of Good Women*. The temple seen by the dreamer is decorated by a series of lovers depicted on its walls. Within it, Pallas Athene kneels before Venus and voices a complaint about love's power. A disconsolate lover next complains of doubt and despair. The goddess encourages him to declare his passion to the lady concerned, who gives an encouraging response. Both lovers glorify Venus and her might. The whole is utterly conventional but possesses a degree of second-hand charm.

Reson and Sensuality [21] (about 1408), a courtly allegory left unfinished, has a rather more moralistic bent. It was translated by Lydgate from a French text (*Les Échecs amoureux*), written in the medieval-Platonic tradition of Alanus de Insulis but adapted, as in the *Roman de la Rose*, for courtly purposes. Nature is described as the source of beauty and harmony in the universe of physical and subhuman biological creation:

> 363   For this lady, fresshest of hewe
> Werketh euer and forgeth newe,
> Day and nyght, in her entent,
> Wevyng in her garnement
> Thynges dyuers ful habounde [abundant].

This same Nature advises the author to follow the way of virtuous Reason as opposed to that of Sensuality. Reason is Nature's sister, she says, and always agrees with her. The poet, however, deviates somewhat from the thornier path pointed out, and makes a detour into the confines of Love's well-known magic garden. Here it is that he finds his lady-love and enters into a game of chess with her which, in an allegorical sense, signifies the moves played by courtly humans in the game of love.

The very long *Pilgrimage of the Life of Man* [22] (1426—30), about 24,000 lines translated from the works of Guillaume de Déguileville (see ch. 8, sec. 5) is didactic allegory of the religious, non-courtly type. Though unoriginal, the English version is important as a summation of ideas on human life and destiny that had been current through all the medieval centuries. Again we have the abstract figures of Reason, Nature, Penance, Grace-Dieu (capable of performances beyond Reason's comprehension), Labour, Idleness, and many other abstract companions of Man on his pilgrimage through life. There are simplified discussions on such matters as the relation of body to soul, of faith to reason, of sin to penance, of the three estates to one another: in short, all the chief problems vexing medieval theorists. The need for different occupations among people is used to justify the theoretical need for a class society. Yet it is recognised here (as often elsewhere) that manual labour upholds the entire social structure:

> 11,369   Yiff all ffolk in a regioun
> Hadden on occupacioun
> In the rychest crafft of alle,
> Deme thanne what sholde falle:
> Thanne al ylyche (yiff thow tok hed)
> The ffoot as good as ys the hed;

<blockquote>
A knaue also by hys werkyng,
Sholde ben egal wyth the kyng;
The wych (who wysly kan espye)
Ne wer no maner polycye,
But rather a confusioun
11,380   In euery maner regioun.
</blockquote>

[on = one;   ylyche = alike;   hed = heed;   hed = head]

Hence each should function to his degree in society, and remain within it:

<blockquote>
11,386   And swych as myghty ben, & strong,
And Wyth myghte lat hem the lond dyffende;
And clerkys to ther studye entende;
And labourerys, lat hem werche;
11,390   And spyrytuall ffolk of the cherche,
Lat ther occupacioun
Ben in contemplacioun,
In deuocioun & prayere;
Voyde hem from offyce seculer;
Lat hem go lyue lyk ther bond;
And swyche ffolk as tyle the lond,
Lat hem do trewly ther labour,
Bothe in drought & ek in shour;
Ffor trewly (yiff I rekne shal)
11,400   Carte & plowh, they ber up al
The clergye & the cheualrye...
</blockquote>

[lyk ther bond = according to their pledge]

Among romances of classical origin, Lydgate produced an expanded version of Guido delle Colonne's *Historia Troiana* under the title of *Troy Book*[23] (1412—20), over 30,000 lines in length. When he reaches the story of Troilus and Criseyde, however, the English poet amplifies the theme, making use of Chaucer and offering a defense of women in reply to Guido's attack upon them for infidelity. *The Siege of Thebes*[24] (1420), a free treatment of the epic material inherited from Statius, was apparently based upon some abbreviated form of the Old French *Roman de Thèbes*. Lydgate added some moralising passages to the courtly descriptions of love and warfare. The most interesting aspect of the whole is his effort to attach the romance to Chaucer's *Canterbury Tales*: he represents himself as joining the pilgrims and offering the *Siege* as his contribution after a boisterous welcome (not badly imagined) by the Host.

The Fall of Princes[25] (1431—38) is a treatment of Boccaccio's *De Casibus Virorum Illustrium*, based on a French translation by Laurent de Premierfait (done in 1405—09). The gloomy tone had been heightened in the French version, thus reducing the humanistic effect and heightening the medieval. Here again Lydgate evinces a strong interest in political problems such as a king's responsibility, the need for order and subordination in the relations of the estates, and the disastrous results of civil war.[26] This last theme engaged his attention separately in his prose work *The Serpent of Division*,[27] an eclectic account of the struggle between Julius Caesar and Pompey for mastery of the Roman world.

Among the purely religious poems by Lydgate the one long text is a *Life of Our Lady*, numbering about 6000 lines, which is now being edited.[28]

Besides all these more ambitious works, Lydgate contrived to produce an imposing number of shorter poems: lyrics, fables, courtly love eulogies and laments, occasional and religious pieces. Some of them, like *The Black Knight* and *The Flour of Curteysie*, were mistakenly attributed to Chaucer by early editors.[29] The lyrics both secular and religious[30] are quite conventional; some are decorative and possess a degree of musical quality. A very few of them have some slight pretensions to humour.

Thomas Hoccleve or Occleve (ca. 1370—1454), another English Chaucerian, was far less productive than Lydgate. A member of London's middle class, he held a government post as clerk of the Privy Seal, and received benefits from noble patrons. His works are conventional enough in type. What makes them interesting is the series of autobiographical passages and personal comments interspersed in them. The confessional poem *La male règle de Thomas Hoccleve*[31] (written in English, despite the title, in 1406) admits to extravagance and riotous living, and it affords some precious glimpses of contemporary London at work and play. The translation (1412) of Egidio Colonna's *De Regimine Principum* (composed ca. 1280) as *The Rule of Princes* also contains original interpolated material on contemporary English life. A poem addressed to Sir John Oldcastle (1415) exhorts him to repent of his heresy, objecting especially to the Lollards' denial of the pope's authority and their desire to introduce community of goods among members of the sect. Hoccleve also wrote pious tales and religious poems, and some courtly ones too, such as his exhortation to chivalry, addressed to the Knights of the Garter.

A London Lickpenny, once attributed to Lydgate and included among his works, is an anonymous satire rather in the vein of Hoccleve. It deals with the power of money in various quarters, especially among lawyers.

Far more than either of the chief English followers of Chaucer, it was his Scottish admirers who were able to capture something of their master's poetic skill and occasionally to apply it to original themes of their own choice. The purely romantic aspect of Chaucer is imitated in *The Kingis Quair* (i.e., Book)[32] almost certainly written by King James I of Scotland (ca. 1420) and based upon his experiences as a prisoner of war taken by the English. The hero of the poem is also a prisoner and—like Palamon or Arcite in Chaucer's Knight's Tale—he falls in love with a lady seen in the garden outside his place of confinement. He has a dream-vision peopled by figures of myth and allegory in the approved literary mode; somewhat unusually, however, the love-languishing is eventually crowned by a proper marriage. Curiously enough, the real hero, King James, imitated art in his own life, for he conceived just such a romantic love for Joan Beaufort while in captivity and married her before returning to Scotland. Some shorter poems of his, though following a well-established pattern of another sort, treat with verve the uncourtly theme of peasant brawling and merry-making.

Robert Henryson, a schoolmaster of Dumferling (died before 1508), shows still greater originality within the Chaucerian tradition.[33] His most ambitious work was *The Testament of Cressid*, a continuation of Chaucer's poem which portrays the faithless heroine being smitten with leprosy as a punishment. Though some creaking machinery of the courts is brought into action for this poem—the author falling asleep over a book, a vision of mythological deities, a formal lament pronounced by Cressid—the language is infused with remarkable vitality. One does not forget the spectacle of this once beautiful and pampered lady now horribly transformed and compelled to beg by the roadside with clapper and bowl while her heart-broken lover, riding by, casts alms to her without recognising her. The entire scene is sketched with fidelity to contemporary scenery and customs.

Vigorous too and marked with notable originality is Henryson's treatment of *The Moral Fables of Esope*. More than most fabulists, the Scottish writer has conveyed through the animal tales an essential vision of the conrete life of his own age and country. Not only is the Wolf often made to stand for a type of grasping monk and the Fox for a wily layman—this had been done before—but the various beasts are also displayed as prototypes of extortionate landlords, tricky and corrupt judges, brutal sheriffs and (in contrast) miserable downtrodden peasants. The poor sheep, Henryson says, represent the commons of Scotland:

> This selie scheip may present the figure
> Of pure commounis, that daylie ar opprest
> Be tirrane men, quhilkis settis all thair cure
> Be fals meinis to mak ane wrang conquest.

[pure = poor; tirrane = tyrant; quhilkis = who]

In another fable, the commons are identified with timid mice, neglected by their slothful ruler. In the one about Chanticleer and the Fox, the picture of a poor widow's barnyard is strongly reminiscent of Chaucer's in the Nun's Priest's Tale, but while making use of his master's example

Henryson has at the same time written with his eye on reality as it existed around him in Scotland.

In some of his other shorter poems Henryson is also able to imbue trite themes and forms with a breath of reality, as in the little idyll of Robin and Makyn, modelled on French *pastourelles* of the type of "Robin et Marianne." At other times he descends to the most arid of imitations, as in his moral allegorical "Garment of Gude Ladies" or the disputation called "A Reasoning betwix Aige and Youth." Stylistically he lapses sometimes into the over-ornate style, full of artificial Latinity, which was called "aureate English" at this time. It represents an exaggerated imitation, to the point of absurdity, of Chaucer's occasional dignified clustering of polysyllables derived from Latin through French. It also uses and abuses, to the reader's weariness, the jaded divinities of classical myth. A glaring instance of Henryson's stylistic distortion is to be found in his "Prayer for the Pest," which begins as a solemn appeal to heaven in the time of plague, and then descends to precious word-play like this:

65   Superne lucerne, guberne this pestilens,
      Preserve and serve, that we not sterve [i. e., die] thairin,
      Declyne that pyne, by thy devyne prudence.
      O trewth, haif rewth...

and so on. The blight of "aureate" composition extended far and persisted long, damaging the work of some really talented and original poets.

William Dunbar, another Scottish Chaucerian (ca. 1460—ca. 1530) wrote with greater literary independence. He was a Franciscan friar who performed services for the royal court and after 1500 derived a pension from it. He lived in the strife-torn age which culminated in the disastrous defeat of Scottish by English forces at Flodden. He saw with open eyes the wasteful baronial feuds, the grinding poverty of the masses, the church corruption which was calling forth a tide of bitter protestant sentiment decades before the official Reformation began. His short poems are written in two styles. In the more traditional vein Dunbar[34] was able to turn a graceful courtly compliment (such as "The Thistle and the Rose," celebrating a royal marriage), or put together an aureate religious poem ("Ane Ballat of Our Lady," written in highly artificial style), or a debate of birds ("The Merle and the Nightingale") or a moral allegory (e.g., "The Dream," and "The Golden Targe"). But these routine exercises are far from showing his real talent.

It is Dunbar's trenchant satire, written in his second, more original style, that gives him his eminence in the generations of imitators. He attacks the degeneracy of his own order on one occasion by placing an obviously ironic eulogy of it into the mouth of a fiend. On others,

he attacks — sometimes by name — charlatans and ambitious adventurers
at the court; he reproaches the merchants of Edinburgh for disfiguring
the city with their brawls, their cheating, and the stinking dirt (realistically described) of their fish-market. He pours out a torrent of earthy
popular words, many of them rare on the printed page, in the dialogue
reported between "The Twa Marrit Wemen and Wedo" (i.e., widow) —
a discussion conceived in the manner of the Wife of Bath, but more
concentrated and more daring. Burlesque is employed in order to make
fun of chivalry and courtly love. The juxtaposition of physiological details
with chivalrous forms and conventions is used to bring off the effect
in one case ("Ane Brash Wowing," i.e., wooing); and in another, tournaments are ridiculed in the absurd jousting of a tailor and a cobbler
("The Justis betwix the Teleȝeour and the Sowtar").

Like Henryson, Dunbar had a sombre vein revealed in his poems
on death and the world's instability. His "Lament for the Makaris"
(i.e., poets) is accompanied by a tolling funereal refrain: *"Timor mortis
conturbat me."* The lament contains valuable allusions to contemporary
poets, whose works have in great part perished: from one, Walter Kennedy (ca. 1460 — ca. 1508), some poems have survived. [35]

4. FURTHER CONTINUATIONS OF COURTLY LITERATURE

The lengthy romances treated by Lydgate are a testimony to the
persisting vogue of chivalrous literature, and a number of anonymous
metrical tales of chivlary continued to be composed in the old style down
through the 15th century. Typical examples are: *Eger and Grime,* [36]
Ponthus and Sidone, [37] *Melusine* [38] and *Parthenope of Blois.* [39] An unusual
instance of persistent themes is to be found in the two prolix and laboured
compositions by Harry Lovelich (ca. 1450) on *Merlin* and *The Holy
Graal.* [40] Dull and unoriginal as these may be, they are remarkable because
they were composed by a member of the Skinners' Guild of London,
at the suggestion of the city mayor, and thus reflect the shift of class
patronage going on beneath the continuity of subject matter. In contrast
to Lovelich's work, an anonymous Scottish treatment of Carolingian
epic, *Rauf Colȝear (Ralph the Collier),* [41] is exceptionally original. It tells
how Charlemagne, in disguise, learned some practical wisdom from one
of his worker subjects. The Scots metrical *Lancelot of the Laik* [42] is distinguished by an elaborated passage of political theory expounding the king's
duties to his subjects in preserving peace and order.

Besides metrical romances, courtly dream visions and debates also
continued to manifest old influences, in this case stemming from the

Caxton Presenting to Margaret of York His
Recuyell of the Historyes of Troye

Romance of the Rose. For instance, *The Flower and the Leaf,* purporting to be by a woman, described two types of lovers — the chaste and steadfast contrasted with the frivolous — by symbolic means and with unusual stylistic (if mannered) charm, despite the conventional setting. *The Assembly of Ladies,* a more abstract allegory, is heavily indebted to Chaucer and the *Romance.* The dialogue entitled *La Belle Dame sans Merci,* translated from the French of Alain Chartier, occurs between a lover and his pitiless mistress; *The Court of Love* embodies a quest for an ideal mistress; *The Cuckoo and the Nightingale,* by Thomas Clanvowe (ca. 1403), formally presents the negative and positive attitudes to courtly love. *The Isle of Ladies* received the title *Chaucer's Dream* and was attributed to him. Obviously, these texts[43] belong within the school imitative of Chaucer's earlier work. Courtly style pervades many secular lyrics too, though in this genre the popular element was strong, even outside of the ballads.[44]

The feudal ideological impulse actuating such narrative and lyrical poems was of course much enfeebled by this time, both in France and England. Persons of nobility and royalty continued to write love poems, to fight tournaments, to pretend to chivalrous behaviour while the foundations of privilege were being swept away from beneath them, and their own activities often glaringly contradicted their claims to refinement.[45] The mannerisms of knighthood lasted in both life and art down into the Tudor period. The most impressive monument of late chivalrous literature belongs however to the latter 15th century: the *Morte d'Arthur* of Sir Thomas Malory (died 1471), which is both the *summa* and the swan-song of English Arthurian fiction.

Its author[46] was a knight who served under the Duke of Warwick after his lord had joined the cause of Lancaster, and he shared the defeat and penalties suffered by the losing faction. Malory's last years were spent in prison, charged not only with political but also serious civil crimes reflecting the disorder of the war period. For these he was never brought to trial. His own deeds may or may not have been exceptionally lawless, but in any event his literary labours in prison formed a vast prose panegyric on the dying institution which had attempted at least to inculcate principles of loyalty, generosity and bravery among feudal aristocrats. His own comments and additions show that he looked backwards with nostalgia to an imagined age when he fancied these public virtues to have been exemplified by members of his class. As material he chose a series of French prose romances of the 13th century (*Merlin, Tristan, Queste del Graal, Lancelot, Mort Artu*; probably some lost texts as well), and two Middle English metrical romances (the alliterative and stanzaic poems on Arthur's death (see ch. 9, sec. 3).

Considering the complexity and bulk of his sources, written by many different hands with inevitable overlappings and inconsistencies, Malory was surprisingly successful in creating an orderly, unified and impressive work. The style possesses great dignity without being over-heavy. Through all its divagations the action progresses with a sense of masterly guidance.

Sir Thomas Malory, *Morte d'Arthur*. A woodcut

Now that we possess a manuscript of the author's own version, untouched by his publisher's editorial changes,[47] we can more clearly trace the sense of his cuts and modifications. Their general result is to exalt the active role of men like Arthur and Lancelot as leaders of a fellowship opposed to the chaos of barbarism. The author's cutting reduced the mystical and supernatural elements while making use of them to heighten the imaginative effects. Malory points out the negative consequences of courtly love for its adherents, while conceding to it the function of refining manners. The following words of his King Arthur are significant of Malory's attitude throughout (they are spoken on hearing of knights killed by Lancelot during his rescue of Guinevere): "And much more I am soryer [sorrier] for my good knightes losse than for the losse of my fayre queene; for queenes I myght have inow, but such a felyship of good knyghtes shall never be togydirs in no company" (Vinaver ed., p. 1184).

The last sentences of Malory's prose epic rise gradually to a momentous climax and catastrophe which appears to embrace a whole scheme of society. It does not, of course. The partial society shown in the *Morte d'Arthur* lacks a foundation: its wandering knights and fair ladies and cruel villains move endlessly from castle to castle, through enchanted forests remote from towns, rarely if ever encountering the traders, the peasants, the craftsmen who created the material culture on which they lived. Their isolation had to be sure been still more complete in the French sources; Malory succeeds in diminishing somewhat their distance from reality. But the world of knighthood is involuntarily shown to be shadowy and archaic in the very work which invests it with its greatest attraction. No wonder that after Malory, chivalrous romance becomes practically extinct as a living form in English. Translations, redactions, copies and feeble imitations are all that survive from the last part of the 15th and the first of the 16th century, though these did continue to be read widely for a long time, especially in the form of popular prose chap-books.[48]

5. RELIGIOUS AND DIDACTIC LITERATURE

Conventional saints' lives, collections of *exempla* and books of both religious and secular instruction were multiplied throughout the 15th century. (For Caxton's contributions in this field, see the following section.) A large collection of preacher's *exempla* was put together under the title of *Jacob's Well*; the *Gesta Romanorum* and *An Alphabet of Tales* were Englished from the Latin.[49] Among hagiographers, the Augustinian frair Osbern Bokenham (died 1447) produced a group of legends dealing with saintly women, and John Capgrave, member of the same order (diep 1464), treated the *vitae* of St. Augustine and St. Catherine of Alexandra.[50] General religious instruction was represented by the verse writings of John Mirk composed soon after 1400 (ch. 9, sec. 5). Didactic allegory and philosophical dialogues were also cultivated in the traditional vein. Boethius was translated afresh by John Walton (about 1410); the philosopher's influence had been apparent late in the preceding century in *The Testament of Love*[51] by Thomas Usk, who wrote it, Boethius-like, in prison before his execution (1388). *The Court of Sapience*[52] by an anonymous Chaucerian (formerly ascribed to Lydgate), demonstrates the perennial charm exercised by didactic allegory. Though burdened by a dead weight of catalogues and citations, it makes its point about the relation of learning to religion with some skill and imagination. There are faint, probably accidental similarities to Dante, as when the author describes his dream of a fearful waste land (the world) in which he is lost at the beginning of his vision, and the inscription on the bridge over the River of Quiet leading to the abode of Sapience: "Who dredeth God, com yn and right well-come; / For drede of God is wey of all wysdome." The catalogues themselves were inserted for a reason: to offer instruction; and the description of the Seven Arts as allegorical ladies—testifying to the long-range influence of Martianus Capella—contains some curiously edifying details. Philosophy is thus presented:

> 1562   She ys clepyd also the Arte of Artes,
> And eke of dethe the meditacioun,
> Hyr beyng eke yset [ys] in two partes:
> In pure science, and opinacioun;
> Science thyng teccheth by certayn resoun,
> Opynyon ys in vncertaynte,
> Whan thyng by reason may nat prouyd be.

The old medieval contrast between vices and virtues continued to be elaborated in moral treatises based on the one which Chaucer used in his Parson's Tale,[53] and the four-fold allegorical interpretation of Scripture was further expounded in the traditional style.[54] *The Mirour of Man's Saluacioune*,[55] from an anonymous Latin tract, is typical of the moral *specula* already current for centuries. A moral theme frequently stressed in the 15th century was the admonitory reflection upon death: not a new subject, certainly, but one constantly being brought home by visitations of war and pestilence. Dunbar reveals signs of this preoccupation; it appears in an anonymous *Of the Craft of Dying* (*Ars Moriendi*),[56] and will be found supremely exemplified in the morality play of *Everyman* (see ch. 14, sec. 2).[57] The tradition of 14th-century mystical writings like those of Richard Rolle was carried on by his translators (for instance, Richard Misyn), by the translators of Thomas à Kempis,[58] and by that strangely hysterical woman of the middle class, Margery Kempe, whose outpourings have interest from the psychological and linguistic points of view as well as the literary. Her record of visions, pilgrimages and private religious experiences exemplifies the anarchic tendency implicit in mysticism, making it *a priori* rather suspect to church authority.[59] The contrasting intellectual tendency appears in the work of Reginal Pecock, already mentioned (see above, sec. 1).

Books of secular instruction are especially interesting in the 15th century because they throw into relief the efforts of newly prosperous families and newer members of the aristocracy to impove their manners and augment their knowledge. The desire to increase refinement and education was in fact general, and many of the works published by Caxton were designed to meet that need. There are a number of short tracts on manners, written for children and especially concerned with their behaviour at table [60]. Parental instructions, chiefly moral, were given by Peter Idley in an earnest if unoriginal book of *Instructions to his Son*; an anonymous Scottish writer composed the same sort of advice in *Ratis Raving* (both ca. 1450). [61] The similar work of the French Knight of La Tour Landry, written for his daughters, was translated into English prose: a curious combination of practical advice and moral instruction, studded with anecdotal *exempla*. [62] There are also shorter tracts of the type, full of common sense and practical wisdom.

Among the various branches of learning then treated in the vernacular, historiography is most important and closest to literature. Latin was still used, but was more extensively supplanted by the vernacular in a number of important works. [63] In Scotland the writing of verse chronicles in vigorous native verse had been initiated by Barbour's *Bruce* late in the 14th century; it was carried forward by Andrew of Wyntoun in *The Orygynalle Chronykil of Scotland* (ca. 1424) and by Henry the Minstrel ("Blind Harry") in his biographical poem on *Sir William Wallace* (ca. 1482). In England, the capital city of London became a centre of historical writing, with important contributions made by Capgrave (the hagiographer mentioned above), Robert Bale, Fabyan, John Stow, the anonymous author of *The Brut*, and others.

Political and legal theory also made a marked advance, chiefly in the work of Sir John Fortescue (died ca. 1476). Sir John was an adherent of the losing side of Lancaster and he lived for some time in exile, but his gifts later won him a place in the royal council of Edward IV. In his Latin *De Natura Legis Naturae* and *De Laudibus Legum Angliae* [64] he stressed the factor of consent by the people as a basis for sound government. *The Governance of England*, [65] written in English, is a eulogy of limited monarchy (*jus politicum et regale*) as opposed to absolute monarchy (*jus regale*), as found in France. Fortescue recognised that it was the English warfare in France which had given French kings the chance to establish absolutism there. With sympathy he paints the miserable condition of the French masses, resulting from the English invasions. At the same time he reproaches the French people for their passivity, their failure to rebel against arbitrary taxation and other oppressions. Poverty, he claims, and the misfortunes of war have made them spiritless. It would be a tragedy for England if the commons there were reduced to such servility. "Ffor than thai wolde not rebelle, as now thai done oftentymes; wich the commons of Ffraunce do not, nor mey doo; ffor thai haue no wepen, nor armour" (Plummer ed., p. 137). The English tradition of rebellion deserves credit, says Fortescue, for producing the blessings of a limited monarchy. His writings have historical importance because they were used by English political theorists of the 17th century in their struggle against the absolutism of the Stuart monarchy.

Miscellaneous information, scientific and pseudo-scientific, was treated in numerous writings. A short handbook of general knowledge, the *Secreta Secretorum* popularly attributed to Aristotle, was seven times translated into English. Handbooks on hunting and agriculture, on chivalric usage and military art also appeared in English versions, original or translated. They do not have great literary significance but they further testify to the hunger for popular instruction.

6. CAXTON AND HIS WORK

The activities of William Caxton (1422—91), first English printer, subsume all of the chief intellectual interests of his time. He moved in the orbit of the two main social groups then sharing secular power: the wealthy merchants of the towns, and the circles of royalty and nobility who still adhered to feudal forms of culture.[66] He rose from a mercer's apprentice to merchant in the wool trade, and became governor of the English company of Merchant Adventurers resident in the Low Countries. While at Bruges he became absorbed in the new art of printing, which he learned by practical experience at Cologne. After 1469 he combined this interest with literary activity. He entered the service of the English-born Duchess of Burgundy (a sister of Edward IV), and thus found himself in the midst of a circle distinguished not only by wealth but also by literary and artistic activity. Among his colleagues were such outstanding Flemish painters as the van Eyk brothers and Roger van der Weyden. The Duchess gave Caxton access to one of the best of Western European libraries, and encouraged him to undertake translations from French into English. Returning to England about 1476, Caxton set up a printing establishment in Westminster, close to the court and to the centre of the nation's wool trade. The location was symbolic. The pioneer printer continued to enjoy royal and noble patronage, and supplemented it by commissions executed for members of the middle class, aldermen and merchants. Among the assistants he trained were Wynkyn de Worde, Pynson and Copland, who carried on the new craft after him.

The invention which made possible the rapid and cheap production of books, as compared with the laborious older system of hand copying, was destined to have profound effects on literary culture. It meant that that culture would be able to penetrate to wider circles of the masses than ever before in written form. It meant, in fact, that the written form would increasingly displace the oral for popular as well as aristocratic entertainment. Coming on the eve of the age of humanism and

Reformation, it was at once a symptom of the vast transformations already being prepared, and also a factor contributing to their realisation.

Yet Caxton and his assistants were probably only slightly aware of the cultural revolution they were initiating. Technological conservatism was apparent (as often in such cases) in the very nature of the characters used for printers' type. The letters were made heavy in style, imitating the thick black down-strokes of a scribe's pen, though the new process might have favoured the immediate use of clear slender lines such as we use today. Moreover, the range of subject matter reflected medieval interests expressed in traditional forms through well-established texts. It was the quantitative amount of distribution which came first, followed later by qualitatively different materials appropriate to a new era.

The output of Caxtons' press was great, and a number of the works printed were translated into English by the owner himself. He was very sensible of his responsibilities as a stylist, rendering new services to literary English as a vehicle of expression. His prefaces and epilogues[67] frequently inform us of his doubts and debates with himself over such matters as the fittest choice of words or the sentence structure best adapted to his purpose. His own remarks indicate that he was dissatisfied with the results. At times he is over-faithful to his original, rendering French or Latin idioms and constructions literally; at times he uses two synonyms connected by "or" for one word in the original, out of anxiety apparently to reproduce the meaning accurately. To a certain extent he realised and acted on the need to "modernise" Middle English texts. Aware that he was playing an important part in establishing a norm for the rising national language, he seriously discussed the problem of local dialects — which he quaintly attributed to changeability in the English character, due to the influence of the moon. Though his style in both original and translated writings is sometimes repetitious and awkward, such defects are not due entirely to unskilled naiveté. They represent lapses from a standard of very considerable skill and dignity. His constructions show the influence of rhetorical teachings and the imitation of rhetorical models. Nevertheless the style is best where such influence is least obvious. Caxton was striving to benefit from classical doctrine without damage to native linguistic structure. Though his success was imperfect, he made a greater contribution than he himself could have realised to the shaping of modern literary English.[68] His orthography achieved the status, more or less, of a standard, unfortunately preserved by later generations long after it had become archaic.

By grouping Caxton's main publications under appropriate headings, we may see the leading interests reflected in them.

The traditional forms of medieval religious and moral instruction were represented by allegories, tracts and saints' lives. Jean de Gallopes' French prose redaction of Déguileville's *Pilgrimage of the Soul* was put into English, thus supplementing Lydgate's *Pilgrimage of the Life of Man* (above, sec. 3). The allegorical *Court of Sapience* was also printed by him. The *Doctrinal of Sapience*, on the other hand, represents religious instruction pure and simple, without narrative framework. Various books of prayer and meditation were published, including (among others) tracts such as *The Art and Craft to Know Well to Die* (from the *Ars Moriendi* already mentioned), St. Bonaventura's *Speculum Vitae Christi* (done into English by Nicholas Love from the French of Jean de Gallopes) Hagiography was represented by the *Festial* of John Mirk, giving homiletic materials for the year's calendar of feast-days, by the bulky translation of Jacobus de Voragine's *Legenda Aurea* (with many additions and some omissions), and by the *Vitae Patrum* already known in Anglo-Saxon England. For his *Golden Legend* Caxton used both an earlier English and a French translation. [69] His *Royal Book* treated (once again) the theme of vices and virtues from the source used by Chaucer in the Parson's Tale.

Out of the stock of feudal romances Caxton made liberal contribution for the entertainment of his readers. In addition to Malory's monumental treatment of the Arthurian cycle, Caxton printed (for a noble patron) an English version of a Carolingian *chanson de geste*, namely *The Four Sons of Aymon*. [70] The crusading theme had all but died out in English literature, but when the Turks threatened to capture Rhodes (1480), an effort was made to revive it for the occasion. Caxton sponsored two works designed to support an unpopular crusade: *Charles the Great*, a prose compilation using both history and fiction as sources in order to glorify the Frankish champion against the Saracens; and *Godefroy of Boulogne*, written "to th'ende that every cristen man may be the better encoraged tenterprise warre for the defense of Christendom." [71] Two shorter and less famous romances, *Blanchardyn and Eglantine* and *Paris and Vienne*, [72] treat the familiar theme of young knights winning fair ladies by brave adventures.

Classical myth, filtered through romantic versions, inspired a prose translation of part of Ovid's *Metamorphoses* from a French prose version. [73] On the occasion of Edward IV's becoming a member of the Burgundian Order of the Golden Fleece (1477) Caxton offered a translation of a French book on *Jason*. [74] The story was a tribute to the Order, which by its very theme reminded its members how wool formed the basis of Flemish prosperity. The French text had been composed by Raoul Lefèvre, who drew on Guido delle Colonne for its material, and also for the general

of feed that
wel weyed
whan it shold
come in to the
myddle and
half waye
thurgh of
therthe / there
ryght shold
it abyde, and
holde hym for
it myght ne-
ther go lower

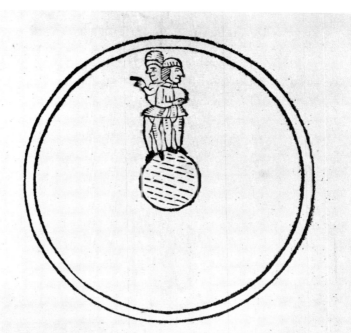

ne arise hyer / but yf it were that by the force of the grete
heyght it myght by the myght of the waight in fallyng
falle more depe than the myddle, but anon it shold
arise agayn in suche wise that it shold abyde in the myddle of therthe / ne neuer after shold meue thens / ffor thenne
shold it be egally ouerall vnder the firmament whiche
torneth nyght & daye, And by the vertue and myght of
his tornyng nothyng may approche to it that is pyssant
and heuy / but withdraweth alway vnder it, of whiche ye
may see the nature and vnderstondyng by this present
figure / on that other side /

a   Nd yf the erthe were perced thurgh in two places
of whiche that on hole were cutte in to that other
lyke a crosse, and foure men stoden right at the foure hee-
des of thise ij holes, on aboue / and another bynethe / and

The knowledge of history was disseminated by Caxton in several publications. *The Chronicles of England* (to 1461) was a composite affair using an English version of *The Brut* expanded from London chronicles, popular poems and eye-witness accounts. Trevisa's Middle English translation of Higden's *Polychronicon* (see ch. 9, sec. 5) was also modernised and provided with a supplement to include later events. The description of Britain belonging to it was also issued separately. The *Statutes* of Henry VII represent a contribution to legal history.

Secular instruction in general holds a more restricted place in Caxton's output than the didactic works on religion and morals. Nevertheless the text books on science and worldly arts have a prophetic significance out of all proportion to their actual bulk. The *Nova Rhetorica*, also called the *Margarita Eloquentiae* (*Pearl of Eloquence*), foretells that new passion for the study of classical rhetoric which was to affect so profoundly the creative English writing of the 16th century. On a more elementary, practical level Caxton also furnished his patrons with vocabulary-builders and simple dialogues in French and English to help travelers acquire the language of the neighbouring country. Elementary hygiene and some medical lore were offered in the prose *Governayle of Helthe*, to which was appended a verse *Medicina Stomachi*.

The most ambitious service to popular science was Caxton's *Mirrour of the World*,[82] the first illustrated book in English print (1481?). It was translated from a French prose work called *L'Image du Monde*, redacted from a long encyclopedic poem of the 13th century. The original was written by a certain Gauthier or Gossouin of Metz, and it existed in two versions, the later being much amplified from the first. Its popularity is attested by the fact that two Hebrew renderings of it were done in the Middle Ages. The poem belongs among the pioneering efforts made towards secularising learning 200 years before Caxton: the same impulse, probably, which inspired Jean de Meun's encyclopedic digressions on the *Roman de la Rose*. What Caxton gave his public was not far advanced over Jean's information, but his giving it was a very significant act. It has a fine appropriateness coming from one who himself learned the art of printing, as Wynkyn de Worde later reported, by working at Cologne on the printed encyclopedic *De Proprietatibus Rerum* of Bartholomew the Englishman. Both works may be thought of as inaugurating the procession of seriously written "popular science" books continuing to our own day.

The theological element in Caxton's *Mirrour*, its divisions corresponding to the seven arts of the schools, the solemn recapitulation of ancient errors, all make the book seem distinctly medieval to us. But the translator's evident care to be clear, his use of diagrams, his very willingness to give general readers some factual picture of the world they lived in—limited as it may have been—strikes us as very modern in spirit. The great age of discovery and exploration, anticipated by the more fanciful *Travels of Sir John Mandeville*, is now felt to be close. The epoch-making voyage of Columbus lay ahead but one year more than a decade. To Caxton's readers at least the view of the world as spherical would come as no surprise, for he had effectively disseminated the doctrine which the best-informed if not numerous medieval thinkers had always surmised. His account had also made available a rudimentary conception of the operation of earth's gravitational pull:

And yf it were so that by aduenture two men departed that one fro that other, and that one went alle way toward the eest and that other to ward the weste, so that bothe two wente egally, it behoued that they shold mete agayn in the opposite place fro where as they departed....
In lyke wise shold they goo aboute therthe, as they that contynuelly drewe them right to ward the myddle of therthe, for she fastneth alle heuy thyng to ward her. And that most weyeth, moste draweth and most ner holdeth to ward the myddle.... Yf the erthe were departed right in the myddle, in such wyce [wise] that the heuen myght be seen thurgh, and yf one threwe a stone or an heuy plomette of leed that wel weyed, whan it shold come in to the myddle and half waye thrugh of therthe, there ryght shold it abyde and holde hym (Prior ed., p. 52 f.).

William Caxton was not only a great innovator in technology, a man of wide culture and discriminating taste, a voluminous translator and one who contributed to the shaping of English literary style. He was also very eminently a teacher and a populariser of knowledge, the first one able to begin to reach out to the masses of the people. For these broader services he has received insufficient recognition. Only in our own times are their fruits beginning to reach the multitudes all over the world, to whom they properly belong.

[1] Georg Schanz, *Englische Handelspolitik gegen Ende des Mittlealters*, 2 vols. (Leipzig, 1881); Lipson, *Economic History*, II; Dobb, *Studies*, ch. 3.

[2] K.H. Vickers, *England in the Later Middle Ages* (London, 1919); A.R. Myers *op. cit.*, Part ii; Sylvia Thrupp, *The Merchant Class of London* (Chicago, 1948).

[3] C.L. Kingsford, *Prejudice and Promise in 15th Century England* (Oxford, 1925), ch. 3; J.E.T. Rogers, *A History of Agriculture and Prices in England* (Oxford, 1866—1902), IV, introd.; G.M. Trevelyan, *Illustrated English Social History*, II (London, 1944). Trevelyan points out, p. 54 f., that actual campaigns and battles involved combatants numbering no more than from two to ten thousand.

[4] Dobb, *Studies*, p. 121.

[5] Clara P. McMahon, *Education in Fifteenth Century England* (Baltimore: Johns Hopkins University Press, 1947).

[6] J.E.T. Rogers, *History of Agriculture*, IV, pp. 23 ff.

[7] G.G. Coulton, *Five Centuries of Religion*, IV: *The Last Days of Medieval Monasticism* (Cambridge University Press, 1950), pp. 499 ff.

[8] Johann Loserth, *Huss und Wiclif* (Berlin, 1925) prints two letters sent by Oldcastle to Bohemia, pp. 210—13.

[9] Andrzej Gałka, "Pieśń o Wiklifie," see ch. 10, n. 10.

[10] See note 59.

[11] Reginald Pecock, *The Reule of Crysten Religioun*, ed. William Cabell Greet, EETS, OS, No. 171 (1927); *The Donet*, ed. Elsie Vaughan Hitchcock, EETS, OS, No. 156 (1921); *The Folewer to the Donet*, ed. Hitchcock, *ibid.*, No. 164 (1924).

[12] *Pierce the Plowman's Creed*, ed. W.W. Skeat, EETS, OS, No. 30 (1867).

[13] *Mum and the Sothsegger*, ed. Mabel Day and Robert Steele, EETS, OS, No. 199 (1936 for 1934). *Richard the Redeless* is edited by Skeat as an appendix to his *Piers Plowman*.

[14] Ruth Mohl, "Theories of Monarchy in *Mum and the Sothsegger*," *PMLA*, LIX (1944), 26 ff.

[15] Ed. Skeat, *Chaucerian and Other Pieces*, in *The Works of Geoffrey Chaucer*, VII (Oxford, 1897).

[16] *God Speed the Plow*, *ibid.* (citation from p. 70).

[17] *Jack Upland*, *ibid.*

[18] *Ane Plesant Satyre*, ed. David Laing in Lyndsay's *Works*, II (1879); also in EETS, OS, No. 37 (1869 and 1883) and separately by James Kinsley (London, 1954).

[19] A preliminary biographical sketch of Lydgate was made by J. Schick in the introduction to his edition of *The Temple of Glas* (see n. 20). A recent complete study

is Walter F. Schirmer, *John Lydgate: Ein Kulturbild aus dem 15. Jahrhundert* (Tübingen, 1950).

[20] *The Temple of Glas*, ed. J. Schick, EETS, ES, No. 60 (1891).

[21] *Reson and Sensuality*, ed. Ernst Seiper, *ibid.*, Nos. 84 and 89 (1901, 1903),

[22] *Pilgrimage of the Life of Man*, ed. Katherine B. Locock, *ibid.*, Nos. 77, 83, 92 (1899—1904). Use of capitals has been normalised in the citations.

[23] *Troy Book*, ed. H. Bergen, *ibid.*, Nos. 97, 103, 106, 126 (1906—35).

[24] *Siege of Thebes*, ed. Eilert Ekwall and A. Erdman, *ibid.*, No. 125 (1930).

[25] *The Fall of Princes*, ed. H. Bergen, *ibid.*, Nos. 121—24 (1918—19).

[26] What Lydgate says on these topics is largely commonplace. W. Schirmer tends to overstate the poet's claim to modern democratic sentiments; see his article on *The Fall* in *Anglia*, LXIX (1950), 301—24.

[27] *The Serpent of Division*, ed. Henry Noble MacCracken (Oxford University Press, 1911).

[28] See Ralph A. Klinefelter, "A Newly Discovered Fifteenth-Century English Manuscript," *Modern Language Quarterly*, XIV (1953), 3—6.

[29] Published by Skeat in *Chaucer's Works*, VII.

[30] Lydgate, *Minor Poems: Religious*, EETS, ES, No. 107 (1910); *Secular, ibid.*, OS, No. 192 (1933).

[31] This and other poems by Hoccleve in his *Works*, ed. F.J. Furnivall, EETS, ES, Nos. 61 and 72 (1892, 1897).

[32] *The Kingis Quair*, ed. W.M. MacKenzie (London, 1939); this and other texts ed. C. Rogers, *Poetical Remains of James the First* (Edinburgh, 1873). On the peasant poems see George Fenwick Jones in *PMLA*, LXVIII (1953), 1101—25.

[33] For biographical study see Marshall Stearns, *Robert Henryson* (Columbia University Press, 1949); the works edited by G. Gregory Smith, Scottish Text Society, Nos. 45—47 (1906—14); *Poems and Fables*, ed. H. Harvey Wood (Edinburgh, 1933),

[34] *The Poems of William Dunbar*, ed. Bellyse Baildon (Cambridge University Press, 1907); also by J. Schipper for the Scottish Text Society. On the satire in Dunbar's "Twa Marrit Wemen" see James Kinsky in *Medium Aevum* XXII (1954), 31—35.

[35] *The Poems of Walter Kennedy*, ed. J. Schipper (Vienna, 1901).

[36] *Eger and Grime*, ed. J.R. Caldwell (Harvard University Press, 1933).

[37] *Ponthus and Sidone*, ed. F.J. Mather in *PMLA*, XII (1897), 1—50.

[38] *Melusine* (in prose), ed. A.K. Donald, EETS, ES, No. 68 (1895).

[39] *Parthenope of Blois*, ed. A.T. Bödtker, *ibid.*, No. 109 (1911).

[40] Lovelich's *Merlin*, ed. E.A. Koch, EETS, ES, Nos. 93 and 112 (1904, 1913) and OS, No. 185 (1930); *The History of the Holy Graal*, ed. F.J. Furnivall, EETS, ES, Nos. 20, 24, 28, 30 (1874—78); introductory volume by Dorothy Kempe, *ibid.*, No. 95 (1905).

[41] *Rauf Colzear* ed. S.J. Herrtage, EETS, ES, No. 39 (1882); discussion by H. Smyser in Harvard *Studies and Notes*, XIV (1932), 135—50.

[42] *Lancelot of the Laik*, ed. M.M. Gray, Scottish Text Society, (1912).

[43] These courtly poems are all edited by Skeat, *Chaucer's Works*, VII.

[44] For texts see R.H. Robbins, *Secular Lyrics of the XIVth and XVth Centuries*

(Oxford, 2nd ed., 1955); Carleton Brown, *Religious Lyrics* (Oxford, 1939) E.K. Chambers and F. Sidgwick, *Early English Lyrics* (London, 1937); for discussion, E.K. Chambers, *English Literature at the Close of the Middle Ages* (Oxford, 1945).

[45] Raymond Lincoln Kilgour, *The Decline of Chivalry as Shown in the French Literature of the Late Middle Ages* (Harvard University Press, 1937), defines tendencies characteristic of English literature also.

[46] Biographies by Edward Hickes, *Sir Thomas Malory* (Harvard University Press, 1928) and by Eugene Vinaver, *Malory* (Oxford, 1929). See also the introductory study by Vinaver in his three-volume edition of *The Works of Sir Thomas Malory* (Oxford, 1947).

[47] Discussed by Vinaver, Malory's *Works*, introd.

[48] For bibliography see Arundell Esdaile, *A List of English Tales and Prose Romances Printed before 1740* (London, 1912).

[49] *Jacob's Well*, ed. Arthur Brandeis, EETS, OS, No. 115 (1900); *Gesta Romanorum*, EETS, ES, No. 33 (1879); *An Alphabet of Tales*, EETS, OS, Nos. 126—27 (1904—05).

[50] Bokenham's *Lives of Holy Women* ed. M.S. Sergeantson, EETS, OS, No. 206 (1938); Capgrave's *Lives*, ed. C. Horstmann, *ibid.*, No. 100 (1893); by J. Munro, *ibid.*, No. 140 (1910).

[51] Usk's *Testament of Love* is edited by Skeat in *Chaucer's Works*, VII.

[52] *The Court of Sapience*, ed. Robert Spindler (Leipzig, 1927).

[53] One English version of Friar Lorens's *La Somme des vices et des vertus* is edited by W.N. Francis, EETS, OS, No. 217 (1942).

[54] See R.H. Bowers, "A Middle English Treatise on Hermeneutics," *PMLA*, LXV (1950), 590—600.

[55] *The Mirour of Man's Saluacioune*, ed. A.H. Huth for the Roxburghe Club (1888).

[56] *The Crafte of Dying*, ed. C. Horstmann in *Yorkshire Writers*, II (1895), 406—20.

[57] See James M. Clark, *The Dance of Death in the Middle Ages and the Renaissance* (Glasgow University Press, 1950).

[58] Misyn's translations of Rolle's *Incendium Amoris* and *De Emendatione Vitae*, ed. R. Harvey, EETS, OS, No. 106 (1896); *The Imitation of Christ* in two versions ed. by J.K. Ingram, EETS, ES, No. 63 (1893) and by P.B.M. Allan (1923).

[59] *The Book of Margery Kempe*, ed. S.B. Meech and Hope Emily Allen, EETS, OS, No. 212 (1940).

[60] For several such texts see Furnivall's *Manners and Meals in Olden Times*, OS, No. 32 (1868).

[61] Peter Idley's *Instructions*, ed. Charlotte d'Evelyn (Boston and London, 1935); *Ratis Raving*, ed. R. Girvan, Scottish Text Society, XI (1939).

[62] A translation of *The Book of the Knight of La Tour Landry* was published by Caxton in 1484. For an earlier translation see the one edited by Thomas Wright for the EETS, OS, No. 33 (1868), revised by J.J. Munro (1906).

[63] Charles L. Kingsford, *English Historical Literature in the Fifteenth Century* (Oxford, 1913).

[64] John Fortescue, *De Laudibus Legum Angliae*, ed. S.B. Chrimes (Cambridge University Press, 1942). His collected works have been edited by Thomas Fortescue (1869).

[65] John Fortescue, *The Governance of England*, ed. Charles Plummer (Oxford, 1885).

[66] A useful survey is given by Nellie Slayton Aurner, *Caxton: Mirrour of Fifteenth Century Letters* (Boston, 1926).

[67] W.J.B. Crotch, *The Prologues and Epilogues of William Caxton*, EETS, OS, No. 176 (1929).

[68] For general discussion see Samuel K. Workman, *Fifteenth Century Translations as an Influence on English Prose* (Princeton University Press, 1940); J.W.H. Atkins, *English Literary Criticism: The Medieval Phase* (Cambridge University Press, 1943), ch. 8.

[69] Discussed by Sister Mary Jeremy, "Caxton's *Golden Legend* and Varagine's *Legenda Aurea*," *Speculum*, XXI (1946), 212–31.

[70] *The Foure Sonnes of Aymon*, ed. Octavia Richardson, EETS, ES, Nos. 44–45 (1884–85).

[71] *Charles the Grete*, EETS, ES, Nos. 36–37 (1881); *Godefroy of Boloyne*, ed. Mary Noyes Colvin, *ibid.*, No. 64 (1893).

[72] *Blanchardyn and Eglantine* ed. Leon Kellner, EETS, ES, No. 58 (1890); *Paris and Vienne*, ed. W.C. Hazlitt for the Roxburghe Club (1868), but no critical edition exists.

[73] Caxton's *Metamorphoses* of Ovid ed. (but without critical apparatus) S. Gaselea and H.F.B. Brett-Smith (1924).

[74] *The History of Jason*, ed. John Munro, EETS, ES, No. 111 (1913 for 1912).

[75] *The Recueil of the Histories of Troy*, ed. Oskar Sommer, 2 vols. (1894).

[76] *Eneydos*, ed. M.T. Culley and F.J. Furnivall, EETS, ES, No. 57 (1890).

[77] *Aesop*, reprinted in the Bibliothèque Carabas, V (n.d.); *Reynard the Fox* ed. W.J. Thoms for the Percy Society (1844), neither in a modern critical edition.

[78] *The Book of the Ordre of Chyualry*, ed. Alfred T.P. Byles, EETS, OS, No. 168, (1926), *The Game and Play of Chess*, ed. W.E.A. Axon (1883), but no critical edition.

[79] *The Faits of Arms and Chivalry*, ed. A.T.P. Byles, EETS, OS, No. 199 1932).

[80] *The Curial*, ed. Paul Meyer and F.J. Furnivall, EETS, ES, No. 54 (1888) without critical apparatus.

[81] See Curt F. Bühler, *The Dictes and Sayings of the Philosophers*, EETS, OS, No. 211 (1941), introd. An early, native English collection existed under the title of *Proverbs of Alfred* (early 13th century), ed. Helen South (New York, 1931).

[82] *The Mirrour of the World*. ed. Oliver H. Prior, EETS, ES, No. 110 (1913 for 1912).

CHAPTER XIV

THE EARLY TUDOR PERIOD: AN AGE OF TRANSITION

1. THE FOUNDATIONS OF RENAISSANCE ENGLAND

A shift of power and prestige from the old feudal circles of English landowning nobles into the hands of city merchants had been in process for some time before 1500, and the arts had been responding to that shift by certain changes in themes, subject matter, mode of treatment and general allegiance: that is, in the type of patronage sought. Until the reigns of Henry VII and Henry VIII (from 1485 to 1547), however, the modifications in the cultural world had been relatively slow. The last preceding chapters have pointed out more than once that an obstinate vitality was maintained by early medieval forms such as allegory, dream-vision, scholastic and quasi-scholastic debate and chivalric romance, over a span of many centuries. Apart from the work of an exceptional genius like Chaucer, the changes may be said to have been inconspicuous. With the transition from the 15th to the 16th century, however, the factors causing cultural transformations begin to move at a much more rapid tempo. In literature specifically the slow accumulation of minor changes is replaced by conspicuous metamorphoses affecting not only style and subject matter but also general ideological orientation. An extensive public able to read and correspond, to appreciate literature and to make amateur contributions to it, had emerged from both the landed gentry[1] and the commons of the cities.

The sum total of these essential quickened changes defines the transition from late medieval to Renaissance culture. Before attempting to explain what this much-disputed term means with reference to English literature, however, it is necessary to review the course of external events affecting the change.

Two main factors determined the course of economic history under the Tudors. The first is the triumphant, even dazzling expansion of merchant capital, deeply affecting the social structure of the ruling class in all its layers and elements; the second is the crisis and transformation of agriculture, with consequences affecting English general welfare for centuries to come.

Mercantilism, the whole sphere of trading activity, was conditioned of course by patterns of regulation and control already set in the Middle Ages. Weaving and dyeing and manufacturing had improved in the 15th century, and it was now finished cloth more than raw wool that was exported. The merchants of the several coastal cities still strove however to direct the export and to obtain monopoly privileges at the expense of other towns.[2] The range of monopolies began to extend beyond the narrow confines of the guilds. Profits made in trading flowed into nascent industries. Farming for profit led to investments by landowners in trading enterprises. These tendencies at the beginning of the century were a forecast of the large-scale monopolies, the vastly expanded trade by navigation, and the feverish speculation which characterised the reign of Queen Elizabeth.

Under her father and grandfather, however, the greatest economic transformations occurred in the field of agriculture. A large-scale expropriation of small holders from their land, initiated early in the 16th century, created the two essential preconditions for the development of modern industrial capitalism. It had a dual consequence: it enriched the wool-producers, thus endowing them with surplus capital for investment; and it uprooted a large section of the rural population, driving them off the land and turning them into a drifting army of the unemployed. These destitute people migrated naturally towards the towns and cities, where they became the nucleus of the modern proletariat — workers possessing neither land nor tools nor any other instruments of their own for purposes of production.

The expropriation of land from small holders took several forms. Individual farms rented or held by traditional right from landlords were now thrown together and converted from tillage into grazing lands as a result of the profits obtainable from the wool and cloth industry. The inhabitants of the farms were expelled, the farm-houses were allowed to fall into decay. At the same time the practice of open-field farming in separate strips was more and more relinquished for the cultivation of large, single, fenced-in tracts. The older system, based on the rotated individual use of individual strips (when not lying fallow) had insured a certain distribution of risks and other disadvantages. To this extent it had retarded the development of social and economic inequalities in the class of peasants. But the open-field system had obvious shortcomings from the point of view of efficiency and productivity. Rising prices, population increase, and the desire for profit impelled farmers to a consolidation of multiple holdings into one. In some instances, open-field strips were thrown together into enclosures for the purpose of improving the land by drainage, or increasing the yield from tillage, and these consolidations were approved by community sentiment. But the people as a whole condemned the enclosures changing arable into pasture land, causing depopulation of the country-side; and these were the ones most numerous and extensive.

Another deprivation was visited upon the peasants at this time when the common lands formerly used by all villagers for grazing domestic animals, were fenced in by the landlords for their sheep, and the traditional rights to use meadowlands and forests for fuel, turf, peat and building materials were likewise restricted.

Nor was this all. The victims of enclosure, the expropriated peasants, were not only rendered destitute but with fantastic social injustice, adding torture to injury, they were thereupon treated as criminal outcasts, as if blameworthy for the calamity which had overtaken them. The ruling class feared the mass of beggars and vagabonds they themselves had created. "The fathers of the present working class," says Marx, "were chastised for their enforced transformation into vagabonds and paupers. Legislation treated them as 'voluntary' criminals, and assumed that it depended on their own goodwill to go on working under conditions that no longer existed."[3] When they were unable to perform this miracle, they were by a law of Henry VIII (1530) subjected, as "sturdy vagabonds," to whipping and imprisonment; upon second arrest there was more whipping and cutting off of half an ear; and upon the third—execution. Such ferocious laws were reaffirmed and re-enacted throughout the 16th century. Though legislators perceived the catastrophic social consequences of enclosure for agriculture, and tried to stem the movement by laws, their acts were seldom enforced. The justices of the peace in the shires, themselves belonging to the class reaping profit from it, generally ignored the statutes.

Private ownership of land was further aggrandised and made more profitable when the large and exceptionally productive tracts belonging to the monasteries were expropriated by Henry VIII and promptly transferred to noble and ennobled families at very advantageous rates. The social gap between landlords and poor peasants was thus widened still further; depopulation extended to villages formerly attached to church holdings. Monastic institutions were largely corrupt, wealthy and socially irresponsible, beyond question; the records of investigations on the eve of dissolution leave no doubt that reform was urgently needed. But what was done with them gave no help to the victims of the agricultural system. What should have been a taking over of title by the rightful owners—the workers on the church-owned estates, who cultivated them from time immemorial—was replaced by the expulsion of large numbers of those same workers. To quote Marx again:

The suppression of the monasteries, etc., hurled their inmates into the proletariat. The estates of the church were to a large extent given away to rapacious royal favourites, or sold at a nominal price to speculating farmers and citizens, who drove out, *en masse*, the hereditary subtenants and threw their holdings into one. The legally guaranteed property of the poorer folk in a part of the church's tithes was tacitly confiscated (*loc. cit.*).

By the law suppressing monasteries, the rural population was also deprived of the elementary social services traditionally administered by their agency. Food and a minimal relief for the destitute, shelter and some kind of hospital care for the sick, had been provided by monastic orders of men and women, often through special foundations they administered. Though inadequate and granted as unpalatable charity, not as an ensured service due out of the communities' tithes and savings, still these services had been the only ones of the kind available to the population. Their cancellation meant further deprivation, further misery to the dispossessed.

The Reformation was introduced by Henry VIII from above for motives of immediate policy. Nevertheless it answered to certain popular demands long since expressed in anti-papal satire and protest, beginning with the Lollards. There were positive aspects to offset some of the damages caused by its economic methods. It produced a fever of discussion on the theoretical questions involved, it enhanced the interest in the national vernacular language as an instrument for translations of the Bible; it voiced criticism of a certain type of authoritarian theology and the terrors connected with it (though efforts were soon made to put new terrors in place of the old ones). The reform movement attacked the political role of the papacy with especial vehemence. It reinforced nationalism in culture as it also did, for good and ill, in politics and economics. Though the new state church tried to claim absolute powers like the old, it could not succeed. Popular protest had been too active to yield to complete conformity once more. The Acts of Reformation in Parliament (1534) had been preceded five years before by a bill of grievances against the clergy, originating in the Commons and not with the King. The step was therefore not unprepared, though carried out by royal initiative.

Although considerable numbers of people resisted the change and adhered to the old forms at the risk of death, the majority were apparently ready for a drastic reformation of some sort to do away with the accu-

mulated glaring abuses of centuries. The immediate aim of Henry was
a consolidation of absolute power. He received at least passive support
from most of the nation, and the list of those who suffered the death
penalty for resistance, though including some distinguished names like
that of Sir Thomas More, was not a long one.[4]

The dissociation of the English church from Rome, its full integration
into the state apparatus, the expropriation of the monasteries and their
lands, all occurred at ε time when England was beginning to respond
fully to the artistic and intellectual stimuli of the European Renaissance.
To that great general movement (see below, sec. 7) the special studies
of the English humanists made a unique contribution. The economic
prosperity of the wealthy commons, and the new relations of production
obtaining among them—no matter how brutally achieved by expropriation
and merciless inner competition—gave the foundation for the whole
impressive superstructure created in the latter 16th century. Taken
together, all of these transformations signalise the end of the Middle
Ages far more truly than the mere cessation of baronial struggles after
the War of the Roses.[5]

2. POPULAR LITERATURE: EARLY DRAMA
AND THE BALLADS

The growth of towns, and with them the growth of craft guilds,
had for some time before 1500 been fostering the development of a popular
drama. During the Middle Ages, mimetic performances in Latin had
been attached to embellished liturgical rituals of the church. Questions
and answers introduced into the authorised liturgy as "tropes" or ampli-
fications on the text were at first merely ornamental. They did not become
dramatic until an element of impersonation was made a feature of the
dialogue. This innovation came quite early on the continent, in connection
with the Easter mass. An 11th-century text of Monte Cassino in Italy,
for instance, tells something of the arrangements for a dialogue supposed to occur before Christ's sepulchre:

Finita tertia, uadat unus sacerdos ante altare, alba uesta indutus,
et uersus ad choram dicat alta voce:

Quem queritis?

Et duo alii clerici stantes in medio chori respondeant:

Jesum Nazarenum.

Et sacerdos:

Non est hic, surrexit.

Illi uero conuersi ad chorum dicant:

Alleluia, resurrexit Dominus.

Post hec incipiatur tropos. Sequatur introitus: Resurrexi.[6]

Translated, this means:

When terce has been finished, let one priest go before the altar, dressed in white, and having turned towards the choir let him say with a clear high voice:

Whom seek ye?

And let two other priests standing in the middle of the choir answer thus:

Jesus of Nazareth.

And the one priest:

He is not here; He is risen.

And they, turning to the choir, shall say:

Halleluliah, the Lord is risen.

After this, let the trope begin. The introit "Resurrexi" should follow.

Elsewhere too it was incidents connected with the Easter story which were the first to be elaborated into dialogues with impersonation, including representation of the Marys and an angel, the apostles Peter and John, and the risen Christ. A text from Cracow, for instance, gives a lyrical elaboration with antiphones.[7] After the Easter ritual, other occasions were marked by dialogues with impersonation: incidents of the Passion, Ascension and Nativity. Christmas ritual was amplified by the introduction of personages to represent the Magi, the shepherds, and Herod, besides members of the Holy Family. All this occurred within the church.

Our knowledge of the Latin liturgical dialogue in England is less abundant than for other countries. We do know, however, that the preparation of mimetic performances was eventually assumed by lay organisations such as guilds and secular fraternities, and the vernacular language was substituted for Latin. At the same time the performances were no longer within the interior of the church but on the steps or in an open square. In England it was French which appeared first instead of Latin in a performance of this sort, probably as a result of practices transferred directly from Normandy (see ch. 7, sec. 1). Some scattered dialogues composed in Middle English—for instance, a religious piece on the Harrowing of Hell, and a secular conversation between a clerk and a maiden ("De Clerico et Puella")—were probably intended for private recitation and not public acting.[8] Out-of-doors dramatic performances were apparently current and in laymen's hands by the 14th century, perhaps earlier, but our evidence about them is indirect: the Wycliffite *Tretise of Miraclis*

Playing[9], certain passages in Robert Manning of Brunne's *Handlyng Synne* (also denunciatory), a few references by Chaucer, and so on. Of the separate texts themselves we have little surviving.

From the late 14th century into the early 16th there came the development of ambitious cycles of religious plays based on the Bible. In scope they covered the outstanding events from Creation to Resurrection, even to the coming of Anti-Christ and the Last Judgment. The acting was done on platforms mounted on wheels, called "pageants," which could be drawn from place to place. Thus the people living in a set of neighbouring villages were able to watch the same series of playlets as they arrived and passed on, one after another in sequence. Not all the available scenes were necessarily enacted each year, however. The coming of the series of pageants was announced by standard-bearers called *vexillatores*. Judging from prologues and directions in the manuscripts, the relation between amateur actors and audiences in the market places was quite informal. Villainous characters like Satan, Herod and Pontius Pilate, though condemned, were popular; they were sometimes instructed to rage about in the street as well as on the stage. The guildsmen were chosen to enact scenes appropriate to their daily work; for instance, at York the plasterers undertook to show God creating the earth; the shipwrights to reproduce the construction of Noah's ark; and the bakers to stage the scene of the Last Supper. In creating their processional plays, writers of the time may at certain points have drawn upon festival games and rituals of folklore, such as spring-time celebrations of nature's resurrection which antedate the Christian religion in England. In general however the affinity of such pagan themes is closer to the folklore of miracle plays based on saints' lives, a form of religious drama less developed in England than in France. The extent of the indebtedness to folklore is a matter of dispute. [10]

The language of the Biblical plays was fitting to the broad, non-courtly audiences of town and village. The verse was simple: not polished, but lively and easy to deliver. Comic passages were not infrequent. The words and expressions used were at times colloquial to the point of rudeness, but the phraseology could also achieve a simple elevated dignity. These collective undertakings were the most impressive flowering of popular late medieval literature to proceed from the stimulus of town life.

Two extant cycles of plays belong to the Northern districts and are closely connected in origin. These are the York cycle, begun in the middle 14th century, and the related cycle of Wakefield (also called the "Towneley Plays" from the name of the family owning the manuscript of them). [11] Five of the Wakefield plays coincide with those from York except for minor deviations, and there are scattered passages elsewhere

that agree verbally. In dealing with scenes from the Passion, both alike
were influenced by the metrical narrative called the *Northern Passion*
(see ch. 9, n. 63). Both also used the Middle English apocryphal Gospel
of Nicodemus. The most probable theory is that the two cycles represent
separate developments of one shorter series of plays, worked up independently in two different localities. [12] The York cycle maintains a generally
serious tone, while that of Wakefield is marked by striking admixtures
of broad comedy, probably introduced by a writer of the early 15th century.
The famous *Second Shepherd's Play* is a burlesque episode describing
how a peasant named Mak tries to save a stolen lamb from confiscation
by having his wife take it to bed with her and pretend that it is her new-
born baby. By juxtaposition with the perfectly serious Nativity play
of the cycle, this realistic pastoral sketch attains an effect of increased
hilarity through contrast. The scene between Cain and Abel also reflects
contemporary life in a realistic style. Cain's crudely voiced protest at
the need to make offerings has obvious reference to the oppressive exaction
of tithes by the church. Beside it, his killing of Abel is made a matter
of reduced importance. The Wakefield master tended to transform his
devils into jesters, as in the character of the merry Titivillus who enlivens
the Last Judgment. The clown-like devil is a figure who persists into
Elizabethan drama, as for instance in Ben Jonson's *The Devil is an Ass*
and other satiric comedies.

The Chester cycle of plays, [13] dating from the 15th century, was
designed to cover three days. It shows some influence from the York
cycle, but is more unified in tone and more consistently didactic in intention. Nevertheless it has its own humorous elements as in the scene —
enacted by "the watter leaders and drawers of Dee" — between Noah
and his shrewish wife. The lady does not wish to enter the ship without
her "gossips," and must be haled aboard forcefully by her sons. The
humour is nevertheless kept decorous and subordinate throughout.

The *Ludus Coventriae* or the Coventry Plays [14] represent a 15th-
century compilation of the Northeast Midlands, including some plays
previously acted separately and some written especially for it. There
are some passages of unabashed vulgarity, while the didactic commentary
is supplied by an allegorical personage named Contemplation. Other
allegorical figures appear in the cycle, contrasting with the more realistic
ones conceived as individuals.

Pure allegory in the drama took the form of morality plays, in which
all the personages represented qualities or ideas. The schemes resembled
the narrative allegories already known for centuries, depicting quests,
combats, sieges and other generalised experiences in which good and
bad traits of humanity were deployed against one another. Whereas

the mysteries or Biblical plays, and the miracle plays based on saints' lives, were dropped soon after the Reformation, the allegories were continued for some time afterwards. Dealing with abstract moral concepts as they did, they were not subject to Protestant charges of mishandling the Bible or inculcating idolatry.

The conflict of vice and virtue, that popular theme of preachers for many centuries, was presented in three plays surviving in a single manuscript, called the Macro text. They are: *The Castle of Perseverance*; *Mind, Wit and Understanding*; and *Mankind*. In *Mundus et Infans* (*The World and Youth*), as in *The Castle*, a theme of subjective conflict is cast in the form of an individual's education by experience during successive phases of his life. [15] The finest morality of all is *Everyman*, now conceded by most critics to be indebted to the Middle Dutch *Elkerlijk* (first printed in 1495). It follows a typical human being through the experiences of fear, despair and comfort in the closing scenes of his life. The action extends from the time when he receives Death's first warning until he is ready to quit this world with his soul prepared and fortified for the one he expects to enter. Kinship with the Dance of Death theme is clear, but the morality play avoids horror and stresses the mood of steadfast hope.

Biblical parables using didactic allegory were treated by Protestant writers who avoided or condemned the use of other Biblical narrative. The story of the Prodigal Son, for instance, having been treated several times in continental Latin plays, was adapted in English in the anonymous *Nice Wanton* and in Thomas Ingeland's *Disobedient Child* (texts first printed about 1560). [16] Morality writing was extended to ambitious satire in David Lyndsay's *Three Estaitis* (ch. 13 sec. 2), and in Skelton's *Magnificience* (see below, sec. 3). Later, the revival of Seneca's Latin tragedies and the comedies of Plautus and Terence led to some dramatic treatments of Biblical parable and history in a learned rather than a popular style.

The period of the rise of English drama also witnessed the rise of another popular form: the ballad, associated in its later career rather with village life, but known also in town and castle in the Middle Ages. As contrasted with courtly and religious lyrics, the ballad uses a simpler technique and is always, not merely on occasion, anonymous. Its substance is narrative and its point of view is objective. It tells an uncomplicated story by means of sequent incidents abruptly introduced; it makes much use of repetition and refrain. In the simplest form of all it may build up a series of almost identical verses in which the changing of no more than a single phrase in each is the means of leading to a climax. For instance, in "A Maid Saved from the Gallows," [17] a young girl asks a number

Sir Thomas Wyatt
by Johann Holbein, Jr.

3. COURTLY LITERATURE, OLD STYLE

As might be expected in a period of rapid change, literature adhering faithfully to old forms is still to be found beside the first products of vigorous innovation. [21]

Stephen Hawes (1474—1523), who was attached to the court of Henry VII, followed the old style of didactic allegory. His first work, *The Example of Virtue*, is mere homily in a slight narrative framework. The second, *The Pastime of Pleasure*, [22] is didactic allegory cast in the form of a quest. Graunde Amour, the hero, resembles the dreamer in *The Court of Sapience* (ch. 13, sec. 5). He receives instruction from ladies representing the seven liberal arts; he kills allegorical monsters and visits mythological dwellings like the pre-Spenserian warrior he is; and he thus wins the shadowy Belle Pucelle as his lady-love. There is little in this poem of that vernal literary charm which had pervaded the *Romance of the Rose*, its remote ancestor, and still less of the splendid language, the fantasy and the intelligence characterising its famous successor, *The Faery Queene*. The verse is pedestrian, marked by caesuras falling with deadly regularity. At best the work is reminiscent of no greater master than Lydgate. But the end especially has an admonitory earnestness that belongs peculiarly to Hawes. Instead of concluding the poem with the nuptials of hero and heroine, the poet goes on to tell how Graunde Amour succumbed to the results of old age, died and was buried, and how Fame's effort to keep alive at least the memory of his exploits was thwarted by Time. To balance this destruction, Eternity appears in a "fayre whyte vesture," and the poem concludes with an apostrophe to her.

Alexander Barclay (1475—1552) was a priestly author credited with the translation of a French allegory of the medieval type, Pierre Gringoire's *Castle of Labour* (first printed 1505). More noteworthy is his translation of the German satirical poem, Sebastian Brant's *Narrenschiff*, as *The Ship of Fools*. Barclay more than doubles the length of his text as he embroiders on its theme and makes it more English. This work establishes him as a pioneer in contacting German culture directly, for he tells us that he used the original "in plain and common speech of Doche" besides a French translation and one in Latin upon which he chiefly depended. The subject is a panoramic view of follies in all levels of society, akin to the more famous treatment by Erasmus of Rotterdam in his *Encomium Moriae* or *Praise of Folly*. The *Eclogues* of Barclay, although imitative of classical and humanist Italian models, are adapted to an English environment in many concrete details. [23]

John Heywood (?1497-ca. 1580), was a satirist and dramatist (see sec. 5) who weathered the changes at three Tudor courts and remained a Catholic throughout his life. His long satirical poem *The Spider and the Fly*[24] has something about it of the medieval heritage of beast-epic, debate and allegory, but likewise something of the classical mock-epic and parody. The Spider in question is clearly the Protestant Archbishop Cranmer, while the Fly seems to represent the commons of England. The maidservant who at the end liberates the captive Fly with her broom and crushes the Spider may be identified with Queen Mary.

John Skelton (ca. 1460—1529) is the most interesting and original of the satirical poets. As tutor to Henry VIII he wrote a Latin didactic manual entitled *Speculum Principis* (*The Prince's Mirror*), which follows conservative medieval doctrines. His allegories in rime royal, *The Bowge of Court* and *The Garland of Laurel*,[25] also follow medieval patterns in external form, but they are infused with a spirit which is Skelton's own. *The Bowge* (that is, the free banquet or rations given to court retainers) portrays the malicious gossip and the denunciations current among court folk. The characters bear allegorical names like Riot, Dissimuler and Disdain. They appear as attendants upon Lady Peerless, on whose ship the dreamer-hero Dread has embarked in order to obtain some of her bounty—Court Favour. Each of the back-biters denounces one of the others to Dread, and then denounces Dread himself to another in gossip which Dread overhears. The hero awakens with his own desperate effort to leap off the ship. *The Garland of Laurel*, a poem written under the influence of Chaucer's *House of Fame*. embodies a graceful compliment to the Countess of Surrey.

In *Magnificence* Skelton produced an allegory in the form of a morality play, but not a religious one. As with Lyndsay's *Satyre of the Thrie Estaitis*, the theme is political: an admonition to a young prince on the dangers besetting his rule. Despite the good advice of Liberty and Felicity, the titular hero is lured into extravagance by Fancy, Counterfeit Countenance (a personage resembling Faux-Semblant or Hypocrisy in the *Romance of the Rose*) and others. When Adversity and Poverty overthrow the king, he succumbs before Despair, but Redress and Goodhope bring about his restoration. Though written with some force, *Magnificence* can not compete with the mordant verve in Lyndsay's satire.

In his shorter satirical pieces Skelton used a rapid-moving line of two stresses with rime. Skeltonic verse, as it is called from his name, is a vernacular adaptation of the riming short lines of medieval Latin also used for early humanistic satire. The English poet handled it with much virtuosity. He drew many racy words and phrases from popular speech and cast them into verse that is by turns biting, rollicking, tender and disdainful. After the formal aureate writers, his language has the impact of homely reality. The tumbling lines possess an air of spontaneity, but in their own kind they are wrought with care. A fine example is the sketch called *The Tunning of Eleanor Rumming*, in which a crew of tavern-haunting villagers, more or less unsavoury, come scurrying forward at the tidings that the hostess has a supply of freshly brewed ale. Here are a few of the unsparing lines devoted to Hostess Eleanor herself:

> 12 Her loathly lere
> Is nothing clear,
> But ugly of cheer,
> Droopy and drowsy,
> Scurvy and lousy;
> Her face all bousy
> Comely crinkled,
> Wondrously wrinkled,
> Like a roast pig's ear
> Bristled with hair....
>
> 27 Her nose somedele hooked,
> And camously crooked
> Never stopping,
> But ever dropping;
> Her skin, loose and slack,
> Grained like a sack;
> With a crooked back....

[lere = face;   bousy = drunken;   camous = upturned]

In the same lively vein Skelton denounces the wealthy clergy, the degenerate friars, the ambitious political bishops. He uses as mouthpiece a fictitious "Colin Clout" who wanders among people observing and commenting on abuses. Though not mentioned by name, Cardinal Wolsey is here the object of much denunciation by Skelton. The attack is made more direct in *Why Come Ye not to Court* and *Speak, Parrot!* Skelton remained aloof from the Reformation, but his pungent criticism of the clergy, his burlesque of the church burial service for the dead in *Philip Sparrow* and his general uninhibited boldness of denunciation led Barclay, among others, to charge him with heterodoxy.

Besides Skelton, others were cultivating the rich veins of language adapted to satire, and thus successfully breaking away from both Lydgate's mediocrity and the excesses of aureate verse. The Scottish poet David Lyndsay (already mentioned) was one of these, a worthy successor to Henryson and Dunbar. The London printer Robert Copland pictured scenes of dirt, crime and misery in his *Highway to the Spital-House*[26] (i.e., hospital-almshouse). His harshly sombre language is lacking in form and movement when compared with Skelton's, but it shows a like striving for honesty. All these efforts announce a fervid new desire to experiment with non-courtly language, to break away from the pallid imitations of the 15th century. The origins of the satiric school were in large part learned and traditional, but it drew vitality from great resources of popular vocabulary and expression. Its innovations opened the way to much powerful writing later in the 16th century.

4. THE POETRY OF WYATT AND SURREY

With the names of Sir Thomas Wyatt and Henry Howard, Earl of Surrey, we reach the very threshold of the great new age of poetry. Both of them, especially Wyatt, incorporated in their poems the dual tradition of popular simplicity combined with courtly style found in their best medieval predecessors; both, in addition, were deeply influenced by the verse of the Italian Renaissance, particularly by Petrarch. Both were courtiers and moved in the circle of talented personalities gathered about Henry VIII.

Thomas Wyatt[27] (1503—42), like Chaucer before him, served his king on missions abroad which took him to Spain, Italy and France. He suffered eclipse and imprisonment at the time when his patron Thomas Cromwell fell out of royal favour, but his eloquent self-defense (the text of which survives) was accepted, and he was released. A tradition of some plausibility — but unverifiable — states that he had been a lover of Anne Boleyn before the King wooed her. His untimely death was caused by fever. Surrey, on the other hand, a very tempestuous character, was executed for treason at the age of thirty (1547).

Both poets show some awkwardness in their experimental grafting of alien forms (such as Dante's *terza rima* and the Petrarchan sonnet) upon the medium of English verse. Wyatt, however, has merits of sincerity, musicality and unhackneyed felicity which place him in a sphere by himself. Though many of this sonnets are based on originals by Petrarch, Aretino, Clement Marot and others, he is much more than a translator. Critics applying a mechanical standard have exaggerated the metrical "roughness" of his lines, but recent studies correct the unjust, or at least extreme, criticism.[28] Wyatt's lines should not be scanned apart from the music that was meant to go with them, and the music is able to introduce those compensatory delays, pauses and minor stresses which cancel the seeming inadequacies of the words considered in isolation.

Even without music, the lines of Wyatt are often as hauntingly melodious as they are striking in their fresh-minted newness. At his best Wyatt sings as if no poet before him had already exploited the emotions of love and time's change, friendship and patriotism. There are anticipations of Shakespeare's soul-searching directness in lines like these:

> Disdain me not without desert,
> > Nor leave me not so suddenly;
> Since well ye wot that in my heart
> > I mean ye not but honestly.
> > > Disdain me not....
>
> Disdain me not that am your own:
> > Refuse me not that am so true:
> Mistrust me not till all be known:
> > Forsake me not ne for no new.
> > > Disdain me not.   (Tillyard ed. No. 10;
> > > > Muir No. 177)

Or this:

> There was nothing more me pained,
> > Nor nothing more me moved,
> As when my sweetheart her complained
> > That ever she me loved.
> > > Alas the while!   (Tillyard No. 14; Muir
> > > > No. 38)

Or the puzzling poem that begins:

> They flee from me that sometime did me seek,
> > With naked feet stalking in my chamber...
> > > (Tillyard No. 13; Muir No. 37)[29]

Wyatts' adaptation of the Horatian fable about a town and a country mouse (previously treated by Robert Henryson also) is an example of language admirably fitted to its theme. The opening lines set the tone with effortless skill; the *terza rima* flows easily:

> My mother's maids, when they did sew and spin,
> > They sang sometime a song of the field mouse,
> That forbecause her livelihood was but thin
> > Would needs go seek her townish sister's house...

Such artful simplicity is not often encountered in the lyrics of Surrey, a number of which, like Wyatt's, are based on Petrarch's sonnets. The younger poet is also less original in his phraseology, which while unquestionably delightful often echoes that of Chaucer and other medieval lyricists:[30]

> The sun hath twice brought forth the tender green
> And clad the earth in lively lustiness,
> Once have the winds the trees despoiled clean,
> And once again begins their cruelness....

Or this:

> The soote season, that bud and bloom forth brings,
> With green hath clad the hill, and eke the vale.
> The nightingale with feathers new she sings;
> The turtle to her make hath told her tale.

[turtle = turtledove;   make =mate]

When Surrey writes the seven-stressed long line (septenarius), he is so far from Wyatt's freedoms and irregularities that he makes his stresses and caesuras fall with a stultifying monotony. Nevertheless he too has the gift of happy phrase, and in the blank verse which he used, first of all English poets, to translate a part of the *Aeneid*, he achieves subtle musical effects by the discreet introduction of assonance, occasional rime (internal and external), consonance, alliteration and other sound effects. There is an unusual concentration of these echoes in the following lines:

> With this the sky gan whirl about the sphere:
> The cloudy night gan thicken from the sea,
> With mantles spread that cloaked earth and skies,
> And eke the treason of the Greekish guile.
> The watchman lay disperst, to take their rest,
> Whose wearied limbs sound sleep had then oppresst.

(Book ii)

(Notice assonance in *sphere:sea* and also in *spread:earth:treason* according to 16th-century pronunciation; assonance likewise in *skies:guile*; alliteration in *Greekish guile*; rime in *rest:oppresst*.)

The origin of Surrey's acoustic decorations appears to spring from the practice of Italian poets writing Latin verse: Petrarch, for instance, used them, as did Italian translators of Virgil (Ippolito dei Medici and Carlo Piccolomini). [31]

The poems of both Wyatt and Surrey waited for publication until the appearance of Tottel's *Miscellany* (1557), the famous collection which marks the beginning of the Elizabethan age of song. The 16th-century editor did not print all the poems even then, and he modified the texts in order to make them smoother. Their true significance as pioneer works can only be appreciated, however, when read as they were written. The original form, with all the defects of groping experiment and archaism, merely throws into sharper relief the new vigour and intensified feeling which animates the work as a whole.

5. THE ENGLISH HUMANISTS

Among the intellectual currents bringing new interest and vitality to 16th-century England, the revived study of classical authors is a conspicuous force. [32] In a sense of course all of Western medieval literature had always been steeped in Latin literary influences, despite loss of direct contact with the Greek. Virgil, Ovid, Lucan, Cicero and Boethius exercised an unfailing spell, and the classical scholarship of a man like the

12th-century John of Salisbury was, in view of the sources available to him, very impressive. But it was one thing to read Virgil's poems for hidden Christian symbolism, or Ovid's to the accompaniment of a moralising interpretation, and quite another to strip away medieval commentaries and try to re-establish imaginatively the pagan world in which these masters had lived. Moreover, as trade bloomed and mercantile wealth accumulated, there was more and more demand for texts to be owned and enjoyed by worldly purchasers indifferent to medieval sermonising. Libraries in Italy and elsewhere were ransacked, and throughout the 15th century newly recovered treasures were constantly being brought to light. Love poems of a Catullus or a Propertius, books on style, rhetoric and oratory, long-lost Roman authors like Plautus and eventually Greek ones too, offered a wealth of fresh models and instruction which led to imitation and to creative efforts in the vernacular languages. The change was not merely one of quantity, of adding a certain number of new items to old collections. It was also qualitative: the recently discovered authors and the familiar ones were regarded as a source of aesthetic pleasure which, though most esteemed when serving moral ends, did not need to be justified in addition by constant sermonising and allegorical commentaries reaching out beyond life to the "four extremes" of death, judgment, heaven and hell. Literary warrant was found close at hand, in the activities of humanity itself; hence the contrast implied in the term *litterae humaniores* (the "humanities") as a study distinct from theology. Correspondingly, non-ecclesiastical patrons, merchant princes and noblemen, now aspired to assume the function of Maecenases and to encourage writing comparable to that of Rome's pagan geniuses. Moral-didactic elements do not by any means disappear in humanistic literature, but they are now coloured less by medieval patristic and more by Aristotelian ethical concepts. In this general tendency Italy led the way.

The forerunners of humanism in 15th-century England had already begun to show some interest in the acquisition of recovered ancient classics and there were patrons of literature like Cardinal Beaufort and Humphrey Duke of Gloucester who imitated their Italian peers in the expectation of a like flattering recognition from their protégés. Their attitudes were still medieval, however. Poggio Bracciolini, invited to England by the English Cardinal (1418), had complained in a letter that the monastery libraries there were provided with little besides "recent" writers' works, mostly ecclesiastical, while their inventories showed nothing worthy of humane studies. Pagan authors were woefully lacking.[33] Other Italians visited England, partly as a result of contacts made at the Councils of Constance and Basle; some patrons—Duke Humphrey and Bishop Thomas Bekynton among them—had agents in Italy who purchased

Sir Thomas More

by Johann Holbein, Jr.

for its time, the Vulgate nevertheless contained some original errors, and through much copying and recopying, with concomitant additions and omissions, the texts in circulation at the end of the Middle Ages had become modified and more or less corrupted.

The required editorial labour was boldly undertaken by Erasmus for the text of the New Testament in Greek, which he prepared in large part in Cambridge (published 1519). With still greater courage William Tyndale put the Greek into English and published it abroad. He also translated the Pentateuch, but his premature efforts led to exile, persecution and execution at the hands of the Inquisition in Antwerp (1535). Even the Greek edition by Erasmus was regarded askance by the orthodox. Scholars who recognised its merits were afraid of its unsettling effects, since the critical method here applied to a sacred text was precisely the same as that used for any pagan classic. Despite the protestations and defenses of the editor and his friend Sir Thomas More,[36] the procedure did in fact tend indirectly to weaken the unquestioning fideism of the Middle Ages. It was not part of the editor's intention to undermine Catholic orthodoxy, any more than the Protestant translators of the Bible into the vernacular—Luther in Germany, Cheke, Tyndale and Coverdale in England—desired to weaken the newer types of orthodoxy they were trying to erect in place of the old. Nevertheless the multiplication of versions and translations did tend to undermine the more solid unity of doctrine which, despite heresies, had ruled in previous ages.

Translation became a great and rewarding activity in the 16th century.[37] Medieval romanticised versions of classical epics like the *Aeneid* were rejected for new ones like Surrey's, more faithful to the originals. In this sense even Gavin Douglas (1475—1522), who has been reckoned as a belated Scottish Chaucerian on the basis of his early conventional allegories, deserves to be classified as a humanist for his direct rendering of Virgil's poem and his sharp criticism of Caxton's medieval distortion of it.[38] Translators of outstanding literary ability in the Tudor age gave to the public readable and quite faithful versions of classical texts in English, which later served to enrich the creative work of Shakespeare and his contemporaries. The pedagogical interest of the humanists was continued in further translations from Xenophon and Plutarch, Lucian and Cicero, with Plato casting an enduring spell upon them all.

A less direct but very important influence of the new learning and the new religious issues was felt in the plays of the early 16th century. The old moralities were modified further and were adapted to private court entertainments as interludes. The pride of a new nationalism was inculcated in the anonymous *Wealth and Health* (ca. 1551), which introduces the satirical figure of a clownish Dutch merchant; and the New World is described in Rastell's *Interlude of the Four Elements* (before 1535), with an expression of regret that England could not claim the honour of first discovery. John Bale (died 1563) used both Biblical and morality materials shaped into argumentation for the Protestant cause (e.g., *Three Laws* and *God's Promises*). In *King John* he combined the old type with elements of chronicle history, prophetic of a new form to be created by Shakespeare's immediate predecessors. [36]

At this time the earlier discovery of Plautus (1427) began to have a profound effect on English comedy, introducing some new concepts of form and typical characters. The amorous and boasting soldier or *miles gloriosus*, made proverbial by Plautus, was acclimatised in a supremely English setting by the schoolmaster Nicholas Udall in his *Ralph Roister Doister* (dated variously from ca. 1535 to 1550). [40] Some of the Tudor interludes recall the old medieval debates in their form, but at the same time they display the new passion for rhetorically embellished argument. A good example was provided by Henry Medwall's *Fulgens and Lucrece* (ca. 1497), based on a kind of Ciceronian *controversia* by the Italian Latinist Buonaccorso. The result is less drama than an exercise in rhetoric. John Heywood, already mentioned as the author of the satiric *Spider and the Fly*, wrote interludes using themes of debate combined with *fabliau* situations for purposes of courtly entertainment: for instance, *The Four P's* and *The Play of the Weather*. [41] He also drew on French farces for some of his materials, as in *Johan Johan*.

6. SIR THOMAS MORE

Not only among his contemporaries but among English writers of all time, Sir Thomas More (1478—1535) occupies a singularly lofty position. He possessed that rare combination, the imagination, wit and intellect of a genius on the one hand, and on the other a character of generous and affectionate humanity, of luminous integrity, modesty and steadfast devotion to principle, which in the end made him a martyr to his convictions at the hands of an absolutist monarch.

More was descended from a middle-class family and moved in a circle of cultivated Londoners. [42] The son of a lawyer, he himself studied jurisprudence and rose high in the legal profession. Having served with exceptional honesty and disinterestedness as justice of the peace, member of Parliament, and judge, he eventually became Chancellor of the realm (1529). His attitude to the state which he served was ambiguous, and at the same time typical of other English humanists. As a middle class man he felt the need to push forward out of the confines of an atomistic feudal-hierarchical society, to consolidate a strong—and he hoped, an enlightened—national goverment; but as a humane thinker he was revolted by the ruthless measures being taken by the new ruling class through the state apparatus of the Tudors.

Though personally deeply religious and in fact inclined to a voluntary asceticism in his own life, More had no greater sympathy than did his friend Erasmus for the vulgar superstititions which passed under the name of religion: the crass thaumaturgy, the cult of relics and wonder-working images and pilgrimages, the credulity that was both shared and exploited by many members of the clergy.[43] As with Erasmus, however, More's scholarly and humanistic criticism remained within the limits of Catholic doctrine, and he replied to the challenge of Luther's Protestantism with a long and vehement tract in Latin (*Responsio ad Convitia Martini Lutheri*, ca. 1522). He broke with Henry VIII over the issue of secular headship for the English church, and it may well be that his theoretical religious opposition was fortified by some apprehension that (as history was to show) the middle class was paying too high a price in allying itself with royal absolutism in order to put a check on the landlord class.

In this connection More's biography of Richard III, twice written (both in Latin and in English), may be regarded as a political sermon.[44] The obvious moral is a warning against the unscrupulous and bloody careerism of which More's period offered many examples. Richard's well-known use of London's merchant-citizens to advance his drive for power might serve as a warning for contemporaries of Henry VIII. More sharpens his portraiture by a rhetorical denigration of the King's character, producing an image of villainy heightened beyond any warrant of historical foundation. Adapted to the later compendious *Mirrour for Magistrates* and incorporated in Holinshed's *Chronicle*, More's study became the source inspiring Shakespeare's play *Richard III*, in which the political sermon is heightened still further by the blood-and-thunder of Senecan tragedy.

The English text of More's biography is particularly significant in the history of English literary prose. As a type of writing it represents a break with the tradition of hagiography—the chief biographical form of the Middle Ages—and a return to classical models, in which issues of politics and ethics predominate. The supernatural element is conspicuously absent from *Richard III*, and religious judgments are subordinated to estimates in the manner of Plutarch or Suetonius. There is also a marked debt to classical rhetoric and oratory, which had laid down principles about the manner of presenting an eminent person's character, appearance and career, whether for purposes of praise or blame.[45] The very sentence structure of his biography testifies to a humanistic interest in refinement of the vernacular, for More was here clearly trying to shape English, carefully yet unpedantically, into a dignified medium of literary expression. He succeeded in attaining eloquence in some of the inserted speeches. We may regret that he did not leave us an English version also of his short discourse, a distillation of his own high principles on the need to remain firm in faith even to death ("Quod Mors pro Fide non sit Fugienda"). His English *Dialogue of Comfort against Tribulation* is Boethian in style and conception, very fitted to the author and his situation.

More's great work, which elevates him to a position of world fame in progressive thought, is of course his *Utopia* (written in Latin, 1515—16). This sketch of an ideal commonwealth is developed in an imaginary conversation supposed to have been held between More and friends of his, in Antwerp, with a Portugese voyager named Raphael Hythlodaye, a companion of Amerigo Vespucci. More at times acts as an *advocatus diaboli* and thus draws out Hythlodaye's information and opinions the more effectively. The returned voyager, with his skill in classical languages, his learning and his noble humanitarianism, is obviously also a projection of the author. There is no foundation for the attempts sometimes made to set More in opposition to Hythlodaye, and thus to "purge" More of advocating a certain type of communism as both desirable and practicable.[46] It is More himself, not a character disowned by him, who is here a worthy fountainhead of modern communist thought: directly of the utopian socialist school, indirectly of the scientific.

Difficult it would be to say which part of the *Utopia* is the more valuable: Book i, with its description of England's actual economic misery as More saw it and understood it, or the earlier-composed Book ii, with its attractive and (for its times) astonishingly convincing, circumstantial picture of a human society rationally and harmoniously organised. For his devastating picture of contemporary England, More drew on his own observation and knowledge, and he unerringly placed his finger on the important causes. The abandonment of tillage for sheep raising, the enclosure of land and the expulsion of peasant cultivators was recognised by him as the main source of social maladjustment. The landlords—including abbots, he remarks parenthetically, who are "holy men, no doubt," but bent on profit like the rest —

not contenting them selfes with the yearely revenues and profytes, that were wont to grow [to] theyr forefathers and predecessours of their landes, nor beynge content that they liue in rest and pleasure nothinge profiting, yea much noying the weale publique: leaue no ground for tillage, thei inclose al into pastures: thei throw doune houses: they plucke downe townes, and leaue nothing standynge, but only the churche to be made a shepehowse....47

As a result, More continues, of one "cormoraunte's" parasitic greed—

the husbandmen be thrust owte of their owne, or els either by coueyne and fraude, or by violent oppression they be put besydes it, or by wronges and iniuries thei be so weried, that they be compelled to sell all: by one meanes therfore or by other, either by hooke or crooke they muste needes departe awaye, poore, selye, wretched soules, men, women, husbands, wiues, fatherlesse children, widowes, wofull mothers, with their yonge babes, and their whole houshold smal in substance, and muche in numbre, as husbandrye requireth manye handes. Awaye thei trudge, I say, out of their knowen and accustomed houses, fyndynge no place to rest in...

No better, no more vivid literary account has ever been given of the agrarian dislocations which created an uprooted population as precursors of the modern proletariat. The author of *Utopia* also perceived other important causes of unemployment, rootlessness and despair: the dismissal of many returned soldiers, which marked the end of a century of feudal warfare; the replacement of large-scale feudal levies by modern professional armies; and especially the dismissal of whole households of retainers as the old aristocracy was bought out by new merchant landlords. The savage laws inflicted upon the dispossessed victims were condemned by More with a burning indignation that remains unparalleled in England until the satire of a Fielding or a Swift (concealed only in part by irony) again called attention to the degradation of the masses and the injustice of the laws turned against them.

After the sombre depiction of contemporary England, the positive image of a collectivist Utopia gleams the more brightly. Obviously it is indebted to what More knew of earlier speculation and experiments in communal living, whether Platonist, Stoic or early monastic. Obviously too his understanding of the problem of production is limited. Whereas he carries far the community of ownership in goods and commodities, in a manner somewhat suggestive of primitive tribal communism, he permits the basic process of production—the one dealt with first of all by modern states moving toward communism—to retain features of class exploitation. There are bondsmen in Utopia. True it is that their status is temporary and punitive; true it is that a bondsman's condition in Utopia, with its prospects of eventual freedom and advance, was more attractive than the condition of most free citizens in 16th-century Europe. Nevertheless Utopia depends on its bondsmen to do oppressive labour. It is here that we see the limitations of his era imposing themselves to a degree on More's thinking. Only modern industry and modern machinery in the hands of its workers as owners could conceivably handle the problems of economic production and distribution underlying a workable communist state. Yet the striking thing about More's class system is that it sits lightly upon the people and could obviously be corrected.

Many aspects of Utopian civilisation reveal the noble character of More himself: the scorn of show and needless expenditure, the esteem for fraternal cooperation, the high value placed on a rational education for both men and women,—an education undistorted by medieval defects such as scholastic logic-chopping and astrological superstitions. The hatred of war and aggression, of conquests and colonial exploitation is several times expressed. Most striking of all, perhaps, is the non-dogmatic deism which More ascribes to his happy islanders instead of a formal theology or an institutionalised cult. Their system of beliefs sounds a bit like revived Epicurean philosophy, even more like an anticipation of 18th-century rationalism. More must not be supposed, of course, to have considered the Utopian doctrines superior to revealed Christianity. He attributed to the citizens of his ideal commonwealth the highest level of virtues attainable by enlightened pagans, while showing them ignorant of the specifically Christian virtues until instructed in these by Hythlodaye. The trenchant point of More's satire is this: that, even though they lacked the supreme benefit (as he saw it) of Christian ideology, the Utopians were able unaided to rise so high above the bloody and greedy culture of Christian Europe in the age of colonial conquests and mass expropriations. They did so precisely because, having surmounted the handicap of private property, they could develop the virtues of pagan enlightenment to their fullest extent, and More shows how far these could take them.

In the *Utopia* for the first time in history, human aspirations toward a fraternal way of life were united with an extensive and rational system of proposals about its realisation, based on a pre-condition of communal ownership and collective work. The vision which, though imprecise and mystically obscured, had attracted the finest thinkers among the early Anglo-Saxon converts to Christianity and, through the ages, the most magnanimous of their successors, was now argued convincingly to be capable of approximation in future real experience, if once the underlying economic dilemmas could be solved. Unwittingly, More was showing the way to liberty and equality as well as fraternity. The atmosphere of 1789 and beyond is already about his thinking. Furthermore, he was also, despite all historical limitations, casting one of the first strong rays of light forward to the concept of a classless society to be realised ultimately by communism in the modern sense of the word.

Sir Thomas More, scholar, humanist and martyr for the sake of his principles, was a prophetic social thinker of towering proportions, embracing vast perspectives of hope for an improved humanity in his vision of a better life to be lived here on earth.

7. CONCLUSION: THE COMING OF FULL RENAISSANCE

Humanistic learning, the inspiration of Italian art, the Reformation, the discovery of the geographical New World and of the Copernican new heavens in the early 16th century—all these tremendous modifications in the European world view add up to what is called the distinctive age of the Renaissance. Considered by themselves the cultural transformations loom so large that they might well appear to defy explanation, the more so since they were carried out by men of such impressive stature as Thomas More and Nicholas Copernicus, to name but two. It was, in the well-known phrase of Engels, an age that demanded giants and created them.[48] But we have seen the slow accumulation of change from the beginnings of urban life and trade and maritime commerce which, gathering momentum through the later Middle Ages, opened the way for a consummated qualitative change in the reign of Queen Elizabeth. The transformation, when it came, was no miracle.

It has been the fashion among certain recent writers to deny or minimise the importance of that European cultural revolution which, since the time of the art historian Jacob Burckhardt (1860), has generally gone by the name of Renaissance. Some have claimed that the term and the concept are a 19th-century invention not corresponding to historical reality. To an extent Buckhardt himself made this challenge possible, for he concentrated on art history to the neglect of its economic basis, often interpreting it idealistically in primary terms of personalities and their influences. Besides, those with a vested interest in the Middle Ages, so to speak, or with other special reasons for exalting that period at the expense of others, have been eager to prove that the "real" Renaissance occurred in the 12th or the 13th century;[49] or, conversely, that the Middle Ages did not stop at the time here indicated. By choosing special evidence and concentrating on certain aspects of cultural history, to the exclusion of others, it is possible to argue for such theses with some show of reason. A preliminary burgeoning did occur in the 12th century, as we have seen, when the early expansion of city life and trading was accompanied by very considerable advances in learning and by great achievements in art (especially in architecture). Moreover, the medieval forms, habits of thought and preoccupations did persist, not only into the 16th century but for some time after.[50] There is much of the medieval heritage surviving in Shakespeare, for instance, along with his supreme innovations, and a knowledge of it helps us to understand many of the sources of conflict in his creative work.

But to admit these facts does not mean a denial that deep-going and essential changes occurred in the 16th century. Much of the argumentation on the other side results from an over-narrow specialisation and from conservative apologetics for a previous *status quo*. When the view is expanded to embrace humanity's multiple activities as a whole, then the evidence for profound qualitative change is found to be overwhelming.[51] The period was one of enormous quickening, of new powers and new realms of vision and creation. If the term Renaissance is justly to be criticised, it is because it suggests no more than a rebirth of what had been lost, disregarding the addition of what was unprecedented and truly new. Yet the age of Shakespeare, for all its indebtedness to classical antiquity and to the recent Middle Ages, was about to enter upon a distinctly new era in man's age-long struggle to conquer nature and his own social organisation for the ultimate purposes of fraternal, collective living. The new literature was rapidly to become a grandly orchestrated symphony accompanying and interpreting a new age.

¹ For instance, the Paston family of Norfolk, whose 15th-century correspondence is an invaluable source of information for the social background. The *Letters* have been edited by James Gairdner in six vols. (London, 1904).

² Lipson, *Economic History*, III, ch. 5; Eli Heckscher, *Mercantilism* (London, 1938).

³ Marx, *Capital*, I, Part viii, ch. 28. New evidence on the desperate plight of 16th century agriculture is given by M. Beresford, *The Lost Villages of England* (New York, 1954).

⁴ Coulton, *Last Century of English Monasticism*, pp. 631 ff. The general situation is discussed by Karl Kautsky in his book on Sir Thomas More; Polish translation as *Tomasz More i Jego Utopia* (Warsaw, 1948).

⁵ This point is made by Myers, *op. cit.*, though he does not of course express it in Marxist terms.

⁶ Karl Young, *The Drama of the Medieval Church*, 2 vols. (Oxford, 1933), I, p. 214; Hardin Craig, *English Religious Drama of the Middle Ages* (Oxford, 1955).

⁷ E.K. Chambers, *The Mediaeval Stage*, 2 vols., II (Oxford, 1903).

⁸ Wilhelm Creizenach, *Geschichte des neueren Dramas* (Halle, 1911), I, pp. 154 ff. For fragments of plays from Shrewsbury composed partly in Latin and partly in English, see K. Young, *op. cit.*, II, pp. 514—23.

⁹ Ed. E. Mätzner in *Altenglische Sprachproben*, I, Part ii (Berlin, 1869). For surviving separate pieces see O. Waterhouse, *The Non-Cycle Mystery Plays*, EETS, ES, No. 104 (1909).

¹⁰ Chambers, *op. cit.*, I; the claim for such elements was recently restated by Arthur Brown, *Folklore*, LXIII (1952), 65—78.

¹¹ *The York Mystery Plays*, ed. Lucy Toulmin Smith (London, 1885); *The Towneley Plays*, ed. George England and A.W. Pollard, EETS, ES, No. 71 (1897).

¹² Marie C, Lyle, *The Original Identity of the York and Towneley Cycles*, University of Minnesota *Research Publications*, VIII, No. 3 (1919). On the Wakefield author see M.G. Frampton in *PMLA*, L (1935), 631—60; on the Second Shepherd's Play see R.C. Cosley, "The Mak Story and its Folklore Analogues," *Speculum*, XX (1945), 310—17.

¹³ *The Chester Plays*, ed. H. Deimling and G.W. Matthews, EETS, ES, Nos. 62, 111, 115 (1893, 1916 and 1926).

¹⁴ *The Coventry Plays*, ed. K.S. Block, EETS, ES, No. 120 (1922). Discussion by Esther L. Swenson, *An Inquiry into the Composition of the* Ludus Coventriae, University of Minnesota *Studies in Language and Literature*, I (1914). Timothy Fry finds a doctrinal unity underlying the play; see *Studies in Philology*, XLVIII (1951), 527—70. The diversity of popular elements is stressed by Joseph Allen Bryant, Jr.,

in "The Function of *Ludus Coventriae* 14," *Journal of English and Germanic Philology*, LII (1953), 340—45.

[15] *The Macro Plays*, ed. F.J. Furnivall and A.W. Pollard, EETS, ES, No. 91 (1904).

[16] See Joseph Herrlich, *Das englische Bibeldrama zur Zeit der Renaissance und Reformation* (Munich diss., 1907). Allegorical interludes also had religious-political significance: T.W. Craik in *Review of English Studies*, N.S., IV (1953), 98—108.

[17] For this and other ballads see the *English and Scottish Popular Ballads* collected by Francis James Child, 5 vols. (Boston, 1882—98); one-volume selection with introduction by G.L. Kittredge (1904). A general survey of ballad literature is given by E.K. Chambers, *English Literature at the Close of the Middle Ages* (Oxford, 1945), ch. 3.

[18] By F.B. Gummere in *The Popular Ballad* (London, 1907); also by Kittredge as cited in note 17.

[19] Represented by Louise Pound in her book *Poetic Origins and the Ballad* (1921); also her discussion of the term "communal," *PMLA*, XXXIV (1924), 440—54.

[20] Alexander Keith, "Scottish Ballads: Their Evidence of Authorship and Origin," *Essays and Studies* by Members of the English Association, XII (1926), 100—19.

[21] For general discussion see Book ii of Baugh's *Literary History of England*, written by Tucker Brooke; also John M. Berdan, *Early Tudor Poetry* (New York, 1920)—useful despite a superficial introductory analysis.

[22] Stephen Hawes, *The Pastime of Pleasure*, ed. William E. Mead, EETS, OS, No. 173 (1928 for 1927). The influence of Boccaccio on this poem is discussed by C.W. Lemmi, *Review of English Studies*, V (1929), 195—98.

[23] Barclay's *Ship of Fools*, ed. T.H. Jamieson, 2 vols. (London, 1874); the *Eclogues* ed. B. White, EETS, OS, No. 175 (1928).

[24] John Heywood, *The Spider and the Fly*, ed. A.W. Ward for the Spenser Society (1894).

[25] Skelton's *Complete Works* ed. Philip Henderson (London, 1931) with modernised spelling, based on the still standard edition by A. Dyce (1843). For general study see H.R.L. Edwards, *Skelton: The Life and Times of an Early Tudor Poet* (London, 1949), containing fresh biographical material.

[26] Ed. A.V. Judges in *The Elizabethan Underworld* (London, 1930); discussed by W.G. Moore in the *Review of English Studies*, VII (1931), 406—18.

[27] Ed. E.M. Tillyard, *The Poetry of Thomas Wyatt* (London, 1929); Sir Thomas Wyatt, *The Collected Poems*, ed. Kenneth Muir (Harvard University Press, 1949).

[28] Robert O. Evans, "Some Aspects of Wyatt's Metrical Technique," *Journal of English and Germanic Philology*, LIII (1954), 197—213, supplementing and partly correcting Alan Swallow, "The Pentameter Lines in Skelton and Wyatt," *Modern Philology*, XLVII (1950—51), 1—11. Most recent discussion of Wyatt's possible relations with Anne Boleyn is by Richard C. Harrier, *Journal of English and Germanic Philology*, LIII (1954), 581—85. Evidence hitherto accepted as valid is here proved to be unsound.

[29] Arthur K. Moore, "The Design of Wyatt's 'They Flee from Me'," *Anglia*, LXXI (1952), 102—11, gives an explication of the poem in the light of its rhetorical structure; not entirely convincing.

30 Surrey's poems are here cited from the edition by Gerald Bullett in *Silver Poets of the Sixteenth Century* (London: Everyman's Library, 1947). The complete works have been edited by Frederick Morgan Padelford (University of Washington Press, Seattle, 1920).

31 Ants Oras, "Surrey's Technique of Phonetic Echoes," *Journal of English and Germanic Philology*, L (1951), 289—308. Surrey was also somewhat indebted to the translation of the *Aeneid* by Gavin Douglas. See note 38 below.

32 General discussion by А. А. Аникст in *История Английской Литературы*, ed. Алексеев, (1943), pp. 258 ff.

33 "Monasteria sunt hic opulentissima, sed novae fundationis... Quod si qua sunt antiquiora, ea carent libris gentilibus, referta novis doctoribus, et maxime ecclesiasticis. Vidi praeterea inventaria diligenter facta, in quibus nihil erat dignum studiis humanitatis," *Epistolae*, ed. Th. de Tonellis (Florence, 1832—61), I, 31; quoted by Walter Schirmer, *Der englische Frühhumanismus* (Leipzig, 1931), p. 19. The present discussion of 15th-century precursors is based on Schirmer's study. See also Lewis Einstein, *The Italian Renaissance in England* (Columbia University Press, 1902).

34 A continental edition of Linacre's *De Emendenda Structura* (Leipzig, 1545), contains an interesting commendatory epistle by Melanchthon. The contribution of such early works to literary theory is discussed by J.W.H. Atkins, *English Literary Criticism: The Renaissance* (London, 2nd ed., 1951), For Thomas Lupset see the *Life and Works* by J.A. Gee (Yale University Press, 1928).

35 A convenient edition of Elyot's *Book Named the Governour* is by Foster Watson (London: Everyman's Library, 1937).

36 See More's letter to his contemporary Dorpius, who had expressed the fear "ne variae translationes dubios faciant animos infidelium." Yet More pointed out that Jerome's text, on the translator's own admission, needed to be subjected to critical editing: "Mutavit vero Hieronymus, ut ipse fatetur, si quid in sensu fuit, quo Latinus codex discreparet a Graeco," The letter is printed in More's *Opera Omnia* (Frankfurt and Leipzig, 1689), pp. 276—82.

37 Henry Burrowes Lathrop, *Translations from the Classics into English from Caxton to Chapman* (University of Wisconsin, 1933), chs. 1—2.

38 Gavin Douglas, *Poetical Works*, ed. John Small, 4 vols. (Edinburgh, 1874). On Douglas as a humanist see Bruce Dearing, "Gavin Douglas' Aneados," *PMLA*, LXVII (1952), 845—62.

39 Discussion in W. Creizenach, *op. cit.*, III, pp. 418—513. On political aspects of *Wealth and Health*, see T.W. Craik as cited in note 16. On the continuity of morality tradition to Shakespeare, see D.C. Boughner, "Vice, Braggart and Falstaff," *Anglia*, LXXII (1954), 35—61.

40 The earlier date for *Ralph Roister Doister* is supported by C.G. Child in his edition (London, 1913); the later by T.W. Baldwin and M.C. Linthicum in *Philological Quaterly*, VI (1927).

41 There is no collected edition of Heywood's plays. See Tucker Brooke in Baugh's *Literary History of England*, p. 361, n. 8. On the source of *Johan Johan* see S. Sultan in *Journal of English and Germanic Philology*, LIII (1954), 23—37.

42 Russell Ames, *Citizen Thomas More and His Utopia* (Princeton University Press, 1949). This biography stresses the milieu of mercantile prosperity surrounding More and his friends. The medieval heritage is stressed, on the other hand, by R.W.

Chambers in his *Thomas More* (London, 1935), and by A.P. Duhamel in *Studies in Philology* LII (1955), 90—126.

[43] A lively picture is given in the chapter on "Stulta Superstitio" in the *Encomium Moriae* or *Praise of Folly* by Erasmus.

[44] The English text of More's life of Richard III, published in 1513, is edited by J. Rawson Lumby (Cambridge, 1883). See also the collected *English Works of Sir Thomas More*, ed. by W.E. Campbell and A.W. Reed (London, 1931).

[45] On this problem see Marie Schütt, *Die englische Biographik der Tudorzeit* (Hamburg, 1930). More's description of Richard follows the order recommended by classical writers: *res externae, bona corporis, bona animi*, etc. (though here *mala animi* would be a more apt term). Erasmus' description of More himself, in a famous letter to Ulrich von Hutten, follows the same scheme.

[46] H.W. Donner, *Introduction to Utopia* (London, 1945), is one who has tried to purge More of Hythlodaye's ideas. In reply see Edward L. Surtz, S.J., "Thomas More and Communism," *PMLA*, LXIV (1949), 549—64, effectively arguing that More supported Hythlodaye's position on communism in property ownership. See also J.H. Hexter, *More's* Utopia: *The Biography of an Idea* (Princeton University Press, 1950), and the introductory essay by V.P. Volgin to the Russian translation from the Latin (Moscow: Soviet Academy of Sciences, 1947). A.L. Morton, *The English Utopia* (London, 1952) places More's work in the perspective of other utopian writings.

[47] Citations follow the English translation of More's Latin text made by Ralph Robinson (2nd revised ed., 1556). For confirmation of More's picture see Beresford as cited above, n. 1.

[48] Friedrich Engels, *The Dialectics of Nature*, tr. Clemens Dutt (New York, 1940), introd., p. 2.

[49] Charles Haskins, *The Renaissance of the 12th Century*, criticised and somewhat modified (under the influence of Toynbee) by Urban T. Holmes, Jr., in *Speculum*, XXVI (1951), 643—51.

[50] Pearl Kibre, as one of many, points to the continuity of themes in her study "The Intellectual Interests Reflected in Libraries of the Fourteenth and Fifteenth Centuries," *Journal of the History of Ideas*, VII (1946), 257 ff.

[51] Cf., for instance, B.L. Ullman, "Renaissance—the Word and the Underlying Concept," *Studies in Philology*, XLIX (1952), 105—18; Wallace Ferguson, *The Renaissance and Historical Thought* (Boston, 1948). The characteristics of the age are sketched by Engels, *The Peasant War in Germany* (New York, 1934), ch. 1.

INDEX

INDEX TO THE FOOTNOTES

NOTE: The following index will serve at the same time as bibliography, since information is given about each book or article in the first footnote in which it is referred to. Items are normally entered by title as well as author or editior. Abbreviations have been avoided in footnotes except in a few instances well established in usage:

- EETS, ES and OS, means Early English Text Society, Extra Series and Original Series respectively;
- PMLA (now officially used by the journal itself) refers to the *Publications of the Modern Language Association of America*;
- SATF refers to the volumes published by the Société des Anciens Textes Français.

In accordance with general library practice, names of medieval personages are indexed under given names, disregarding epithets and places of origin; after about 1500, when family names became common, these are the forms indexed. Thus Ailred of Rievaulx is indexed under A, but Thomas More under M. A few well-known instances like Geoffrey Chaucer (under C) are exceptional.

Topics separately listed in the table of contents (e.g., Chaucer's *Troilus and Criseyde*) are not repeated in the index.

The first number given indicates the chapter; the second, following a period, the note in the chapter.